A BIBLIOGRAPHY OF PHILOSOPHICAL BIBLIOGRAPHIES

A BIBLIOGRAPHY OF PHILOSOPHICAL BIBLIOGRAPHIES

Edited and compiled by

Herbert Guerry

GREENWOOD PRESS
Westport, Connecticut • London, England

Library of Congress Cataloging in Publication Data

Guerry, Herbert.
A bibliography of philosophical bibliographies.

Includes index.
1. Bibliography--Bibliography--Philosophy.
2. Philosophy--Bibliography. I. Title.
Z7125.A1G83 [B53] 016.0161 77-71862
ISBN 0-8371-9542-X

Library of Congress Catalog Card Number: 77-071862
ISBN: 0-8371-9542-X

First published in 1977

Greenwood Press, Inc.
51 Riverside Avenue, Westport, Connecticut 06880

Printed in the United States of America

Contents

	Acknowledgments	vii
	Introduction	ix
I	Bibliographies of Individual Philosophers	1
II	Subject Bibliographies	179
	Index	313

Acknowledgments

A number of people are due recognition and thanks for their help with this work, especially my parents for their kind support of my research and travels. For help with compiling the work, I thank Min-Hong Choi, Jean G. Gamble, Gregory Kohlbach, and Francine Rainone. For help with translations, I am indebted to Theodore T. Boushy, John Chay, Lawrence Feinberg, Madeline Levine, Augustín Maissen, George Schlesigner, and Victor W. Wolf. Others who have given valuable help are David Bolig, Avery J. Butters, June Chay, Ruth Gladstone, James B. Graves, my daughter Elizabeth, Milton Wolf, Peter Petcoff, L. Miles Raisig, P. Albert Studdard, and especially my wife. My editor, James T. Sabin, and an unknown reviewer are also due thanks for valuable suggestions, and Pat Blunden and Judy Horning are to be commended for their typing skills.

The following libraries and their staffs graciously opened their collections to me: Bibliothèque National (Paris), Bodleian Library, British Museum, Cambridge University, Duke University, Library of Congress, Pembroke State University, Saint Andrews Presbyterian College, University of Michigan, and the University of North Carolina.

For any errors in the text, I would like very much to blame the machinations of malignant, or at least mischievous, cosmic forces against which human resistance is utterly and hopelessly futile. Since this is not a live option nowadays, I concede that responsibility for such errors lies on my shoulders alone.

Introduction

The present work attempts to list philosophical bibliographies published in all countries since about 1450, when printing was invented, through the year 1974. Nonspecialists and undergraduates will find references to the standard bibliographical aids appropriate to their interests and courses. Advanced scholars are directed to the more specialized and abstruse bibliographies.

My aim has been to include only bibliographies that have been published separately or appeared as contributions to journals, though I have included a few significant bibliographies which were published as appendixes to monographs or as parts of larger bibliographies. This restriction was necessary in order to make the task of compiling the bibliography manageable. Bibliographies are always incomplete, and all subject bibliographies are slightly out of date from the time of publication. The present volume is no exception. Like Mozart's Don Giovanni, I have tried to make my collection as extensive as possible, knowing all the while that true completeness is a daydream. Moreover, when I began my work, I had intended to describe each work cited. As the number of entries grew, it became clear, given my present circumstances, that the annotation of each item would be impossible. I therefore elected to write as many annotations as I could for the present edition and complete them in a subsequent larger work.

The bibliographies in this volume are divided into two alphabetically arranged lists, numbered consecutively. The first list (1-1395) contains bibliographies on the works of, and literature about, individual philosophers. The second list (1396-2353) contains bibliographies on philosophical topics. Bibliographies that cover more than one topic are cross-indexed; thus a bibliography on the doctrine of Platonic ideas appears under the subject heading "Ideas (Platonic)," but is also referred to *by number* in the entries under the author heading "Plato." Bibliographies of works on or within a school of philosophy bearing the name of an individual (for example,"Cartesianism," "Cartesians,"

"Marxism," "Marxism-Leninism") are listed among the bibliographies on that individual (for example, under "Descartes, Réne," or "Marx, Karl").

The reader who wants an overview of the bibliography of philosophy, or who wants to know what was considered to be philosophically important at various times since the mid-fifteenth century, should consult the bibliographies listed under the heading "General." As an aid to the reader, these bibliographies and others under headings encompassing a large number of works are arranged chronologically according to the periods of time covered. Readers who need information about available bibliographical indexes in philosophy, or about indexes to the contents of specific journals, should consult the section of the present work entitled "Indexes." Together, the sections "Indexes" and "General" provide the most comprehensive (in terms of the number of works cited) accumulation of references to general philosophical bibliographical materials yet assembled. Probably little or nothing of philosophical importance since the Dark Ages, except possibly some doctoral dissertations, escapes reference in one or another of the works listed in these two sections.

I have not translated the titles of bibliographies written in the major European languages. For bibliographies in other Roman alphabet languages, I have listed the title in the original language and provided an English translation. For bibliographies in non-Roman alphabets (Russian, Hebrew, Arabic, Japanese, and so on), I have given a transliteration of the title into the Roman alphabet followed by a translation into English. I have also identified the language (for example, "[In Arabic]").

The prefixes of surnames (for example "Mc", "O' ", "Di", and "D' ") have been treated as the first component of the name, and names with such prefixes have been alphabetized accordingly. German surnames are the exception. Following custom, I have listed them according to the main element. For example, "von Sternberg" appears under "Sternberg."

As this work is exclusively a bibliography of bibliographies, it complements rather than replaces research guides such as Richard De George's *Guide to Philosophical Bibliography and Research*,[1] Henry J. Koren's *Research in Philosophy; a Bibliographical Introduction to Philosophy and a Few Suggestions for Dissertations,*[2] Wilhelm Totok's *Handbuch der Geschichte der Philosophie,*[3] and Gilbert Varet's *Manuel de bibliographie philosophique.*[4] Although most of the bibliographies found in these works are repeated here, the reader will find much else in them that is of use.

A number of sources of bibliographical material in philosophy now exist. Books and periodicals are now being indexed by several periodicals, notably *The Philosopher's Index* (Bowling Green), *Repertoire bibliographique de la philosophie* (Louvain), *Bulletin signaletique: Philosophie* (Paris), *Bibliographie Philosophie mit Autoren und Sach Register* (Berlin), *Philosophischer Literaturanzeiger* (Meisenheim am Glan), and *Philosophical Books* (Leicester). Lists of philosophical journals may be found in the first four of the above-mentioned works, as well as in *Ulrich's International Periodicals Directory* (New York and London), David Baumgardt's *Philosophical Periodicals,*[5] and Hogrebe, Kamp, and Konig's *Periodica Philosophica.*[6]

The numerous national bibliographies provide another source of useful, general bibliographical information on philosophy. These are described in such works as Constance M. Winchell's *Guide to Reference Books,*[7] and its supplementary volumes by E. P. Sheehy. General bibliographical journals such as the *Bibliographic Index* (New York) and the *Bibliographische Berichte* (Frankfurt am Main) contain much that is helpful. The former is good for its coverage of bibliographies in monographs; the latter is good for European works (about one-third of its contents is devoted to Eastern European materials).

The difficulty of giving a precise definition of "bibliography" requires some comment. A simple list of works is a bibliography, as is a list with brief annotations. A list with extensive annotations is still a bibliography. Nevertheless the annotated list merges imperceptibly into a "survey of the literature," which itself develops by stages into a full-fledged history. The main histories of philosophy are not bibliographies; yet they contain bibliographies. "Histories" that contain a preponderance of bibliographical material, such as Friedrich Ueberweg's *Grundriss der Geschichte der Philosophie*, are perhaps more valuable as bibliographies than as histories. In general, I have excluded histories of philosophy from this work, except ones such as Ueberweg's. I have not actively sought out surveys of the literature, but I have included most of those I came across. Similarly, although I have made no systematic effort to collect references to book sellers' catalogs, I have printed those I found that seemed most useful. Nor have I attempted to seek out bio-bibliographies.

The difficulty of defining "philosophy" also requires a few remarks. According to the old joke, in most countries "Yankee" means the same thing as "from the United States"; in the United States a Yankee is someone from the Northeast; in the Northeast, it is a New Englander; in New England, a Vermonter; and in Vermont, a Yankee is sometimes said to be anyone who eats apple pie for breakfast. Likewise, philosophy, when seen from too near, can be defined as a very narrow subject, comprising, for example, only what is being published in a handful of journals. I try to avoid such narrowness of definition.

The definition of "philosophy" is complicated by the fact that much of what used to count as philosophy no longer does. The *Bibliotheca Philosophica* by Paulus Bolduanus in 1616 and the work of the same name by Burkhard Gotthelf Struve in 1804 contain much that we would not call philosophy today. Some of what Europeans in the last hundred years have called philosophy, Americans now term psychology or sociology or educational theory. Some of what has passed for philosophy in Britain and America in the last fifty years would not be recognized as such in other countries.

The implication is that one must define "philosophy" broadly. The meanings of words change not only from time to time but also from place to place. Words are in some respects like natural species, neither being static. In some organisms that reproduce asexually (some bacteria, for example), the differentiation of one species from another is somewhat subjective. Similar problems arise in differentiating the more complex forms of life that reproduce sexually. The ability to cross usually is taken as the identity mark of species, yet there exist "distinct species" of plants and animals that cannot cross with one another, but can both cross with a third "species." Problems concerning the delimitation or specification of concepts are analogous.

My criteria for the philosophical, therefore, have been rather broad. If a bibliography covers a thinker or a topic that might be considered in a philosophy course or in a work on the history of philosophy, or if the bibliography has been published in a journal that appears in any of the lists of philosophical journals, then I have tended to include it. Nevertheless, I have eliminated some bibliographies that seemed to me to be purely in the field of religion, which comprises its own distinct area of scholarship. I have not restricted myself solely to Western philosophy. If Western thinkers preponderate here, it is because the materials available to me dealt almost exclusively with Western works and because non-Western patterns of scholarship have not produced much in the way of bibliographies. If there is a disproportionately large number of bibliographies on semi-philosophical figures and problems, this is a reflection of the work previously done by compilers of bibliographies: the large number of people interested in *belles-lettres*, for example, insures that the number of Voltaire bibliographies will be large; the zeal that so often accompanies faith in an idea (Christianity, Marxism, occultism) guarantees that the number of bibliographies of works related to these faiths will be large.

Four centuries ago Montaigne, lamenting an affliction endemic to scholarship, wrote: "There is more ado to interpret interpretations than to interpret the things, and more books upon books than upon all other subjects; we do nothing but comment upon one another."[8] Nevertheless, I offer the reader not only another book about books, but in effect, *a book about books about books.* My purpose, of course, is to make the vast literature of philosophy more open to philosophers and students of philosophy, many of whom probably would write better in the end if they would read a little more and write a little less.

NOTES

1. New York: Appleton-Century-Crofts, 1971.
2. Pittsburgh: Duquesne University Press, 1966

3. Frankfurt am Main: V. Klostermann, 1964-.
4. Paris: Presses Universitaires de France, 1956.
5. Washington: Library of Congress, 1952.
6. Dusseldorf: Philosophia Verlag, 1972.
7. Chicago: American Library Association, 1967.
8. Montaigne, *Essays*, Bk. III, Ch. 13.

BIBLIOGRAPHIES OF INDIVIDUAL PHILOSOPHERS

ABBAGNANO, NICOLA

1. "Bibliografia su Nicola Abbagnano," in Scritti scelti con introduzione di Norberto Bobbio a cura di Giovanni de Crescenzo e Pietro Faveglia. Torino: Taylor, 1967, pp. 165-171.

See also: "Nota bio-bibliografica" in the same work, pp. 259-264.

2. Maiorca, Bruno. Bibliografia degli Scritti di e su Nicola Abbagnano (1923-1973). Torino: Giappichelli, 1974, 222 pp.

AJDUKIEWICZ, KAZIMIREZ

3. Angelelli, I. "K. Ajdukiewicz: biografía y bibliografía de sus obras," Revista de filo sofía (La Plata), no. 14 (1964), pp. 57-65.

ALAIN (i.e., ÉMILE AUGUSTE CHARTIER)

4. Savin, Maurice. Texte présenté avec une biographie et une bibliographie d'Alain et une table analytique des propos par Maurice Savin. Paris: Gallimard, 1956, 1370 pp.

ALBALAG, ISSAC

5. Vajda, Georges. Issac Albalag, averroiste juif. traducteur et annotateur d'al-Ghâzalî. Paris: Librairie philosophique, J. Vrin, 1960. 289 pp.

Contains a bibliography of works on Albalag.

ALBERT THE GREAT

6. Daley, Charles Maric. "Incunabula of Albertus Magnus in the Library of Congress," Catholic Historical Review (Washington), vol. 17 (1932), pp. 444-463. Reprinted: Washington, D. C.: 1932.

7. Weiss, Melchoir. Primordia Novae Bibliographiae b. Albert. Magni Ratisbonensis Episcopi, Ordinis Praedicatorum; Ed. 2, Aucta et Emendata. Parisiis: apud Ludovicum Vivès, 1905. 120 pp.

8. Meersseman, Gérard Gilles. ["A Bibliography of Albert the Great"] in Opera Omnia B. Alberti Magni. Bruges: C. Beyaert, 1931, "Introduction," pp. ix-x.

9. Van Steenberghen, Fernand. "La Littérature albertino-thomiste (1930-1937)," Revue Néoscholastique de Philosophie (Louvain), vol. 41 (1938), pp. 126-161.

10. Brounts, Simon. "Albertus Magnus-literature," Tijdschrift voor Philosophie (Leuven), vol. 14 (1952), pp. 87-96.

11. Catania, Francis J. "A Bibliography of St. Albert the Great," The Modern Schoolman (St. Louis, Mo.), vol. 37 (1959), pp. 11-28. Addenda: Vol. 39 (1961), pp. 61-64.

12. Schooyans, Michel. "Bibliographie philosophique de saint Albert le Grand (1931-1960)," Revista da Universidade católica de São Paulo (São Paulo), vol. 21 (1961), pp. 36-88.

ALEXANDER OF HALES

13. Herscher, I. "A Bibliography of Alexander of Hales," Franciscian Studies (New York), vol. 5 (1945), pp. 434-454.

ALEXANDER, SAMUEL

14. Alexander, Samuel. Philosophical and Literary Pieces, Edited, with a Memoir by his Literary Executor (John Laird). London: Macmillan, 1939.

Includes a bibliography of his works, "Elenchus Operum," on pp. 387-390.

AL-FĀRĀBĪ

15. Rescher, Nicholas. Al-Fārābī: an Annotated Bibliography. Pittsburgh: University of Pittsburgh Press, 1962. 54 pp.

References to about 300 works arranged alphabetically. Also includes a "Topical register of Al-Fārābī studies" which serves as an index. Includes a list of about a dozen bibliographies. Also: the review by W. I. Quinn in The New Scholasticism, vol. 37 (1963), pp. 528-533 for a supplement and corrections.

16. Cunbur, Müjgân. Fârâbi bibliyografyası, kitap-makale (Dogumunun 1100 üncü yıldonümü münasebetiyle). (Basbakanlık kültür müstesarliğl. Cumhuriyet'in 50. yildönümü yayınları: 4) [Fârâbi bibliography, books, articles (In connection with the 1100th anniversary of his birth). (Culture Secretariat of the Prime Minister's Office. Publications of the Republic's 50th anniversary, no. 4) [In Turkish]]Ankara: Basbakanlık Basımevi, 1973. 115 pp.

AL-GHAZALI. See also 5.

17. Bouyges, Maurice. Essai de chronologie des oeuvres de Al-Ghazali (Al-Gazel), édité et mis à jour par Michel Allard. (Institut de lettres orientales de Beyrouth, 14). Beyrouth: Imprimerie catholique, 1959. 204 pp.

18. Badawī, 'Abd al-Rahmān. Mu'allafāt al-Ghazālī [In Arabic]. Added title page: Les oeuvres d'al-Ghazali, étude bibliographique par 'Abdurrahmân Badawi. (Series: United Arab Republic. al-Majis al-A'la li-Ri'āyat al-Funūn wa-al-Adāb wa-al-'Ulūm al-Ijti mā'īyah. al-Matbū'āt, 22). Cairo: [prob. Higher Council for the Supervision of Arts, Literature, and Social Science], 1961. 567 pp.

A large bibliography on al-Ghazâli.

19. Van Leeuwen, A. P. "Essai de bibliographie sur Al-Ghazzali," Ibla. Institut des Belles Lettres Arabes (Tunis), vol. 21 (1958), pp. 221-227.

AL-KINDĪ

20. Rescher, Nicholas. Al-Kindī: An Annotated-Bibliography. Pittsburgh: University of Pittsburgh Press, 1964. 55 pp.

About 500 entries alphabetically arranged. Topic index.

ALONSO ALONSO, MANUEL

21. Gómez Nogales, Salvador, "Nota bio-bibliográfica [: Mañuel Alonso Alonso]," Pensamiento (Madrid), vol. 25 (1969), pp. 5-20.

ALTANER, BERTHOLD

22. "Bibliographie Berthold Altaner (Abgeschlossen 6. April 1958)," Goerres-Gesellschaft zur Pflege der Wissenschaft in katholischen Deutschland. Historischen Jahrbuch (Bonn), vol. 77 (1958), pp. 576-600.

ANDERSON, JOHN

23. Anderson, John. Studies in Empirical Philosophy with an Introduction by John Passmore. Sidney: Angus and Robertson, 1962. 389 pp.

Contains an Anderson bibliography, pp. 375-378.

AQUINAS, THOMAS. See also: 9, 226, 962.

24. Quetif, J. and J. Echard. Scriptores Ordinis Praedicatorum. Vol. 1-2, Paris: 1719-1721. Vol. 3 by R. Coulton and A. Papillon, Paris: 1910-1934. Vol. 1: to 1500; Vol. 2: to 1720; Vol. 3: 1700-1750.

25. Chevolier, Cyr Ulysse Joseph. Catalogue critique des oeuvres de st. Thomas d'Aquin. Romans: Imp. R. Sibillat André, 1886. 16 pp.

26. Domet de Vorges, Cte. "Bibliographie de la philosophie thomiste de 1877 à 1887," Annales de philosophie chrétienne (Paris), n.s. vol. 18 (1888), pp. 577-602.

27. Domet de Vorges, Cte. "La Philosophie thomiste pendant les années 1888-1898," Compte-rendu des travaux du Congrès bibliographique international tenu à Paris du 13 au 16 avril 1898. Paris: Société Bibliographique, 1900. Vol. 1, pp. 84-108.

28. Viel, A. "Le Mouvement thomiste au XIXe siècle. Apercu d'après ses historiens," Revue Thomiste (Paris), (1909), pp. 733-746; (1910), pp. 95-108.

29. Mandonnet, P. Des Ecrits authentiques de St. Thomas, 2. éd., (Extrait de la Revue thomiste, 1909, 1910). Frilbourg, Switz.: Convict Albertinum, 1910. 142 pp. Also: 2. éd. revue et corrigée. Fribourg (Suisse): Impro. de l'Oeuvre de Saint-Paul, 1910. 158 pp.

30. Michelitsch, Anton. Thomasschriften; Untersuchungen über die Schriften Thomas' von Aquino. Graz und Wien: Verlagsbh. "Styria," 1913. 252 pp.

31. Grabmann, Martin. Die echten Schriften des heiligen Thomas von Aquin. Münster i. W.: Aschendorff, 1920. 275 pp. Also: Second edition, Die Werke des heiligen Thomas von Aquin, Münster i. W.: 1931.

32. Mandonnet, P. and J. Destreg. Bibliographie thomiste (Revue des Sciences Philosophiques et Théologiques, supplement). Kain, Belg.: Le Saulchoir, 1921. 116 pp. 2nd ed.: Completed and revised by M. D. Chenu, Paris: J. Vrin, 1960, 119 pp.

Covers the period, 1800-1920. Continued by V. J. Bourke "Thomistic bibliography, 1920-1940" and by Bulletin Thomiste, vols. 1 (1924)-7 (1930) published in the Revue Thomiste (Paris), vols. 8 ff. published separately. 2219 entries.

33. Kowalski, K., "Przeglad liter. neotomist. ostatn. lat. [Survey of Neo-Thomist Literature of Recent Yeras [In Polish]]," Przeglad filozofski, vol. 33 (1930), pp. 161-173.

34. Bulletin thomiste (Paris), vol. 1 (1924)--[to date]. Vols. 1-7 (1924-1930) are in Revue thomiste; vol. 8 (1931) published separately.

Contains bibliographies in section "Bibliographie critique."

35. Labergie, firm, booksellers, Paris. [Catalogue de librairie, methodique et pratique] octobre, 1932. Bordeaux: J. Biere, 1932. 165 pp.

Classified in two parts: A: Bibliothèque d' initiation et de doctrine thomistes; B: Bibliothèque dominicaine.

36. Van Steenberghen, Fernand. "La Litterature thomiste récente," Revue Neoscholastique de Philosophie (Louvain), vol. 42 (1939), pp. 591-608.

37. Bourke, Vernon J. "Thomistic bibliography, 1920-1940," The Modern Schoolman, Supplement to vol. 21. St. Louis, Mo.: 1945. 312 pp.

4764 entries.

38. Wyser, Paul. Thomas von Aquin (Bibliographische Einführungen in das Studium Der philosophie, 13/14). Bern: A. Francke, 1950. 78 pp.

About 900 entries giving good coverage of various aspects of Aquinas' philosophy, but without annotations. Analytical subject headings.

39. Wyser, Paul. Der Thomismus (Bibliographische Einführungen in das Studium der Philosophie, 15/16). Bern: A. Francke, 1950. 120 pp.

About 1500 entries. Nice coverage of the tradition since Aquinas. Index.

40. Rondet, Louis. "Saint Thomas," (Bulletin de Theologie Historique. Etudes Médiévals, II). Recherches de Science Religieuse, (Paris) vol. 38 (1951), pp. 144-160.

41. De Raedemaeker, F. "Tomistische Literatuur," Katholiek cultureel tijdschrift streven (Amsterdam), vol. 2 (1949), pp. 1188-1200; vol. 5 (1951-1952), I, pp. 45-56.

42. Rossi, Giovanni Felice. Antiche e nuove edizioni degli opuscoli de san Tommaso d'Aquino e il problema della loro authenticità. (Monografie del Collegio Alberoni, n. 22). Piacenza: Collegio Alberoni, 1955. 73 pp.

43. Eschmann, I. T. "A Catalogue of St. Thomas's Works: Bibliographical Notes," in E. Gilson, The Christian Philosophy of St. Thomas Aquinas, New York: Random House, 1956, pp. 381-439.

98 entries, a few of which the authenticity is debatable. Aims at being complete. Detailed annotations that give editions and translations.

44. De Raedemaker, F. "Kroniek van Thomistische Literatur, II," Bijdragen; tijdschrift voor Filosofie en Theologie (Amsterdam), vol. 17 (1956), pp. 280-302.

45. Sanchez, J., and C. Ferreira. "Rassegna bibliografica sul pensiero di S. Tommaso," Filosofia e Vita (Torino), vol. 1 (1960), pp. 68-82.

46. Van Steenkiste, C. "Codici tomistici della Biblioteca Domenicana di Vienna," Angelicum (Rome), vol. 38 (1961), pp. 133-165.

47. "Select Bibliography on Teaching Thomism Today," in G. F. McLean, ed., Teaching Thomism Today. Washington: The Catholic University of America Press, 1963, pp. 375-378.

ARDIGÒ, ROBERTO

48. Levi, Alessandro. "Bibliografia ardighiana," Rivista di Filosofia (Torino), vol. 19 (1928) pp. 400-429; vol. 20 (1929), pp. 171-196, 395-420.

49. "Appendice alla bibliografia ardighiana," Rivista di filosofia (Torino), vol. 31 (1940), pp. 56-65.

An appendix to Levi's bibliography.

ARISTOTLE. See also 118, 120, 1234, 1235.

50. Moraux, Paul. Les Listes anciennes des ouvrages d'Aristote. Pref. par Augustin Mansion. Louvain: Editions Universitaires de Louvain, 1951. 391 pp.

Bibliographical footnotes plus a bibliography, pp. 347-359.

51. Mioni, Elpidio. Aristotelis Codices Graeci qui in Bibliothecis Ventis Adservantuer. (Miscellanea Erudita, vol. VI.) Patavii: In Aedibus Antenoreis, 1958. 162 pp.

52. Siwek, Paul. Le De anima d'Aristote dans les manuscrits grecs (Studi e testi, 241). Citta del Vaticano: Biblioteca apostolica vaticana, 1965. 196 pp.

53. Minio-Paluello, Lauerentius. Aristoteles Latinus Codices: Supplementa Altera. Bruges et Paris: de Brouwer, 1961.

Adds 182 codices and some emendations to the Lacombe work. Index.

54. Wingate, Sybil Douglas. The Mediaeval Latin Versions of the Aristotelian Scientific Corpus, with Special Reference to the Biological Works. London [etc.]: The Courier Press, 1931. 135 pp.

With bibliographical notes.

55. Legowicz, Jan. "Projet d'inventaire des commentaires medievaux d'Aristote," in La Filosofia della natura nel medioevo (atti del Terzo congresso invernaxionale de filosofia medioevale passo della Mendola (Trento). Milano: Società Editrice Vita e pensiero, 1966, pp. 777-787.

56. Lohr, Charles H. "Medieval Latin Aristotle Commentaries, Authors: Narcissus-Richardus," Traditio (Bronx, N.Y.), vol. 28 (1972), pp. 281-396.

Alphabetical listing of medieval commentaries continuing that in earlier issues of Traditio.

57. Markowski, Mieczyslaw. Repertorium Commentariorum Medii Aevi in Aristotelem Latinorum que in Bibliotheca Iegellonica Cracoviae Asseorvantur/Composuerunt Miecislaus Markowski, Sophia Wlodek. Wrocw: Zaklad Narodowy im. Ossolínskich, 1974. 210 pp.

Contains indexes.

58. De Raedemaeker, Jozef. "Une Ebauche de catalogue des commentaires sur le De anima parus aux XIIIe XIVe et XVe siècles," Bulletin de philosophie mediévale edité par la société internationale pour l'étude de la philosophie médiévale (Louvain), vol. 6 (1964), pp. 119-134.

59. De Raedemaeker, Jozef. "Une Ebauche de catalogue des commentaires sur les Parva Naturalia parus aux XIIIe, XIVe, et XVe siècles," Bulletin de philosophie medievale édité par la société internationale pour l'étude de la philosophie medievale (Louvain), vol. 7 (1965), pp. 95-108.

60. Cranz, P. Edward. A Bibliography of Aristotle Editions 1501-1600. (Bibliotheca Bibliographica Aureliana, 38). Baden-Baden: V. Koerner, 1971. 187 pp.

Composed of the entries on Aristotle in the Index Aureliensis. With an introduction and indexes.

61. Labbé, Philippe. Aristotelis et Platonis Graecorum Interpretum Typis Hactenus Editorum Brevis Conspectus. Ex Athenaea Philosophico, seu Bibliotheca Aristotelis & Platonis Interpretum Omniúmque Cuiuscumque Sectae Philosophorum, qui Gracaè aliquid Scripsisse Noscuntur, aut Praelo Excusum, aut in Mss. Codicibus ad hune Vsque diem Reconditum. Lvtetiae Parisiorum: ex Officina Cramosiana, 1657. 31 pp.

61. (Continued)

329 entries.

62. Pennsylvania University Library. Aristotle Texts and Commentaries to 1700 in the University of Pennsylvania Library; a Catalogue by Lyman W. Riley. Philadelphia: University of Pennsylvania Press, 1961. 109 pp.

First appeared in five installments in the University of Pennsylvania Chronicle, vols. 22 (1956) to 24 (1958).

63. Buhle, Johann Gottlieb Gerhard. De Distributione Librorum Aristotelis in Exotericos et Acroamaticos eiusque Rationibus et Causis. Gottingae: J. C. Dieterich, 1786. 97 pp.

64. Chandler, Henry William. A Catalogue of Editions of Aristotle's Nicomachean Ethics and of Works Illustrative of Them, Printed in the Fifteenth Century. Oxford: "Not published," 1869. 47 pp. Also: Corrections and Additions: Oxford, 1878.

Twenty-five copies printed.

65. Chandler, Henry William. Chronological Index of Editions of Aristotle's Nicomachean Ethics, and of Works Illustrative of Them, from the Origin of Printing to the Year 1799. Oxford: E. P. Hall and J. H. Staey, Printers, 1878. 45 pp.

Fifty copies printed.

66. "Bibliography of Aristotle," Journal of Speculative Philosophy (St. Louis, Mo.), vol. 20 (1886), pp. 439-443.

67. Oxford University. Pembroke College library. A Catalog of the Aristotelian and Philosophical Portions of the Library of the Late Henry William Chandler. Oxford: 1891.

68. Paris. Bibliothèque nationale. Department des impremés. Aristote. Supplément au catalogue précédement publié des oeuvres de cet auteur conservées au Départment des imprimés de la Bibliothèque nationale. Paris: Imprimerie nationale, 1896. 37 pp. Also: 1901, etc.

69. Schwab, Moïse. Bibliographie d'Aristote. Paris: Welter, 1896. 380 pp. Reprinted: New York: B. Franklin, 1967.

Contains 3742 entries. Fairly complete for the period covered.

70. Dyroff, A. "Jahresbericht über die deutsche Literatur zur Nacharistotelischen Philosophie (1897-1903)," Archiv für Geschichte der Philosophie (Berlin), vol. 17 (1903-1904), pp. 144-157, 275-287.

71. Grabmann, Martin. Forschugen über die lateinischen Aristotelesübersetzungen des XIII. Jahrhunderts. Münster: Aschendorff, 1916. 270 pp.

72. Cooper, Lane, and Alfred Gudeman. A Bibliography of the Poetics of Aristotle (Cornell Studies in English, no. 11). New Haven: Yale University Press; London: Humphrey Milford, Oxford University Press, 1928. 194 pp.

About 1590 entries. References to Greek texts, translations, commentaries, etc. No annotations, name index. Supersedes Cooper's bibliography in his booklet on the Poetics in the "Our Debt to Greece and Rome" series. 1923. 750 titles.

73. British Museum. Department of Printed Books. Aristole: an Excerpt from the General Catalog of Printed Books in the British Museum. London: W. Clowes and Sons, 1933. 170 cols. Also: 1884, 110 cols.

74. Berlin. Preussische Staatsbibliothek. Deutscher Gesamtkatalog. Aristoteles. [Gesamtkatalog der Pressischen Bibliotheken mit Nachweis des identischen Besitzes der Bayrischen Staatsbibliothek in München und der National-Bibliothek in Wien, Aristoteles]. Berlin: Preussische Druckerei- und Verlags-Aktiengesellschaft, 1934. Also published as: Aristoteles [:Bibliographie]. Berlin: 1934. 156 pp.

About 1400 entries of editions and translations.

75. Lacombe, Georgius. Aristoteles Latinus. Roma: La Libreria dello stato, 1939. 763 pp. Reprinted: Cambridge, England: Cambridge University Press, 1955; Paris and Bruges: de Brouwer, 1957.

1120 entries. Contains select bibliography of works on Aristotle manuscripts in Latin, plus locations of extant manuscripts.

76. Philippe, Marie-Dominique. Aristoteles. (Bibliographische Einführungen in das Studium der Philosophie, 8). Bern: A. Francke, 1948. 48 pp.

About 480 entries. Good on editions, and commentaries; few works in English. Index.

77. De. Vleeschauwer, Herman Jan. L'Odyssée de la bibliothèque d'Aristote et ses répercussions philosophiques. (Mousaion. Bolk-en biblioteekwese. Books and Libraries. Nr. 24-25.) Pretoria: 1957. 2 vols.

78. Long, Herbert S. "A Bibliographical Survey of Recent Work on Aristotle," Classical World (New York), vol. 51 (1957-1958), pp. 47-51, 57-60, 69-76, 96-98, 117-119, 160-162, 167-168, 193-194, 204-209.

79. Mansion, Auguste. "Travaux d'ensemble sur Aristote, son oeuvre et sa philosophie," Revue Philosophique de Louvain (Louvain), vol. 57 (1959), pp. 44-70.

80. Moraux, Paul. "Errichtung eines Aristoteles-archivs an der Freien universität Berlin," Scriptorum (Bruxelles), vol. 20 (1966), p. 71.

81. Rhode, Gisela. Bibliographie der deutschen Aristoteles-Übersetzungen vom Beginn d. Buchdrucks bis 1964. Frankfurt am Main: Klostermann, 1967. 104 pp.

82. Lohr, Charles H. "Aristotle in the West: Some Recent Books," Traditio (Bronx, N.Y.), vol. 25 (1969), pp. 417-431.

Discusses books published in the 1960s on the history of Latin Aristotelianism from the 12th to the 16th century.

83. Schmitt, Charles B. A Critical Survey and Bibliography of Studies on Renaissance Aristotelianism, 1958-1969. (Saggi e testi, 11) Padova: Antenore, 1971. 196 pp.

84. Cosenza, Paolo. "Studi su Aristotele nel secolo XX," Logos (Napoli), (1972), pp. 265-282.

85. Erickson, Keith. Aristotle's Rhetoric: Five Centuries of Philogical Research/Compiled with an Introduction by Keith V. Erickson. Metuchen, N. J.: Scarecrow Press, 1975. 187 pp.

ARON, WILLY

86. German Jewish Publishers of New York. A Bibliographical Essay, Containing an Account of Books, Treatises, Essays and Articles Written by Willy Aron, also Extracts from a Philosophical Correspondence between Albert Einstein and Willy Aron Relating to the Problems of Space and Time, and Spinoza's Cogitato et Extensio. New York: the German-Jewish Publishers of America, Section: Science and Literature, 1935. 10 pp.

ASCHERI, CARLO

87. "Bibliografia degli scritti di Carlo Ascheri," in Studi in memoria di Carlo Ascheri, Urbino: Argalià, 1970, pp. xv-xvi.

ASÍN, MIGUEL

88. Longas, Pedro. "Bibliografía de don Miguel Asín," Al-Andalus (Madrid), vol. 9 (1944), pp. 293-319.

ASPELIN, GUNNAR

89. Aspelin, Inga-Lill. "Bibliography of Writings Published 1917-1962 by Gunnar Aspelin," in Philosophical Essays Presented to Gunnar Aspelin on his Sixty-fifth Birthday. Lund: C. W. K. Gleerup, 1963, pp. 319-364.

ASTI VERA, ARMANDO

90. García Bazan, F. "Bibliografía de Armando Asti Vera," Stromata (San Miguel, Arg.), Vol. 28 (1972), pp. 261-262.

ATTISANI, ADELCHI

91. Lisi, E. "Adelchi Attisani pensatore, studioso e educatore. Profilo bibliografico-critico, con appendice bibliografica: a) Scritti di Adelchi Attisani; b) Scritti su Adelchi Attisani," in Umanità e storia. Scritti in onore di Adelchi Attisani. Napoli: Giannini, 1971, vol. 2, pp. 785-804.

AUER, ALBERT

92. "Bibliographie von Univ.-Prof. Dr. P. Albert Auer, O. S. B.," in Festschrift für Albert Auer: Salzburger Jahrbuch für Philosophie (Salsburg), vols. 5-6 (1961-1962), pp. 9-12.

AUGUSTINE OF HIPPO

93. Lowe, Elias Avery. A List of the Oldest Extant Manuscripts of Saint Augustine, with a Note on the Codex Bambergensis. (Estratto dalla Miscellanea Agustiniana, vol. 2) [Roma]: Tipografia poliglotta vaticana, 1931, pp. 235-251.

Includes only manuscripts in uncial and half-uncial script.

94. Zumkeller, Adolar. "Manuskripte von Werke der Autoren des Augustinerere mit Enordens in mitteleuropäischen Bibliotheken (Fortsetzung folgt)," Augustiniana (Heverlee und Leuven), vol. 11 (1961), pp. 27-86, 261-319, 478-532; vol. 12 (1962), pp. 27-92, 299-357, vol. 13 (1963), pp. 418-473.

95. Nebreda, Eulogius. Bibliographia Augustiniana seu Operum Collectio, quae Divi Augustini Vitam et Doctrinam Quadantenus Exponunt. Romae: Cuore di Maria, 1928. 272 pp. Reprinted: Dubuque, Iowa: Wm. C. Brown Reprint Co., 1965.

About 930 entries. Topic index, author index, chronological index. Annotated, with introductory remarks after each subject heading.

96. Raimundo González, P., "Bibliografía Agustiniana del Centenario," in San Agustin en el XV Centenario de su Muerte (430-1930) (Separata del Número extraordinario de Religión y Cultura), El Escorial: Monasterio de El Escorial, 1930, pp. 461-509.

574 Entries. Supplements Nebreda for 1928-1931.

97. Berlin. Staatsbibliothek. Gesamtkatalog der preussischen Staatsbibliothek, Sp. 477-588. Sonderheft. Berlin: Preussiche Druckerei- und Verlagaklien-Gesellschaft, 1935.

98. Perini, D. A. Bibliographia Augustiniana cum Notis Biographicus. (Scriptores Itali, 3). Firenza: Libreria editrice fiorentina, 1936. 316 pp.

99. Gutiérrez, David. "La Bibliografía del último decinio en torno a la escolástica agustiniana," La Ciudad de Dios (Madrid), vol. 156 (1944), pp. 17-46.

100. Sciacca, Michele Federico. Augustinus. (Bibliographische Einführungen in das Studium der Philosophie, 10) Bern: A. Francke, 1948. 32 pp.

100. (Continued)

Chronological chart of his works, plus about 250 entries, primarily books on Augustine. Index.

101. Rondet, Henri. "Etudes augustiniennes," Recherches de sciences religieuses (Paris), vol. 37 (1950), pp. 619-633.

102. De Veer, Albert C. and G. Folliet. "Bulletin augustinien pour 1950," L'Année théologique (Paris), vol. 12 (1951), pp. 359-388.

103. Revue des études augustiniennes (Paris), vol. 1 (1956) --[to date].

Regularly carries a bibliographical "Bulletin augustinien." Continues the Année théologique augusustinienne, vol. 1 (1940)-14 (1954).

104. Boyer, Charles. "Bulletin Augustinien," Gregorianum (Romae), vol. 38 (1957), pp. 134-142.

105. Van Bavel, Tarsicius. "Répertoíre bibliographique de saint Augustin," Augustiniana (Heverlee und Leuven), vol. 10 (1960), pp. 462-546.

See also below: Répertoire bibliographique de Saint Augustin, 1950-1960. The Hague: Nijhoff, 1963.

106. Rondet, Henri. "Bulletin augustinien," Recherches de sciences religieuses (Paris), vol. 50 (1962), pp. 290-302.

107. Andressen, Carl. Augustinus-Gespräch der Gegenwart, Verbunden mit Augustinus-Bibliographie. Köln: Wienand-Verlag, 1962. 583 pp.

108. Lamirande, Emillen. Un Siécle et demi sur l'ecclesiologie de saint Augustin. Essai bibliographique. Paris: Etudes augustiniennes, 1962. 125 pp.

109. Andressen, Carl. Zum Augustingespräch. Mit Bibliographie. (Wege der Forschung, 5) Darmstadt: Wissenschaftl. Buchgesellschaft, 1962. 583 pp.

110. Van Bavel, Tarsicius J. Répertoire bibliographique de saint Augustin, 1950-1960. Avec la collaboration de F. van der Zande. The Hague: M. Nijhoff, 1963. 991 pp. Also: Augustiniana (Leuven), vols. 1-8 (1951-1958) for a serialized version of this bibliography.

Review: C. Van Steenkiste, Angelicum, 1964, pp. 257-258. Van Bavel's work is an exhaustive coverage of the work on Augustine for the period

110. (Continued)

covered, containing 5502 entries of books, journal articles, and editions of Augustine's works. Most entries are annotated and evaluated. Necessary for any serious work on Augustine.

111. Capánaga, Victorino. "Boletín agustiniano," Augustinus (Madrid), vol. 9 (1964), pp. 387-397.

112. Institut des etudes augustiniennes. Fichier augustinien (Augustine bibliography). Paris: 4 vols. 2675 pp. Reprint: Boston: G. K. Hall, 1972.

About 63,000 entries.

113. Andresen, Carl. Bibliographia Augustiniana, 2. völlig. neubearb Anfl. Darmstadt: Wissenschaftliche Buchgesellschaft, 1973. 317 pp. Also: 1962 ed. 127 pp.

AUROBINDO GHOSE (i.e., SRI AUROBINDO). See also 1397.

114. Kaul, H. K. Sri Aurobindo: A Descriptive Bibliography. New Delhi: Munshiram Manoharlal, 1972. 222 pp.

About 1800 entries arranged by topic, name and title indices. Dedicated to all those who live and seek the truth.

115. Mannohan Reddy, Vedre. Sri Aurobindo: a Bibliography. Hyderabad: Institute of Human Study, 1973. 48 pp.

AUSTIN, JOHN LANGSHAW

116. Fann, K. T., ed. Symposium on J. L. Austin. New York: Humanities Press: 1969. 486 pp.

Bibliography, pp. 469-482.

AVERROES (i.e., IBN-RUSHD). See also 5, 1936.

117. Bouyges, Maurice. Notes sur les philosophes arabes connus de Latins au moyen âge, vol. 4. Inventaires des textes arabes d'Averroès in mélanges de l'Université saint-Joseph. Beirut: 1922, vol. 8, Fascicle 1.

118. Wolfson, H. A. "Plan for the Publication of a *Corpus Commentariorum Averrois in Aristotelem*," *Speculum* (Cambridge, Mass.), vol. 6 (1931), pp. 412-427.

119. Gauthier, Léon. *Ibn Rochd (Averroès)*. Paris: Presses universitaires de France, 1948.

"Oeuvres d'Ibn Rochd," pp. 12-16.

120. Wolfson, H. A. "Revised Plan for the Publication of a *Corpus Commentariorum Averrois in Aristotelem*," *Speculum* (Cambridge, Mass.), vol. 38 (1963), pp. 88-104.

121. Vennebusch, Joachim. "Zur Bibliographie des psychologischen Schrifttums des Averroes," *Bulletin de Philosophie Médiévale édité par la Société internationale pour l'étude de la philosophie médiévale* (Louvain), vol. 6 (1964), pp. 92-100.

AVICEBRON (i.e., SOLOMON BEN JUDA IBN-GEBIROL)

122. Munk, Salomon. *Mélanges de philosophie juive et arabe, renfermant des extraits méthodiques de la source de vie de Salomon ibn-Gebirol (dit Avicebron) . . . accompagnés de notes critiques et explicatives;--un mémoire sur la vie, les écrits et la philosophie d'ibn-Gebirol*. Paris: A. Franck, 1859. 536 pp. Also: Paris, G. Gamber, 1927; Paris: J. Vrin, 1955.

123. Kohlmeier, Johann. "Bibliographie zu Ibn Gabirol," *Freiburger Zeitschrift für Philosophie und Theology* (Freiburg), vol. 13-14 (1966-1967), pp. 207-209.

AVICENNA (i.e., IBN-SĪNĀ)

124. Anawati, Georges C. *Mu'allafāt Ibn Sīnā. Essai de bibliographie avicennienne*. Cairo: Dar-al-Maaref, 1950. 20 pp. [French], 31-435 pp. [Arabic].

125. Naficy, Said. *Bibliographie des principaux travaux européens sur Avicenne*. Téhéran: Université de Téhéran, 1953. 30 pp.

About 300 entries.

126. Mehdawi, Yaha. *Bibliographie d'Ibn Sīnā*. (Series: Tehran Dānishgāh Intishārāt, 206). Teheran: 1954.

127. Ergin, Osman. *Ibni Sina: Bibliografyasi/ Bibliographie d'Avicenne*. (Istanbul üniversitiesi tip fakültesi Yayinlarindan, no. 20). Istanbul: Osman Yalçin

127. (Continued)

Matbaasi, 1956. 168 pp.

About 230 entries. Titles in Arabic; manuscript locations in Turkish. Only works by Avicenna. In six parts: his known works; attributed works; translations, summaries, etc. made by him; editions of his works from 1939 to 1955; titles known to him; and different titles of works attributed to him.

BAADER, FRANZ VON

128. Jost, Johannes. Bibliographie der Schriften Franz von Baaders, mit kurzem Lebensabriss. Bonn: F. Cohen, 1926. 24 pp. Reprint from Rheinischer Buch-Anzeiger, Heft 4.

BACHELARD, GASTON

129. Rummens, Jean. "Gaston Bachelard: une bibliographie," Revue Internationale de Philosophie (Bruxelles), vol. 17 (1963), pp. 492-504.

130. "Gaston Bachelard (1884-1962)," Annales de l'Université de Paris (Paris), vol. 33 (1963), pp. 5-9.

131. Aron, Raymond. Notice sur la vie et les travaux de Gaston Bachelard (1884-1962) (Institut de France. Académie des sciences morales et politiques--1965, 7). Paris: impr. Firmin-Didot, 1965. 22 pp.

132. Dagognet, Francois. Gaston Bachelard. Sa vie, son oeuvre avec un exposé de sa philosophie. Paris: Presses universitaires de France, 1965. 116 pp.

BACON, FRANCIS

133. British Museum. Department of Printed Books. Catalog of Printed Books. [Francis] Bacon. London, 1884. 24 cols.

134. Woodward, Parker. Francis Bacon's Works (Acknowledged, Visared, or Suspected). London: Sweeting and Co., 1912. 105 pp.

135. Spedding, James. The Collection of Books Used by James Speeding as his Working Library in Preparing his

135. (Continued)

Edition of the Works of Sir Francis Bacon. London: Strangeways and Sons, Printers, 1916. 24 pp.

136. Livingston, Dorothy F., and M. M. Patton. "Contributions to a Bibliography of Francis Bacon; Editions before 1700 in Yale Libraries," in Papers in honor of Andrew Keogh. New Haven: Privately printed, 1938, pp. 95-143.

67 entries with brief descriptions.

137. Gibson, R. W. Francis Bacon: a Bibliography of his Works and of Baconiana to the Year 1750. Oxford: Scrivener Press, 1950. 369 pp.

________. Supplement. (Privately issued under the auspices of the Francis Bacon Foundation of Pasadena, California). Oxford: Bruning Copyflex reproduction of typescript privately issued, 1959.

About 700 entries, including about 440 works on Bacon. Annotated with index. Period covered: 1597-1750.
Supplement contains about 240 additions to the above work. Index.

138. Rossi, Paolo. "Per una bibliografia degli scritti su Francesco Bacone (1800-1956)," Rivista critica di storia della filosofia (Milano), vol. 12 (1957), pp. 75-89.

139. Patrick, J. Max. Francis Bacon. British Council: British Book News, Bibliographical Series of Supplements, no. 131, 1961. 43 pp.

140. Vickers, Brian. Essential Articles for the Study of Francis Bacon. London: Sidgwick and Jackson, 1972. 323 pp.

BACON, ROGER

141. Easton, Stewart Copinger. Roger Bacon and his Search for a Universal Science. Oxford and New York: Columbia University Press, 1952. 255 pp.

Contains annotated bibliographies, pp. 236-244.

142. Alessio, F. "Un seculo di studi su Ruggero Bacone (1848-1957)," Rivista critica di storia della filosofia (Firenze), vol. 14 (1959), pp. 81-108.

BAILEY, SAMUEL

143. Ireland, A. "Bailey of Sheffield," Notes and Queries (London), 9 March, 16 March, 27 April, 1878; 21 June, 1879.

BALFOUR, ARTHUR JAMES

144. Robertson, John M. "The Right Hon. Arthur James Balfour . . . 'Bibliography'," English Illustrated Magazine (London), new series, vol. 29 (1903), pp. 436, 442.

BALIĆ, CHARLES

145. Barnabas, Hechich. "Bibliographia P. Caroli Balić OFM Systematico Ordine Digesta," in Studia Mediavalia et Mariologica. P. Carolo Balić OFM Septuagesimum Explenti Annum Dicata. (Pontificium Athenaeum "Antonianum") Romae" Ed. Antonianum, 1971, pp. 37-63.

BALMES, JAIME

146. De Mendosa, Juan. "Bibliografía balmesiana. Ediciones y estudios," Analecta Sacra Tarraconiensa (Barcelona), vol. 33 (1960), pp. 1-272.

147. De Dios Mendoza, Juan. Bibliografía balmesiana. Ediciones y estudios. (Biblioteca histórica de la Biblioteca Balmes. Serie II. Vol. XXIV) Barcelona: Editiones Balmes, 1961. 272 pp.

BARDILI, CHRISTOPH GOTTFRIED

148. Garbein, F. W. "Bibliographie Ju Christoph Gottfried Bardili. Ans den Quellen ermittelt und historisch-kritisch erläutert," Wiener Jahrbuch für Philosophie (Wien), vol. 7 (1974), pp. 7-59.

BARDY, GUSTAVE

149. De Veer, Albert C. "Bibliographie choisie des travaux de M. Gustave Bardy," Review des études augustiniennes (Paris), vol. 2 (1956), pp. 9-37.

BARION, JAKOB

150. Baumanns, Peter. "Ausgewählte Bibliographie der Veroffentlichugen von Jakob Barion," Zeitschrift für philosophische Forschung (Meisenheim am Glan), vol. 22 (1968), pp. 463-466.

BARTH, TIMOTHEUS

151. Reuter, Ottfried. "Zum Schrifttum des P. Timotheus Barth O.F.M.," Wissenschaft und Weisheit (Freiburg i. Bremen), vol. 30 (1967), pp. 205-212.

BARZIN, MARCEL

152. Paumen, Jean. "Bibliographie: Travaux de M. [Marcel] Barzin," Revue de l'Université de Bruxelles (Bruxelles), vol. 13 (1960-1961), pp. 340-342.

BASTIDE, GEORGES

153. ["Principal books and articles: Georges Bastide,"] in G. Deladalle and D. Huisman, eds., Les Philosophes français d'aujourd'hui [n.p., n.d.], pp. 260-261.

BATAILLE, GEORGES

154. "Bibliographie, I: Oeuvres de Georges Bataille," Critique (Paris), vol. 19 (1963), pp. 195-196.

155. "Bibliographie, II. Etudes et articles sur Georges Bataille," Critique (Paris), vol. 19 (1963), pp. 803-832.

BAYER, RAYMOND

156. ["Bibliographie: Raymond Bayer,"] in G. Deledalle and D. Huisman, eds., Les Philosophes francais d'aujourd'hui, [n.p., n.d.], pp. 193-195.

Six books mentioned.

BAYLE, PIERRE

157. Labrousse, Elisabeth. *Inventaire critique de la correspondance de Pierre Bayle.* (Bibliothèque d'histoire de la philosophie). Paris: Librarie philosophique J. Vrin, 1961. 413 pp.

About 2000 entries arranged chronologically and alphabetically, with introduction.

BEARD, CHARLES A. See 159.

BECCARIA, GIAMBATTISTA

158. Balbo, P. *Catalogo delle opere di Giambattista Beccaria.* Firenze: Sansoni, 1961. 17 pp.

BECKER, CARL L.

159. Rule, John C. and Ralph D. Handen. "Bibliography of Works on Carl Lotus Becker and Charles Austin Beard, 1945-1963," *History and Theory* (Den Haag), vol. 5 (1966), pp. 302-314.

BECKER, KARL FERDINAND

160. Weigand, Georg. *Karl Ferdinand Becker, ein hessischer Pädagoge und Sprach-Philosoph des 19. Jahrhunderts.* Frankfurt am Main: Diesterweg, 1966. 102 pp.

Contains a Becker bibliography.

BECKER, OSKAR

161. Zimny, Leo. "Oskar Becker--Bibliographie," *Kant-Studien* (Bonn), vol. 60 (1969), pp. 319-330.

BEDE (THE VENERABLE)

162. Berlin. Preussische Staatsbibliothek. *Deutscher Gesamtkatalog.* *Beda Venerabilis [:Bibliographie].* Berlin: Preussische druckerei-und Verlags-A. G., 1938. 12 pp.

BELLARMINE, ROBERTO F. R.

163. "A Bellarmine Bibliography," in Gerard Smith, ed., Jesuit Thinkers of the Renaissance. Milwaukee: Marquette University Press, 1939, pp. 242-254.

BELLO, ANDRÉS

164. Grases, Pedro. "Bibliografía de Andres Bello," Revista Nacional de Cultura (Caracas), no. 172 (1965), pp. 153-169.

BENEŠ, ÉDOUARD

165. Îakovenkoh, Borīs Valentīnovīch. La Bibliographie d'Édouard Beneš. Prague: Imprimé chez "Blahoslav," 1936. 123 pp.

BENTHAM, JEREMY

166. Everett, C. W. "Bibliography [of and on Jeremy Bentham]," in Elie Halévy, The Growth of Philosophical Radicalism. London: Faber and Faber, 1928, pp. 522-546.

> 170 entries by Bentham (including editions, translations). 60 works on Bentham. Annotated. Exhaustive coverage on Bentham's works in various editions up through about 1925. Good.

167. Muirhead, Arnold Meadowcroft. "A Jeremy Bentham collection," The Library (London), fifth series, vol. 1 (1946), pp. 6-27. "Transactions of the bibliographical society."

168. Milne, Alexander Taylor. Catalogue of the Manuscripts of Jeremy Bentham in the Library of University College London. 2nd ed. London: University of London, Athlone press, 1962. 104 pp.

BERGER, GASTON

169. Bayen, Maurice. "Gaston Berger (1896-1960)," Revue de l'Enseignement supérieur (Paris), vol. 5 (1960), pp. 5-10.

BERGSON, HENRÍ. See also 962.

170. Columbia University. Libraries. A Contribution to a Bibliography of Henrí Bergson. I. G. Mudge, ed. New York: Columbia University Press, 1913. 56 pp.

171. Coviello, Alfredo. El Proceso filosófico de Bergson y su bibliografía. 2nd ed. Tucumán, Argentina: Revista Sustáncia, 1941. 117 pp.

172. J. L. "Bibliographie [de Bergson]," Revue internationale de philosophie (Bruxells), vol. 3 (1949), pp. 459-478.

173. Millet, Louis. "Note pour une bibliographie bergsonienne," in Les Etudes bergsoniennes, vol. 4. Paris: Albin Michel, 1956, pp. 243-244.

174. Mossé-Bastide, R.-M. ["Bibliographie bergsonienne, 1945-1952"], in Les Etudes bergsoniennes, vol. 4. Paris: Albin Michel, 1956, pp. 245-254.

175. Casas, M. G. "Bibliografia bergsoniana in Spagna e nell'America latina," Giornale di metafisica (Torino), vol. 14 (1959), pp. 866-872.

176. Mathieu, V. "Bibliografia bergsoniana in Francia (1945-1959)," Giornale di metafisica (Torino), vol. 14 (1959), pp. 835-856.

177. Paris. Bibliothèque nationale. Henri Bergson; exposition du centeraire. Paris: 1959. 54 pp.

178. Bréhier, Emile. "Notice sur la vie et les travaux de Henrí Bergson," in his Etudes de Philosophie moderne. Paris: Presses universitaires de France, 1965, pp. 129-144.

179. Kremer-Marietti, Angèle. "Bibliographie: Bergson dans l'histoire," Les Etudes bergsoniennes, vol. 10 (1973), pp. 189-195.

180. Gunter, P. A. Y. Henrí Bergson: A Bibliography. Bowling Green, Ohio: Philosophy Documentation Center, 1974. 457 pp.

> 470 entries by Bergson and about 4000 entries about him. Indexed.

181. Washington, D. C. Library of Congress. References on Henrí Bergson. 3 pp.

BERKELEY, GEORGE

182. Mead, Herman Ralph. . . . A Bibliography of George Berkeley, Bishop of Cloyne. (University of California. Library Bulletin No. 17). Berkeley, California: The University Press, 1910. 46 pp.

183. Archibald, R. C. "Bibliography of George Berkeley." Scripta Mathematica (New York), vol. 3 (1935), pp. 81-83.

184. Dublin University. Trinity College. Library. Catalog of the Manuscripts, Books, and the Berkeleiana Exhibited in the Library of Trinity College, Dublin, on the Occasion of the Commemoration of the Bicentenary of the Death . . . Dublin: Dublin University Press, 1953. 35 pp.

Annotated list of 137 items.

185. Lameere, J. [et al.] "Bibliographie [Berkeley]," Revue internationale de philosophie (Bruxelles), vol. 7 (1953), pp. 152-156.

A supplement to Jessop for 1934-1953.

186. Leroy, A. L. "Etudes berkeleyennes récentes," Revue philosophique de la France et de l'étranger (Paris), vol. 83 (1958), pp. 352-362.

187. Turbayne, C. M. and Robert X. Ware. "A Bibliography of George Berkeley, 1933-1962." Journal of Philosophy (New York), vol. 60 (1963), pp. 93-112.

188. Jessop, Thomas Edmund. "George Berkeley: A Select Bibliography," in W. E. Steinkraus, ed., New studies in Berkeley's Philosophy. New York: Holt, Rinehart, and Winston, 1966, pp. 173-180.

189. Jessop, Thomas Edmund. A Bibliography of George Berkeley . . .with an Inventory of Berkeley's Manuscripts Remains by A. A. Luce. Oxford: Oxford University Press; London: Humphrey Milford, 1934. 99 pp. Reprint: New York: B. Franklin, 1968. 2nd. ed: The Hague: M. Nijhoff, 1973, 155 pp., revised and enlarged.

Aims at completeness for works, posthumously published works, translations, manuscripts. Also has about 517 works on Berkeley, 1707-1733.

BERNARD OF CLAIRVAUX

190. Janauschek, Leopold. Bibliographia Bernardian; qua Sancti Bernardi, Primi Abbatis Claravallensis, Operum cum

190. (Continued)

Omnium tum Singulorum, Editiones ac Versiones, Vitas et Tractatus, de eo Scriptos Quotquot usque ad Finem Anni MDCCCXC Reperire Potuit Collegit et Adnotavit P. Leopoldus Janauschek . . . Vindobonae: in Commissis apud A. Hölder, 1891. 558 pp. Also: Hildesheim: G. Olms, 1959.

Continued by Bouton's bibliography.

191. Van Gassel, E. "Bibliographie over de H. Bernardus," in Sint Bernardus van Clairvaux. Rotterdam: Forel, 1953, pp. 337-350.

Works, biographies, studies of his works.

192. Talbot, C. H. "Bibliografia di s. Bernardo," Rivista di storia della Chiesa in Italia (Roma), vol. 8 (1954), pp. 438-442.

193. Bouton, Jean de la Croix. Bibliographie bernardine, 1891-1957. Paris: P. Hethielleux, 1958. 164 pp.

A continuation of L. Janauschek's Bibliographia Bernardina.

194. Leclercq, Jean. Recueil d'études sur saint Bernard et ses écrits, I. Roma: Edizioni di storia e letteratura, 1962. 369 pp.

BERTALANFFY, LUDWIG VON

195. Laszlo, Ervin. The Relevance of General Systems Theory: Papers Presented to Ludwig von Bertalanffy on his Seventieth Birthday. New York: George Braziller, 1972.

Pp. 203-204 contain a list of 41 selected recent books on general systems theory; pp. 205-206 contain a list of 15 books by von Bertalanffy.

196. Gray, William, and Nicholas D. Rizzo, eds. Unity through Diversity: a Festschrift in Honor of Ludwig von Bertalanffy. New York, London, and Paris: Gordon and Breach, 1973, 2 vols.

Contains a bibliography of about 280 entries consisting of von Bertalanffy's works.

BETH, E. W.

197. Staal, J. F. "Bibliography of E. W. Beth," Dialectica (Neuchâtel), vol. 19 (1965), pp. 166-179.

198. Staal, J. F. "Bibliography of E. W. Beth," Synthése (Amsterdam), vol. 16 (1966), pp. 90-106.

BINSWANGER, LUDWIG

199. Sneessens, Germaine. "Bibliographie de Ludwig Binswanger," Revue philosophique de Louvain (Louvain), vol. 64 (1966), pp. 594-602.

BIRKENMAJER, ALEXANDRE

200. "Choix de la bibliographie des oeuvres d'Alexandre Birkenmajer," Mediaevalia Philosophica Polonorum (Warszawa), no. 10 (1961), pp. 9-21.

BLOCH, ERNST

201. Bloch (Ernst). Wissen und Hoffen, Auszüge aus seinen Werken 1918-1955, Festgabe zum 70 Geburtstag von Ernst Bloch am 8. Juli 1955. Berlin: Aufbau-Verlag, 1955. 90 pp.

Introduction to his work and bibliography.

202. "Verzeichnis der Schriften Ernst Blochs," Ernst Bloch zum 70. Geburtstag; Festschrift. Berlin: Deutscher Verlag der Wissenschaften, 1955, pp. 13-15.

203. "Vorläufige Bibliographie [: Ernst Bloch]," in Siegfried Unseld, ed., Ernst Bloch zu Ehren, Frankfort am Main: Suhrkamp verlag, 1965, pp. 395-413.

204. Wren, Thomas E. "An Ernest Bloch Bibliography for English Readers," Philosophy Today (Celina, Ohio), vol. 14 (1970), pp. 272-273.

BLONDEL, MAURICE

205. "Maurice Blondel (1961-1949)," Ciencia y fe. (San Miguel, FCSM, Argentina), vol. 5 (1949), pp. 8-10.

Bibliography of his principal works.

206. Crippa, Romeo. "Rassegna di bibliografia blondeliana," *Giornale di metafisica* (Torino), vol. 6 (1951), pp. 602-638.

Also: Torino: Società editrice internazionale, 1952.

207. Hayen, André. "Bibliografia blondélienne (1888-1951)," *Teoresi* (Catania), vol. 7 (1952), pp. 5-87.

208. Hayen, André. *Bibliographie blondélienne, 1888-1951*. Extrait de la revue Teoresi. (Museum Lessianum, section philosophique, no. 38). Bruges et Paris: De Brouer, 1953. 95 pp.

About 1100 entries. Very exhaustive coverage through 1951. Writings by Blondel and commentaries grouped chronologically and by subject. Index of authors.

209. Crippa, Romeo. "Bibliografia blondeliana," *Giornole di metafisica* (Genova e Torino), vol. 16 (1961), pp. 631-659.

210. Costa, Antonina. "Bibliografia Blondeliana," *Teoresi* (Messina), vol. 16 (1962), pp. 295-320.

211. Costa, Antonina. "Un Decennio di bibliografia blondeliana (1951-1961)," *Teoresi* (Catania), vol. 17 (1962), pp. 295-320.

212. Gómez Caffarena, José. "Publicaciones sobre Blondel en el primer centenario de su nacimiento," *Pensamiento* (Madrid), vol. 18 (1962), pp. 317-327.

213. Raffelt, Albert. "Bibliografía blondeliana: mais um decenio, 1962-1972," *Revista protuguesa de filosofia* (Braga), vol. 29 (1973), pp. 434-444.

Continues the bibliographies of Hayen and Costa. Covers the period 1961-1972.

BÖHME, JAKOB

214. British Museum. Department of Printed Books. *Jacob Boehme; an Extract from the Catalogue of Printed Books of the British Museum*. London: Printed by W. Clowes and Sons, Ltd., 1922. 13 pp.

215. Buddecke, W. *Verzeichnis von Jakob Böhme--Handschriften*. Göttingen: Häntzschel, 1934. 143 pp.

216. Popp, K. R. *Jakob Böhme und Issac Newton*. *Mit einem Verzeichnis der deutschen Böhme--ansgaben seit 1624 und der englischen Böhme-uebersetzungen seit 1645*. (Studien und

216. (Continued)

Bibliographien zur Gegenwartsphilosophie, 12). Leipzig: Hirzel, 1935. 104 pp.

Reviewed by: Schmitz, Hermann, in Scholastik (Eupen).

217. Buddecke, W. Die Jakob Böhme-Ausgaben. Ein beschreibendes Verzeichnis, Teil I. Die Ausgaben in deutscher Sprache. (Hainberg-schriften, 5). Gottingen: Häntzschel, 1937. 225 pp.

218. De Vooys, C. G. N. "Nederlandsche Vertalingen van Jacob Böhme's Geschriften," De Nieuwe taalgids (Groningen), vol. 37 (1943), pp. 246-250.

BOHME, RUDOLF

219. Dresden. Stadt-und Bezirks-Bibliothek. Bibliographie Rudolf Böeme. Selbständige Schriften, Zeitschriftenaufsätze, Rezensíonen, Bibliographien. Anlässl. 3. 65. Geburtstages hersg. Dresden: 1972. 28 ll.

BOEZIO, SEVERINO

220. Obertells, Luca. Severino Boezio, II. Geneva: Accademia Ligure di Scienze e Lettere, 1974. 325 pp.

Vol. II is a bibliography.

BOFILL, JAIME

221. "Bibliografia filosofica de Jaime Bofill," Convivium (Barcelona), no. 21 (1966), pp. 5-6.

BOLLNOW, OTTO FRIEDRICH

222. Rodi, Frithjob. "Otto Friedrich Bollnow: Schriftenverzeichnis." Zeitschrift für philosophische Forschung (Meisenheim am Glan), vol. 22 (1968), pp. 298-309.

BOLZANO, BERNARD

223. "Bolzano-bibliographie und Editionsprinzipien der Gesamtausgabe," in Eduard Winter, ed., Bernard-Bolzano-Gesamtausgabe, Einleitungsband II. Stuttgart bad Connstatt: Frommann, 1972. 180 pp.

BONAVENTURE

224. Bougerol, J. Guy. Introduction à l'étude de S. Bonaventure (Bibliothèque de théologie. Série I. Théologie dogmatique, vol. 2). Tournai-Paris: Desclée et Co., 1961. 270 pp.

225. Wenin, Christian. "Bibliographie bonaventurienne. Saint Bonaventure à l'heure de l'electronique," Actes du Colloque saint Bonaventure 9-12 septembre 1968, Orsay (Etudes franciscaines, vol. 18 (1968), Supplement annual). Paris: Etudes franciscaines: Librairie mariale et franciscaine, 1968. 187 pp.

226. Vatican. Biblioteca Vaticana. Saint Thomas and St. Bonaventure in the Vatican Library: Exhibit on their Seventh Centenary (1274-1974): Catalogue. Vatican City: Biblioteca Apostolica Vaticana, 1974. 121 pp.

227. Etudes franciscaines (Paris).

Carries an annual Bonaventure bibliography since 1964.

228. Bougerol, Jacques Guy, et al. S. Bonaventura (1274-1974), V: Bibliographia Vonaventuriana (c. 1850-1973). Grottaferrata: Collegio S. Bonaventura, 1974. 704 pp.

BOSANQUET, BERNARD

229. "Bernard Bosanquet [: a bibliography]," in George Watson, ed. The New Cambridge Bibliography of English Literature. Cambridge: Cambridge University Press, 1969, vol. 3, cols. 1519-1522.

Approximately 110 entries of works by and about Bosanquet.

230. Newcastle upon Tyne. University. Library. Bosanquet Papers: Handlist. Newcastle upon Tyne, 1974. 4 l.

BOYLE, ROBERT

231. Keynes, Geoffrey Langton. The Honourable Robert Boyle, a Handlist of his Works. London: "G. L. K. for and from J. F. F.," 1932. 13 l.

232. Fulton, John Farquhar. A Bibliography of the Honourable Robert Boyle, Fellow of the Royal Society. 2nd ed. Oxford: Clarendon Press, 1961. 218 pp.

541 entries.
Reviews: Book Collector, vol. 10 (1961), pp. 344-348; Library, series 5, vol. 17 (1962), pp. 164-166; Papers, Bibliographical Society of America (New York), vol. 56 (1962), pp. 68-70. This work supersedes Fulton's A Bibliography of the Honourable Robert Boyle, Fellow of the Royal Society. Oxford: Oxford University Press; New Haven: Privately printed, 1932, 171 pp.; with addenda in Oxford Bibliographical Society, Proceedings and Papers, vol. 3, part 3 (1933) pp. 339-365; ibid., new series, vol. 1 (1947), pp. 33-38.

BOZZETTI, GIUSEPPE

233. Riva, Clemente. ["Bibliografia di G. Bozzetti"], Rivista rosminiana di filosofia e di cultura (Pallanza), vol. 50 (1956), pp. 161-173.

234. Riva, Clemente. "P. Giuseppe Bozzetti [: note di bibliografia]," Giornale di metafisica (Torino), vol. 12 (1957), pp. 196-199.

BRADLEY, FRANCIS HERBERT

235. "Francis Herbert Bradley [: a Bibliography]," in George Watson, ed., The New Cambridge Bibliography of English Literature. Cambridge: Cambridge University Press, 1969, vol. 3, cols. 1522-1525.

About 70 entries of works by and about Bradley.

236. Taylor, Alfred Edward. "Francis Herbert Bradley, 1846-1924," Proceedings of the British Academy, vol. 11 (1924-1925), pp. 458-468.

"Bibliography" of his books and articles found on pp. 466-468.

BRAHE, TYCHO See 483.

BRÉHIER, EMILE

237. "Bibliographie des oeuvres d'Emile Bréhier," Revue Internationale de philosophie (Bruxells), vol. 6 (1952), pp. 4-11.

BRENTANO, FRANZ

238. Gibson, Lucie. Méthode et Metaphysique selon F. Brentano. Paris: J. Vrin, 1955. 286 pp.

Bibliography, pp. 15-23.

239. Mayer-Hillebrand, Franziska. "Rückblick auf die bisherigen Bestrebungen zur Erhaltung und Verbreitung von Fr. Brentanos philosophischen Lehren und kurze Darstellung dieser Lehren," Zeitschrift für philosophische Forschung (Wurzach), vol. 17 (1963), pp. 146-169.

BRITO, FARIAS

240. De Mattos, Carlos Lopes. "Bibliografia de centenario de Farias Brito," Revista brasileira de filosofia (São Paulo), vol. 14 (1964), pp. 603-604.

BROAD, CHARLIE DUNBAR

241. Lewy, C. "Bibliography of the Writings of C. D. Broad to the End of July 1959," in P. A. Schilpp, ed., The Philosophy of C. D. Broad. New York: Tudor Publishing Co., 1959, pp. 831-852.

BROWN, THOMAS M. D.

242. Welsh, David. Account of the Life and Writings of Thomas Brown, M.D. [1778-1820]. Edinburgh: 1825. 525 pp.

BRUNO, GIORDANO

243. Salvestrini, Virgilio. Bibliografia di Giordano Bruno (1582-1950). (Biblioteca bibliografica italica).

243. (Continued)

Firenze: Sansoni antiquariato, 1958. 407 pp. Also an earlier edition: Bibliografia delle opere di Giordano Bruno e degli scritti. Pisa: V. Salvestrini, 1926. 377 pp. Index. 1238 entries.

1750 entries including about 1500 works about Bruno. Annotated, with index of Bruno's writings and name index.

BUBER, MARTIN

244. Catanne, Moshe. A Bibliography of Martin Buber's Works (1897-1957). Jerusalem: Biadik Institute, 1958. 142 pp.

245. Friedman, Maurice. "Bibliography of the writings of Martin Buber," in P. A. Schilpp, ed., The Philosophy of Martin Buber, La Salle, Ill.: Open Court; London: Cambridge University Press, 1967, pp. 747-786.

Chronologically lists about 500 entries.

246. Weltsch, Robert. "Martin Buber--Bibliographie," in Martin Buber. L'Homme et le philosophe. Bruxelles: Editions de l'Institut de sociologie de l'Universite libre de Bruxelles, 1968. 76 pp.

BURKE, EDMUND

247. Cordasco, Francesco G. M. Edmund Burke, a Handlist of Critical Notices and Studies. (Eighteenth Century Bibliographical Pamphlets, no. 12). New York: B. Franklin for Long Island University Press, 1950. 12 pp.

248. Todd, William Burton. "The Bibliographical History of Burke's Reflections on the Revolution in France," Library (London), series 5, vol. 6 (1951), pp. 100-108.

249. Copeland, Thomas Wellsted. A Checklist of the Correspondence of Edmund Burke, Arranged in Chronological Order and Indexed under the Names of 1200 Correspondents, by Thomas W. Copeland and Milton Shumway Smith. Cambridge: Printed for the Index Society at the University Press, 1955. 481 pp.

250. Todd, William Burton. A Bibliography of Edmund Burke. (Soho Bibliography, no. 17). London: Rupert Hart-Davis, 1964. 312 pp.

Burke's works, primarily Reflections [etc.], from 1748 to 1827 when his collected works were printed Index.

BURTT, EDWIN A.

251. Stainton, Elsie Myers. "E. A. Burtt: Bibliography," Philosophy East and West (Honolulu), vol. 22 (1972), pp. 461-465.

A complete bibliography of Burtt's works.

CAILLOIS, ROGER

252. ["Bibliographie: Roger Caillois"], in G. Deladalle and D. Huisman, eds., Les Philosophes francais d'aujourd'hui [n.p., n.d.], pp. 391-394.

40 works. Annotated.

CAJETAN (i.e., GAETANUS, TOMMASO DE VIO)

253. Marega, Isnardus M. "Operum Caietani Indices. Bibliographiae Specimen," in Thomas de Vio Cardinalis Caietanus. Scripta Philosophica. Commentaria in Porphyrii Isagogen ad Praedicamenta Aristotelis. Romae, Collegium Angelico, 1934, pp. lxx-lxxvii.

Reviewed by M. D. Chenu, Bulletin thomiste (Paris), vol. 4 (1936), pp. 843-844.

254. Congar, M.-J. Bio-bibliographie de Cajétan. Saint-Maximin (Var): Edit. de La Revue Thomiste, 1935. 47 pp.

Originally appeared in the Revue Thomiste, vol. 17 (1934-35), pp. 3-39.

255. De Meyer, A. Registrum Litterarum Fr. Thomas de Vio Cietani O. P., Magistri Ordinis, 1508-1513. (Monumenta Ordinis Fratrum Praedicatorum, 17). Romae: Santa Sabina, 1935. About 680 pp.

256. Frénand, G. "Les inédits de Cajétan," Revue thomiste (Saint-Maximin), vol. 19 (1936), pp. 331-366.

256. (Continued)

Reviewed by M. D. Chenu, *Bulletin thomiste*, vol. 4 (1936), pp. 848-849.

CALAMANDREI, PIERO

257. Mandolfo, A. and Cappelletti, M. *Bibliografia degli scritti di Piero Calamandrei*. Firenze: La Nouva Italia, 1960. 110 pp.

CALLUS, DANIEL

258. "A Bibliography of the Published Writings of Daniel Callus," in *Oxford Studies Presented to Daniel Callus* (Oxford Historical Society, New Series, 16). Oxford: Clarendon Press, 1964, pp. 313-319.

CAMERON, JOHN

259. Swinne, Axel Hilmar. *John Cameron Philosophe und Theologe (1579-1625) Bibliographie-krit. Analyse d. Hand-- und Druckschriften sowie d. Cameron Literature.* Marburg: Elwert, 1968. 367 pp.

CAMPANAGA, P. V.

260. "Bibliografía del P. V. Campanaga," *Augustinus* (Salamanca), vol. 12 (1967), pp. 17-26.

CAMPANELLA, THOMAS

261. Grillo, Francesco. *Tommaso Campanella in America: A Critical Bibliography and a Profile*. New York: S. F. Vanni, 1954. 109 pp.

209 entries. Good annotations.

262. Firpo, Luigi. *Bibliografia degli scritti di Tommaso Campanella. Pubblicazione promossa dalla Reale academia della scienze di Torino nel 3. centenario della morte di Tommaso Campanella.* Torino: Bona, 1940. 225 pp.

263. Amerio, Romano. "Correzioni alla bibliografia campanelliana," Rivista di filosofia neo-scholastica (Milano), vol. 31 (1939), p. 428.

264. Firpo, Luigi. "Cinquant'anni di studi sul Campanella (1901-1950)," Rinascimento (Milano), vol. 6 (1955), pp. 209-348.

265. Grillo, Francesco. Tammaso Campanella in America. A Supplement to the Critical Bibliography. New York: S. F. Vanni, 1957. 48 pp.

91 entries. Corrects and augments the original. Annotated, name index.

266. Grillo, Francesco. Bibliografia di Tommaso Campanella in America, (Secondo supplemento). Cosenza: Tip. Editrice MIT, 1968. 57 pp.

178 entries. Annotations. Name index.

267. Demattei, Rodolfo. "Le Edizioni inglesi della 'Monarchia di spagna' di Tommaso Campanella," Giornale critico della filosofia italiana (Firenze), vol. 23 (1969), pp. 194-205.

CAMPBELL, ALEXANDER

268. Spencer, Claude E. "A Comprehensive Bibliography of Alexander Campbell's Writings" in Samuel Morris Eames, ed., The Philosophy of Alexander Campbell, Bethany, W. Va.: Bethany College, 1966. 110 pp.

CAMUS, ALBERT

269. Crepin, Simone. Albert Camus: Essai de Bibliographie. (Memorie presente à l'Ecole provinciale de bibliothecaires du Brabant--session 1959). Bruxelles: Commission belge de bibliographie, 1960. 240 pp.

1151 entries arranged without annotation according to topics, by years. Hard to find things in. Name index.

270. Fitch, Brian T. Albert Camus: Essai de bibliographie des études en langue francaise consacrées à Albert Camus (1937-1962). Paris: Minard, 1965. 231 pp.

271. Hoy, Peter Charles. Camus in English, an Annotated Bibliography of A. Camus's Contributions to English and American Periodicals and Newspapers. Wymondham, Eng.: Brewhouse, 1968. 31 pp. Also: Folcroft, Pa.: Folcroft Press, 1969. 29 pp; Paris: Lettres modernes, 1971, [n.p.].

272. Roeming, Robert F. Camus: A Bibliography. Madison, Milwaukee, and London: The University of Wisconsin Press, 1968. 298 pp.

> 3432 entries. Author, journal, and chronological indexes. Editions and translations of Camus' works. No annotations.

273. Fontinell, Eugene. "A Tribute to Camus: Recent Studies of his Work," Cross Currents (New York?), vol. 10 (1969), pp. 283-289.

CARINS, DORIAN

274. "Bibliography of the Writings of Dorian Cairns," in Marvin Farber, ed., Philosophical Essays in Memory of Edmund Husserl. Cambridge, Mass.: Harvard University Press, 1940, pp. 263-264.

CARLYLE, THOMAS

275. Shepherd, Richard Herne. The Bibliography of Carlyle; a Bibliographical List, Arranged in Chronological Order, of the Published Writings in Prose and Verse of Thomas Carlyle (from 1820-1881). London: E. Stock, 1881. 60 pp.

> Reprinted: New York: Haskell House Publishers, 1970.

276. Michigan University. Library. A Catalogue of the Dr. Samuel A. Jones Carlyle Collection, with Additions from the General Library; comp. by Mary Eunice Wead . . . Ann Arbor: University of Michigan, 1919. 119 pp. Reprint: Folcroft, Pa.: Folcroft Library Editions, 1973.

277. Dyer, Issac Watson. A Bibliography of Thomas Carlyle's Writings and Ana. Portland, Me.: Southworth Press, 1928. 587 pp. Reprinted: New York: Octagon Books, 1968. Also reprinted: New York: Burt Franklin, 1968 (Burt Franklin Bibliography and Reference series, #177).

278. Sanders, Charles Richard. Carlyle's Letters to Ruskin: a Finding List with some Unpublished Letters and Comments. Folcroft, Pa.: Folcroft Library Editions, 1974. 31 pp.

278. (Continued)

Reprint of the 1958 ed. published by the Librarian, the John Rylands Library, and Manchester University Press, Manchester.

Includes bibliographical references.

CARNAP, RUDOLPH

279. Pasquinelli, Alberto. "Contributi bibliografici [: Rudolph Carnap]," Rivista critica di storia della filosofia (Milano), vol. 10 (1955), pp. 462-478.

Writings by and about Carnap, plus translations of his works.

280. Benson, Arthur. "Bibliography of the Writings of Rudolph Carnap," in P. A. Schilpp, ed., The Philosophy of Rudolph Carnap. La Salle, Ill.: Open Court, 1963, pp. 1015-1070.

Comprised of his published writings, works edited by him, and reviews of Carnap's writings. About 350 works by Carnap, 5 works edited by him, 400 reviews.

CARPENTER, NATHANAEL

281. Dredge, John Ingle. "A Few Sheaves of Devon Bibliography, . . . the Third Sheaf . . . Nathanael Carpenter . . . ," Plymouth: W. Brendon, Printers, 1889-1896. 5 parts. 250 l. [Not published]

CARRERAS ARATU, JOAQUIM

282. Cuellar-Bassoes, Luis. "Nota bibliografica sobre el Dr. Joaquim Carreras Aratu," Convivium (Barcelona), no. 17-18 (1964), pp. 19-22.

CARRERAS-ARATU, TOMÁS

283. "Bibliografía [: T. Carreras Aratu]," Convivium (Barcelona), vol. 1 (1956), pp. 11-18.

CARUS, PAUL

284. Carus, Paul. Philosophy as a Science; a Synopsis of the Writings of Dr. Paul Carus, Containing an Introduction Written by Himself, Summaries of his Books, and a List of Articles to Date. Chicago: The Open Court Publishing Co., 1909.

CASSIRER, ERNST

285. Klibansky, Raymond and W. Solmitz. "Bibliography of E. Cassirer's Writings," in R. Klibansky and H. J. Paton, eds., Philosophy and History. Essays Presented to Ernst Cassirer. Oxford: Clarendon Press, 1936, pp. 339-346. Revised edition: New York: Harper and Row, 1963, pp. 338-353.

286. Hamburg, C. H. and W. M. Solmitz. "Bibliography of the Writings of Ernst Cassirer to 1946," in P. A. Schilpp, ed., The Philosophy of Ernst Cassirer, Evanston, Ill.: Library of Living Philosophers, 1949, pp. 881-910.

287. Nadean, Robert. "Bibliographie den textes sur Ernst Cassirer," Revue Internationale de Philosophie (Bruxelles), vol. 28 (1974), pp. 492-510.

Aims at completeness.

CATTANEO, CARLO

288. Armani, Giuseppe. Gli scritti su Carlo Cattaneo. Saggio di una bibliografia (1836-1972). (Domus mazziniana, Pisa. Collana scientifica, 13). Pisa: Nistri-Lischi, 1973. 243 pp.

CAYRÉ, FULBERT

289. "Bibliographie du R. P. Fulbert Cayré," Recherches augustiniennes (Paris), vol. 2 (1962), pp. 7-14.

CHALMERS, WILLIAM

290. Ferrier, Francis. William Chalmers (1596-1678) Etude bio-bibliographique avec des textes inédites. (Le Mouvement des idées au XVII siecle, 7). Paris: Presses universitaires de France, 1968. 196 pp.

CHARTIER, ÉMILE AUGUSTE. See Alain

CHENU, M. D.

291. Duval, André. "Bibliographie du P. Marie-Dominique Chenu (1921-1965)," in Melanges offerts à M.-D. Chenu, maître en théologie (Bibliothèque thomiste, 37), Paris: J. Vrin, 1967, pp. 9-29.

CHIAVACCI, GAETANO

292. Faucci, Dario. "L''Attualismo' di Gaetano Chiavacci," Filosofia (Turin), vol. 21 (1970), pp. 49-72.

Commentary on Chiavacci's works.

CHIOCCHETTI, EMILIO

293. Gemelli, Agostino. "In memoria di P. Emilio Chiocchetti, O. F. M. [con una] Bibliografia degli scritti di P. E. Chiocchetti," Rivista di filosofia neo-scholastica (Milano), vol. 43 (1951), pp. 367-372.

CICERO, MARCUS TULLIUS

294. Deschamps, Pierre Charles Ernest. Essai bibliographique sur M. T. Cicéron, par P. Deschamps. Avec une préface par J. Janin. Paris: L. Pothier, 1863. 184 pp.

295. Hubner, Emil. The Epistles of Cicero; Bibliography and Hints for Study. Baltimore: Publication Agency of the Johns Hopkins University, 1888. 11 pp.

296. British Museum. Department of Printed Books. Cicero, an Excerpt from the General Catalog. London: printed by W. Clowes, 1944. 196 cols.

CLARKE, SAMUEL

297. Hoadly, Benjamin. ["An Account of the Life, Writings and Character of Samuel Clarke"], in Samuel Clarke: Works, with an Accounts of the Author. London: J. and P. Knapton, 1738. 4 vols.

298. Gay, John H. "The Idea of Freedom as the Basis of the Thought of Samuel Clarke." Unpublished Columbia University (N.Y.) thesis, 1959.

Bibliography found on pp. 245-253.

CLASEN, SOPHRONIUS

299. Gimmnich, Otho. "Bibliographie der veröffentlichungen von P. Sophronius Clasen O.F.M.," Wissenschaft und Weisheit (Düsseldorf), vol. 37 (1974), pp. 83-89.

COHEN, MORRIS RAPHAEL

300. Kuhn, M. A. Raphael Cohen. A Bibliography. New York: City College Library, 1957. 44 pp. Also: supplement to Journal of the History of Ideas (New York), 1957.

COIMBRA, LEONARDO

301. Ribeiro, Alvaro. Leonardo Coimbra: Apontamentos de biografia e de bibliografia. Lisboa: Editorial Empério, 1945. 93 pp.

COLERIDGE, SAMUEL TAYLOR

302. Kennedy, Virginia Wadlow. Samuel Taylor Coleridge: A Selected Bibliography of the Best Available Editions of his Writings, of Biographies and Criticisms of him, and of References Showing his Relations with Contemporaries. Baltimore: The Enoch Pratt Free Library, 1935. 151 pp.

About 750 annotated entries, including 29 bibliographies. Index.

COMENIUS, JOHANN AMOS

303. Pilz, Kurt. Comenius. Die Ausgaben des Orbis Sensualium Pictus. Eine Bibliographie (Beitrage zur Geschichte und Kultur der Stadt Nürnberg, 14). Nürnberg: Stadtbibliothek Edelmann in Komm, 1967. 447 pp.

304. "Bibliographia Comeniana," Studia Comeniana et Historica (Uherský Brod), vol. 1 (1971), pp. 99-109; vol. 2 (1972), pp. 77-86, 86-111.

COMTE, AUGUSTE

305. Catalogue des livres positivistes appartenant à la société des exécuteurs testamentaires d'Auguste Comte. Paris: Emprimé par E. Thunot: 1860, 7 pp.

306. Ostwald, Friedrich Wilhelm. Auguste Comte, der Mann und sein Werk. Leipzig: Verlag Unesma, g.m.b.h., 1914. 288 pp.

307. Ducassé, Pierre. La Méthode positive et l'intuition comtienne; bibliographie. Paris: Alcan, 1939. 172 pp.

CONFUCIUS

308. Martí Brugueras, María Montserrat. Confucio, los cuatro libros clásicos. estudio preliminar y bibliografía. Barcelona: Bruguera, 1974. 436 pp.

CONRAD-MARTIUS, HEDWIG

309. Dempf, A. "Veröffentlichungen von Hedwig Conrad-Martius," Philosophisches Jahrbuch (München), vol. 66 (1957), pp. 2-5.

64 titles.

310. Festschrift für Hedwig Conrad-Martius, ed. Aloys Wenzl. Freiburg und Munich: Karl Alber, 1958.

Contains a bibliography of Conrad-Martius' writings.

COPERNICUS, NICOLAUS

311. Poznanski, Marceli. "Bibliografie kopernowskie," Bibliotekarz (Warszawa), vol. 20 (1953), pp. 89-92.

312. Rosen, Edward. "Copernicus bibliography (1539-1958)," in his Three Copernican Treatises. 2nd ed. New York: Dover Publications, 1959.

313. Baranowski, Henryk. Bibliografia kopernikowska, 1509-1955 [Copernican Bibliography, 1509-1955 [In Polish]] (Burt Franklin: Bibliography and Reference Series, 393. Science Classics, 5). New York: Lenox Hill, 1970. 448 pp. Also: Warszawa: Pánstwowe Wydawn. Naukowe, 1958-

About 3750 entries.

314. Łódź, Poland. Miejska Biblioteka Publiczna. Copernica w zbiorach miejskiej Publicznej. [Copernicus in the Collections of the City Public Library [In Polish]]. Łódź: 1971. 30 pp.

315. Biskup, Marian. Regesta Copernicana (Studia Copernicana, 7) Wrocław: Zakład narodowy im. Ossolińskich, 1973. 241 pp.

CORSANO, ANTONIO

316. "Bibliografia degli scritti di Antonio Corsano," in Studi in onore di Antonio Corsano, Manduria: Lacaita, 1970, pp. 861-869.

CROCE, BENEDETTO

317. Castellano, G. Benedetto Croce. Il filosofo. Il critico. Lo storico. Seconda ed. con l'aggiunta di una <<bibliografia cronologica>> degli scritti del Croce. (Bibliografia di cultura moderna). Bari: Laterza, 1936. 208 pp.

318. L'Opera filosofica, storica e letteraria di Benedetto Croce. Saggi di scrittori italiani e stranieri e bibliografia dal 1920 al 1941. (Bibliografia di cultura moderna, 367) Bari: Laterza, 1942. 360 pp.

319. Flora, Francesco. "Bibliografia intorno alle opere di Benedetto Croce dal 1941 al 1953," in Benedetto Croce, Milano: Malfase, 1950, pp. 573-615.

Divided according to topics.

320. Nicolini, Fausto. L'Editio ne varietur delle opere di Benedetto Croce. Saggio bibliografico con taluni riassunti o passi testuali e ventinove fuori testo. Napoli: L'Arte tipografica, 1960. 539 pp.

321. Borsari, Silvano. L'Opera di Benedetto Croce. (Istituto italiano per gli studi storici). Napoli: "Nella sede dell'istituto," 1964. 619 pp.

4651 entries of works by Croce, including books, articles, personal letters, "letters to the editor," translations, editions. Name index.

322. Cione, Edmondo. Bibliographia crociana. Rome: Bocca, 1965. 481 pp.

323. Stella, Vittorio. "Il Giudizio su Croce; consuntivo di un centenario," Giornale di metafisica (Genova), vol. 22 (1967), pp. 643-711.

324. Brescia, Giuseppe. "Note di bibliografia crociana. IV: Altre correzioni ed aggiunte. V: Ancova di Valdemaro Vecchi," Rivista di studi crociana (Napoli), vol. 9 (1972), pp. 202-208.

325. Brescia, Giuseppe. "Note di bibliografia crociana: VI: Casamicciola," Rivista di studi crociana (Napoli), vol. 11 (1974), pp. 224-226.

326. Caserta, Ernesto G. "Studi crociani negli Stati Uniti (1964-1971)," Rivista di studi crociani (Napoli), vol. 11 (1974), pp. 217-223.

327. Conrieri, Davide. "Contributo alla bibliografia crociana: le varie eduzioni del saggio su tischbein," Rivista di studi crociana (Napoli), vol. 11 (1974), pp. 227-229.

328. Franchini, Raffaello. "Contributo alla bibliografia crociana," Rivista di studi crociana (Napoli), vol. 10 (1973), pp. 11-17, 177-183, 279-287; vol. 11 (1974), pp. 22-28, 137-141.

CUDWORTH, RALPH

329. Passmore, John A. "A Cudworth Bibliography," in Ralph Cudworth, an Interpretation. Cambridge: 1951. 118 pp.

Chronological list of works and miscellaneous writings.

CURTIUS, ERNST ROBERT

330. Boehlich, Walter. "Bibliographie des oeuvres de Ernst Robert Curtius," in Max Rychner and Walter Boelich, eds., Freundesgabe für Ernst Robert Curtius zum 14. April 1956. Munich: Leo Lehen; Bern: Francke, 1956, pp. 213-234.

DABIN, JEAN

331. "Bibliographie [de J. Dabin]," in Mélanges en l'honneur de Jean Dabin, vol. 1, Bruxelles: Etablissements Emile Bruylant; Paris: Editions Sirey, 1963, pp. xi-xx.

DANILEVSKII, NOCOLAI IAKOVEVICH

332. MacMaster, Robert E. "Danilevsky's writings," in his Danilevsky: a Russian Totalitarian Philosopher, Cambridge, Mass.: Harvard University Press, 1967, pp. 313-319.

DANTE ALIGHIERI. See also 1689.

333. Katushina, L. Ot Dante do Tasso [From Dante to Tasso [In Russian]], Leningrad: Akademica nauk, Institut istorii [Academy of Sciences, Institute of History], 1972. 107 pp.

DAS, BHAGAVAN

334. Dr. Bhagavan Das, 1869-1969: A Centenary Volume. Varanasi: Kashi Vidyapith, 1969. 519 pp.

Annotated bibliography, pp. 485-511.

DE BEAUVOIR, SIMONE. See 1679.

DE CORDEMOY, GERAULD

335. Clair, Pierre, and François Girbal. Gerauld De Cordemoy. Ourvres philosophiques avec une étude bio-bibliographique (Le Movement des idées au XXIIe siècle, 6) Paris: Presses universitaires de France, 1968. 384 pp.

DE GHELLINCK, JOSEPH

336. Demortier, Roger. "Bibliographie du R. P. Joseph de Ghellinck," in Mélanges Joseph de Ghellinck, Tome I: Antiquité. (Museum Lessianum. Section historique, no. 13). Gembloux: J. Duculot, 1951. 403 pp.

DE GUAITA, STANISLAS

337. De Guaita, Stanislas. Catalogue de livres et manuscrits relatifs au sciences occultes . . . provenant de la Bibliothèque de feu Stanislas de Guaita, et portant, pour la plupart, sur les feuillets, de garde, des annotations de sa main. Paris: Librairie Dorbon, 1898-1899. 272 pp.

337. (Continued)

Also issued as: Stanislas De Guita et sa bibliothèque occulte. Paris: Dorbon, 1899. 299 pp.

References to 2227 items offered for sale.

DE KRONIC, CHARLES

338. Gagné, Armand. "Bibliographie de Charles de Konick de 1933 à 1965," in Mélanges à la memorie de Charles de Kronick. Québec: Presses de l'Université Laval, 1968.

DELACROIX, HENRI

339. Meyerson, I. "Bibliographie de l'oeuvre d'M. Henri Delacroix," Annales de l'Université de Paris (Paris), vol. 13 (1938), pp. 20-24.

DE LA FORGE, LOUIS

340. Clair, Pierre. Louis de la Forge. Oeuvres philosophiques avec une étude bio-bibliographique. (Le mouvement des idées au XVIIe siècle, 9) Paris: Presses universitaires de France, 1974. 424 pp.

DEL-NEGRO, WALTER

341. "Del-Negro: Philosophische Schriften," Zeitschrift für philosophische Forschung (Meisenheim am Glan), vol. 22 (1968), pp. 466-467.

DE LUBAC, HENRI

342. Haulotte, Edgar. "Bibliographie du Père Henri de Lubac," in L'Homme devant Dieu. Mélanges offerts au Père Henri de Lubac, Paris: Aubler-Montaigne, 1964, vol. 3, pp. 347-356.

DEL VECCHIO, GIORGIO

343. Orecchia, Rinaldo. Bibliografia di Giorgio del Vecchio con cenni biografici. Bologna: Licinio Cappelli, 1941. 152 pp.

DE MORGAN, AUGUSTUS

344. Jevons, William Stanley. "De Morgan, Augustus," Encyclopaedia Britannica, 11th ed., vol. 8, pp. 8-10.

A sketch of his life and writings.

DESCARTES, RENÉ

345. De Giuli, G. "Edizioni e studi cartesiani," Rivista di filosofia (Torino), vol. 25 (1934), pp. 165-169.

346. Olgiati, Francesco. Cartesio. Milano: Vita e pensiero, 1934. 329 pp.

References to about 200 modern works on Descartes.

347. De Guili, G. "Rassegna cartesiana," Rivista di filosofia (Torino), vol. 26 (1935), pp. 258-364.

348. Keeling, S. V. "Philosophy in France. Recent Interpretation of Cartesianism," Philosophy (London), vol. 11 (1936), pp. 336-340.

349. "Autour du Discours de la méthode," Archives de philosophie (Paris), vol. 13 (1937), cah II. 247 pp.

350. "Bibliografía sumaria de los estudios cartesianos (1925-1936)," Estudios (Buenos Aires), vol. 57 (1937), pp. 548-556.

351. Bergmann, E. "Les Principaux ouvrages sur Descartes publiés en Allemagne depuis 1900," Revue de synthèse (Paris), vol. 14 (1937), pp. 98-102.

352. Bontadini, G. "Les Ouvrages italiens sur Descartes et le cartésianisme publiés depuis 1900," Revue de synthèse (Paris), vol. 14 (1937), pp. 87-97.

353. Bontadini, G. "Annotazione ad alcuni scritti italiani su Cartesio," in Cartesio. Nel terzo centenario del Discorso del metodo (Pubblicazione a cura della Facolta di filosofia dell' Università cattolica del Sacro cuore) (Rivista di filosofia neo-scholastica, supplement to vol. 20). Milano: Vita e pensiero, 1937, pp. 85-104.

354. Boorsch, Jean. Etat présent des études sur Descartes. Paris: Las Belles lettres, 1937. 197 pp.

About 200 entries in the bibliography. Good discussions of the state of Cartesian scholarship at the time.

355. Chiriotti, E. "Stato attuale degli studi cartesiani in Italia," in Congrès Descartes. Travaux du IXe Congrès international de philosophie. Paris: Hermann, 1937, pp. 127-133.

356. D'Alverny, Marie Thérèse. Descartes; notices bibliographiques et iconographiques. Paris: Bibliothèque nationale, 1937. 170 pp.

About 800 entries.

357. Giacon, Carlo. "Le Pubblicazioni dell' Università cattolica del Sacro coure per celebrare il centenario cartesiano," Gregorianum (Romae), vol. 18 (1937), pp. 599-603.

358. Keeling, S. V. "Livres et articles en langue anglaise sur Descartes et le cartésianisme depuis 1900," Revue de synthèse (Paris), vol. 14 (1937), pp. 109-111.

359. Krüger, G. "Descartes-Bibliographie," in C. A. Emge, ed., Dem Gedächtnis au René Descartes (300 Jahre Discours de la méthode). Berlin: Verlag für Staatswissenschafte und Geschichte, 1937, pp. 203-204.

360. "La Littérature cartésienne au XXe siècle," Revue de synthèse (Paris), vol. 14 (1937), pp. 67-114.

Broad coverage of works in various languages.

361. Lubnici, N. "Les Travaux cartésiens polonais depuis 1900 environ," Revue de synthèse (Paris), vol. 14 (1937), pp. 103-108.

362. Milhaud, Gérard. "La Littérature cartésienne au XXe siècle. I. Descartes vu par la génération française contemporaine. II. Bibliographie," Revue de synthèse (Paris), vol. 14 (1937), pp. 67-86.

363. Paris. Bibliothèque nationale . . . Descartes, exposition organisée pour le IIIe Centenaire du Discours de la méthode. Paris, 1937. 170 pp.

364. Pos, H.-J. and C.-A. Steenberger. "Les Ouvrages sur Descartes publiés dans les Pays-Bas de 1910 à 1937," Revue de synthèse (Paris), vol. 14 (1947), pp. 112-114.

365. Colombo, C. "Pubblicazioni in occasione del centenario cartesiano," Rivista di filosofia neo-scholastica (Milano), vol. 30 (1938), pp. 62-85.

366. Robinson, D. S. "The Cartesian Studies of the Ninth International Congress of Philosophy," The Journal of Philosophy (New York), vol. 35 (1938), pp. 180-183.

367. Cassirer, Ernst. Die Philosophie im XVII. und XVIII. Jahrhundert. Paris: Hermann, 1939. 94 pp.

138 bibliographical entries. A survey of the 1937-1938 Descartes and Malebranche anniversary literature.

368. Bar, A. "Kartezjusz w Poloce [Descartes in Poland [In Polish]]," Kwartalnik filozoficzny, vol. 19 (1950), pp. 151-160.

Works in Polish by and about Descartes.

369. Dibon, Paul. "Notes bibliographiques sur les cartésiens hollandais," in E. J. Dijksterhuis, Descartes et le cartésianisme hollandais, Paris: Presses universitaires de France, 1950, pp. 261-300.

370. Ferro, Carmelo. "Intorno ad alcune recenti interpretazioni de pensiero cartesiano," Rivista di filosofia neo-scholastica (Milano), vol. 42 (1950), pp. 194-221.

371. Ware, C. S. "The Influence of Descartes on Locke: A Bibliographical Study," Revue internationale de philosophie (Bruxelles), vol. 4 (1950), pp. 210-230.

372. Rodis-Lewis, Geneviève. "Bilan de cinquante ans d'-études cartésiennes," Revue de philosophie de la France et de l'étranger (Paris), 76th year, no. 141 (1951), pp. 249-267.

Surveys the literature of the first half of the 20th century. Good.

373. British Museum. "Descartes, René," in General Catalogue of Printed Books. London: Trustees of the British Museum, 1954, vol. 51, pp. 224-257.

Long list of works on Descartes.

374. Sebba, Gregor. Descartes and his Philosophy; a Bibliographical Guide to the Literature, 1800-1958. Athens: University of Georgia, College of Business Administration, Bureau of Business Research, 1959.

375. Croissant, Jeanne. "Bibliographie cartésienne, 1," Morale et enseignement (Bruxelles), vol. 9 (1960), pp. 44-50.

376. Sebba, Gregor. Bibliographia Cartesiana; a Critical Guide to the Descartes Literature, 1800-1960 (Archives internationales d'histoire des idées, 5). The Hague: Nijhoff, 1964. 510 pp.

3612 entries. The place to go for the period covered. Contains references to 33 oyher selected bibliographies.

377. L'Equipe Descartes (C.M.R.S.). "Bibliographie critique des études cartésiennes pour l'année 1971. A Critical Bibliography of Cartesian Studies for 1971," Archives de philosophie (Paris), vol. 36 (1973), pp. 431-495. For 1970: vol. 35 (1972), pp. 263-319.

An annual bibliography.

378. Sebba, Gregor. "Descartes [: an Annotated Bibliography]," in A Critical Bibliography of French Literature, ed. by D. C. Cabeen. Syracuse, N. Y.: Syracuse University Press, 1957-1961, vol. 3, pp. 504-556.

Detailed annotations of about 300 recent works on Descartes with lists of reviews of these works. Excellent, but not exhaustive.

379. Vandenbulcke, Jaak. "Duitse Descartes - Literatuur uit het begin van de Zeventigerjaren," Tijdschrift voor Filosofie (Leuven), vol. 37 (1975), pp. 95-111.

DE STRYCKER, E.

380. Van de Wiele, R. "Keuze uit de bibliografie van E. de Strycker," in Zetesis. Album Amicorum door vrienden en collega's aangeboden aan Prof. Dr. E. de Strycker. Antwerpen and Utrecht: De Nederlandsche Boekhandel, 1973, pp. 20-23.

DE TOCQUEVILLE, ALEXIS

381. Mayer, Jacob Peter. Alexis de Tocqueville. A Bibliographical Essay in Political Science. Trans. by M. M. Bozman and C. Hahn. New York: The Viking Press, 1940. 233 pp.

DE UNAMUNO Y JUGO, MIGUEL. See UNAMUNDO Y JUGO, MIGUEL DE

DEUSTUA, ALEJANDRO O.

382. Barboza, Enrique. Bibliografía de las obras del Dr. Dn. Alejandro O. Deustua. Lima: Gil, 1939. 29 pp.

DEWEY, JOHN

383. Mayerohoff, Milton. et al. "Contributi bibliografici [: John Dewey]," Rivista critica di storia della filosofia (Milano), vol. 6 (1951), pp. 442-453. I: Opere di Dewey (1939-1951); II: Traduzioni italiane di scritti di Dewey (1913-1951); III: Studi italiani su Dewey (1921-1951); IV: Studi stranieri su Dewey (1939-1951).

384. "Bibliography of the Writings of John Dewey," in P. A. Schilpp, ed. The Philosophy of John Dewey, 2nd ed., La Salle, Ill.: Open Court, 1951, pp. 609-686.

About 800 works chronologically arranged.

385. Thomas, Milton Halsey. A Bibliography of John Dewey to July, 1929. New York: Columbia University Press, 1929. 151 pp.

386. Thomas, Milton Halsey. John Dewey: a Centennial Bibliography. Chicago: University of Chicago Press; Toronto: University of Toronto Press, 1962. 370 pp. Also: 1957 ed.

About 2900 entries about and by Dewey. His writings arranged by year, others by author. Indexes.

387. Boydston, Jo Ann. John Dewey; a Checklist of Translations, 1900-1967. Compiled and Edited by Jo Ann Boydston, with Robert L. Andresen. Carbondale, Ill.: Southern Illinois Press; London: Feffer and Simons, 1969. 123 pp.

With an index.

388. Boydston, Jo Ann. Guide to the Works of John Dewey. Carbondale, Ill.: Southern Illinois University Press, 1970. 396 pp.

A collection of 12 essays on various aspects of Dewey's thought. A guide to his writings. Index.

389. Boydston, Jo Ann and Kathleen Poulos. Checklist of Writings about John Dewey, 1887-1973. Carbondale, Ill.: Southern Illinois University Press, 1974. 396 pp.

DIDEROT, DENIS

390. Leyds, J. J. C. Principaux écrits relatifs à la personne et aux oeuvres, au temps, et à l'influence de Diderot. Paris: [n.p.], 1887 [1877?]. 39 pp.

391. Dieckmann, Herbert. Stand und Probleme der Diderot-Forschung. Ein Beitrag zur Diderot-Kritik. Bonn: Cohen, 1931. 40 pp.

A selective, annotated work.

392. Dieckmann, Herbert. "Bibliographical Data on Diderot," in Studies in Honor of Frederick W. Shipley. St. Louis: Washington University Studies, new series, Language and Literature, no. 14 (1942), pp. 181-220.

The best to 1942.

393. "Les Traductions polonaises de l'oeuvre de Diderot et les etudes polonaises le concernant," Bulletin. Centre polonais de recherches scientifiques de Paris (Paris), vol. 8 (1950), pp. 32-34.

394. Dieckmann, Herbert and Norman L. Toerey. "Diderot [: a critical bibliography]," in D. C. Cabeen and J. Brody, gen. eds. A Critical Bibliography of French Literature, vol. 4. Syracuse, N.Y.: Syracuse University Press, 1951, pp. 252-265.

Contains 140 entries. Annotated.

395. Dieckmann, Herbert. Inventaire du fonds Vandeul et inédits de Diderot. Geneva: Droz, 1951. 282 pp.

396. Niklaus, Robert. Diderot, Denis: Pensées philosophiques (Textes littéraires français, 36), Genève: Droz, 1957.

Bibliography pp. 49-69.

397. Vercruysse, J. "Recherches bibliographiques sur les Pensées philosophiques de Diderot," Dix-Huitième siècle (Asnières), (1972), no. 4, pp. 374-378.

398. Knock, Ann. Diderot: Handlist of Books by and Qabout Denis Diderot in the [Birkbeck] College Library. (Birkbeck College Library Publications, no. 33). London: Birkbeck College Library, 1973. 11 pp.

DIÈS, AUGUSTE

399. "Bibliographie de Mgr. Diès," in Mélanges de philosophie grecque offers à Mgr. Diès. Paris: J. Vrin, 1956, pp. 17-20.

DILTHEY, WILHELM

400. Zeeck, Hans. "Im Druck erschienene Schriften von Wilhelm Dilthey," *Archiv für Geschichte der Philosophie* (Berlin), vol. 25 (1912), pp. 154-160.

401. De Cerio, Franco Diaz. "Bibliografia de W. Dilthey," *Pensamiento* (Madrid), vol. 24 (1968), pp. 195-258.

402. Herrmann, Ulrich. *Bibliographie Wilhelm Dilthey. Quellen und Literatur*. (Pädagogische Bibliographien, Reihe A., Bd. 1). Berlin; Basel: Beltz, 1969. 237 pp.

DINGLER, HUGO

403. "Bibliografia di Hugo Dingler," *Methodos* (Milano), vol. 4 (1952), pp. 221-222.

404. "Publikationen Hugo Dinglers," in *Hugo Dingler. Gedenkbuch zum 75. Geburtstag*, ed. by Wilhelm Krampf. München: Eidos-Verlag, 1956. 222 pp.

DIONYSIUS THE AREOPAGITE.

See "Pseudo-Dionysius the Areopagite

DOOYEWEERD, HERMAN

405. "Bibliography [: H. Dooyeweerd]," in *Philosophy and Christianity. Philosophical Essays Dedicated to Professor Dr. Herman Dooyeweerd.* Kampen: Uitg. J. H. Kok; Amsterdam: North-Holland Publishing Co., 1965, pp. 449-452.

DUCASSE, CURT JOHN

406. "Publications of Curt John Ducasse," in *Current Philosophical Issues. Essays in honor of Curt John Ducasse.* Springfield, Ill.: Charles C. Thomas, 1966, pp. 242-257.

DUMÉRY, HENRY

407. Scheire, Urbain. "L'Oeuvre de Henry Duméry. Relevé bibliographique," in G. Thils and R. E. Brown, eds., *Exégèse et théologie. Les Saintes écritures et leur interprétation théologique*, vol. III, Gembloux: J. Duculot, 1968, pp. 315-327.

DUNS SCOTUS, JOHN. See also 1606

408. Minges, P. "Die skotistische Literatur des 20 Jahrhunderts," Franziskanische Studien (Münster i. w.), vol. 4 (1917), pp. 49-67, 177-198.

409. "Bibliographie scotiste de langue française (1900-1934)," in Congrès des lecteurs franciscains de langue--française . . . quatrieme, Lyon. Paris: Editions Franciscains, 1934, pp. 190-259.

410. Amedeus a Zedelgem. "Joannis Duns Scoti Operum Absolutae Editionis Efficax Propositum," Collectanea Franciscana (Assisii), vol. 5 (1935), pp. 261-274.

411. Lime, V. "Bibliographie scotiste de langue française (1900-1934)," La France franciscaine (Paris), vol. 18 (1935), pp. 292-361.

412. Longpré, E. "Nouveaux manuscrits des reportations de Duns Scot (à suivre)," Wissenschaft und Weisheit (Freiburg in Breisgan), vol. 2 (1935), pp. 229-236.

413. Schwitzer, R. "Die skotische Bibliothek in Salsburg," Franziskanische Studien (Werl in Westfalen), vol. 22 (1935), pp. 348-363.

414. Grajewski, Maurice. "Scotistic Bibliography of the Last Decade (1929-1939)," Franciscan Studies (New York), vol. 22 (1941), pp. 55-62, 71-76; vol. 23 (1942), pp. 61-71, 156-173.

415. Smeets, Uriel. Lineamenta Bibliographiae Scotisticae. Pro Manuscripto ad usum Commissionis Scotisticae. Romae: Typograf. Augustiniana, 1942. 182 pp.

416. Bettoni, Efrem. Vent'anni di studi scotisti (1920-1940). Saggio bibliografico. Quaderni della Rivista di fil filosofia neo-scholastica. Milan: Via Ludovico Necchi, 1943. 105 pp.

417. Meier, Ludger. "Vier Jahre Skotusforschung in deutschen Bibliotheken," Zentralblatt für Bibliothekswesn (Leipzig), vol. 60 (1943), pp. 145-167.

418. Schäfer, Odulf. Johannes Duns Scotus (Bibliographische Einführungen in das Studium der Philosophie, 22). Bern: A. Francke, 1953. 34 pp.

About 300 entries arranged by topic. Index.

419. Schäfer, Odulf. Bibliographia de Vita, Operibus et Doctrina Iohannes Duns Scoti, Doctoris Subtilis ac Mariani, Saec. XIX-XX. Romae: Orbis Catholicus-Herder, 1955. 223 pp.

About 4500 entries.

420. Markowski, Mieczyslaw, and Zofia Wtodek. "Les Oeuvres de Jean Duns Scot et de ses adhérents dans les manuscrits mediévaux de la Bibliothèque jagellone à Cracovie," in De doctrina Ioannis Duns Scoti. Acta Congressus Scotistici Internationalis Oxonii et Edimburgi 11-17 Sept. 1966 celebrati, I: Documenta et Studia in Duns Scotum Introductoria; Cura Commissionis Scotisticae (Studia Scolastico-Scolistica, 1), Romae: 1968, pp. 375-394.

421. Schmidt, M. A. "Literatur zu Johannes Duns Scotus (seit 1935) (Wird fortgesetzt)," Theologische Rundschau (Tübingen), vol. 34 (1969), pp. 1-48.

DUPRÉEL, EUGÈNE

422. Colloque Eugène Dupréel (1879-1967). Brussels: Edition de la Revue Internationale de philosophie. 260 pp.

Contains a bibliography of the works of Dupreel for 1949-1967.

DURKHEIM, EMILE

423. Barcani, N. "Bibliographie durkheimienne," Archives internationales de sociologie de la coopération (Paris), no. 28 (1970), pp. 161-223.

EBBINGHAUS, JULIUS

424. Kempski, J. von. "Vervöllstandigte Bibliographie Julius Ebbinghaus [bis 1959]," in Julius Ebbinghaus, Gesammelte Aufsätze Vortrage und Reden. Hildesheim: Georg Olms, 1968.

ECKHART, MEISTER

425. Van de Vyver, E. "Meester Eckhart," Tijdschrift voor philosophie (Leuven), vol. 18 (1956), pp. 666-680.

426. Schaller, Toni. "Die Meister Eckhart-Forschung von der Jahrhundertswende bis zur Gegenwart," Freiberger Zeitschrift für Philosophie und Theologie (Freiburg, Switz.), vol. 15 (1968), pp. 262-316.

EDWARDS, JONATHAN

427. U. S. Library of Congress. Reading Room. . . . A list of Printed Materials on Jonathan Edwards, 1703-1758, to be Found in the Library of Congress; Including Biographies, Appreciations, Criticisms, and Fugitive References, with Supplementary Lists of Material not in the Library and of Notes on his Manuscripts and Works. Compiled in the office of the Superintendent of the Reading Room, Nov., 1934. Washington, 1934. 29 l.

Typed manuscript.

428. Faust, C. H., and T. H. Johnson. Jonathan Edwards. Representative Selections, with Introduction, Bibliography, and Notes. New York: American Book Company, 1935. 434 pp.

429. Johnson, Thomas H. The Printed Writings of Jonathan Edwards, 1703-1758: A Bibliography. Princeton: Princeton University Press; London: H. Milford, Oxford University Press, 1940. 136 pp.

346 entries, plus information on editions. Index of titles.

EHRLICH, W.

430. "Bibliographie W. Ehrlich," Zeitschrift für philosophische Forschungen (Meisenheim am Glan), vol. 20 (1966), pp. 331-332.

EINSTEIN, ALBERT. See also 85

431. Boni, Nell. A Bibliographical Checklist and Index to the Collected Writings of Albert Einstein, Compiled by Nell Boni, Monique Russ, and Dan H. Laurence. (Readex Microprint ed.). New York: Readex Microprint Corp., 1960. 84 pp. Also: Paterson, N. J.: Pageant Books, 1960.

432. Shields, Margaret C. "Bibliography of the Writings of Albert Einstein to May, 1951," in P. A. Schilpp, ed. Albert Einstein: Philosopher--Scientist, Third Edition. La Salle, Ill.: Open Court; London: Cambridge University Press,

432. (Continued)

1970, pp. 689-760.

Chronologically arranged. 445 entries plus additional interviews, letters, speeches, telegrams, etc.

EMERSON, RALPH WALDO

433. Cooke, George Willis. A Bibliography of Ralph Waldo Emerson. New York: Kraus Reprint Corp., 1966. Originally published: Boston: Houghton-Mifflin, 1908. 340 pp.

ENGELS, FRIEDRICH. See also: MARX, KARL, AND 565.

434. Berlin. Stadtbibliotek. Friedrich Engels. [Anlässlich des 150. Geburtstages von Friedrich Engels am 28. 11. 1970 Zusammengestellt von Lieselotte Stöhr] (Bibliographische Kalenderblätter. Sonderblatt, 30). Berlin, 1970. 72 pp.

435. Rakhnev, Slavi and Velcho Vŭlkov Kovachev. Fridrikh Engels. 1820-1970. Metod. i bibliogr. materiali po sluchaĭ 150 g. ot rozhdenieto [Freidrich Engels. 1820-1970. Methodological and bibliographical materials on the occasion of the 150th anniversary of his birth [In Bulgarian]]. Sofia: Nar. bibl. Kiril i Metodii, 1970. 138 pp.

EPICTETUS

436. Oldfather, W. A. Contributions toward a Bibliography of Epictetus. (University of Illinois bulletin, vol. 25, no. 12). Urbana, Ill.: University of Illinois, 1927. 201+ pp.

About 1200 entries. Editions, translations, works about.

437. Harman, Marian. Contributions toward a Bibliography of Epictetus . . . a Supplement, Edited by Marian Harman, with a Preliminary List of Epictetus Manuscripts by W. H. Friedrich and C. U. Faye. Urbana, Ill.: University of Illinois Press, 1952. 177 pp.

Supplements Oldfather's bibliography.

EPICURUS. See also 809.

438. De Lacy, Phillip. "Some Recent Publications on Epicurus and Epicureanism (1937-1954)," Classical Weekly (Pittsburgh), vol. 48 (1955), pp. 169-177.

ERASMUS, DESIDERIUS

439. Van der Halghen, Ferdinand. . . . Bibliotheca Erasmiana. Bibliographie des oeuvres d'Erasme . . . Gand: C. Vyt, 1897-1919. 10 vols. Reprinted: Nieuwkoop: B. De Graff, 1961.

440. Rotterdam. Bibliothek en leeszalen der gemeente. Catalogus van geschriften over liven en werken van Desiderius Erasmus aanwezig in de Bibliotheek der gemeente Rotterdam. Rotterdam: 1937. 97 pp.

441. Margolin, Jean Claude. Douze années de bibliographie érasmienne, 1950-1961. Paris: Vrin, 1963. 204 pp.

442. Centre universitaire de l'etat a Mons. Bibliothèque centrale. Editions anciennes d'Érasme. Exposition organisée dans les salons de l'hôtel de ville . . . [etc.]. Préfait de Léon-E. Halkin. Mons: Centre Universitaire d'État, 1967. 71 pp.

443. Devueux, E. J. A Checklist of Erasmus to 1700 (Oxford Bibliographical Society. Occasional Publication no. 3). Oxford: Oxford Bibliographical Society, 1968. 40 pp.

444. Erasmus en Leuven. (In het kader van de Nederlandse Universitaire week te Leuven ingericht door de Katholieke Universiteit te Leuven, in samenwerking met de Stad Leuven). Leuven: Stedelÿk Museum, 1969. 456 pp.

445. Erasmus en zijn tijd. Catalogus van de tentoonstelling [in het] Museum Boymans-van Beuningen . . . etc. Rotterdam: Boymans-van Beunigen, 1969. 2 vols.

446. Margolin, Jean Claude. Quatorze années de bibliographie érasmienne, 1936-1949. Paris: J. Vrin, 1969. 431 pp.

About 1200 entries. Annotated.

447. Paris. Bibliothèque nationale. Catalogue des ouvrages d'Érasme, conservés au Departement des imprimés. Paris: Imprimerie nationale, 1912. 136 cols.

958 entries.

ERIGENA, JOHN SCOTUS

448. Cappuyns, M. Jean Scott Erigène, sa vie, son oeuvre, sa pensée. Louvain: Abbaye du Mont César; Paris: de Brouwer, 1933. 410 pp.

449. Sheldon-Williams, I. P. "A List of the Works Doubtfully or Wrongly Attributed to Johannes Scottus Eriugena," Journal of Ecclesiastical History (London), vol. 15 (1964), pp. 76-98.

ESPINAS, ALFRED

450. Ostrowski, Jean J. "Notes biographies et bibliographiques sur Alfred Espinas," Revue philosophique de la France et de l'étranger (Paris), vol. 62 (1967), pp. 385-391.

EUSEBIUS

451. Quasten, J. ["Bibliography on Eusebius"], Patrology (Utrecht), vol. 3 (1960), pp. 309-345.

FALCHI, ANTONIO

452. "Pubblicazione di Antonio Falchi," in Scritti in memoria di Antonio Falchi (Universita degli studi di Genova. Annali della facolta di giurisprudenza. Anno III, fasc. I), Milano: Giuffre, 1964, pp. 1-4.

FEIBLEMAN, JAMES K.

453. "Writings by James K. Feibleman," Studium generale (Berlin), vol. 24 (1971), pp. 842-850.

FENSTAD, JENS ERIC. See 2115.

FEUERBACH, LUDWIG ANDREAS

454. Jodl, Friedrich. Ludwig Feuerbach. Stuttgart: F. Frommans, 1904. 135 pp. Pp. 131-133: "Verzeichness der wichtigsten . . . Schriften Feuerbachs;" pp. 134-135

454. (Continued)

"Literatur uber Feuerbach." Also: 1921 ed. with longer bibliography.

455. Bolin, W., and Friedrich Jodl. _Feuerbach: Sämliche Werke, vol. 11_. Stuttgart: Fromann, 1964.

Pp. 341 ff. contain a bibliography.

FICHTE, JOHANN GOTTLIEB

456. Baumgartner, Hans M. and Wilhelm G. Jacobs. _J. G. Fichte-Bibliographie_. Stuttgart-bad-Caanstatt: Friedrich Frommann (Günther Holzboog), 1968. 346 pp.

3827 entries. Includes editions of his works. The Fichte literature, name index, key word index, year index. Works arranged by topic.

457. Zahn, Manfred. "Die erste Fichte-Bibliographie," _Zeitschrift für philosophische Forschung_ (Meisenheim am Glan), vol. 23 (1969), pp. 407-416.

FINK, EUGEN

458. Giannarás, Anastasios, and Friedrich-Wilhelm von Herrmann. "Bibliographie: Eugen Fink," in _Beispiele. Festschrift für Eugen Fink_, Den Haag: Martinus Nijhoff, 1965, pp. 309-314.

459. Herrmann, Friedrich Wilhelm von. _Bibliographie Eugen Fink_. Den Haag: Nijhoff, 1970. 47 pp.

FLOISTAD, GUTTORM. See 2115.

FOLLESDAL, DAGFIN. See 2115.

FOREST, AIMÉ. See also 958.

460. ["Bibliographie: Aime Forest"], in G. Deledalle and D. Huisman, eds., _Les Philosophes français d'aujourd'hui_. [n.p., n.d.], pp. 179-185.

80 unannotated entries.

461. Vito, Orlando. "Aimé Forest: una filosofia che traduce una vita. Rapporto tra vita e pensievo in Forest--Bibliografia di A. Forest," Aquinas (Roma) vol. 16 (1973), pp. 281-287.

FOUCAULT, MICHEL

462. Lapointe, François A. "Michel Foucault: a Bibliographic Essay," The Journal of the British Society for Phenomenology (Manchester), vol. 4 (1973), pp. 195-197.

463. Lapointe, François H. and Walter Seittler. "Bibliographie der Schriften über Michel Foucault," Philosophischen Jahrbach (Munchen), vol. 81 (1974), pp. 202-207.

FRANK, PHILLIPP

464. "A Bibliography of Philipp Frank. Selected Writings on the Philosophy of Science," in Boston Studies in the Philosophy of Science, vol. 2. In Honor of Philipp Frank. (Proceedings of the Boston Colloquium for the Philosophy of Science, 1962-1964). New York: Humanities Press, 1965, pp. xxxi-xxxiv.

FRANKL, VIKTOR E.

465. Fizzotti, Eugenio. "Saggio di bibliografia italiana su Viktor E. Frankl," Teoresi (Catania), vol. 29 (1974), pp. 71-74.

FREGE, GOTTLOB

466. Stroll, Avrum. "On the First Flowering of Frege's Reputation," Journal of the History of Philosophy (Claremont, Calif.), vol. 4 (1966), pp. 72-81.

Bibliography of 1950-1965 articles on Frege, pp. 79-81.

FREUD, SIGMUND

467. Dufresne, Roger. Bibliographie des écrits de Freud, en français, allemand, et anglais (Collection science de l'Homme). Paris: Payot, 1973. 268 pp.

FRIES, JACOB FRIEDRICH

468. "Verzeichnis aller im Druck erschienenen Schriften und Aufsätze von Jacob Friedrich Fries," Abhandlungen der Fries'schen Schule (Berlin), vol. 6 (1937), pp. 473-495.

GABRIEL, A. L.

469. Domonkos, L. S. "A Chronological Bibliography of the Works of Dr. A. L. Gabriel," in L. S. Domonkos and R. J. Schneider, eds., Studium Generale: Studies Offered to Astrik L. Gabriel (Texts and Studies in the History of Mediaeval Education, 11). Notre Dame, Ind.: Mediaeval Institute, University of Notre Dame, pp. xv-xxxi.

GAETANUS, TOMMASO DE VIO. See Cajetan.

GALILEO GALILEI

470. Riccardi, Pietro. Bibliografia Galileiana. Modena: Tipog. di L. Gaddi già Soliani, 1872.

A reprint, with preface and name index, of the article "Galilei" in vol. 1 of the author's Biblioteca Mathematica Italiana (1870-1876).

471. Favaro, Antonio. Per la edizione nazionale delle opere di Galileo Galilei; materiali per un indice dei manoscritti e documenti galileiani, non posseduti dalla Biblioteca nazionale di Firenze. Venezia: Tip. Ferrari, 1894. 127 pp.

472. Carli, Alarico. Bibliografia Galileiana (1568-1895) raccolta ed illustrata da A. Carli ed A. Favaro. Roma: Firenze, Tip. dei Fratelli Bencini, 1896. 402 pp. Supplement, 1896-1940: Rome: Libreria dello stado, 1943-

2108 titles, including references to periodicals, chronologically arranged.

473. Favaro, Antonio. . . . Vent' anni di studi galileiani. Firenze e Roma: Tip. dei Fratelli Bencini, 1896. 26 pp.

100 entries.

474. Favaro, Antonio and Alarico Carli. Bibliografia Galileiana: 1568-1895. Roma: Ministero della pubblica instruzione, 1896.

2129 items. Works by or on Galileo.

475. Lier, R., and Co. booksellers, Florence. Unique Collection of Editiones Principes of Works of Galileo Galilei, Offered for Sale by R. Lier and Co., . . . Firenze . . . Firenze: Tip. B. Coppini and Co., 1931. 2 pp.

476. Vismara, Silvio. "Bibliografia Galileiana," in Nel terzo centenario della morte di Galileo Galilei. Saggi e conferenze. (Pubblicazione dell' Univ. del Sacre Cuore. Scienze storiche, 20). Milano: Vita e pensiero, 1942, pp. 407-426.

477. Boffito, Giuseppe. Bibliografia Galileiana: 1896-1940. Roma: Ministero della educazione nazionale, 1943.

1747 entries of works by or on Galileo and his followers. Some annotations. 170 additions to the Carli-Favaro bibliography. Index of authors and topics for the Boffito and Carli-Favaro volumes.

478. Rocco di Torrepadula, Giampaolo. Biblioteca Galileiana. (Contributi alla Biblioteca bibliografica italica, 15). Firenze: Sansoni, 1957. 393 pp.

479. Drake, Stillman. "Galileo Gleanings IV: Bibliographical Notes," Isis (Washington), vol. 49 (1958), pp. 409-413.

480. Drake, Stillman. "Galileo Gleanings XI: Further Bibliographical Notes," Physis (Firenze), vol. 4 (1962), pp. 33-38.

481. Turina, Irina A. and Usher I. Frankfurt. ["Bibliography of Russian Works Pertaining to Galileo"] in A. J. Ishlinsley, ed., Galileo Galilei: Izbrannye Trudy. Moscow: 1964.

186 entries for the period 1779 to 1964.

482. Gentili, Elio. "Bibliografia Galileiana, fra i due centenari (1942-1964)," La Scuola cattaolica (Varese, It.), vol. 92 (Suppl.) (1964), pp. 267-308. Supplement. Vol. 93 (1965), pp. 82-86. Also: (Hildephonsiana, 8). Varese: Venegono inferiore, Seminario arcivescoirle di Milano, Editrice La Scuole cattolica, 1966. 132 pp.

988 entries.

483. Crowe, Michael J. "Annotated List of Works by Galileo and his Contemporaries," in Ernan McMullin, ed., Galileo: Man of Science, New York and London: Basic Books, 1967, pp. lxxxiii-xciii.

Twelve works by Galileo, a note on editions and the history of his manuscripts (the heirs of Viviani, his pupil to whom the over 300 volumes

483. (Continued)

were trusted, were selling them to a butcher for wrapping paper), about 60 "Early works of Galileo interest" by Kepler, Copernicus, Brahe, Napier, etc.

484. McMullin, Ernan. "Addenda to the Carli-Favaro (1564-1895) and Boffito (1896-1940) Bibliografia Galileiana," in E. McMullin, ed., _Galileo: Man of Science_, New York and London: Basic Books, 1967, pp. lxx-lxxxii.

Lists about 400 additions to the above-mentioned bibliographies.

485. McMullin, Ernan. "Bibliografia Galileiana, 1940-1964," in E. McMullin, ed., _Galileo: Man of Science_, New York and London: Basic Books, 1967, pp. i-lxix.

Lists 1740 items, has a subject index. Continues the Boffito and Carli-Favaro bibliographies.

486. Russo, Francois. "Bulletin de l'actualité philosophique. Chronique galiléenne," _Archives de philosophie_ (Paris), vol. 31 (1968), pp. 640-647.

GANDHI, MOHANDAS K. See also 2110.

487. Deshpande, P. G. _Gandhiana; a Bibliography of Gandhian Literature_. Ahmedabad: Narajivan Publishing House, 1948?. 239 pp.

488. Sharma, Jagdish Saran. _Mahatma Gandhi; a Descriptive Bibliography_. Foreword by U. N. Dhebar (National Bibliographies, no. 1). Delhi: S. Chand, 1955. 565 pp. 2nd. ed. 1968.

A thesis at the University of Michigan.

489. Pontara, Giuliano. "Bibliografia gandhiana," _Rivista di filosofia_ (Bologna, Torino), vol. 53 (1962), pp. 308-312.

490. Kovalsky, Susan Joan. _Mahatma Gandhi and his Influence in South Africa, 1893-1413, a Selective Bibliography_. Johannesburg: University of Witwatersrand, Dept. of Bibliography, Librarianship and Typography, 1971. 27 pp.

491. Dharma Vir. _Gandhi Bibliography_. _With a Foreword by Zahir Husain_. Chandigarh: Gandhi Smarak Nidi; Punjab: Haryana and Himachal Pradesh, 1967. 575 pp.

GAOS, JOSÉ

492. "Bibliografía de José Gaos (1900-1969)," Bibliografía filosofica mexicana (México), vol. 2 (1971), pp. 49-94.

414 entries: Books and articles, translations, works on him.

493. Solayar, Rafael, and E. Bustainente. "Bibliografia del filósofo José Gaos (1900 - 1969)," Libro anvol (ISEE, México), vol. 1 (1971-1972), pp. 223-259.

GARIN, EUGENIO

494. Bibliografia degli scritti di Eugenio Garin. Bari: G. Laterza, 1969. 207 pp.

GARRIGOU-LAGRANGE, RÉGINALD MARIE

495. "Essai de bibliographie du R. P. Garrigou-Lagrange," Angelicum (Roma) vol. 14 (1937), pp. 5-37.

496. "Le Père Garrigou-Lagrange: bibliographie," Itinéraires (Saint-Brieuc), no. 82 (1964), pp. 127-136.

497. Zorcolo, B. "Bibliografia del P. Garrigou-Lagrange," Angelicum (Roma), vol. 42 (1965), pp. 200-272.

GEHLEN, ARNOLD

498. "Die Schriften von Arnold Gehlen," Zeitschrift für philosophische Forschung (Meisenheim am Glan), vol. 18 (1964), pp. 333-338.

GEMELLI, P. A.

499. Mattesini, F. "Bibliografia su P. A. Gemelli (1959-1961)," Studi Francescani (Firenze), vol. 60 (1962), pp. 84-92.

GENTILE, GIOVANNI

500. Bellezza, Vito A. Bibliografia degli scritti di Giovanni Gentile. Firenze: Sansoni, 1950. 141 pp. Also

500. (Continued)

issued as vol. III of Opere complete di Giovanni Gentile. Firenze: Sansoni.

501. Bellezza, Vito A. "L'Estetica e la critica letteraria del Gentile," Giornale critico della filosofia italiana (Firenze), vol. 23 (1969), pp. 446-468.

Recent work on Gentile's aesthetics.

GEORGE, STEFAN

502. Bondi, G. Erinnerungen an Stefan George mit einer Bibliographie. Berlin: Bondi, 1934. 31 pp.

GEULINEX, ARNOLD

503. Vander Haeghen, Victor. "Bibliography," in his Geulinex: Etude sur sa vie, sa philosophie et ses ouvrages. Ghent: 1886, pp. 197-224.

GHERSI, GUIDO

504. Pellegrino, G. "Bibliografia di Guido Ghersi," Theoresi (Messina), vol. 14 (1959), pp. 282-291.

GILLES DE VITERBE

505. Astruc, Charles, and Jacques Monfrin. "Livres latins et hebreux du Cardinal Gilles de Viterbe," Bibliothèque d'humanisme et renaissance (Paris), vol. 23 (1961), pp. 551-554.

GILSON, ÉTIENNE

506. Edie, Callistus James. "The Writings of Étienne Gilson Chronologically Arranged," in Mélanges offerts à Etienne Gilson de l'Academie française, Toronto: Pontifical Institute of Medieval Studies, 1959, pp. 15-58.

GODWIN, WILLIAM

507. Pollin, Burton R. Godwin Criticism: A Synoptic Bibliography. Toronto: University of Toronto Press, 1967. 659 pp.

4200 entries. Annotated coverage of books and articles for the period 1783-1966. Numerous indexee indexes. Good.

GOETHE, JOHANN WOLFGANG VON. See also 775.

508. Weinhandl, F. "Goethe. Zu den Erscheinungen des Goethejahres 1932," Blätter für deutsche Philosophie (Berlin), vol. 8 (1934), pp. 418-430.

509. Schmid, Günther. Goethe und die Naturwissenschaften. Eine Bibliographie. Hrsg. im Namen der kaiserlichen Leopoldinisch-Carolinisch deutschen Akadamie der Naturforscher von E. Abderholden. Halle: Deutsche Akadamie, 1940. 620 pp.

510. Stäglich, Hans. Johann Wolfgang von Goethe und Arthur Schopenhauer. Eine . . . Bibliographie einschlägeger Literatur. Bonn: Rheim, 1960.

147 entries. A reprint of an earlier (1932) work.

GOLDMANN, LUCIEN

511. Tell, Eduard. "Bibliographie de Lucien Goldmann," Revue de l'Institut de sociologie (Bruxelles), (1973), no. 3-4, pp. 787-806.

GOMPERZ, HEINRICH

512. Gomperz, Heinrich. Autobiographical Remarks [n.p., n.d.], 19 pp. Caption title: "Reprinted from the Personalist, vol. 24, no. 1, summer 1943. Originally written for Luminar in the spring of 1942." Bibliography: pp. 18-19.

GONZALEZ, CEFERINO

513. Díaz de Cerio, Franco. "Bibliografía del Cardinal Ceferino González," Pensamiento (Madrid), vol. 20 (1964), pp. 65-69.

GRABMANN, MARTIN

514. "Verzeichnis der von Martin Grabmann verfassten Artikel und Bücher," in Aus der Geisteswelt des Mittelalters, Münster i. W.: Aschendorff, 1935, pp. XXIII-XXXV.

GREDT, JOSEPH

515. Borne, Petro. "Scripta R. P. Josephi Gredt," in Miscellanea Philosophica R. P. Joseph Gredt. Rome: Pontifico ateneo di s. Anselmo. Facolta di filosofia, 1938, pp. 3-5.

GREEN, THOMAS HILL

516. "Thomas Hill Green [: a Bibliography]," in George Watson, ed., The New Cambridge Bibliography of English Literature. Cambridge: Cambridge University Press, 1969, vol. 3, cols. 1533-1534.

About 60 works by and about Green, mostly about him.

GRENIER, JEAN

517. "Jean Grenier, notice biographique et bibliographique," Annales de l'Université de Paris (Paris), vol. 33 (1963), pp. 83-85.

GROTIUS, HUGO

518. Rogge, Hendrik Cornelis. Bibliotheca Grotiana. Hugonis Grotii Operum Descriptio Bibliographica in qua omnes Editiones et Versiones, Argumenti Ratione Habita, Secundum Temporis Ordinem Recensentur. Hagae Comitum: apud M. Nijhoff, 1883. 76 pp.

Pars 1. [Limited to the works of Grotius.]

519. Reeves, Jesse Siddall. Grotius, De Jure Belli ac Pacis: a Bibliographical Account . . . New York, 1925, pp. 251-262.

520. Ter Meulen, Jacob. Concise Bibliography of Hugo Grotius. Leyden: Pub. for the Library of the Palace of Peace by A. W. Sijthhoff's Publishing Co., 1925. 88 pp.

A supplement to the H. C. Rogge bibliography. Itself supplemented by Grotiana, 1 (1928)-?, published by the Veneeniging voor de uitgave van Grotius, The Hague. An annual list containing new editions of Grotius' works and the literature about him. Review: Rivista di filosofia (Bologna; Torino), vol. 42 (1951), pp. 296-302.

521. Burgersdijk and Niermans, firm, booksellers, Leyden. Grotiana; catalogue de livres en verte aux prix marqués. Leiden: Burgersdijk and Niermans [Pays-Bas], 1929. 21 pp.

522. Ter Meulen, Jacob, and P. J. J. Diermanse. Bibliographie des écrits imprimés de Hugo Grotius. Le Haye: M. Nijhoff, 1950. 708 pp.

523. Ter Meulen, Jacob and P. J. J. Diermanse. Bibliographie des écrits sur Hugo Grotius imprimés au XVIIe siécle. Le Haye: Martinus Nijhoff, 1961. 224 pp.

About 500 entries, annotated, arranged by subject, indices of editions, titles and subjects, names. Well done.

GUARDINI, ROMANO

524. Waltmann, H. "Verzeichnis der Schriften und Aufsätze Romano Guardinis 1911-1935," in K. Schmidthus, ed., Christliche Verwirklichung. Romano Guardini zum 50. Geburtstag, Rothenfels a. M.: Burgverlag, 1935, pp. 319-330.

GUSDORF, GEORGES

525. "Bibliographie [: Georges Gusdorf"], in G. Deladalle and D. Huisman, eds., Les Philosophes français d'aujourd'hui [n.p., n.d.], pp. 361-363.

37 unannotated entries of works by him.

GUZZO, CORDELIA

526. Guzzo, Augusto. "Bibliografia di Cordelia Guzzo," Filosofia (Torino), vol. 25 (1974), pp. 303-304.

HÄBERLIN, PAUL

527. "Verzeichnis der Veröffentlichungen von Paul Häberlin," in Im Dienste der Warheit, Paul Häberlin zum 80 geburtstag. Bern: A. Francke, 1958.

528. Kamm, Peter. "Paul Häberlin, Zum 2. Todestag am 29. September d. J.," Zeitschrift für philosophische Forschung (Schledorfam i. Kochelsee), vol. 16 (1962) pp. 413-428.

Pp. 417-428 contain a list of Häberlin's works.

HAEZRAHI, PEPITA

529. Haezrahi, Pepita. "Bibliography of Pepita Haezrahi's Works (in Hebrew) Iyyun (Jerusalem), vol. 24 (1973), pp. 307-309.

Complete bibliography.

530. Haezrahi, Pepita. "Select Bibliography of Articles on Pepita Haezrahi (in Hebrew)," Iyyun (Jerusalem), vol. 24 (1973), pp. 310-311.

HALL, EVERETT W.

531. "The Writings of Everett W. Hall," in E. M. Adams, ed., Categorial Analysis: Selected Essays of Everett W. Hall. Chapel Hill: University of North Carolina Press, 1964, pp. 344-347.

HALL, MANLY P.

532. Hall, Manly Palmer. Great Books on Religion and Esoteric Philosophy . . . With a Bibliography of Related Material Selected from the Writings of Manly P. Hall. Los Angeles: Philosophical Research Society, 1966. 85 pp.

HAMILTON, WILLIAM

533. "Sir William Hamilton [: a Bibliography]," in George Watson, ed., The New Cambridge bibliography of English Literature. Cambridge: Cambridge University Press, 1969, vol. 3, cols. 1535-1536.

About 50 works by and about Hamilton.

HARTMANN, NICOLAI

534. Balluf, Theodor. "Hartmann-Bibliographie," in Nicolai Hartmann. Der Dinker un sein Werke. Göttingen: Vandenhoeck und Ruprecht, 1952, pp. 286-308.

535. Wirth, Ingeborg. Realismus und Apriorismus in Nicolai Hartmanns Erkenntnistheorie. Mit eine Bibliographie d. seit 1952 über Hartmann erschienenen Arbeiten. Berlin: De Gruyter, 1965. 154 pp.

HARTSHORNE, CHARLES

536. Hartshorne, Mrs. Charles. "Published Writings of Charles Hartshorne," in William L. Reise and Eugene Freeman, eds., Process and Divinity; the Hartshorne Festschrift. La Sallè, Ill.: Open Court, 1964. P. 579 ff.

537. Fowler, Dean R. "A Bibliography of Dissertations and Theses on Charles Hartshorne," Process Studies (Claremont, Calif.), vol. 3 (1973), pp. 304-307.

538. Hartshorne, Dorothy C. "Charles Hartshorne: a Secondary Bibliography," Process Studies (Clarement, Calif.), vol. 3 (1973), pp. 179-227.

HEGEL, GEORG WILHELM FRIEDRICH. See also 1404.

539. Rosenkranz, Karl. "Alphabetische Bibliographie der Hegel'schen Schule," Der Gedanke. Philosophische Zeitschrift (Berlin), vol. 1 (1860-1861), pp. 77-80, 183-184, 256-264.

540. Croce, Benedetto. Ciò che è vivo e ciò che è morto della filosofia di Hegel; studio critico sequito da un saggio di bibliografia hegeliana. Bari: G. Laterza e Figli, 1907. 282 pp.

541. Hellersberg, Firm, Booksellers, Berlin. *Hegel und die Hegelianer; eine Bibliothek*. Charlottenburg: Dr. Hellersberg Antiquariat und Verlag, g.m.b.h., [1972?]. 39 pp.

851 titles of a collection since acquired by the New York University Washington Square College Library.

542. Janeff-Sofia, Janko. "Bibliographie der ausländischen Hegel-Literatur," *Literarische Berichte aus dem Gebiete der Philosophie* (Erfurt), vol. 23 (1930), pp. 40-48.

543. Janeff-Sofia, Janko. "Bibliographie der deutschen Hegel-Literatur für hundert Jahre (1828-1928)," *Literarische Berichte aus dem Gebiete der Philosophie* (Erfurt), vol. 24 (1931), pp. 35-49.

544. Cogni, G. "Studi hegeliani (continua)," *Giornale critico della filosofia Italiana* (Firenze), vol. 15 (1934), pp. 295-311.

545. Koyré, A. "Hegel à Iéna. (A propos de publications récentes)," *Revue de philosophie de la France et de l'étranger* (Paris), vol. 118 (1934), pp. 274-283.

546. Kühler, Otto. *Sinn, Bedeutung, und Auslegung der heiligen Schrift in Hegels Philosophie; mit Beiträgen zur Bibliographie über die Stellung Hegels (und der Hegelianer zur Theologie, insbesondere) zur heiligen Schrift*. Leipzig: S. Hirzel, 1934. 110 pp.

547. Nadler, K. "Wandlung des Hegelbildes in Deutschland seit der Jahrhundertwende; zur deutschen Hegel-Bibliographie von 1900-1933," *Idealismus, Jahrbuch für die Idealistiche Philosophie* (Zurich), vol. 1 (1934), pp. 227-257.

548. Cogni, G. "Studi hegeliani, (continuazione, continua)," *Giornale critico della filosofia Italiana* (Firenze), vol. 16 (1935), pp. 152-168.

549. Haering, Th. "Neue Hegelliteratur," *Blätter für deutsche Philosophie* (Berlin), vol. 9 (1935), pp. 85-91.

550. Hyppolite, J. "Les Travaux de jeunesse de Hegel d'après des ouvrages récents," *Revue de metaphysique et de morale* (Paris), vol. 42 (1935), pp. 399-426, 549-578.

551. Koyré, A. "Hegel à Iéna. (A propos de publications récentes)," *Revue d'historie de la philosophie religieuse* (Strasbourg), vol. 15 (1935), pp. 420-458.

552. Cogni, G. "Studi hegeliani (continuazione e fine), *Giornale critico della filosofia Italiana* (Firenze), vol. 17 (1936), pp. 12-25.

553. Contri, S. "Bollettino di filosofia hegeliana. Prima puntata," Sophia (Napoli), vol. 4 (1936), pp. 251-262; ". . . Seconda puntata," vol. 5 (1937), pp. 72-82.

554. Merker, Nicolao. "A proposito di due annuari tedeschi su Hegel," Rivista critica di storia della filosofia (Milano), vol. 16 (1961), pp. 448-463.

555. Bredenfeld, Hermann. "Dissertationen über Hegel und seine Philosophie (Deutschland, Oesterreich, Schweiz)," Hegel-Studien (Bonn), vol. 2 (1963), pp. 424-441.

556. Nicolin, F. "Nachdrucke und Neuanflagen hegelscher Texte," Hegel-Studien (Bonn), vol. 3 (1965), pp. 323-325.

557. Nürnberg. Stadtbibliothek. Georg Wilhelm Friedrich Hegel (1770-1831) in Nürnberg 1808-1816. Ausstellung. Eröffuet am 15. Sept. 1966. (Einrichtung der Ausstellung und Katalog: Franz Xaver Prö ll). Nürnberg: Stadtbibliothek, 1966.

558. Kern, Walter. "Hegel-Bücher 1961-1966; ein Auswahlbericht," Theologie und Philosophie (Freiberg i. Bremen), vol. 42 (1967), pp. 79-88, 402-418.

559. Krońska, Irena. "Neuere polnische Hegel-Literatur," Hegel-Studien (Bonn), vol. 4 (1967), pp. 317-321.

560. Noica, Constantin. "Hegel-Literatur in rumänien," Hegel-Studien (Bonn), vol. 4 (1967), pp. 321-322.

561. Kern, Walter. "Hegel-Buecher. 1961-1968: ein Auswahlbericht, 4," Theologie und Philosophie (Freiburg i. Bremen), vol. 46 (1971), pp. 71-87.

562. Kern, Walter. "Hegel-Buecher 1961-1971: ein Auswahlbericht," Theologie und Philosophie (Freiburg i. Bremen), vol. 48 (1973), pp. 398-409.

563. Weiss, Frederick G. "Hegel: A Bibliography of Books in English, Arranged Chronologically," in J. J. O'Malley [et al], ed., The Legacy of Hegel. Proceedings of the Marquette Hegel Symposium 1970, The Hague: Nijhoff, 1973, pp. 298-308.

564. Hegel-Studien (Bonn), vol. 1 (1961)--[to date].

Each volume carries an "abhandlungen zur Hegel-Forschung" for the previous year or so.

565. "Bibliographie sur Hegel, Marx, Engels," Recherches hégéliennes (Poitiers), (1973), no. 8, pp. 30-35.

HEIDEGGER, MARTIN

566. Lübbe, Hermann. "Bibliographie der Heidegger-Literatur 1917-1955," Zeitschrift für Philosophische Forschung (Meisenheim am Glan), vol. 11 (1957), pp. 401-452. Also: Separately printed, Meisenheim am Glan: A. Hain, 1957, 52 pp.

880 unannotated entries. Name index.

567. Schneeberger, Guido. Ergänzungen zu einer Heidegger-Bibliographie. Mit vier Beilagen und einer Bildtafel. Bern: (Private printing), 1960. 27 pp.

Continuation of Hermann Lübbes "Bibliographie der Heidegger-Literatur, 1917-1955."

568. Panmen, Jean. "Elëments de bibliographie heideggerienne," Revue internationale de philosophie (Bruxelles), vol. 14 (1960), pp. 263-268.

569. Schneeberger, Guido. Nachlese zu Heidegger. Dokumente zu seinem/Eben und Denken. Bern: [88, Hochfeldstrasse], 1962. 288 pp.

570. Sass, Hans-Martin. Heidegger-Bibliographie. Meisenheim am Glan: Anton Hain, 1968. 181 pp.

About 2500 entries, including Heidegger's works and those of his critics and commentators. Name index. Works arranged by year.

571. Pereboom, Dirk. "Heidegger-Bibliographie 1917-1966," Freiburger Zeitschrift für Philosophie und Theologie (Freiburg, Switz.), vol. 16 (1969), pp. 100-161.

572. Martín, Victor R. "Martin Heidegger. Elementos de bibliografía," Philosophia (Mendoza ?), (1971), no. 37, pp. 125-171.

573. Landolt, Eduard. "Rassegna heideggeriana," Teoresi (Catania), vol. 27 (1972), pp. 261-280.

574. Hoeller, Keith. "Heidegger: Bibliography of English Translations," Journal of the British Society of Phenomenology (Manchester), vol. 6 (1975), pp. 206-208.

575. Sasn, H. M. et al. Matuiolien zur Heidigger-Bibliographie 1917-1972. Meisenheim am Glan: Verlag Anton Hain, 1975. 225 pp.

HEIMSOETH, HEINZ

576. Nicolin, Friedhelm. "Die Schriften Heinz Heimsoeths. Eine Bibliographie," Zeitschrift für Philosophische Forschung (Meisenheim am Glan), vol. 15 (1961), pp. 579-591.

577. ["Bibliographie Heinz Heimsoeth"], in Friedrich Kaulbach and Joachim Ritter, eds., Kritik und Metaphysic. Studien Heinz Heimsoeth zum 80. Geburtsdag. Berlin: De Gruyter, 1966, pp. 387-395.

HEINEMANN, FRITZ

578. "Die Schriften von Fritz Heinemann," Zeitschrfit für philosophische Forschung (Meisenheim am Glan), vol. 19 (1965), pp. 153-158.

HELLESNES, JOHN. See 2114.

HELVÉTIUS, CLAUDE-ADRIEN

579. Smith, D. W. "A Preliminary Bibliographical List of Editions of Helvétius's Works," Australian Journal of French Studies (Melbourne), vol. 7 (1970), pp. 299-347.

HENNEMANN, GERHARD

580. Hennemann, Gerhard. "Gerhard Hennemann: Bibliographie," Zeitschrift für philosophische Forschung (Meisenhein am Glan), vol. 24 (1970), pp. 449-454.

HERACLITUS

581. Roussos, Evangelos N. Heraklit-Bibliographie. Darmstadt: Wissenschaftliche Buchgesellschaft, 1971. 164 pp.

Texts, criticism, 1499-1970. Index. A good work, but no annotations. About 1250 entries.

HERBART, JOHANN FRIEDRICH

582. Allihn, F. H. Th. "Ueber das Leben und die Schriften J. F. Herbart's, nebst einer Zusammenstellung der Literatur seiner Schule," Zeitschrift für exacte Philosophie im Sinne des neuern philosophischen Realismus (Leipzig), vol. 1 (1860), pp. 44-99.

HERBARTIANI, HERBART E.

583. De Cumin, Nicola Siciliani. "Herbart E. Herbartiani alla scoula di Bertrando Spaventa," Giornale critico della filosofia italiana (Firenze), vol. 52 (1973), pp. 517-561.

HERBERT OF CHERBURY, EDWARD

584. Palmer, George Herbert. "A Herbert Bibliography, being a Catalogue of a Collection of Books Relating to George Herbert . . . ," Cambridge, Mass. [Privately printed], 1911, 61 l.

HERMANN, WILHELM

585. Fischer-Appelt, Peter. Metaphysik im Horizont der Theologie Wilhelm Hermanns. Mit eine Hermann-Bibliographie. (Forschungen zur Geschichte und Lehre des Protestantismus. Reine 10, Bd. 32). München: Ch. Kaiser, 1965. 258 pp.

HILDEBRAND, DIETRICH VON

586. "Bibliography of Dietrich von Hildebrand's Works," in Baldwin V. Schwarz, ed., The Human Person and the World of Values. Westport, Conn.: Greenwood, 1972, pp. 193-210. Also: New York: Fordham University Press, 1960.

HILDEBRANDT, KURT

587. "Nachtrag zur Bibliographie von Kurt Hildebrandt Erschienen 1962 als Anhang zu seinen Buch Ein Weg zu Philosophie," Zeitschrift für philosophische Forschung (Meisenheim am Glan), vol. 21 (1967), p. 151.

HIORTH, FINNGEIR. See 2115.

HIPPLE, ERNST VON

588. "Bibliographie Ernst von Hippel," in Carl Joseph Hering, ed., Staat, Recht, Kultur. Festgahe für Ernst von Hippel. Bonn: Röhrscheid, 1965, pp. 345-358.

HOBBES, THOMAS

589. Cambridge University Library. "A Catalogue of First and Early Editions of the Works of Thomas Hobbes Forming Part of the Library Bequeathed by John Maynard, Baron Keynes of Tilton, to King's College, Cambridge." Cambridge: Cambridge University Library, 1949. 42 pp.

Typescript with illustrations of the large Keynes collection on Hobbes. Early editions of his works plus about a dozen works about his work (especially about Leviathan) by his contemporaries.

590. Polin, R. ["Hobbes Bibliography"], Revue internationale de philosophie (Bruxelles), vol. 4 (1950), pp. 460-461.

591. Macdonald, Hugh, and Mary Hargreaves. Thomas Hobbes; a Bibliography. London: The Bibliographical Society, 1952. 83 pp.

108 entries. Notes on all editions of works to 1725, translations to 1700, and collected editions to 1952. Reviews: Times Literary Supplement, 24 April 1953, p. 276; ibid., 8 May 1953, p. 307; ibid., 5 June 1953, p. 365; Review of English Studies, new series, vol. 5 (1954), pp. 83-85; Book Collector, vol. 2 (1953), pp. 83-85.

592. Pacchi, A. "Bibliografia hobbesiana dal 1840 al oggi," Rivista critica di storia della filosofia (Milano), vol. 17 (1962), pp. 528-547.

593. Jessop, Thomas Edmund. Thomas Hobbes (Bibliographical Series of Supplements to British Book News on Writers and Their Work, no. 130). Harlow, Eng.: Published for the British Council and the National Book League, by Longmans Green, 1968. 40 pp. Also: 1960 edition.

594. Valls, Francisco Javier. "Bibliografía sobre Hobbes, 1960-1974," Anales de la Catedra Francisco Suárez (Banco de Vizcaya) vol. 14 (1974), pp. 187-203.

595. Valls, Francisco Javier. "Bibliografía sobre Hobbes, 1960-1974," in H. C. W. Sigwart, ed., Vergleichung der Rechts - und Staats - theorien des B. Spinoza und des Th. Hobbes, Aalen: Scientia - Verlag, 1974, pp. 187-203.

HOCKING, WILLIAM ERNEST

596. Gilman, Richard C. "The Bibliography of William Ernest Hocking from 1898 to 1951. Compiled by Richard C. Gilman, Colby College, Waterville [Maine], 1951. 63 pp. "Pro manuscript."

597. Gilman, Richard C. "The Bibliography of William Ernest Hocking, from 1898 to 1964," in Philosophy, Religion, and the Coming World Civilization: Essays in Honor of William Ernest Hocking, The Hague: Martinus Nijhoff, 1966, pp. 469-504.

HOLBACH, PAUL HENRI THIRY, BARON D'

598. Vercruysse, Jeroom. Bibliographie descriptive des écrits du Baron d'Holbach. Paris: Minard (Lettres modernes), 1971. No pagination for the body of the work. About 250 pages.

Editions and translations of Holbach's works through 1970. Index.

HOOK, SIDNEY

599. Crowley, John Dennis. "Sidney Hook: a Bibliography," Modern Schoolman (St. Louis, Mo.), vol. 44 (1966-1967), pp. 331-374.

HOOKER, RICHARD

600. Hill, William Speed. Richard Hooker, a Descriptive Bibliography of the Early Editions: 1593-1724. Cleveland: Press of Case Western Reserve University, 1970. 140 pp.

601. Grislis, Egil, and W. Speed Hill. Richard Hooker: a Selected Bibliography. (Bibliographia Tripotamopalitana, no. 4), Pittsburgh: Clifford E. Barbour Library, Pittsburgh Theological Seminary, 1971. 58 pp.

HUGH OF ST. VICTOR

602. Hauréau, Barthelemy. Les Oeuvres de Hughes de Saint-Victor; essai critique . . . Nouv. éd. Paris: Hachette et cie., 1886. Reprinted: Frankfurt am Main: Minerva-Verlag, 1963.

A bibliography.

HUME, DAVID. See also 1860.

603. Metz, Rudolf. "Bibliographie der Hume-Literatur," Literarische Berichte aus dem Gebiete der Philosophie (Erfurt), vol. 15/16 (1928), pp. 39-50.

604. Jessop, Thomas Edmund. A Bibliography of David Hume and of Scottish Philosophy from Francis Hutcheson to Lord Balfour. London and Hull: A. Brown and Sons, 1938. 201 pp.

Works by Hume by year, on Hume by topic, plus brief bibliographies on perhaps 80 Scottish philosophers for the period from about 1725 to about 1830. Good, with interesting introductory remarks for each work. About 2000 entries.

605. Lameere, J. "Notes bibliographiques," Revue internationale de philosophie (Bruxelles), vol. 6 (1952), pp. 250-253.

Writings on David Hume, 1938-1952.

606. Matczak, Sebastian A. "A Select and Classified Bibliography of David Hume," Modern Schoolman (St. Louis, Mo.), vol. 42 (1964-1965), pp. 70-81.

607. Hall, Roland. A Hume Bibliography from 1930. York, End.: Ronald Hall, 1971. 80 pp.

About 800 entries. No annotations. Index.

608. Hall, Roland. "More Hume Bibliography," Philosophical Quarterly (Edinburgh), vol. 26 (1976), pp. 92-101.

HUSSERL, EDMUND

609. Fries, Horace S. "Husserl's Unpublished Manuscripts," The Journal of Philosophy (New York), vol. 36 (1939), pp. 238-239.

610. Patocka, Jan. "Husserl. Bibliographie," Revue internationale de philosophie (Bruxelles), vol. 1 (1939), pp. 374-397.

611. "Les Archives Husserl à Louvain. Leur état actuel," Revue néo-scholastique de philosophie (Louvain), vol. 43 (1945), pp. 346-350.

612. Raes, Jean. "Supplément à la bibliographie de Husserl," Revue internationale de philosophie (Bruxelles), vol. 4 (1950), pp. 469-475.

613. Van Breda, H. L. "Note sur les archives Husserl à Louvain," in Problèmes actuels de la phénoménologie (Actes du Colloque international de phénoménologie, avril 1951 (Collection Textes et études philosophiques)). Paris: De Brouwer, 1952, pp. 155-159.

614. Van Breda, H. L. "Bibliographie der bis zum 30. Juni 1959 veröffentlichten Schriften Edmund Husserls," in Edmund Husserl, 1859-1959 (Phaenomenologica. Collection publiée sous le patronage des Centres d'archives-Husserl, IV). La Hage: Martinus Nijhoff, 1959, pp. 289-306.

615. Valori, P. "Recenti studi sulla fenomenologia husserliana," Civiltà catolica (Roma), vol. 122 (1961), pp. 278-285.

616. Bona, Ida. "Su alcuni manoscritti di Husserl," Aut Aut (Milano), no. 75 (1963), pp. 7-15.

617. De Lellis, Enzo. "Bibliografia degli studi husserliari in Italia: 1960-1964 (La Fenomenologia in Italia, II," Revue internationale de philosophie (Bruxelles), vol. 19 (1965), pp. 71-72, 140-152.

618. Maschke, Gerhard, and Iso Kern. "Husserl. Bibliographie," Revue internationale de philosophie (Bruxelles), vol. 19 (1965), pp. 153-202.

619. Noack, Hermann. "Bibliographie" in his Husserl (Wege der Forschung, 40) Darmstadt: Wissenschaftliche Buchgesillschaft, 1973, pp. 325-331.

620. Allen, Jeffner. "Husserl: Bibliography of English Translations," Monist (La Salle, Ill.), vol. 59 (1975), pp. 133-137.

HUSSERL, GERHART

621. "Verzeichnis der Werke von Gerhart Husserl," in Phänomenologie, Rechtsphelosophie, Jurisprudenz. Festschrift für Gerhart Husserl zum 75. Gebrutstag. Hrsg. von Thomas

621. (Continued)

Würtenberger. Frankfurt am Main: Klostermann, 1969, pp. 274-276.

IBN AL-JAWZĪ

622. Al-Alwajī, 'Abd al-Hamīd. Mu'allafāt Ibn al-Jawzī [The writings of Ibn al-Jawzi [In Arabic]], Baghdad: Republican House for Publishing and Printing, 1965. 209 pp.

IBN GABIROL. See AVICEBRON.

IBN KHALDŪN

623. Badawi, 'Abd al-Rahman. Mu'allafāt Ibn Khaldūn. [The Writings of Ibn Khaldun [In Arabic]] (Cairo, Egypt, Information House 1962 series of the National Center for Social and Criminal Studies). 338 pp.

See pp. 251-313 for "Documentation on his [Ibn Khaldun's] bibliography with the opinions of his contemporaries."

624. Cairo. Dār al-kutub al-Misrīyah. Ibn Khaldun. A Bibliographical List and some References Written about him Issued on the Occasion of the Symposium by the National Center of Social and Criminological Research, January 2-6, 1962. Cairo. 1962. 58 pp.

Publications in Arabic and in western languages.

625. Lababi, Mohamed-Aziz. Ibn-Khaldûn. Presentation, choix de textes, bibliographie. (Philosophes de tous les temps, 47). Paris: Segners, 1968. 192 pp.

IBN SINA. See AVICENNA.

INGARDEN, ROMAN

626. ["Bibliography of Roman Ingarden's Publications from 1915 to 1963"], in Szkice filozoficzne. Romanowi Ingardenowi w darze [Philosophical essays dedicated to Roman Ingarden [In Polish]]. Warsaw: Panstwowe wydawnictwo naukowe, 1964. 511 pp.

627. Petsch, Danuta. "Roman Ingarden's Works Published by the Rolish Scientific Publishers," Dialectics and Humanism (Firenze) vol. 2 (1975), pp. 123-124.

IQBAL, MOHAMMED

628. Ghani, Abdul, and Khwaja Nur Ilaha. Bibliography of Iqbal. Lahore: Bazm-i-Iqbal, [1955?]

About 250 items by or about Iqbal.

ISADORE OF SEVILLE

629. Segovia, A. "Informe sobre bibliografía isidoriana (1936-1960)," Estudios eclesiásticos (Madrid), vol. 36 (1961), pp. 73-126.

JACOBY, GÜNTHER

630. Freytag-Löringhoff, B. von. "Günther Jacoby 80 Jahre alt," Zeitschrift für philosophische Forschung (Meisenheim am Glan), vol. 15 (1961), pp. 237-250.

JACQUES, AMÉDÉE FLORENT

631. Carballal de Torres, Maria Teresa. "Escritos montevideanos de Amadeo Jacques (1852-1853)," Cuadernos uruguayos de filosofía (Montevideo), vol. 4 (1966), pp. 149-153.

632. Roig, Arturo Andres. "El Pensamiento de Amadeo Jacques. Sus fuentes y su evolución. Apendice: bibliografía de Amédée Florent Jacques," Cuadernos Uruguayos de Filosofía (Montevideo), vol. 4 (1966), pp. 5-44.

JAEGER, WERNER

633. Schadewaldt, Wolfgang. Gedenkrede auf Werner Jaeger, 1888-1961 . . . Mit einem Verzeichnis der Schriften Werner Jaegers. Berlin: de Gruyter, 1963. 39 pp.

634. Baldassari, Mariano. "Complemento alla bibliografia degli scritti di W. Jaeger," Rivista filosofia neoscholastica (Milano), vol. 58 (1966), pp. 507-508.

JAENSCH, E. R.

635. Fischer, G. H. Verzeichnis der Schriften von E. R. Jaensch und Mitarbeitern. Marburg: Ebel, 1935. 35 pp.

636. "Verzeichnis der Arbeiten von E. R. Jaensch und Mitarbeitern," Zeitschrift für Psychologie (Leipzig), vol. 148 (1940), pp. 49-90.

JAMES, WILLIAM

637. James, Henry, Jr., and Edwin B. Holt. "A list of the Published Writings of William James," Journal of Philosophy, Psychology, and Scientific Method (New York), vol. 18 (1911), pp. 157-165.

Superseded by the Perry bibliography on James.

638. Perry, Ralph Barton. Annotated Bibliography of the Writings of William James. New York [etc.]: Longmans, Green and Co., 1920. 69 pp. Reprinted: Folcraft, Pa.: Folcraft Library editions, 1973.

About 300 entries arranged by year. Index of names and topics.

639. McDermott, John J. The Writings of William James, a Comprehensive Edition. New York: Modern Library, 1967.

Contains an annotated bibliography of James' writings, pp. 811-858.

JANET, PIERRE

640. Ellenberger, H. F. "Pierre Janet philosophe. Bibliographie de P. Janet," Dialogue (Montréal), vol. 12 (1973), pp. 254-260, 260-287.

The article contains a complete bibliography of Janet's works.

JANKÉLÉVITCH, VLADIMIR. See also 958.

641. Jerphagnon, Lucien. Vladimir Jankélévitch ou de l'effectivite presentation, choix de textes, bibliographie. (Philosophes de tous les temps, 49), Paris: Seghers, 1969. 192 pp.

JANSEN, CORNELIUS

642. Labbe, Philippe. Bibliotheca anti-Janseniana; sive, Catalogus Piorum Eruditorumque Scriptorum qui Corn. Jansenii . . . et Janseniarum Haereses, Errores, Ineptiasque Oppugnarunt. Paris: Ex Officina Cramosiana, 1654. 104 pp.

JASKOWSKI, STANISLAW

643. Dublikajtis, Lech. "The Life and Works of Stanislaw Jaskowski," Studia Logica (Wroclaw), vol. 34 (1975), pp. 109-116.

JASPERS, KARL

644. "Bibliographie Karl Jaspers," in Festschrift für Karl Jaspers, München: Piper, 1953, pp. 449-458.

Chronological bibliography with contents of some books given.

645. Rossmann, Kurt. "Bibliography of the Writings of Karl Jaspers to Spring 1957," in P. A. Schilpp, ed., The Philosophy of Karl Jaspers, New York: Tudor Publishing Co., 1957, pp. 871-886.

Lists works by year. 109 entries.

646. Karl Jaspers, sein Werke, eine Übersicht im Jahr seines 75. Geburtstages. Münich: Piper and Co., 1959. 31 pp.

With a bibliography of the published works of Jaspers.

647. Bentz, Hans W. Karl Jaspers in Uebersetzungen. Karl Jaspers. Translated. Karl Jaspers traduit. Eine Bibliographie seiner in Buchform und Anthologien erschienenen Uebersetzungen 1945 bis 1960. (Weltliteratur in Uebersetzungen. Reihe I: Deutschsprachige Autoren, Bd I). Frankfurt am Main: Hans W. Bentz, Verlag, 1961. 30 pp.

648. Saner, H. "[Karl Jaspers:] Bibliographie der Werke und Schriften," in Klaus Piper, ed., Karl Jaspers Werk und Wirkung. Zum 80. Geburtstag von Karl Jaspers, 23. Februar 1963. München: R. Piper, 1963, pp. 173-216.

JESSUP, BERTRAM

649. Alexander, Henry A. and Melvin Rader. "In Memoriam. Bertram Jessup," Journal of Aesthetics and Art Criticism (Baltimore), vol. 31 (1972-1973), pp. 151-152.

These pages contain "Bibliography. Bertram Jessup, publications."

KAHL-FURTHMANN, GERTRUDE

650. "Wissenschaftliche und Philosophische Schriften von Gertrud Kahl-Furthmann," Zeitschrift für philosophische Forschung (Meisenheim am Glan), vol. 22 (1968), pp. 289-290.

KAILA, EINO. See 2115.

KANE, W. H.

651. "The Writings of W. H. Kane, O. P. (1929-1960)," in The Dignity of Science, Washington: The Thomist Press, 1961, pp. 524-526.

KANT, IMMANUEL. See also 1891.

652. Kiesewetter, Johann Gottfried Carl Christian. Darstellung der wichtigsten Wahrheiten der kritischen Philosophie. 4 verb. Ausg. und vermehrt durch einen gedrängten Auszug aus Kant's Critik der reinen Vernunft und einer Übersicht der vollständigen Literatur der Kantschen Philosophie. Nebst einer Lebensbeschresbung des Verfassers, von Christian Gottfried Flittner. Berlin: Flittner'sche Buchhandlung, 1824.

653. Adickes, Erich. "Bibliography of Writings by and on Kant which Have Appeared in Germany up to the End of 1887," Philosophical Review (Ithaca, N.Y.), vol. 2 (1893), pp. 252-292, 426-449, 557-583, 690-709; vol. 3 (1894), pp. 31-55, 176-192, 305-336, 434-458; plus supplement to vol. 4 (1895). Also published as German Kantian bibliography. Boston: Ginn and Co., 1895-1896. 623 pp. Reprinted: New York: B. Franklin, 1970; Wurzburg: A. Hiebing, 1966?.

Extensive coverage of early works. Goes only into the first few years of the nineteenth century.

654. Warda, Arthur. Die Druckshriften Immanuel Kants (bis zum Jahre 1838). Wiesbaden: H. Staadt, 1919. 62 pp.

655. Reicke, Rudolph, and Hans Vaihinger. Die Kant-Bibliographie der Jahre 1882-1889. Königsberg: 1883-1890. Reprinted from Altpreussischen Monatsschrift (Königsberg), vol. 20 (1883)-23 (1886). Also: 1890-1894, 60 pp.

656. Erdmann, Benno. "Jahresbericht über die neuere Philosophie bis auf Kant, für 1886," Archiv für Geschichte der Philosophie (Berlin), vol. 1 (1888), pp. 115-121, 263-264; "Für 1887," vol. 2 (1889), pp. 317-329; "Für 1888 und 1889," vol. 4 (1891), pp. 289-332.

657. Baer, Joseph and Co. Kant-Bibliothek; Schriften von und über Immanuel Kant. Frankfurt am Main: Joseph Baer, 1903. 48 pp.

656 titles now in Union Theological Seminary and Columbia University.

658. Warda, Arthur. Immanuel Kants Bücher. Berlin: Martin Breslauer, 1922. 58 pp.

Annotated listing by topic of about 350 works in Kant's library. Should be useful to the Kant scholar.

659. Kuhn, H. and E. Weil. Berichte der Kant-Studien über Zeitschriften und Bücher aus dem Gebiete der Philosophie. Berlin und Charlottenburg: [n.p.], 1933.

660. Ewing, A. C. "History of Philosophy in England [Kant, period 1934-1935]. Sophia (Padova), vol. 4 (1936), pp. 249-250; [period 1936], vol. 6 (1938), pp. 380-381.

661. Beck, Lewis White. "A Bibliography of Kant's Ethics," Delaware Notes (Newark, Del.), 18th series (1945), pp. 23-43.

662. Lehmann, Gerhard. "Die Kant-Ausgabe der Akadamie," Forschungen und Fortschritte (Berlin), vol. 30 (1956), pp. 145-148.

663. De Vleeschauwer, H. J. Entwurf einer Kant-Bibliographie. (Vortrag vor dem Internationalen Kongress der Kant-Gesellschaft am 30. Juli 1965) Pretoria: Universität von Südafrika, 1965. 34 pp. Also: Kant-Studien (Berlin), vol. 57 (1966), pp. 457-483.

664. Barthelémy-Madaule, Madeleine. Bergson adversaire de Kant. Etude critique de la Conception bergsonienne du Kantisme suivie d'une Bibliographie kantienne. Paris: Presses universitaires de France, 1966. 276 pp.

665. Malter, Rudolf. "Bibliographie der deutschsprachigen Kant-Literatur, 1957-1967," Kant-Studien (Berlin), vol. 60 (1969), pp. 234-264.

666. Martin, Gottfried, Hans Adolf Martin, and Dieter Krallmann. "Probleme und Methoden des allgemeinen Kant-Index," Kant-Studien (Bonn), vol. 60 (1969), pp. 198-209.

667. Kleinschneider, M. "Bibliographie--auswahl deutscher Artikel, 1968," Kant-Studien (Berlin), vol. 61 (1970), pp. 285-287.

668. Buchicchio, Fausto Maria. "Bibliografia italiana su Kant: 1949-1969," in Armando Rigobello, ed., Ricerche sul transcendentale kantiano. (Miscellanea Erudita, 24. Università degli studi di Perugia. Facoltà di lettere e filosofia. Instituo Policattedra di filosofia.) Padova: Editricè Antenore, 1973, pp. 259-271.

669. Richter, Günter. Immanuel Kant: Katalog der Ausstellung: (Ausstellung im Gutenberg-Museum Mainz, 12. März bis 10. April 1974/Günter Richter); Mainz: Gutenberg-Museum, 1974. 90 pp.

670. Diemer, Alwin. Gesamtregister der Kant-Studien. Meisenheim am Glan: A. Hain, 1969-

Vol. 1 covers 1897-1925.

671. Malter, Rudolf. "Kant Bibliographie 1972," Kant-Studien (Berlin), vol. 65 (1974), pp. 491-506; "1971," vol. 64 (1973), pp. 520-530; also additions to earlier (1968-1970) bibliographies: vol. 64 (1973), pp. 531, 532, 533, 534-536; vol. 65 (1974), pp. 507-508, 509-510, 511-512, 513-514.

672. Palacios, Juan Miguel. "Kant en Español," Anales del Seminario de metafisica, (Madrid), vol. 9 (1974), pp. 195-202.

Spanish translation of titles and index of Kants works.

673. Molinuevo, José Luis. "Brevc bibliografía en Castellano sobre Kant (1930-1973)," Anales del Seminario de metafisica (Madrid), vol. 9 (1974), pp. 203-213.

674. Dietzsch, Birgit, and Steffan Dietzsch. "25 Jahre Kant-Literatur in der Deutschen Demokratischen Republik, 1949-1974, eine Bibliographie," Deutsche Zeitschrift für Philosophie (Berlin), vol. 22 (1974), pp. 1485-1495.

KANTHACK, KATHARINA

675. "Die philosophischen Schriften von Katharina Kanthack," Zeitschrift für Philosophische Forschung (Meisenheim am Glan), vol. 21 (1967), pp. 314-316.

KAUFMAN, ARNOLD S.

676. Durbin, Jack D. "Arnold S. Kaufman Bibliography," Social Theory and Practise (Tallahassee, Fla.), vol. 2 (1972), pp. 153-159.

Aims at covering all of Kaufman's works.

KELSEN, HANS

677. Mitall, R. A. "Chronoligsches Verzeichnis der Schriften Hans Kelsens," Revue internationale de la theorie du droit (Brünn), vol. 12 (1938), pp. 217-222.

678. Cavalcanti, Filho. "Hans Kelsen: Bibliografia," Revista brasileira de filosofia (São Paulo), vol. 23 (1973), pp. 210-211.

KEPLER, JOHANN. See also 468.

679. Caspar, Max and Ludwig Rothenfelder. Bibliographia Kepleriana. Ein Führer durch das gedructe Schrifttum von Johannes Kepler. Munich: Beck, 1936. 158 pp.

KERLEE, DIETRICH HEINRICH

680. "Bibliographie Dietrich Heinrich Kerlee," Zeitschrift für philosophische Forschung (Meisenheim am Glan), vol. 21 (1967), pp. 149-150.

KEYSERLING, HERMANN. See 1154.

KIERKEGAARD, SØREN. See also 1599.

681. Preiss, Th. "A propos de Kierkegaard (études critiques)," Revue d'historie de la philosophie religieuse (Strasbourg), vol. 16 (1946), pp. 46-64.

682. Moore, W. G. "Recent studies of Kierkegaard," *The Journal of Theological Studies* (London), vol. 40 (1939), pp. 225-231.

683. Joliret, Régis. *Kierkegaard*. (Bibliographische Einführungen in das Studium der Philosophie, 4). Bern: A. Francke, 1948. 33 pp.

About 220 entries with occasional annotations. Index and introduction.

684. Nielson, Edith Ortman and Niels Thulstrup. *Søren Kierkegaard; contributions toward a bibliography / Søren Kierkegaard; Bidrag til en bibliografi*. Kobenhavn: Munksgaard, 1951. 96 pp.

685. Thulstrup, N. "Theological and Philosophical Kierkegaardian Studies in Scandanavia, 1945-1953," *Theology Today* (Princeton), vol. 12 (1955), pp. 297-311.

686. Delfgaauw, Bernard. "De Kierkegaard--Studie in Scandinavie. III: Bizondere studies, tijdschriften," *Tijdschrift voor philosophie* (Leuven), vol. 18 (1956), pp. 121-129.

687. Fabro, Cornelio. "Note di bibliografia kierkegaardiana," in Cornelio Fabro, ed., *Studi kierkegaardiani*. Bresica: Morcelliana editrice, 1957, pp. 415-433.

688. Theunissen, Michael. "Das Kierkegaardbild in der neueren Forschung und Deutung <1945-1957>," *Deutsche Vierteljahrsschrift für Literatur-wissenschaft und Geistesgeschichte* (Halle), vol. 32 (1958), pp. 576-612.

689. Himmelstrup, Jens. *Søren Kierkegaard; International Bibliographi*. *Under Medvirken af Kield Birket-Smith*. Copenhagen: Nyt Nordisk forlag, Arnold Busck, 1962. 216 pp.

Contains list of works and editions by Kierkegaard, and books, articles, and reviews about him. 6995 entries, but no annotations. Systematically covers up to 1955 with spotty coverage to 1965.

690. Cortese, M. Allessandro. "Una nuova bibliografia Kierkegaardiana," *Rivista di filosofia neoscholastica* (Milano), vol. 55 (1963), pp. 98-108.

156 entries. No annotations. Covers works published in late forties through 1961. Many in Italian. Attempts to complete the *International Kierkegaard bibliography*.

691. Colette, Jacques. "Bulletin d'histoire de la philosophie: Kierkegaard," Revue des sciences philosophiques et theologiques (Paris), vol. 54 (1970), pp. 654-680.

Surveys the literature of the period 1955-1970.

692. Jorgensen, Aage. Søren Kierkegaard-litteratur, 1961-1970: en forelobig bibliografi [Søren Kierkegaard literature, 1961-1970: an outline bibliography [In Danish]]. Aarhus: Akademisk Boghandel, 1971. 99 pp.

693. Delfgaauw, Bernard. "De Kierkegaard-studie in Scandinavie," Tijdschrift voor filosofie (Leuven), vol. 33 (1971), pp. 737-778.

694. Sales, Michel. "Dix ans de publications kierkegaardiennes en langue francaise," Archives de philosophie (Paris), vol. 35 (1972), pp. 649-672.

695. Castagnino, Franco. Gli studi italiani su Kierkegaard, 1906-1966. (Collava del dentro di ricerche di storia della storiografia filosofica, 2). Roma: Edizioni dell'Ateno, 1972, pp. 307.

696. Perkins, Robert L. "Always Himself: A Survey of Recent Kierkegaard Literature," Southern Journal of Philosophy, vol. 12 (1974), pp. 539-551.

A survey of seventeen recent books.

KLAGES, LUDWIG

697. Deussen, J. Klages' Kritik des Geistes. Mit einer monographischen Bibliographie Ludwig Klages'. (Studien und Bibliographien zur Gegenwarts-Philosophie, 5). Leipzig: Hirzel, 1934. 176 pp.

KLIBANSKY, RAYMOND

698. Park, Desiree, and Michael J. Wholley. "Bibliography of Raymond Klibansky," Revue internationale de philosophie (Bruxelles), vol. 29 (1975), pp. 167-174.

KÖHLER, WALTHER

699. Bibliographie Walther Köhler. Zurich: Zwingli-Verein, 1940. 178 pp.

KOESTLER, ARTHUR

700. Miles, John A. Jr., "Arthur Koestler./Part One," Zygon (Chicago), vol. 9 (1974), pp. 339-351; "Part Two," vol. 10 (1975), pp. 191-211.

A review of his works.

KOLBENHEYER, ERWIN GUIDO

701. Vetterlein, Hans. "Kolbenheyer-bibliographie," Dichtung & Volkstum (Stuttgart), vol. 40 (1939), pp. 94-109.

KOTARBINSKY, TADEUSZ

702. Przymusiała, Andrzy. ["Bibliography"] in Fragmenty filosoficzne, (3rd ser.). Ksiega pamiatkowa ku czci profesora Tadeusza Kotarbinskiego [Philosophical fragments, 3rd. series. In honor of Prof. Thadeuz Kotarbinsky [In Polish]]. Warzawa: Pánstwowe wydawnictwo naukowe, 1967. 677 pp.

Contains a bibliography of Kotarbinsky's works.

KOYRÉ, ALEXANDRE

703. "Principales publications d'Alexandre Koyré" in Mélanges Alexandre Koyré publiés à l'occasion de son 70e anniversaire. Tome I: L'Aventure de la science, pp. xiii-xvii; Tome II: L'Aventure de l'esprit, pp. xix-xxv (Coll. Histoire de la pensée, 12-13). Paris: Hermann, 1964.

KRAFT, JULIUS

704. Kraft, Margit. "Julius Kraft, Verzeichnis seiner Schriften," Ratio (Oxford), vol. 4 (1962), pp. 11-13.

KRAUSE, KARL CHRISTIAN FRIEDRICH

705. Maresca, Mariano. "Aportación a una bibliografía del Krausismo español," Anales de la Catedra Francisco Suarez (Banco de Vizcaya), vol. 11 (1971), pp. 281-336.

KUHN, HELMUT

706. "Bibliographie Helmut Kuhn," in Franz Wiedmann, ed., Epimeleia. Die Sorge der Philosophie um den Menschen, München: Pustet, 1964, pp. 381-389.

707. "Die Schriften von Helmut Kuhn," Zeitschrift für philosophische Forschung (Meisenheim am Glan), vol. 18 (1964), pp. 708-715.

LALANDE, ANDRÉ

708. Lalande, André. André Lalande par liu-mêm. (Coll. "A recherche de la vérité"). Paris: Vrin, 1967. 272 pp.

Contains a bibliography of Lalande's principal articles.

709. ["Bibliographie: André Lalande"], in G. Deledalle and D. Huisman, eds., Les Philosophes francais d'aujourd'hui [n.p., n.d.], pp. 13-20.

85 unannotated entries.

LAMY, BERNARD

710. Girbal, Francois. Bernard Lamy (1640-1715). Etude biographique et bibliographique avec des textes inédits. (Coll. Le Mouvement des idées au XVIIe siècle .2). Paris: Presses universitaires de France, 1964. 194 pp.

LARSEN, HANS

711. Nesselmark. "Bidrag till en bibliografi över Professor Hans Larssons skrifter, 1927-1944," in Yearbook of the New society of Letters at Lund, Lund: Glurup, 1946, pp. 136-159.

LAURENTIUS OF BRINDISI

712. Felix a Mareto. Bibliographia Laurentiana Opera Complectens au. 1611-1961 Edita de Sancto Laurentio à Brindisi Doctore Apostolico. (Subsidia Scientifica Franciscalia, 1) Romae: Institutum Historicum Ord. Fr. Min. Cap., 1962. 286 pp.

LAVELLE, LOUIS. See also 958.

713. "Bibliographie des oeuvres de Louis Lavelle," Les Etudes philosophiques (Marseille), vol. 6 (1951), pp. 134-136.

714. Sanobria, José Ruben. "Bibliografia lavelliana (1921-1964)," Giornale de Metafisica (Genova; Torino), vol. 21 (1966), pp. 562-588.

LEBRETON, JULES

715. "Bibliographie du R. P. Jules Lebreton" in Mélanges J. Lebreton, Tome II, Recherches de Science religieuse. Paris: 15 rue Monsieur, 1952, pp. 446-477.

LECLERCQ, JACQUES

716. "Bibliographie des ouvrages du chanoine Jacques Leclercq," in Jacques Leclercq, l'Homme, son Oeuvere et ses Amis. Tournai: Casterman, 1961, pp. 307-310.

LEE, HAROLD N.

717. Lee, Harold N. "Publications by Harold N. Lee," Tulane Studies in Philosophy (New Orleans), vol. 21 (1972), pp. 191-193.

LEFEBVRE, HENRI

718. "Bibliographie [: Henri Lefebvre]," in G. Deladalle and D. Huisman, eds., Les Philosophes français d'aujourd'hui, [n.p., n.d.], pp. 300-301.

29 unannotated entries of works by Lefebvre.

LEHMANN, GERHARD

719. "Die Schriften von Gerhard Lehmann," Zeitschrift für philosophische Forschung (Meisenheim am Glan), vol. 19 (1965), pp. 348-356.

LEIBNIZ, GOTTFRIED WILHELM

720. "Extrait d'une lettre écrite de C. du 17 may 1701," Mémoires pour l'histoire des sciences et des beaux arts (Trévoux et Paris), vol. 2 (1701), pp. 211-215.

721. "Mémories sur les ouvrages de Mr. Leibniz," Mémories pour l'Histoire des sciences (Trévoux), vol. 5 (1703), pp. 264-267.

722. "Liste des ouvrages de M. de Leibnitz," L'Europe savante (La Haye), vol. 35 (Nov. 1718), pp. 154-159.

This list appeared two years after Leibniz' death.

723. Eckhart, J. G. von [?]. "Specification aller des Seel. hn. von Leibnitz bissher gedruckten Schriften, wie sie nach einander herausgegeben Worden," in Leibniz, Essais de théodicée, Amsterdam: 1720, part 2. Also in Leibnitz, Theodicaea, Hannover: 1735, pp. 961-973.

724. De Jaucourt, Louis. "Catalogue chronologique des ouvrages de Mr. Leibnitz," in Leibnitz: Essays de théodecée. Nouv. ed. Amsterdam: 173[?], vol. 1, pp. 211-245. Also: 1747, vol. 1, pp. 245-282ñ Lausanne: 1960, t. 1, pp. 275-312. German ed.: Geschichte des Herrn von Leibnitz und Verzeichniss seiner Werke. Leipzig: Bey J. S. Heinsii, 1757, pp. 193-227.

725. Steinhofer, Johann Ulrich. "Catalogus Chronologicus Operum ab Auctore Editorum, Succinctis Adnotationibus Historicis Distinctus," in Leibnitius: Fentamina Theodicaeae, Francotfurti et Lipsiae: 1739, pp. 287-380.

Covers German language editions of the Theodicy from 1720 to 1735.

726. Gottsched, Johann Cristoph. "Neueste Zugabe zu dieser fünften Auflage der Théodicée von 1763," in G. W. Leibniz Théodicée; das ist, Versuch von der Güte Gottes, Hannover: Förster, 1763, pp. 865-908.

727. Schaarschmidt, C. "Zur Leibniz-Literatur. Rezensionen," Philosophische Monatshefte (Berlin), vol. 13 (1877), pp. 461-464.

728. Bodemann, Eduard. Der Briefwechsel des Gottfried Wilhelm Leibniz in der Königlichen öffentlichen Bibliothek. Hannover: 1889. 415 pp.

About 15,000 entries.

729. Bodemann, Eduard. Die Leibniz-Handschriften der Königlichen öffentlichen Bibliothek zu Hannover. Hannover: 1895. 339 pp.

About 2500 entries.

730. Ritter, Paul. Kritischer Katalog der Leibniz-Handschriften . . . Erstes Heft (1646-1672). Berlin: 1908. About 570 pp.

1162 entries.

731. Baege, Dr. "Die wichtigsten Schriften von und über Leibniz," Der Bibliothekar: Monatsschrift für Arbeiter-Bibliotheken (Leipzig), vol. 9 (1917), pp. 1022-1023.

732. Groethuysen, Berhard. "Ecrits sur Leibniz parus en Allemange depuis 1914," Revue philosophique de la France et de l'étranger (Paris), vol. 93 (1922), pp. 281-288.

A review of the literature.

733. Ettlinger, Max. "Sammelbericht der Leibniz Literatur seit 1920," Philosophisches Jahrbuch der Göerres-Gesellschaft. (München), vol. 36 (1923), pp. 56-60.

734. Ritter, Paul [et al.]. Catalogue critique des manuscrits de Leibniz. Fascicule II (mars 1642-novembre 1676). Poitiers: 1914-1924. 259 pp.

1578 entries.

735. Levallois, Marie Charles Henri. Catalogue des ouvrages de Leibniz conservés au Département des imprimés et dans les bibliothèques de l'état, à Paris. Paris: Bibliothèque nationale, 1928. 68 cols.

About 400 entries.

736. Gehlen, A. "Bericht über neue Leibniz-Forschungen," Bläetter für deutsche Philosophie (Berlin), vol. 9 (1935), pp. 313-321.

737. De Ruggiero, G. "Correnti della litteratura leibniziana contemporeana," Archivo di storia delle filosfia italiana (Rome), vol. 6 (1937), pp. 1-10.

738. Maier, A. "Leibnizbriefe in italienischen Bibliotheken und Archiven," Quellen und Forschungen aus italienischen Archiven und Bibliotheken (Rome), vol. 27 (1937), pp. 267-282.

739. Ravier, Emile. Bibliographie des oeuvres de Leibniz. Paris, Alcan, 1937. 703 pp. First ed.: Caen: J. Robert et cie, 1927, 102 pp. Reprinted: Hildesheim: George Olms, 1966.

739. (Continued)

Lists many works by and about Leibniz (many by his contemporaries). Indexes. For the serious student of Leibniz.

740. "Oeffentliche Sitzung zur Feier des Leibnitzischen Jahrestages am 30. Juni 1938," Sitzungs Berichte der Bayerischen Akademie der Wissenschaften. Philosophische-historische Abteilung (Munich), nos. 89-125 (1938).

741. Schrecker, Paul. "Une bibliographie de Leibniz," Revue de philosophie de la France et de l'étranger (Paris), vol. 126 (1938), pp. 324-346.

742. Lima-Alceu, Amoroso. "Notas bio-bibliograficos sôbre Leibniz," Verbum (Rio de Janeiro), vol. 3 (1946), pp. 348-362.

743. Bellezza, Vito A. "Gli studi leibniziani in Italia dal 1900 ad oggi," Archivo di filosofia (Roma), vol. 16 (1947), pp. 27-35.

744. Ferro, Carmelo. "Nota bibliografica su Leibnitz," Rivista di filosofia neo-scholastica (Milano), vol. 39 (1947), pp. 330-348.

745. May, Otto Heinrich. "Neues über Leibniz (Letzte Neuerscheinungen in Auswahl)," Niedersächsesches Jahrbuch für Landesgeschichte (Hildesheim), vol. 21 (1949), pp. 232-235.

746. Richter, Liselotte. "Nachlese zum Leibniz-Jubiläum," Theologische Literaturzeitung (Berlin, E. Ger.), vol. 76 (1951), pp. 599-604.

747. De Mullewie, M. "Leibniz," Tijdschrift voor philosophie (Leuven), vol. 19 (1957), pp. 301-318.

748. Richot, B. "Nouveaux travaux sur Leibniz," Revue de synthèse (Paris), vol. 79 (1958), pp. 146-149.

749. Robinet, André. "Philosophie du XVIIe siècle. Bibliographie 1957. 2. Leibniz," Bulletin de la société d'étude du XVIIe siècle (?), no. 4 (1958), pp. 398-400.

750. Bogliolo, Luigi. "Bibliografia essenziale sul trattado di theodicea," Filosofia e Vita (Torino), vol. 5 (1964), pp. 77-97.

751. Jalabert, J. "Bibliographische analyse van de voornaaniste Franse werken over Leibniz' filosofie," Wijsgerig perspectief of maatschappij en wetenschap (Amsterdam), vol. 6 (1965-1966), pp. 246-254.

752. Parkinson, G. H. R. "Bibliographische analyse van de voornaaniste Engelse wirken [over Leibniz]," Wijsgerig perspectief of maatrchappij en wetenschap (Amsterdam), vol. 6 (1965-1966), pp. 241-245.

753. Müller, Kurt. Leibniz-bibliographie. Ein verzeichnis der Literatur über Leibniz. Frankfurt am Main: Vittorio Klostermann, 1967. 478 pp.

Contains 3392 entries covering articles and books, including 31 bibliographies; also has index of names. Work is divided according to topics. Excellent, with occasional annotations.

754. Sticker, Bernhard. "Zum Briefwechsel zwischen Leibniz und Bourgnet," Studia Leibnitiana (Wiesbaden), vol. 1 (1969), pp. 72-73.

755. Untermoehlen, Gerda. "Leibniz-Bibliographie, 1967-1968," Studia Leibnitiana (Wiesbaden), vol. 1 (1969), pp. 293-320.

756. Voise, Waldemar. "Die Polnische Übersetzung des leibnizschen Werkes Specimen Demonstrationum Politicarum," Studia Leibnitiana (Wiesbaden), vol. 1 (1969), pp. 54-60.

757. Koch-Klose, Abel, and Anke Hölzer. "Leibniz-Bibliographie. Neue Titel 1969-1971," Studia Leibnitiana (Wiesbaden), vol. 3 (1971), pp. 309-320.

758. Ekowski, Felix, and Anke Hölzer. "Leibniz-Bibliographie. Neue Titel 1970-1972," Studia Leibnitiana (Wiesbaden), vol. 4 (1972), pp. 304-319.

759. Ekowski, Felix, and Anke Hölzer. "Leibniz-Bibliographie. Neue Titel 1971-1973," Studia Leibnitiana (Wiesbaden), vol. 5 (1973), pp. 301-316.

LENIN, VLADIMIR ILYICH. See also MARX, KARL.

760. Bulgakova, Lidiia V. Materialy dlia bibliografii Lenina [Material for a Bibliography on Lenin [In Russian]], 1917-1923. Leningrad: Priboĭ, 1924. 296 pp.

761. Drahn, Ernst. Lenin, Vladimir Il'ič Ul'janov; eine Bio-Bibliographie. 2., verb. und verm. Aufl. Berlin: R. L. Prager, 1925. 80 pp.

762. Leningrad. Nauchno-issledovatel'skiĭ institut knigovedeniia. Lenin i o Lenine [Lenin and about Lenin [In Russian]]; materialy dlia bibliograficheskogo ukazatelia za 1924 god, pod-red. G. V. Nikol'skoĭ. Leningrad: Gos. izd-vo, 1925. 612 pp.

763. Shneerson, Boris S. Bibliograficheskiĭ ukazatel' k sobranii͡u sochineniĭ N. Lenina (V. Ul'i͡anova) [Bibliographical Index to the Works of N. Lenin [In Russian]], 1893-1923 g.g. Moskva: Gos, izd-vo, 1926. 153 pp.

Contents:--I. Khronologicheskiĭ ukazatel'.--II. Alfavitnyĭ ukazatel'.--III. Soderzhanie sobranii͡a sochineniĭ N. Lenina.

764. Shneerson, Boris S. Bibliograficheskiĭ ukazatel' k XX, dopolnitel'nomu, tomu sobranii͡a sochinenii N. Lenina (V. Ul'i͡anova) [Bibliographical Index to the 20th Supplementary Volume of the Collected Works of N. Lenin [In Russian]], 1895-1922 g.g. So spiskami izdaniĭ, v kotorykh vpervye poiavilis' proizvedenii͡a Lenina [with Lists of the Publications in which Lenin's Works first Appeared and of the Pseudonyms which he Used], i psevdonimov, kotorymi on pol'zovalsia. Moskva: Gos izd-vo, 1927. 60 pp.

765. Kommunisticheskai͡a akademii͡a. Moscow Biblioteka. Lenin i leninizm [Lenin and Leninizm [In Russian]] alfavitno-predmetnyĭ ukazatel' literatury v Biblioteke Kommunisticheskoĭ akademii. [An Alphabetical and Subject Index to the Collection at the Library of the Communist Academy.] Moskva: Izd-vo Kommunisticheskoĭ akademiĭ, 1928. 365 pp.

766. Moscow. Institut V. I. Lenina. Katalog izdaniĭ [Catalog of publications [In Russian]]. Moskva: Gos. izd-vo, 1929. 59 pp.

767. Moscow. Institut V. I. Lenina. Leniniana [Leninism [In Russian]]; pod obshchei red. L. B. Kameneva. Moskva: Gos. izd-vo, 1926- v. 1-

768. Moskovskiĭ rabochiĭ. Proizvedenii͡a Lenina, zhizn' i rabota Lenina, uchenie Lenina (leninizm) [Works of Lenin, his Life and Teaching [In Russian]]. Katalog Leninskoĭ literatury T͡Sentral'nogo knizhnogo sklada Izdatel'stva "Moskovskiĭ rabochiĭ." Moskva: [192-?], 20 pp.

769. Moscow. Institut Marksa-Engel'sa-Lenina. Biblioteka. Lenin na inostrannykh i͡azykakh [Lenin in Foreign Languages [In Russian]]; bibliograficheskiĭ ukazatel' pod obshcheĭ red. M. A. Savel'eva. [Leningrad]; Gos. izd-vo, 1931. 346 pp.

("V sostavlenii . . . prinimali uchastie . . .: I. F. Bakh, E. A. Starosel'skai͡a, Sh. E. T͡Sobel' pod neposredstvennym rukovodstvom A. D. Eĭkhengol't͡sa i obshchim B. P. Birmana." -p. [vi].)

770. Moscow. Institut Marksa-Engel'sa-Lenina. Daty zhizni i deiatel'nosti Lenina [Dates of Life and Works of Lenin [In Russian]], 1870-1924. ("Kniga podgotovlena k pechati Sh. N. Manuchar'iants pod red. G. A. Tikhomirnova," - p. 5.) Izd. 2. ispr. i dop. Moskva: Partiinoe izd-vo, 1933. 307 pp.

771. Belin, Leonid A., and E. Dmitriev. Tematicheskiĭ ukazatel' k sobraniiu sochineniĭ V. I. Lenina po osnovnym problemam politicheskoĭ ekonomiĭ [Subject Index to Basic Problems in Political Economy in the Collected Works of V. I. Lenin [In Russian]]. Leningrad: 1935. 175 pp.

At head of title: Vsesoiuznyĭ kommunisticheskiĭ sel'skokhoziaĭstvennyĭ universitet im. I. V. Stalina.

772. Moskovskiy rabochiy. Publichnaia biblioteka. Chto chitat' o Lenine [What to Read on Lenin [In Russian]]; kratkiĭ rekomendatel'nyĭ ukazatel' liberatury. Sostavili P. V. Zakharevich, S. V. Panova i I. A. Chemeriĭskiĭ, pod red. S. A. Levina. Moskva: 1944. 28 pp.

773. Pelikán, Bohumil. Bibliografie bibliografií dẽl V. I. Lenina a literatura o Leninovi [A Bibliography of Bibliographies of the Works of V. I. Lenin and of Literature on Lenin [In Czech]]. Praha: 1970.

LE SENNE, RENÉ. See 958.

LESSING, GOTTHOLD EPHRAIM

774. Milchsack, G. (Wolfenbüttel. Herzog-August-Bibliothek.) Systematisches Verzeichniss der Lessing-Literatur der Herzogl. Bibliothek zu Wolfenbüttel mit Ausschluss der Handschriften. Wolfenbüttel: J. Zwissler, 1889. 29 pp.

775. Hervey, William Addison. Syllabus and Selected Bibliography of Lessing, Goethe, Schiller, with Topical and Chronological Notes and Comparative Chronological Tables. New York: Lemcke and Buechner, 1918. 148 pp.

776. Seifert, Siegfried. Lessing-Bibliographie. Berlin: Aufbau-Verlag, 1973. 857 pp.

LÉVI-STRAUSS, CLAUDE

777. Caruso, Paolo. "Bibliografia generale degli scritti di e su Claude Lévi-Strauss," Aut Aut (Milano), no. 88

777. (Continued)

(1965), pp. 76-88. Also: L'Arc, no. 26, 1965.

778. "Bibliographie des oeuvres de Claude Lévi-Strauss," in Echanges et communications, I, Mélanges offerts a Claude Lévi-Strauss. Le Haye, Paris: Mouton, 1970, pp. xv-xxiii.

779. Lapointe, François H. "Claude Levi-Strauss: a Bibliographic Essay," Man and World (The Hague), vol. 6 (1973), pp. 445-469.

LEWIS, CLARENCE IRVING

780. Adams, E. M. "The Writings of C. I. Lewis," in P. A. Schilpp, ed., The Philosophy of C. I. Lewis, La Salle, Ill.: Open Court Publishing Co., 1968, pp. 677-689.

781. Parry, William Tuthill. "In Memoriam Clarence Irving Lewis (1883-1964)," Notre Dame Journal of Formal Logic, vol. 11 (1970), pp. 129-136.

Bibliography, pp. 136-140.

LIEBERT, ARTHUR

782. Kropp, Gerhard. "Arthur Liebert in Memoriam. Mit Schriftenverzeichnis," Zeitschrift für philosophische Forschung (Wurzach, Ger.), vol. 3 (1949), pp. 27-35.

LOCKE, JOHN. See also 371.

783. Tagart, Edward. Locke's Writings and Philosophy Historically Considered, and Vindicated from the Charge of Contributed to the Scepticism of Hume. London: Longman, Brown, Green, and Longmans, 1855. 504 pp.

Chronological table of writers on mental and moral philosophy, pp. 496-504.

784. Christopherson, Halfdan Olans. A Bibliographical Introduction to the Study of John Locke. (Skrifter utgitt av det Norske videnskaps-akademi: Historisk-filosofisk klasse. 1930, no. 8). Oslo: J. Dybwad, 1930. 134 pp. Reprint: New York: Burt Franklin (Bibliography and Reference Series, no. 116), 1968.

785. Hughes, H. C. "Locke's Library," Book-Collector's Quarterly (London), vol. 3 (1933), pp. 32-40.

A survey of what Locke probably read.

786. Lough, J. "Locke's List of Books Banned in France in 1679," French Studies (Oxford), vol. 5 (1951).

787. Lough, J. "Locke's Reading During his Stay in France," Library, vol. 8 (1953), pp. 229-258.

788. Hampton, J. "Les traductions francaises de Locke au XVIIIe siècle," Revue de littérature comparée (Paris), vol. 29 (1955), pp. 240-251.

Annotated. Really a survey of the literature.

789. Long, Philip. "A Summary Catalog of the Lovelace Collection of Papers of John Locke in the Bodeleian Library," Oxford Bibliographical Society, Publications (Oxford), n.s. vol. 8 (1959), pp. xii-64.

2000 entries.

790. Laslett, P. "Locke's Books and Papers for his own University," Times Literary Supplement, 11 March 1960.

791. Cranston, Maurice. Locke (British Council: British Book News: Bibliographical Series of Supplements, no. 135). London: Longmans, Green and Co., 1961. 38 pp.

About 100 entries. Annotated.

792. Long, Philip. "The Mellon Donation of Additional Manuscripts from the Lovelace Collection [of the Papers of John Locke]," Bodeleian Library Record (Oxford), vol. 7 (1964), pp. 185-193.

793. Harrison, John and Peter Laslett. The Library of Locke. (Oxford Bibliographical Society. Publications, new series, vol. 13.) Oxford: For the Oxford Bibliographical Society by the Oxford University Press, 1965. 292 pp.

Contains a catalog of Locke's library and an essay by Laslett on "Locke and his Books."

794. Keynes, Geoffrey Langdon. "A Note on Locke's Library," Transactions of the Cambridge Bibliographical Society, vol. 4 (1967), pp. 312-313.

795. Ashcraft, R. "John Locke's Library: Portrait of an Intellectual," Transactions of the Cambridge Bibliographical Society (Cambridge, Eng.), vol. 5 (1969), pp. 47-60.

796. Hall, Roland, and Roger Woolhouse. "Forty Years of Work on John Locke (1929-1969), a Bibliography," <u>Philosophical Quarterly</u> (Edinburgh), vol. 20 (1970), pp. 258-268.

797. Hall, Roland, and Roger Woolhouse. "Addenda to Forty Years of Work on John Locke," <u>Philosophical Quarterly</u> (Edinburgh), vol. 20 (1970), pp. 394-396.

798. Hall, Roland. "Omissions from Christophersen," <u>Locke Newsletter</u> (Heslington, Eng.), (1974), pp. 18-23.

Additions to the Christophersen 1930 Locke Bibliography, works published from 1697-1928.

799. Hall, Roland. "Some more Addenda to the Locke Library," <u>Locke Newsletter</u> (York), (Summer, 1975), pp. 16-22.

800. Hall, Roland. "More Omissions from Christophersen," <u>Locke Newsletter</u> (York), (Summer, 1975), pp. 23-25.

<u>LOISY, ALFRED</u>

801. Houtin, A. and F. Sartiaux. <u>Alfred Loisy, sa vie, son oeuvre</u>. <u>Manuscrit annoté et publié avec une Bibliographie Loisy et un index bio-bibliographique par E. Poulat</u>. Paris: Ed. Centre national de la recherche scientifique, 1960. 421 pp.

<u>LOSSKY, NICHOLAS ONUFRIYEVICH</u>

802. <u>Festschrift N. O. Losskij zum 60. geburtstage</u>. Bonn: F. Cohne, 1934. 175 pp.

Contains bibliography of his writings and about his writings.

<u>LOTTIN, ODON</u>

803. "Bibliographie de Dom Odon Lottin O.S.B." <u>Recherches de théologie ancienne et médiévale</u> (Louvain), vol. 32 (1965), pp. 9-19.

804. Van Steenberghen, Fernand. "In Memoriam Dom Odon Lottin, O.S.B.," <u>Revue philosophique de Louvain</u> (Louvain), vol. 63 (1965), pp. 181-184.

LOTZE, HERMANN

805. Rehnisch, Eduard. "Verzeichniss der literarischen Publicationen Hermann Lotze's," in Lotze, Hermann, Grundzüge der Psychologie. Leipzig: S. Hirzel, 1882, pp. 92-100.

806. Kuntz, Paul G., and Charles Greaves. "Lotze Bibliography," in George Santayana, Lotze's System of Philosophy. Bloomington, Ind. and London: Indiana University Press, 1971.

546 works by and about Lotze. No annotations.

LOWENBERG, JACOB

807. Budge, Edwin S. "Bibliography of the Writings of Jacob Lowenberg," Journal of the History of Philosophy (Berkeley, Calif.), vol. 8 (1970), pp. 431-466.

62 entries of works by Lowenberg.

LUCRETIUS

808. Gordon, Cosmos Alexander. A Bibliography of Lucretius. (Soho Bibliographies, no. 11). London: Rupert Hart-Davis, 1962. 319 pp.

About 600 entries with annotations. Gives text editions, annotated editions, pocket editions, translations, manuscripts, etc. Index. In the period 1473-1961 De Rerum Natura has gone through about 600 editions.

809. Boyancé, Pierre. Lucrèce et l'epicurisme. Paris: Presses universitaires de France, 1963. 347 pp.

Contains a bibliography, pp. 329-347.

810. Conche, Marcel. Lucrèce et l'experience. Presentation, choix de textes, bibliographie. (Philosophes de tous les temps, 34). Paris: Seghers, 1967. 192 pp.

LÜTZELER, HEINRICH

811. Hespe, Roswitha. "Schriftenverzeichnis Heinrich Lützelers," in Der Mensch und die Künste. (Feitschrift

811. (Continued)

für Heinrich Lützeler zum 60. Geburtstage). Düsseldorf: Schwann, 1962. pp. 500-506.

LUKACS, GEORGES

812. Arvon, Henri. Georges Lukacs ou le front populaire en litterature. Presentation, choix de textes, bibliographie (Philosophes de Tous les temps, 41). Paris: Seghers, 1968. 192 pp.

LUKASIEWICZ, JAN

813. "Bibliografia prac Jana Lukasiewicza," Studia logica (Warszawa), vol. 5 (1957), pp. 9-11.

81

LULL, RAMÓN

814. Gottron, Adam. L'Edicio maguntina de Ramón Lull. Amb un apèndix bibliogràfic dels manuscrits i impresos lulians de Maguncia. (Institut d'etudis catalans: Estudis de bibliografía luliana, vol. 1) Barcelona: Institut d'estudios catalans, 1915. 108 pp.

About 100 entries.

815. Batista y Roca, Joseph M. Catêlech de les obras lulianes d'Oxford. Barcelona: imp. de la Casa de Caritat, 1916. 95 pp.

250 entries.

816. Blanco Soto, Pedro. Estudios de bibliografía luliana. Madrid: Revista de arch. bibliotecas y museos, 1916. 118 pp.

500 entries.

817. Rogent, Elíes, and Estanislau Duran. Bibliografía de los impressions lul.lianes. . .Amb un proemi, addicions i index de Ramón d'Allós-Moner. (Institut d'etudis catalans: Estudis de bibliografía lul. liana, vol. 2) Barcelona: 1927. 406 pp.

430 entries.

818. Ottaviano, Carmelo. "L'Ars compendiosa de R. Lulle, avec une étude sur la bibliographie et le fond ambrosien de Lulle," Études de Philosophie Médiévale (Paris), vol. 12 (1930.

About 500 entries.

819. Avinyó, Juan. Les obres autentiques del beat Ramon Lull. Repertori bibliografic. Barcelona: Obradors Horta, 1935. 320 pp.

239 entries.

820. Batllori, Miguel. Introducción bibliográfica a los estudios lulianos. Palma de Mallorca: Escuela lulística de Mallorca, 1945. 23 pp.

About 100 entries.

821. Mendia, Benito. "Bibliografia luliana contemporanea (Años 1935-1950)," Archivum Franciscanum Historicum (Quaracchi), vol. 44 (1951), pp. 436-458.

822. "Bibliografía luliana (año 1960) (continuará)," Estudios lulianos (Palma de Mallorca), vol. 4 (1960), pp. 347-353.

823. Pérez Martínez. Lorenzo. "Los Fondos lulianos existentes en las bibliotecas de Roma," Anthologica Annum (Romae), vol. 8 (1960), pp. 331-480.

824. García, Jesús, and J. N. Hillgarth. "Manuscritos lulianos antiguos de la Biblioteca pública de Palma," Analecta Sacra Tarraconiensia (Barcelona), vol. 35 (1962), pp. 99-182.

825. Llinares, Armand. Raymond Lulle, philosophe de l'-action. Paris: Presses universitaires de France, 1963.

826. García, Jesús, J. N. Hillgarth, and Lorenzo Perez Martinez. Manuscritos lulianos de la Biblioteca publica de Palma. Barcelona: Biblioteca Balmes; Palma de Mallorca: Biblioteca publica de Palma, C. S. de I. C., 1965. 176 pp.

827. Colomer, Euseki. "Situación de Ramon," Pensamiento (Madrid), vol. 26 (1970), pp. 434-451.

Surveys the literature on Ramon Lull from 1958 to 1968.

828. Platzeck, Erhard Wolfram. "Bibliographia Lulliana," Estudios lulianos (Palma de Mallorca), vol. 17 (1973), no. 2-3, pp. i-xi.

LUNSTEDT, VILHELM

829. Holm, O. Förteckning över Professor Vilhelm Lunstedts intill den 11. Sept. 1942 utgivna Skrifter [List of the published writings of Professor Vilhelm Lunstedt until 11 September 1942 [In Swedish]]. Stockholm: Geber, 1942. 55 pp.

MC CORMICK, JOHN F.

830. "A bibliography of the writings of John F. McCormick, S. J." The New Scholasticism (Washington), vol. 18 (1944), pp. 202-206.

MC COSH, JAMES

831. Dulles, Joseph Keatley. "McCosh Bibliography," Princeton College Bulletin (Princeton), vol. 7 (1895), no. 1. Reprint: Princeton, 1895.

832. Dulles, Joseph H. "Bibliography of James McCosh," in William Milligan Sloane, ed., The Life of James McCosh, New York: Charles Schribner's sons, 1896, pp. 269-282.

MC DOUGALL, WILLIAM

833. Smith, May. "William McDougall: A Bibliography," Character and Personality (Durham), vol. 7 (1939), pp. 184-191.

834. Robinson, A. L. William McDougall, M. B., D. Sc., F.R.S. A Bibliography, Together with a Brief Outline of his Life. Durham, N. C.: Duke University Press, 1943. 54 pp.

MACHIAVELLI, NICOLLÒ

835. Gerber, Adolph. Nicollò Machiavelli; die Handschriften, Ausgaben und Übersetzungen seiner Werke im 16. und 17. jahrhundert, mit 147 Faksimiles und zahlreichen Auszügen. Eine kritisch-bibliographische Untersuchung. Gotha: F. A. Perthes, Aktiengesellschaft, 1912-1913. 3 vols. in 1. Reprinted: 1973.

About 400 entries.

836. Norsa, A. Il principio della forza nel pensiero politico di Niccolò Machiavelli. Seguito dan un contributo bibliografico. Milano: Hoepli, 1936. 249 pp.

837. Lenger, Marie Thérèse. Contribution à la bibliographie des éditions anciènnes, XVIe et XVIIe siècles, des oeuvres de Machiavel. Catalogue critique des exemplaires conservés dans les bibliothèques belges. (Archives et Bibliothèques de Belgique. No. spécial, 9) Bruxelles: (bd. de l'Empereur, 4), 1973. 87 pp.

MAC MURRAY, JOHN

838. Nephew, Albert H. "The Writings of John Mac Murray," Listening (River Forest, Ill.) vol. 10 (1975), pp. 109-111.

MAETERLINCK, MAURICE

839. Lecat, Maurice. Bibliographie de Maurice Maeterlinck. Litterature, science, philosophie. (Extrait de Maeterlinckisme). Bruxelles: Castaigne, 1939. 207 pp.

MAIER, ANNELIESE

840. Heimsoeth, Heinz. "Zum Lebenswerk von Anneliese Maier," Studi internazionale di filosofia (Torino), vol. 4 (1972), pp. 3-14.

MAIMONIDES (Moses ben Maimon)

841. Jellinek, Adolf. Kontres ha - RaMBaM. [Commentary on the Rambam [In Hebrew]]. Wien: R. Picker's Buchhandlung, 1878. 32 pp.

842. Gorfinkle, Joseph Issac. A Bibliography of Maimonides. New York: Bloch Publishing Co., 1932. 16 pp.

About 200 entries.

843. Gorfinkle, Joseph Issac. "A Bibliography of Maimonides," in I. Epstein, ed., Moses Maimonides (1135-1204). London: Sancino, 1935, pp. 229-248.

844. Dienstag, Jacob Israel. Be'ur milot ha-higayon [Maimonides' Treatise on Logic: an Annotated Bibliography [In Hebrew]]. Jerusalem?: 1960. 34 pp.

MAIN DE BIRAN

845. Mayjonade, J. B. Main de Biran, étude biographique et bibliographique. Lille: Taffin-Lefort, 1895. 32 pp.

846. Ghio, M. Michaelangelo. "Essai de bibliographie raisonée de Maine de Biran (1766-1824)," in Maine de Biran e la tradizione biraniana in Francia, Torino: Ed. di filosofia, 1962, pp. 181-199.

MALEBRANCHE, NICOLAS. See also 367.

847. Blampignon, Emile Antoine. Bibiographie de Malebranche. Montbéliard: Hoffman, 1882. 11 pp.

About 150 entries.

848. Del Noce, Augosto. "Bibliografia Malebranchiana," in Malebranche nel terzo centenario della nascità, Milan: Vita e pensiero, 1938, pp. 361-380.

849. Gouhier, Henri. "Introduction bibliographique à l'oeuvre et à la pensée de Malebranche," Revue internationale de philosophie (Brussells), vol. 1 (1938), pp. 161-174.

850. Robinet, André. Malebranche vivant. Documents biographiques et bibliographiques. Vol. 20 of Nicholas Malebranche, oeuvres complètes (Bibliotheques des textes philosophiques). Paris: J. Vrin, 1958. 489 pp.

The definitive bibliography of Malebranche's works.

851. Nicolosi, S. "Venti anni di studi malebranchiani (1938-1957)," Sophia (Padova), vol. 27, 1959, pp. 95-102.

852. Sebba, Gregor. Nicolas Malebranche, 1638-1715; A Preliminary Bibliography. Atlanta: Emory University, 1959 (Microfilm). Also: Athens, Ga.: (Mimeographed), 1959. 90 pp.

About 500 entries, cross referenced.

853. Sebba, Gregor. "Malebranche [an Annotated Bibliography]," in A Critical Bibliography of French Literature, ed. by D. C. Cabeen. Syracuse, N. Y. Syracuse University Press, 1957-1961, vol. 3, pp. 490-503.

Extensive annotations on about 75 important works, with lists of reviews.

854. Stieler, Georg. "Malebranche-literatur," Literarische Berichte aus dem Gebiete der Philosophie (Erfurt), nos. 9-10.

MANNHEIM, KARL

855. ["Verzeichnis der Schriften Karl Mannheims und eine Bibliographie die Jahre 1952-1965,"] in Karl Mannheim, Ideologie und Utopie. 4 Aufl., Frankfurt am Main: Schulte-Bulmke, 1965, pp. 269-270, 271-293, 295-300.

MANNOURY, GERRIT

856. "Bibliography of the Writings of Gerrit Mannoury," Synthése (Dordrecht), vol. 10a (1958), pp. 414-415.

MANSER, GALLUS M.

857. "Verzeichnis der wissenschaftlichen Veröffentlichungen von P. Gallus M. Manser," in Studien zur Philosophie und speculativen Theologie festgabe P. Gallus M. Manser, O. P. Freiburg, Swit.: Rütsche und Egloff, 1936, pp. VI-VIII.

MANSION, A.

858. "Bibliographie de Mgr. A. Mansion, complements," Revue philosophique de Louvain (Louvain), vol. 64 (1966), pp. 668-669.

MAO TSE-TUNG

859. "Bibliographie des oeuvres de Mao Tse-tsung," in Courrier communautaire international (Paris), vol. 7 (1972), pp. 437-446.

MARCEL, GABRIEL. See also 903.

860. Troifontaines, Roger. De l'existence à l'être. Louvain: Nauwelaerts, 1953. 2 vols.

Bibliography of Marcel's works to January, 1953, vol. 2, pp. 381-425.

861. Lapointe, Francois H. "Bibliography on Fabriel Marcel," Modern Schoolman (St. Louis, Mo.), vol. 49 (1971), pp. 23-49.

862. Blázquez, Feliciano. "Gabriel Marcel: Ensayo bibliográfico (1941-1972)," Crisis (Madrid), vol. 22 (1975), pp. 29-76.

863. Lapointe, Francois H. "A Selected Bibliography on the Existential and Phenomenological Psychology of G. Marcel and Paul Ricoeur," Journal of Phenomenological Psychology (Pittsburgh), vol. 4 (1973-1974), pp. 363-373.

MARCIC, RENÉ

864. Gabriel, Leo. "René Marcic-fuenfzig Jahre," Wissenschaft und Weltbild (Wien), vol. 22 (1969), pp. 90-91.

MARCUS, HUGO

865. "Die Schriften von Hugo Marcus," Zeitschrift für Philosophische Forschung (Meisenheim am Glan), vol. 19 (1965), pp. 712-713.

MARCUSE, HERBERT

866. Lapointe, Francois A. "Herbert Marcuse: a Bibliographic Essay," The Journal of the British Society for Phenomenology (Manchester), vol. 4 (1973), pp. 191-194.

MARÉCHAL, JOSEPH

867. "Bibliographie du Père J. Maréchal," in Mélanges J. Maréchal (Oeuvres Museum Lessianum. Section philosophique, no. 32). Bruxelles: L'Edition universelle, 1950, vol. 1, pp. 47-71.

MARITAIN, JACQUES

868. Byrns, Ruth. "Bibliography of Jacques Maritain, 1910-1942," Thomist (Washington), vol. 5 (1943), pp.

869. Gallagher, Donald A., and Idella Gallagher. The Achievement of Jacques and Raïssa Maritain: A Bibliography, 1906-1961. Garden City, N.Y.: Doubleday, 1962. 256 pp.

869. (Continued)

Over 7400 entries. Introductory essay plus an index of names and topics. Editions and translations of the Maritains' work and works about them.

870. Evans, Joseph W. "A Maritain Bibliography," The new Scholasticism (Washington), vol. 46 (1972), pp. 118-128.

871. Zarco, Miguel Angel. "J. Maritain: el hombre y su obra. Bibliografía," Revista filosofía méxicana (México), vol. 5 (1972), pp. 139-154, 155-156.

872. "Bibliografia de Jacques Maritain," Convivium S. P. (São Paulo), vol. 12 (1973), pp. 499-504.

MARITAIN, RAÏSSA. See 869.

MARTIN, GOTTFRIED

873. "Bibliographie du Veroffentichungen [Gottfried Martin]," Kant-Studien (Berlin), vol. 57 (1966), pp. 400-415.

MARX, KARL. See also 565, 1167, 1428, 1431, 1437, 1602, 1603, 1683.

874. Kopf, Eike. "Bibliographie zur Wirkungsgeschichte von Karl Marx' Das kapital bis 1872," in Roman Rosdolsky, ed., Genesi e struttura del capitale di Marx. (Biblioteca di cultura moderna, 712). Bari: Laterza, 1971, pp. 223-231.

875. Drahn, Ernst. Marx-Bibliographie. Berlin: Deutsche Verlagsgesellschaft für Politik und Geschichte m.b.h., 1923-

876. Knizhnik, Ivan S. Sistematicheskiĭ ukazatel' literatury po obshchestvennym naukam. Kommunisticheskaia i marksistskaia literatura [Systematic Index to Publications on Social Sciences. Communist and Marxist literature [In Russian]] 1917-1922 gg. Petrograd: Priboĭ, 1923. 206 pp. Cover-title: Chto chitat' po obshchestvennym naukam.

877. Rozanov, IAkov S. Filosofsko-sotsiologicheskaia literatura marksizma za pervoe desiatiletie sovetskoĭ vlasti [Philosophical-Sociological Marxist Literature for the First Decade of the Soviet Power [In Russian]], 1917-1927. Moskva: 1928. 319 pp.

878. Moscow. Institut Karla Marksa i Fridrikha Engel'sa. Katalog izdaniĭ [Catalog of Publications [In Russian]]. Moskva: Gos. izd-vo, 1929-1930. 2 v.

879. Fomin, Aleksandr G. Putevoditel' po bibliografii Marksa, Engel-sa i Lenina [Guide to a bibliography on Marx, Engels and Lenin [In Russian]]; sistematicheskiĭ, annotirovannyĭ ukazatel' russkikh knig i zhurnal'nykh rabot po bibliografiĭ Marksa, Engel'sa i Lenina, napechatennykh v 1907-1934 gg. (S prilozheniem stat'i .N. Berkova "Lenin, Marks i Engel's kak bibliografy-ret͡senzenty.") Leningrad: Izd-vo Akademii nauk SSSR, 1934. 122 pp.

880. "Courte bibliographie du marxisme," La Vie intellectuelle (Paris), vol. 48 (1937), pp. 133-140.

881. Prague. Ústav dějin kommunistické strany Československa. Knihovna. Karel Marx a Bedřich Engels v některých českych a německĭjch dělnickĭjch, sociálně demokratickĭjch a komunistickĭjch časopisech a novínách, rycházejících na našem území v letech 1867-1938. [Karl Marx and Friedrich Engels in Certain Czech and German Workers' Social-Democratic and Communist Periodicals and Newspapers which Appeared in our Country from 1867 to 1938 [In Czech]]. Praha: 1957. 191 pp.

882. Marksistsko-leninskai͡a literatura [Marxist-Lenin literature [In Russian]]; bibliograficheskiĭ bi͡ulleten'. [?] 1936-1939.

Supersedes Literatura i iskusstvo.

883. Kandel', Efim Pavlovich. O publikat͡sii literaturnogo nasledstva K. Marksa i F. Engel'sa [On the Publication of the Literary Legacy of K. Marx and F. Engels [In Russian]]. Moscow: Gos. izd-vo polit. lit-ry. 1947. 47 pp.

884. Lévin, L. A. Bibliografii͡a proizvedeniĭ K. Marksa i F. Engel'sa [Bibliography of the Works of K. Marx and F. Engels [In Russian]]. Moskva: Gos. izd-vo kul'turno-prosvetitel'noĭ lit-ry, 1948. 234 pp.

Annotated.

885. Hubert, F. "Initiation bibliographique à l'oeuvre de Marx et d'Engels," in Le P. Henri-Charles Desroches, Signification du marxisme. Paris: Editions Ouvrires, 1949.

886. Vulchev, Velichko. Literatura vurkhu marksizmo-leninizma; kratuk bibliografski ocherk [Literature on Marxism-Leninism; a Short Bibliographical Outline [In Bulgarian]]. Sofia: 1949. 41 pp.

887. Rossi, Paolo. "Recenti studi sul marxismo," Rivista critica di storia della filosofia (Milano), vol. 5 (1950), pp. 330-340.

888. Warsaw. Biblioteka nardowa. Marks i Engels w Polsce; materialy do bibliografii, 1842-1952 [Marx and Engels in Poland; Materials for a Bibliography, 1842-1952 [In Polish]]. Warszawa: 1953. 111 pp.

889. Prague. Charles University Library. Soupis spisů a čláků Karla Marxe a Bedřicha Engelse z fondů universtudi knihorny a Slovanské knihorny v Praze. [A list of writings and articles by Karl Marx and Friedrich Engels from the collections of the university library and the Slavic library in Prague [In Czech]]. Praze: 1954. 3 pts., 428 pp.

890. Berlin. Institut für Marxismus-Leninismus. Die Erstdrucke der Werke von Marx und Engels; Bibliographie der Einzelausgaben. [1. Aufl.] Berlin: Dietz, 1955. 62 pp.

About 300 entries listed chronologically, with title index.

891. Academia republicii populare Romîne. Biblioteca. Marx si Engels în limba romînă [Marx and Engels in Roumanian [In Roumanian]]. [no place]: Editura Academiei republicii populare Romîne, 1956. 60 pp.

892. Rubel, Maximilien. Bibliographie des oeuvres de Karl Marx avec en appendice un répertoire des oeuvres de Friedrich Engels. Paris: Librairie Marcel Rivière et cie., 1956. 273 pp. Supplement, 1960. 79 pp.

901 entries by Marx, excluding translations and editions. 151 entries by Engels. Annotated. Name indexes. Works arranged by year. Supplement contains list of errata for the original, plus about 100 additional items.

893. Karutsin, Krŭstíu and Velcho Kovachev. Karl Marks i Fridrikh Engels na bulgarski: bibliografia [Karl Marx and Friedrich Engels in Bulgarian: A Bibliography [In Bulgarian]]. Sofia: Nauka i izkustvo, 1961. 198 pp.

894. Misharina, Vladilena Vasil'evna. Osnowopolozhniki nauchnogo kommunizma; chto chitat' o Markse i Engel'se [The Founders of Scientific Communism; What to Read on Marx and Engels [In Russian]]. Moscow: 1961. 39 pp.

895. Bochenski, Innocentius M. et al., eds. Guide to Marxist philosophy: an introductory bibliography. Chicago: Surallons, 1972. 81 pp.

Divided into eight chapters listing books in English. Index. For the beginner.

896. Bratislava. Univerzita. Knižnica. [Bratislava university. library] O marxistickej filozofii a vedeckom komunizme bibliografia [On Marxist Philosophy and Scientific Communism [In Slovak]]. Martine: Matica Slovenská, 1962. 146 pp.

About 450 entries.

897. Bravo, Gian Maria. Marx e Engels in lingua italiana, 1848-1960. (Saggi e documentazioni, 10). Milano: Edizioni Avanti, 1962. First published in the Revista storica del socialismo, 1961, nos. 13-14. Republished in the above edition with additions and corrections.

898. Brno. University. Library. Dialeklický a historický materialismns; výběr literatury ke přednáškám večerní university marxismu-leninismu. Literaturu se signaturami knih z fondů universitní knhovny v Brně vybrala Anna Zykmundová. [Dialectic and Historical Materialism; a Selection of Literature for the Lectures of the Evening University of Marxism-Leninism. Literature Selected by Anna Zykmundová with the Call Numbers of Books in the University Library in Brno [In Czech]]. Brně: 1963.

899. Bütow, Hellmuth G. Die Entwicklung des dialektischen und historischen Materialismus in der Sowjetzone. (Bibliographische Mitteilungen des Osteuropa-instituts an der Freien Universität Berlin, Heft 4). Berlin: in Kommission bei O. Harrassowitz, Wiesbaden, 1960-1963. 3 vols.

900. Herchlova, L. [et al.] Marx-Engels-Lenin; bibliografia, 1913-1962 [In Slovak]. Bratislava: Univerzita. Kniznica [Library], 1963. 187 pp.

901. Literatura po marksistsko-leninskoĭ filosofiĭ i nauchnomre kommunizmu [Literature on Marxist-Leninist Philosophy and Scientific Communism [In Russian]]. Moscow: Izd-vo polit-lit-ry, 1964. 47 pp.

902. Literaturkatalog; klassiker des marxismus-leninismus, philosophie, geschichte. Leipzig: Leipziger kommissions- und gross-Buchhandel, 1964-[to date].

903. Bibliographical Bulletin of Current Marxology (Warzawa), vol. 1 (1965)-[no more published?]

1965 issue titled "Trial Issue", 176 pp.

904. Bütow, Hellmuth G. Philosophie und Geschichte in Marxismus-Leninismus. Zum Stand der Diskussion über Fragen der Klassifikatin und Methodologie der Gesellschaftswissenschaften. (Berichte des Osteuropa-Instituts an der Freien Universität Berlin, Heft 71). Berlin: Freien Universität, Osteuropa-Institut, 1965. 117 pp.

905. Orlov, S. M. and L. G. Kni͡azeva. Spisok literatury kandidatskogo minimuma po marksistsko-leninskoi filosofii [A List of Literature to Satisfy the Minimum Requirement for the Degree of "Kandidat" in Marxist-Leninist Philosophy [In Russian]]. Moscow: Mysl', 1965.

906. Landesberg, Paul Ludwig. "Marx y el problema del hombre," Convivium (Barcelona), no. 23 (1967), pp. 83-95.

907. Munby, Lionel M. and Ernst Wangermann. Marxism and History. A Bibliography of English Language Works. London: Lawrence and Wishart, 1967. 62 pp.

908. Baxandall, Lee. Marxism and Aesthetics; a Selective Annotated Bibliography; Books and Articles in the English Language. New York: Humanities Press, 1968. 261 pp.

909. Berlin. Stadtbibliothek. Karl Marx; zum 150. Geburtstag am 5. Mai. (Bibliographische Kalendarblätter, Sonderblatt, 21). Berlin, 1968.

910. Dortsmund. Stadtbücherei. Karl Marx, 1818-1968: Mensch, Werk, Wirkung; Auswahl der neueren Literatur. Bremen: Volks Büchereien der Freien Hansestadt Bremen, 1968. 63 pp.

911. German Democratic Republic. Ministerium für Auswörtige Angelegenheiten. Sektion Bibliothek. Bibliographie über Äusserungen von Karl Marx zu Fragen der Aussenpolitik und der internationalen Beziehungen. Berlin: Ministerium für Auswärtige Angelegenheiten Sektion Bibliothek der Abteilung Wissenschaftliches Archiv, 1968. 41 pp.

912. Lachs, John. Marxist Philosophy; a Bibliographical Guide. Chapel Hill, N.C.: University of North Carolina Press, 1967. 166 pp. Also: London: Oxford University Press, 1968.

> 38 chapters on "Marxist philosophy" broadly construed. 1557 entries. Each chapter preceded by a few introductory paragraphs. Name index. A useful work.

913. Saf'i͡an, Hdaliĭ Maĭseevich. Tvory Marksa, Enhel'sa, Lenina vydadzenyi͡a ŭ Belarusi u 1917-1967. [Works of Marx, Engels, Lenin Published in Byelorussia from 1917 to 1967 [In Byelorussian]]. Minsk: D zi͡arzhanŭnai͡a bibli͡ateka BSSR, 1968, 127 pp.

914. Varenychenko, K. Karl Marks; pam'jatka chitachevi [Karl Marx; a Guide for the Reader [In Ukrainian]]. Kiev: Molod', 1968. 32 pp.

915. Bigaev, Îusuf Kurbanovich. Izdanic proizvederiĭ K. Marksa, F. Ėngel'sa i V. I. Lenina na îazykakh narodov Dagestana. [Publication of the works of K. Marx, F. Engels, and V. I. Lenin in the Languages of the Peoples of Dagestan [In Russian]]. Makhachkala: Dagknigoizdat, 1969. 31 pp.

916. Paeglis, Jānis. K. Markss, F. Engelss, V. I. Lenins latviešu valodā bibliogrāfija [Lettish Language Bibliography of K. Marks, F. Engels, and V. I. Lenin [In Lettish]] Riga: 1969. 362 pp.

917. Touchlík, Karol. Prehl'adná bibliografia diel K. Marxa, F. Engelsa a V. I. Lenina. K 150 výr. nar. Marxa a Engelsa a k. 100 výr. nar. Lenina [A Survey Bibliography of the Works of K. Marx, F. Engels and V. I. Lenin. On the 150th Anniv. of the Birth of Marx and Engels and the 100th Anniv. of the Birth of Lenin [In Slovak]]. Bratislava: Epocha, 1970. 167 pp.

918. Planty-Bonjour, G. "Bibliographie sur Marx," Recherches Hégéliennes (Cognac), vol. 1, no. 3, (1971).

919. Grin, T͡siliia Iosifovna. Osnovopolozhniki marksizma [The founders of Marxism [In Russian]]. Moscow: Kniga, 1973. 77 pp.

920. Svatošova, Miluše. Průvodce Marxovými a Engelsovými spisy [A Guide to the writings of Marx and Engels [In Czech]]. Prague: Svoboda, 1974. 284 pp.

921. Vrtacic, Ludvik. Einführung in den jugoslawischen Marxismus-Leninismus. Organisation, bibliographie. (Sovietica. Veröffentlichungen des Osteuropa-Instituts. Universität Freiburg, Schweiz.) Dordrecht: D. Reidel. 1963. 208 pp.

MASARYK, TOMÁŠ GARRIGNE

922. Îakovenko [Jakovenko], Boris Valentīnovīch. La Bibliographie de T. G. Masaryk. (Bibliothèque internationale de philosophie. Publication périodique, vol. 1, no. 9/10). Prague: 1935. 92 pp. Also: Ann Arbor, Michigan: University Microfilms, 1969; and Bonn: F. Cohen, 1930. 25 pp.

MASSIGNON, LOUIS

923. Moubarac, Y. "Bibliographie de Louis Massignon," in Mélanges Louis Massignon. Damas: Publiés sous le patronage de l'Institut d'études Islamiques de l'Université de

923. (Continued)

Paris et de l'Institute français de Damas, 1956-1957. Vol. I, pp. 1-56.

924. Moubarac, Y. "Bibliographie [de Louis Massignon]," in Louis Massignon, Opera Minora (Coll. Recherches et documents), Dar-al-Maaref: Esquisses Bibliographlques, 1963. Vol. 1, pp. 627-665.

MASSOLO, ARTURO

925. "Bibliografia di Arturo Massolo," in L. Sichirollo, ed., Studia in onore di Arturo Massolo. (Studi urbinati di storia, filosofia e letteratura, vol. 41 (1967), nuova serie B, no. 1-2), Urbino: Argalia, 1967, pp. 9-16.

MASSON-OURSEL, PAUL

926. Schuhl, P.-M. "Paul Masson-Oursel (Paris, 5 septembre 1882-1918 mars 1956)," Revue de la France et de l'étranger (Paris), vol. 81 (1956), pp. 169-177.

Has a bibliography of Masson-Oursel's principal articles.

MAY, EDWARD

927. "Die philosophischen Schrfiten von Eduard May," Zeitschrift für philosophische Forschung (Meisenheim am Glan), vol. 20 (1966), pp. 324-327.

MAZZINI, GIUSEPPE

928. Grandi, Terenzio. Appunti di bibliografia mazziniana. La fortuna dei Doreri e Mazzini fuori d'Italia: La letteratura mazziniana, oggi. ("Erica", 16). Milano: A.M.I., 1961 169 pp.

MEAD, GEORGE HERBERT

929. Natanson, Maurice. The Social Dynamics of George Herbert Mead. Washington: Public Affairs Press, 1956. 102 pp.

"Bibliography": pp. 96-102.

930. Reck, Andrew. "The Writings of George Herbert Mead," in Andrew J. Reck, ed., George Herbert Mead, Selected Writings. Indianapolis: Bobbs-Merrill, 1964, pp. lxiii-lxix.

MEINONG, ALEXIS

931. Lenoci, Michele. "Bibliografia degli studi su Alexis Meinong," Rivista di filosofia n -scholastica (Milano), vol. 62 (1970), pp. 437-473.

MENDELSSOHN, MOSES

932. Schwab, Moïse. Mendelssohn, sa vie et ses oeuvres, son influence philosophique sur le judaïsme moderne. Paris: A. Wittensheim, 1868. 34 pp.

MENDES, GEORG

933. Lindner, Frank. "Verzeichniss der Publikationen Georg Mendes," Wissenschaftliche Zeitschrift der Friedrich-Schiller-Universität Jena (Jena), vol. 19 (1970), pp. 701-708.

MENÉNDEZ Y PELAYO, MARCELINO

934. Bonillay San Martín, Adolfo. Bibliografía de d. Marcelino Menéndez y Pelayo. Madrid: Suárez, 1911. 33 pp.

935. Bonilla y San Martín, Adolfo. La Filosofía de Menendez y Pelayo. Con un apéndice bibliográfico. Madrid: Revista de archivo, bibliotecas, y museos, 1912. 55 pp.

936. Catálogo da Exposição bibliográfica comemorativa do primeiro centenário do nascimento de Marcelino Menéndez Pelayo (1856-1956). Org.: Emilio Silva. Rio de Janeiro: Biblioteca Nacional, Ministério de Educaçâo e cultura, 1956. 120 pp.

MENGARELLI, CARLO

937. "Notizie biografiche ed elenco dei lavori scientifici di Carlo Mengarelli," Rivista internazionale di scienze sociali e discipline ausiliari (Milano), (1942), [n.p.?].

MENSARD, PIERRE

938. Bibliographie resumée des oeuvres de Pierre Mensard," in G. Deledalle and D. Huisman, eds., Les Philosophes français d'aujourd'hui [n.p., n.d.], pp. 224-226.

62 unannotated entries.

MENZER, PAUL

939. Gerresheim, Eduard. "Bibliographie der Veröffentlichungen von Paul Menzer," Kant-Studien (Köln), vol. 53 (1961-1962), pp. 544-553.

MERLAN, PHILIP

940. "Bibliographie [Philip Merlan] Veröffenlicht aus Anlass des 70. Geburtstag am 20. 12. 1967." Zeitschrift für Philosophische Forschung (Meisenheim am Glan), vol. 22 (1968), pp. 139-145.

MERLEAU-PONTY, MAURICE. See also 1165, 1679.

941. Good, Paul, and Frederico Camto. "Bibliographie des Werkes von Maurice Merleau-Ponty," Philosophisches Jahrbuch (München), vol. 77 (1970), pp. 434-443.

942. Lapointe, Francois H. "A Bibliography of Maurice Merleau-Ponty. Primary Sources: Books, Articles, and Lectures (Published and Unpublished) by Merleau-Ponty," Human Inquiry (i.e., Review of Existential Psychology and Psychiatry), vol. 11 (1971), pp. 63-78.

943. Llavonia, Rafael. "Merleau-Ponty a los diez años de su muerte: ensayo bibliografica," Pensamiento (Madrid), vol. 27 (1971), pp. 255-307.

Contains a bibliography of Merleau-Ponty's published and posthumous writings, translations, works about him, etc.

944. Lapointe, François H. "A Selected Bibliography on the Existential and Phenomenological Psychology of Maurice Merleau-Ponty," Journal of Phenomenological Psychology (Pittsburgh), vol. 3 (1972-1973), pp. 113-130.

945. Lapointe, Francois H. "Selected Bibliography on Art and Aesthetics in Merleau-Ponty," Philosophy Today (Celina, Ohio), vol. 17 (1973), pp. 292-296.

MESSER, AUGUST

946. "Supplement zur Bibliographie August Messer," Zeitschrift für philosophische Forschung (Meisenheim am Glan), vol. 21 (1967), pp. 618-620.

MEYER, HANS

947. "Die Schriften von Hans Meyer," Zeitschrift für philosophische Forschung (Meisenheim am Glan), vol. 19 (1965), pp. 540-542.

MICHELET, KARL L.

948. Fock, Gustav, firm, booksellers. [Catalogue] Philosophie; enthaltend u.a. die Bibliothek des Prof. Karl L. Michelet (Lager-Verzeichnis, 116). Leipzig: 1896.

MICHELIS, P. A.

949. Givone, Sergio. ["Bibliografia delle opere di P. A. Michelis"], Rivista di estetica (Torino e Pandova), vol. 15 (1970), pp. 340-345.

MICHOTTE VAN DU BERCK, ALBERT

950. De Montpellier, Gerard. "Notice sur le baron Albert Michotte van du Berck, membre de l'Academie," Academie royale de Belgique. Annuaire pour 1968. Koninklijke academie van Belgie. Jaarboek voor 1968 (Bruxelles), vol. 134, pp. 191-221.

Bibliography, pp. 213-221.

MIDDLETON, RICHARD OF. See Richard of Middleton.

MIDGAARD, KNUT. See 2114.

MIGUEL, REALE

951. Strenger, Irineu. "Contribuicão de Miguel Reale à teoria do direito e do estado," Revista brasileira de filosofia (São Paulo), vol. 11 (1961), pp. 234-247.

Bibliography, pp. 243-247.

MILL, JOHN STUART

952. MacMinn, Ney. J. R. Hainds, and James McNab McCrimmon. Bibliography of the Published Writings of John Stuart Mill. (Northwestern University Studies in the Humanities, no. 12). Evanston, Ill.: Northwestern University, 1945. 102 pp.

About 600 entries, consisting of Mill's own list of his writings 1822-1873, plus annotations by the editors. In the first entry for 1851, Mill states, "A leading article in the Morning Chronicle of August 28th, 1851, on some cases of wife murder. This, like all my newspaper articles on similar subjects, and most of my articles on all subjects, was a joint production with my wife." Reviews: Modern Philosophy, vol. 43 (1945), pp. 149-150; Times Literary Supplement, 26 January 1946, p. 48; Journal of English and German Philology, vol. 45 (1946), pp. 115-116.

953. Cranston, Maurice. John Stuart Mill. (British Council: British Book News: Bibliographical Series of Supplements, no. 99). London: Longmans, Green and Co., 1958. 34 pp.

954. Amano, Kazuo. Bibliography of the Classical Economics, vol. 3, pt. 4, Mill. Tokyo: 1964.

955. "John Stuart Mill [: a Bibliography]," in George Watson, ed., The New Cambridge Bibliography of English Literature. Cambridge: Cambridge University Press, 1969, vol. 3, cols. 1551-1756.

About 120 works by Mill and 600 works about him. Good coverage.

956. Hascall, Dudley, and J. M. Robson. "Bibliography of Writings on Mill," Mill News Letter (Toronto), vol. 5 (1970), pp. 8-11.

This journal carries bibliographies on Mill.

957. Fukuhara, Gyozo. "Articles on J. S. Mill," Mill News Letter (Toronto), vol. 7 (1971), pp. 16-18.

Covers articles on Mill's political economy.

MINKOWSKI, EUGÈNE

958. "Bibliographie des travaux de Aimé Forest, Vl. Jankélévitch, Louis Lavelle, René Le Senne, Gabriel Marcel, E. Minkowski," Revue internationale de philosophie (Bruxelles), vol. 2 (1939), pp. 128-132.

959. "Bibliographie [Eugène Minkowski]," in Eugène Minkowski. Recueil d'articles 1923-1965, Paris: Librairie le livre psychologique; Lille: Librairie le furet du nors, 1965, pp. 169-175.

MOLINA, LUIS DE

960. "Bibliographical note on Molina," in Gerard Smith, ed., Jesuit Thinkers of the Renaissance: Essays Presented to John F. McCormick, S. J., by his Students on the Occasion of the Sixty-fifth Anniversary of his Birth. Milwaukee: Marquette University Press, 1939.

MONTAIGNE, MICHEL DE

961. Payen, Jean François. Notice bibliographique sur Montaigne . . . avec deux Supplements . . . Paris: Impr. de E. Duverger, 1860. 80 pp.

962. Esquerra, R., J. Sanfeliu, Sever de Montsonís and Agustí de Montclar. "Butlletí d'história de la filosofia: Montaigne, Pascal, Espanyols dels segles XVI-XVII, Tomisme, De Bergson al realisme de Sant Tomàs," Crit[ica?], vol. 12 (1936), pp. 33-45.

963. Tannenbaun, Samuel Aaron. . . . Michel Eyquem de Montaigne (a Concise Bibliography). Elizabethan Bibliographies, no. 24) New York: S. A. Tannenbaum, 1942. 137 pp.

964. Richou, Gabriel Charles Marie. Inventaire de la collection des ouvrages et documents, rénuis par J.-F. Payen et J.-B. Bastide sur Michel de Montaigne. New York: B. Franklin, 1970. Reprint of the Paris, 1878 edition. 396 pp. Also: An 1877 Bordeaux edition. Also: An Amsterdam: B. R. Gruner, 1972, reprint.

MONTESQUIEU (i.e., CHARLES LOUIS DE SECONDAT)

965. Quérard, Joseph Marie. "Montesquieu," in his La France littéraire ou dictionnaire bibliographique. Paris: Didot, 1827-1864, vol. 6, pp. 237-246.

Detailed account of various editions of Montesquieu's works.

966. Dangeau, Louis [Louis Vian]. Montesquieu, bibliographie de ses oeuvres. Paris: Rouquette, 1874. 33 pp. 100 copies printed.

Montesquieu's works only. About 500 entries.

967. Cabeen, David Clark. Montesquieu: a Bibliography. New York: New York Public Library, 1947. 87 pp. Also found in: New York Public Library Bulletin, vol. 51 (1947), pp. 359-383, 423-430, 513-525, 545-565, 593-616.

Annotated entries of about 600 works in various languages by and about Montesquieu. Index.

968. Desgraves, Louis. Montesquieu (1689-1755). Exposition. Bordeaux: 1955. 151 pp.

483 entries.

MOORE, GEORGE EDWARD

969. Buchanan, Emerson, and G. E. Moore. "Bibliography of the Writings of G. E. Moore (to July, 1952)," in P. A. Schilpp, ed., The Philosophy of G. E. Moore, 2nd ed., La Salle, Ill.: Open Court Publishing Co., 1952, pp. 689-699.

MORE, HENRY

970. Landes, Margaret Winifred. "Bibliography: Henry More, 1614-1687," in Flora Isabel MacKinnon, ed., Philosophical Writings of Henry More . . . New York, London [etc.]: Oxford University Press, 1925. 333 pp. Reprinted: New York: AMS Press, 1969.

Bibliography on pp. 233-256.

MORE, THOMAS

971. Sullivan, Frank, and M. P. Sullivan. Moreana, 1478-1945; a Preliminary Check List of Material by and about Saint Thomas More. Kansas City, Mo.: Rockhurst College, 1946. 175 pp.

Duplicated typescript.

972. Gibson, R. W. St. Thomas More: a Preliminary Bibliography of his Works and of Moreana to the Year 1750. With a bibliography of Utopiana Compiled by R. W. Gibson and J. Max Patrick. New Haven and London: Yale University Press, 1961. 499 pp.

Gives locations and descriptions of 895 works. Much material on utopian works written by other authors. The place to look for utopian writings prior to 1750.

973. Sullivan, Frank, and M. P. Sullivan. Moreana: Materials for the Study of Saint Thomas More. Los Angeles: Loyola University of Los Angeles Press, 1964. 4 vols.

Well annotated.

974. Sullivan, Frank, and M. P. Sullivan. Moreana; Materials for the Study of Saint Thomas More, G-M. Los Angeles: Loyola University, 1965. 360 pp.

Duplicated typescript.

MOREAU, JOSEPH

975. "Bibliographie [: Joseph Moreau]," in G. Deladalle and D. Huisman, eds., Les Philosophes français d'aujourd'hui, [n.p., n.d.], pp. 237-241.

81 unannotated entries.

MOSCA GAETANO

976. Delle Piano, Mario. "Bibliografia di Gaetano Mosca," Quaderni di critica (Firenze), vol. 22 (1949).

150 entries.

MOSER, SIMON

977. "Die wissenschaftlichen Schriften von Simon Moser, Zusammengestellt von Ernst Oldemeyer," Zeitschrift für Philosophische Forschung (Meisenheim am Glan), vol. 20 (1966), pp. 327-330.

MOSES BEN NAHMAN

978. Israel. ha-Mahlakah - le - tarbut toranit. ha - Ramban vi - yetsirato [The Ramban and is creation. The literary exhibition on the 700th anniversary of his journeying to the land of Israel [In Hebrew]]. Jerusalem: Office of Education and Culture, Department of Torah Culture, 1967. 22 pp.

MÜLLER, ALOYS

979. Kluge, Fr. Aloys Müllers Philosophie der Mathematik und Naturwissenschaft. Mit vier Abbildungen und einer monographischen Bibliographie Aloys Müllers. (Studien und Bibliographien zur gegenwartsphilosophie, 11). Leipzig: Hirzel, 1935. 108 pp.

MUNRO, THOMAS

980. "Bibliography of Thomas Munro from 1922 to 1964," Journal of Aesthetics and Art Criticism (Detroit), vol. 23 (1964-1965), pp. 7-11.

MURPHEY, ARTHUR E.

981. "Bibliography of the Writings of Arthur E. Murphey," in Reason and the Common Good. Selected Essays of Arthur E. Murphey. Englewood Cliffs, N.J.: Prentice-Hall, 1963, pp. 398-408.

NABERT, JEAN

982. Robberechts, L. "Liste chronologique des publications de Jean Nabert," Les Etudes philosophiques (Paris), vol. 17 (1962), pp. 323-338.

983. Piersol, Wesley. "Selected bibliography on Jean Nabert," Philosophy Today (Celina, Ohio), vol. 11 (1967), p. 224.

NAESS, ARNE

984. Flo, Olav. Bibliografi over Arne Naess' forfatterskap 1936-1970. Bergen, Universitetsforlaget, 1971. 36 pp. (Filosofiske bibliografier, nr. 9).

985. Flo, Olaf. "Arne Naess: Selected List of his Philosophical Writings in the English and German Languages, 1936-1970," Synthèse (Amsterdam), vol. 23 (1971-1972), pp. 348-352.

36 entries selected from Flo's larger bibliography on Naess.

NAHM, MILTON C.

986. "In tribute to Milton C. Nahm: A note on a Fortunate Man: Vita: Bibliography," Journal of Aesthetics and Art Criticism (Baltimore), vol. 30 (1972), pp. 435-440.

NAPIER, JOHN. See 483.

NARCISSUS-RICHARDUS. See 56.

NELSON, LEONARD

987. Hermann, Grete, and Hellmut Bauschenplat. Verzeichnis der Schriften Leonard Nelsons. Gottingen: 1929. 16 pp.

89 entries.

NEWMAN, JOHN HENRY

988. Schiffers, N. and W. Becker. "Newman Bibliographie," in Newman Studien, vol. II, ed. by H. Fries and W. Becker (Veröffentlichungen des Cardinal Newman Kuratoriums). Nürnberg: Glock und Lutz, 1954, pp. 325-343.

989. Boekraad, A. J. "Newman Studien (Part II)," Philosophical Studies (Ireland), (Dublin), vol. 22 (1974), pp. 198-222.

989. (Continued)

A survey of recent literature.

NEWTON, ISSAC. See also 216.

990. Gray, George J. A Bibliography of the Works of Sir Issac Newton, together with a List of Books Illustrating his Works. Second Edition, Revised and Enlarged. Cambridge: Bowes and Bowes, 1907. 80 pp. Also: First ed.: Cambridge: Macmillan and Bowes, 1888. 40 pp. Also: London: Dawson's of Pall Mall, 1967. 80 pp.

412 entries plus name index.

991. Catalogue of the Newton Papers Sold by Order of the Viscount Lymington to whom they have Descended from Catherine Conduitt, Viscountess Lymington, Great-niece of Sir Issac Newton, which will be Sold by Auction by Messrs. Sotheby and Co. London: 34 and 35 New Bond Street, 1936. 144 pp.

992. Pelseneer, Jean. "Lettres inédites de Newton," Osiris (Cambridge, Mass.), vol. 7 (1939), pp. 523-555.

993. Babson Institute. Babson Park, Mass. Library. A Descriptive Catalog of the Grace K. Babson Collection of the Works of Sir Issac Newton and the Material Relating to him in the Babson Institute Library . . . with an Introduction by Roger Babson Webber. New York: H. Reichner, 1950. 228 pp. Supplement, 1955. 91 pp.

994. Hofmann, Joseph Ehrenfried. "Neue newtoniana," Studia Leibnitiana (Wiesbaden), vol. 2 (1970), pp. 140-145.

NICHOLAS OF CUSA

995. Uebinger, J. "Die philosophische Schriften von Nicolas von Cues," Zeitschrift für Philosophie und philosophische Kritik (Leipzig), vol. 103 (1893), pp. 65-121; vol. 104 (1894), pp. 46-106; vol. 105 (1895), pp. 48-102.

996. Rotta, Paolo. Il Cardinale Nicolò di Cusa, la vita ed il pensiero. Milano: Società editrice, "Vita e pensiero," 1928. 447 pp.

"Nota bibliografica," pp. xv-xvi.

997. Ullman, B. L. "Manuscripts of Nicolas of Cues," Speculum (Cambridge, Mass.), vol. 13 (1938), pp. 194-197.

998. Kleinen, H. and R. Danzer. "Cusanus-Bibliographie (1920-1961)," Mitteilungen und Forschungsbeiträge der Cusanus-Gesellschaft. (Mainz), vol. 1 (1961), pp. 95-126.

999. Mantese, Giovanni. "Ein notarielles Inventar von Büchen und Vertgegenständen aus dem Nachlass des Nikolaus von Kues," Mitteilungen und Forschungsbeiträge der Cusanus-Gesellschaft (Mainz), vol. 2 (1962), pp. 85-116.

1000. Danzer, R. "Cusanus-bibliographie. Fortsetzung (1961-1964) und Nachträge," Mitteilungen und Forschungsbeiträge der Cusanus-Gesellschaft (Mainz), vol. 3 (1963), pp. 223-237.

1001. "Bibliografia sobre Nicolau de Cusa," Revista portuguesa de filosofia (Braga), vol. 20 (1964), pp. 467-468.

1002. Bataillon, L. J., and Charles von Schonborn. "Connaissance de Nicolas de Cusa," Revue des sciences philosophiques et théologiques (Paris), vol. 56 (1972), pp. 63-77.

Discusses some recent works on Nicholas of Cusa.

NIETZSCHE, FRIEDRICH

1003. U. S. Library of Congress. Select List of Books on Friedrich Wilhelm Nietzsche. Washington: 1913. 5 ff.

46 entries.

1004. Mette, Hans Joachim. Der handschriftliche Nachlass Friedrich Nietzsches. Leipzig: Verlag Richard Hadl, 1932. 87 pp.

About 400 entries.

1005. Oehler, Max. Deutsche Nietzsche-Literatur von 1890 an. Zusammengestellt in Privatdruck von E. Seidel für das Nietzsche-Gedenkzimmer der Gemeinde Sils-Maria. Jena: Kämpfe, 1938. 52 pp.

1006. Reichert, Herbert W., and Karl Schlechta. International Nietzsche Bibliography. (University of North Carolina Studies in Comparative Literature, vol. 29). Chapel Hill, N. C.: University of North Carolina Press, 1960. 133 pp. Revised and expanded: (University of North Carolina Studies in Comparative Literature, no. 45), 1968. 162 pp. Adds 566 entries.

1007. Loreaux, Max. "Oeuvres de F. Nietzsche traduites en français," Morale et enseignement (Bruxelles), vol. 10 (1961), p. 32.

1008. IJsseling, Samuel. "Kroniek van de Nietzsche-Literatur," Tijdschrift voor filosofie (Leuven), vol. 34 (1972), pp. 550-569.

1009. Krummel, Richard F. Nietzsche und der deutsche Geist: Ausbreitung und Wirkung des Nietzscheschen Werkes im deutschen Sprachraum bis zu seinem Todesjahr: ein Schrifttumsverzeich nis der jahre 1867-1900. (Monographien und Texte zur Nietzsche-Forschung, vol. 83). Berlin: De Gruyter, 1973.

1010. Valadier, Paul. "Bulletin nietzschien," Archives de Philosophie (Paris), vol. 34 (1971), pp. 125-138, 333-340; vol. 36 (1973), pp. 135-150.

1011. Reichert, Hubert W. "International Nietzsche Bibliography 1968 through 1971," Nietzsche-Studien (Berlin, New York), vol. 2 (1973), pp. 320-339.

NORDENSTAM, TORE. See 2114.

NYMAN, ALF

1012. Starfelt, Eric. "Contribution à l'établissment d'une bibliographie des écrits imprimés de M. le Professeur Alf Nyman de 1899 à 1949," Theoria (Göteborg), vol. 15 (1949), pp. 399-423.

OLGIATI, FRANCESCO

1013. Orecchia, Rinaldo. "Bibliografia di F. Olgiati, scritti su F. Olgiati," Rivista internazionale di filosofia del diritto (Milano), vol. 39 (1962), pp. 846-848.

1014. Preto, E. "Publicazioni di Francesco Olgiati," in Studi di filosofia e di storia della filosofia in onore di Francesco Olgiati. Milano: Società editrice Vita e pensiero, 1962, pp. 583-597.

ORESME, NICOLAS

1015. Menut, Albert. "A Provisional Bibliography of Oresmis Writings," Mediaeval Studies (Toronto), vol. 28 (1966), pp. 279-299.

ORTEGA Y GASSET, JOSÉ

1016. Adam, Carlos. "Obras de José Ortega y Gasset publicadas en la Argentina," Revista de filosofía (La Plata), no. 17 (1966), pp. 102-145.

1017. Rukser, Udo. Bibliografía de Ortega. Madrid: Estudios orteguianos, Editiones de la Revista de occidente, 1971. 420 pp.

Worldwide listing of his works and books and articles about him. By country. About 4800 entries.

OWEN, ROBERT

1018. National Library of Wales. A Bibliography of Robert Owen, the Socialist, 1771-1858. Second Edition, Revised and Enlarged. Aberystwyth: National Library of Wales in Association with the Press Board of the University of Wales; London: Humphrey Milford, Oxford University Press Warehouse, 1925. 90 pp. First ed.: Aberystwyth: 1914. 54 pp.

597 entries by and about Owen published up to 1925. Gives books and articles with occasional annotations.

1019. Gotō, Shigeru. Robert Owen, 1771-1858, a New Bibliographical Study. Osaka: Osaka University of Commerce, 1934. 238 pp.

On his works. Notes in Japanese.

1020. London. University. Library. Robert Owen, 1771-1858, Catalog of an Exhibition of Printed Books Held in the Library of the University of London. London: 1959. 40 pp.

PAINE, THOMAS

1021. Clark, Harry Hayden. Thomas Paine. Representative Selections with Introduction, Bibliography and Notes. New York [etc.]: American Book Company, 1944. 436 pp.

PANNENBERG, WOLFHART

1022. North, Robert. "Bibliography of Works in Theology and History," History and Theory (Middletown, Ct.), vol. 12 (1973), pp. 55-133.

1022. (Continued)

About 1000 entries divided into five categories with index.

PARACELSUS

1023. Weimann, Karl-Heinz. Paracelsus-Bibliographie, 1932-1960. mit e. Vers. neu Entdeckter Paracelsus-Handschriften (1900-1960). Im Auftr. d. Paracelsus-Kommission bearb. (Kosmosphie., vol. 2). Wiesbaden: Steiner, 1963. 100 pp.

PARETO, VILFREDO

1024. Bousquet, Georges Henri, and E. Valenti. Bibliographie métodique des écrits de Vilfredo Pareto connus á ce jour. Genova: Università degli Studi: Laboratorio di economia Vilfredo Pareto, 1959. 28 ff.

About 400 entries.

PASCAL, BLAISE. See also 962.

1025. Basse, J. H. "Monographie des éditions des Lettres provinciales, ou catalogue raisonné d'une collection des Lettres provinciales," Bulletin du Bibliophile et due Bibliothécaire (Paris). Supplément. March-April, 1878, pp. 1-72.

Annotated and useful. The result of forty years research.

1026. De Pourtalès, Guy. "Les Editions originales des Pensées," Revue hebdonadaire (Paris), 32nd year, vol. 7 (1923), pp. 278-286.

1027. Maire, Albert. "Essai bibliographique des Pensées de Pascal," Archives de philosophie (Paris), vol. 1, no. 4 (1924), 211 pp.

About 1400 entries. Gives editions, translations, and commentaries.

1028. Maire, Albert. Bibliographie générale des Oeuvres de Blaise Pascal. Paris: L. Giraud-Badin, 1925-1927. 5 vols. I. Pascal savant: Ses travaux mathématiques et physiques; II, III. Pascal pamphlétaire: Les Lettres provinciales; IV. Pascal philosophe: Les Pensées; V. Opuscules, lettres, biographie et iconographie; IV: 420 pp.

1446 entries, 85 page introduction, annotations.

1029. Peyre, H. "Pascal et la critique contemporaine," Romantic Review (New York), vol. 21 (1930), pp. 325-340.

113 selected entries. Works on Pascal from 1910 to 1929.

1030. Paris. Bibliothèque nationale. Départment des imprimés. . . Catalogue des ovurages de Pascal conservés au Départment des impremés. Paris: Imprimerie nationale, 1935. Reprinted from the Catalogue général des Livres imprimés de la Bibliothèque nationale, v. 130.

1031. Flasche, Hans. "Stand, Methoden, und Aufgaben der Pascalforschung," Dichtung und Volkstum (Stuttgart), vol. 27 (1953), pp. 611-635.

Aims at completeness for the period 1939-1952. About 160 annotated entries. Good.

1032. Kruse, Margot. Das Pascal-Bild in der französischen Literatur. Hamburg: Cram, De Gruyter, 1955. 118 pp.

A survey of the literature from Bayle to Claude, but with a good bibliography.

1033. Bishop, Morris, and Sister Marie Louiso Hubert. "Pascal [: an Annotated Bibliography]," in D. C. Cabeen and J. Brody, gen. eds., A Critical Bibliography of French Literature, Syracuse, N. Y.: Syracuse University Press, 1961. Vol. III, pp. 417-456.

Critical evaluations of about 300 works. Very useful.

1034. Morra, Gianfranco. "Studi pascaliani in Italia," in E. Castelli [et al.], eds., Pascal e Nietzsche (Archivo di filosofia (Roma), 1962, no. 3), Padova: Cedam, 1962, pp. 183-195.

1035. Ruiz, Félix. "Repertorio bibliográfico pascaliano en Español," Augustinus (Madrid), vol. 7 (1962), pp. 421-425.

PEIRCE, CHARLES SANDERS

1036. Fisch, Max H. et al. "A Draft of a Bibliography of Writings about C. S. Peirce," in Edward C. Moore and Richard S. Robin, Studies in the Philosophy of Charles Sanders Peirce; Second Series. Amherst, Mass.: University of Massachusetts Press, 1964, pp. 486-514.

1037. Fisch, Max H. "A First Supplement to 'A Draft of a Bibliography of Writings about C. S. Peirce'," Transactions of the Charles S. Peirce Society, vol. 2 (1966), pp. 54-59. Also published as an appendix to the Fisch Bibliography.

1038. Robin, Richard S. Annotated Catalogue of the Papers of Charles S. Peirce. Amherst: University of Massachusetts Press, 1967. 268 pp.

A catalogue of, and guide to, the Peirce papers. About 1700 entries. Analytical table of contents, general index, supplement, chronological list, cor cross-reference index. Very good.

1039. Fisch, Max H. "Supplements to the Peirce Bibliographies," Transactions of the Charles S. Peirce Society (South Hadley, Mass.), vol. 10 (1974), pp. 94-129.

PELSTER, FRANZ

1040. Schönmetzer, Adolf. "Verzeichnis der von Franz Pelster, S. J. verfassten Aufsätze und Bücher," Scholastik (Freiburg i. B.), vol. 31 (1956), pp. 487-495.

PELZER, AUGUSTE

1041. "Bibliographie de monseigneur Auguste Pelzer," in Mélanges Auguste Pelzer, Louvain: Bibliothèque de l'université, Bureau du Recueil, 1947, pp. 17-21.

1042. Pelzer, Auguste. Études d'histoire littéraire sur la scolastique médiévale. Louvain: Publications universitaires, 1964.

"Bibliographie d'Auguste Pelzer," pp. 13-18.

PEPPER, STEPHEN C.

1043. Duncan, Elmer H. "Stephen C. Pepper: a Bibliography," The Journal of Aesthetics and Art Criticism (Cleveland), vol. 28 (1970), pp. 287-293.

A complete list of Pepper's own works and a list of more than fifty works about Pepper's work.

PERELMAN, CHAIM

1044. "Bibliographie de Ch. Perelman," in La Theorie de l'argumentation. Perspectives et applications. Louvain: Ed. Nauwelaerts; Paris: Beatrice-Nauwelaerts, 1963, pp. 604-611. Also published in Logique et Analyse, nouvelle série, 6e année, 1963, nos. 21 to 24.

PETER OF SPAIN. See also 2011.

1045. Grabmann, Martin. Handschriftliche Forschungen und Funde zu den philosophischen Schriften des Petrus Hispanus, des späteren Papstes Johannes XXI (1277). (Sitzungsbericht der Bayerischen Akadamie der Wissenschaften, philosophische-historische Abteilung, Jahrgang, 1936.) München: Bayerischen Akadamic der Wissenschaften, in kommission bei Beck, 1936. 136 pp.

PÉTRONIEVICS, BRANISLAV

1046. Anthony, R. "Resumé des travaux philosophiques et scientifiques de Branislav Pétronievics," Revue générale des sciences pures et appliquées (Paris), vol. 50 (1939), p. 312.

PHELAN, GERALD B.

1047. "Bibliography of the Works--Books, Editions, Articles, Translations and Book Reviews--of Gerald B. Phelan," in Arthur G. Korn, ed., G. B. Phelan: Selected Papers. Toronto: Pontifical Institute of Medieval Studies, 1967, pp. 231-242.

PIAGET, JEAN

1048. Psychologie et epistemologie genetiques. Thèmes piagetiens. Hommage à Jean Piaget avec une bibliographie complete de ses oeuvres. (Sciences du comportement, I). Paris: Dunod, 1966. 444 pp.

PICO DELLA MIRANDOLA, GIOVANNI

1049. Ludovici, Sergio Samek. Catalogo della mostra delle opere di Giovanni Pico della Mirandola. Modena: Biblioteca communale, 1963. 71 pp.

PIEPER, JOSEF

1050. Breitholz, Paul. Das Schrifttum Josef Piepers in den Jahren 1928-1964. Münster: Selbstverl., Mecklenburger Str. 22, 1964. 31 pp.

1051. Breitholz, Paul. Josef-Pieper-Schriften-Verzeichnis. München: Kösel, 1974. 78 pp.

PILCHER, HANS

1052. Jacoby, Günther. "Denkmal Hans Pilchers zum 5. Todestag (2-II-1882 *10-XI-1958) Zeitschrift für philosophische forschung (Meisenheim am Glan), vol. 17 (1963), pp. 462-476.

Contains a bibliography of his works.

PLATO. See also 61, 1234, 1235, 1861.

1053. Alcinous. Alcinoi Disciplinarium Platonis Epitoma. id est. Brevaiarium Incipit. Nürmberg: Anton Koberger, 1472.

1054. Tennemann, Wilhelm Gottlieb. System der Platonischen Philosophie, vol. 1. Leipzig: Barth, 1792.

Pp. xxvi-xxxiii contain a list of writings on Plato and Platonic philosophy. Extensive and good up to about 1790, but not complete for the period.

1055. Teuffel, Wilhelm Sigismund. Übersicht der Platonischen Literatur, Programm-Tübingen (Geburtsfest des Königs Karl von Württemberg). Tübingen: 1874.

About 800 entries.

1056. Ledos, Émile Gabriel. Catalogue des ouvrages de Platon conservés au départment des imprimés et dans les bibliothèques Mazarine, Sainte-Geneviève, de l'Arsenal, de l'université de Paris, de l'Institut Victor-Cousin et de l'École normale supérieure. Paris: Bibliothèque nationale, 1937. 198 cols.

1056. (Continued)

About 1800 entries.

1057. De Strycker, E. "Chronique platonicienne (1929-1934)," L'Antiquité classique (Bruxelles), vol. 4 (1935), pp. 227-243.

Also: Vol. 18 (1949), pp. 95-107.

1058. Sciacca, Michele Federico. "Studi platonici," Logos (Firenze; Hapoli), vol. 20 (1937), pp. 134-142.

1059. Sciacca, Michele Federico. Platone (Guide bibliografiche, 5) Milano: Società editrice "Vita e pensiero," 1945. 58 pp.

366 entries.

1060. Gignon, Olaf. Platon (Bibliographische Einführungen in das Studium der Philosophie, 12). Bern: A. Francke, 1950. 30 pp.

About 300 entries. Gives important editions, ancient and modern commentaries. Solid, worth looking at.

1061. Rosenmeyer, T. G. "Platonic Scholarship, 1945-1955," Classical Weekly, vol. 50 (1957), pp. 173-182, 185-196, 197-201, 209-211.

A selected bibliography, but still quite extensive. Arranged by topics. Annotated. Good.

1062. Cherniss, H. F. "Plato Studies, 1950-1957," Lustrum (Göttingen), vol. 4 (1959), pp. 5-308; vol. 5 (1960), pp. 323-648.

About 2000 entries.

1063. Brumbaugh, Robert S. and Rulon Wells. Plato Manuscripts: a Catalog of Microfilms in the Plato Microfilm Project, Yale University Library. New Haven: Yale University Library, 1962. 2 vols.

See also next entry (which supersedes the above).

1064. Brumbaugh, Robert S. and Rulon Wells. The Plato Manuscripts: a New Index, Prepared by the Plato Microfilm Project of the Yale University Library. New Haven: Yale University Press, 1968. 163 pp.

Indexed list of all pre-1500 Platonic manuscript material.

1065. Rodis-Lewis, Geneviève. Platon et la chasse de l'être. Presentation, choix de textes, bibliographie. (Coll. Philosophes de tous les temps, 19). Paris: P. Seghers, 1965. 192 pp.

1066. Fritz, Kurt. "Der vermeintliche augenarzt Lynkens in Platons siebtem Brief," Archiv für geschichte der Philosophie (New York), vol. 53 (1971), pp. 231-237.

PLATZECK, ERHARDI-WOLFRAM

1067. Spätling, Luchesius. "Bibliographia Erhardi-Wolfram Platzeck, O.F.M.," Antonianum (Roma), vol. 48 (1973), pp. 268-299.

PLOTINUS

1068. Marien, B. Bibliografia critica degli studi Plotiniani con rassegna delle loro recensioni, rev. e curata da V. cilento. Bari: Laterza, 1949. 668 pp.

POLANYI, MICHAEL

1069. Polanyi, J. "Bibliography: Scientific Papers, Books, and Film by Michael Polanyi," in The Logic of Personal Knowledge: Essays Presented to Michael Polanyi on his Seventieth Birthday, 11 March 1961. Glencoe, Ill.: The Free Press; London: Routledge and Paul, 1961, pp. 239-248.

POLIN, RAYMOND

1070. "Raymond Polin (Notice biographique et bibliographique)," Annales de l'Université de Paris (Paris), vol. 32 (1962), p. 61.

POPPER, KARL

1071. Hansen, Troels Eggers. "Bibliography of the Writings of Karl Popper," in P. A. Schilpp, ed., The Philosophy of Karl Popper, La Salle, Ill.: Open Court, 1974, pp. 1199-1287.

PRAWITZ, DAG. See 2115.

PRENTICE, ROBERT P.

1072. Vazquez, Issac. "Bibliography [: Robert P. Prentice, O.F.M. (1928-1974)]," Antonianum (Roma), vol. 49 (1974), pp. 370-372.

PREUSS, K. TH.

1073. Boccassino, R. "Elenco delle publicazioni del prof. Th. Preuss," Rivista di anthropologia (Roma), vol. 32 (1940), pp. 388-396.

PRIESTLEY, JOSEPH

1074. Fulton, John Farquhar, and C. H. Peters. "Introduction to a Bibliography of the Educational and Scientific Works of Priestley," Papers of the Bibliographical Society of America (Chicago), vol. 30 (1936), pp. 150-161.

1075. Crook, Ronald Edward. A Bibliography of Priestley, 1733-1804. (Library Association Bibliographies, no. 6) London: Library Association, 1966. 201 pp.

PRINGLE-PATTISON, ANDREW SETH

1076. "Andrew Seth Pringle-Pattison [: a Bibliography]," in George Watson, ed., The New Cambridge Bibliography of English Literature, Cambridge: Cambridge University Press, 1969, vol. 3, cols. 1579-1580.

About 50 works by and about him.

PRIOR, ARTHUR N.

1077. Flo, Olaf. Bibliography of the Philosophical Writings of A. N. Prior, 1937-1967. Bergen: Universitetsbiblioteket i Bergen, 1969. 23 l. Also: "Bibliography of the Philosophical Writings of A. N. Prior," Theoria (Lund), vol. 36 (1970), pp. 189-213.

PRISCO, GUISEPPE

1078. Orlando, Pasquale. "Bibliografia del cardinale. Guiseppe Prisco (Boscotrecase 8 sett. 1833-4 febbr. 1923)

1078. (Continued)

secondo i documenti. Nel quarantesimo anniversario della morte," Aquinas (Roma), vol. 7 (1964), pp. 76-124.

PRZYWARA, ERICH

1079. Zimny, Leo. Erich Przywara. Sein Schrifttum 1912-1962. Einsiedeln: Johannes Verlag, 1963. 92 pp.

1080. Sánchez Marales, Narciso. "P. Erich Przywara (12.10.-1889-28.9.1972) Nota bio-bibliográfica," Augustinus (Madrid) vol. 18 (1973), pp. 63-67.

PSEUDO-DIONYSIUS THE AREOPAGITE

1081. Hornus, J.-M. "Les Récherches recentes sur le Pseudo-Denys l'Aréopagite," Revue d'historie et de philosophy religieuses (Strasbourg), vol. 35 (1955), pp. 404-448.

Covers publications 1932-1954.

1082. Doherty, Kevin F. "Toward a Bibliography of Pseudo-Dionysius the Areopagite: 1900-1955," Modern Schoolman (St. Louis, Mo.), vol. 33 (1956), pp. 257-268.

1083. Hornus, Jean-Michel. "Les Recherches dionysiennes de 1955 a 1960. [Appendix:] Bibliographie dionysienne, 1954-1959," Revue d'histoire et de philosophie religieuses (Strasbourg), vol. 41 (1961), pp. 22-81.

PUSINERI, P. GIOVANNI

1084. Bergamaschi, Cirillo. "Scritti principali del P. Giovanni Pusineri," Rivista rosminiana di filosofia e di cultura (Domodossola e Milano), vol. 58 (1964), pp. 295-308.

RAMUS, PETER

1085. Ong, Walter Jackson. Ramus and Talon Inventory: a Short-Title Inventory of the Published Works of Peter Ramus (1515-1572) and of Omer Talon (ca. 1510-1562) in their Original and in their Variously Altered Forms, with Related Material. Cambridge, Mass.: Harvard University Press, London: Oxford University Press, 1958. 558 pp.

RASHI (i.e., SOLOMON BEN ISSAC)

1086. Toledano, Jacob Moses. Apiryon [Bibliography of the Works on Rashi's Biblical Commentaries [In Hebrew]]. Jerusalem: [n.p.], 1905. 25 pp.

RAWLS, JOHN

1087. Tattershall, Gerald. "A Rawls Bibliography," Social Theory and Practice (Tallahassee), vol. 3 (1974), pp. 123-127.

REICHWEIN, ADOLF

1088. Henderson, James L. "Veröffentlichungen von Adolf Reichwein," in Henderson, ed., Adolf Reichwein; eine politisch-pädagogisch Biographie. Stuttgart: Deutsche Verlags-Anstalt: 1958, pp. 219-221.

REINER, HANS

1089. "Bibliographie Hans Reiner," Zeitschriften für philosophische Forschungen (Meisenheim am Glan), vol. 21 (1967), pp. 152-158.

RENAN, ERNEST

1090. Cresson, André. Ernest Renan: sa vie, son oeuvre, avec un exposé de sa philosophie. Paris: Presses universitaires de France, 1949. 127 pp.

RESTA, RAFFAELE

1091. "Bibliografia degli studi monografici e degli articoli [R. Resta]," in Gli aspetti essenziali di una vita e di un pensiero. Bari: Editori Aster, 1956, pp. 153-172.

REYMOND, MARCEL

1092. Gavin, Pierre. "Bibliographie des publications de Marcel Reymond," in Marcel Reymond, un philosophe au service des valeurs humaines. Textes et temoignages. Neuchâtel: La Baconniere, 1968, pp. 167-174.

RICHARD OF MIDDLETON

1093. Hocedez, Edgar. Richard de Middleton, sa vie, ses oeuvres, sa doctrine (Spicilegium Sacrum Lovaniesne, Etudes et documents, fasc. 7). Paris: E. Champion, 1925. 555 pp.

A discussion of Richard's works plus a bibliography on pp. xii-xvi.

1094. Zavalloni, Roberto. Richard de Mediavilla et la controverse sur la pluralité des formes. Textes inédits et étude critique. Louvain: Editions de l'Institut supérieur de philosophie, 1951. 551 pp.

Contains a good bibliography, pp. 508-538.

RICOEUR, PAUL. See also 863.

1095. Vansina, Dirk F. "Bibliographie de Paul Ricoeur (jusqu'au 30 juin 1962)," Revue philosophique de Louvain (Louvain), vol. 60 (1962), pp. 394-413.

1096. Vansina, Dirk F. "Bibliographie de Paul Ricoeur. Complements (jusqu'a la fin de 1967)," Revue philosophique de Louvain (Louvain), vol. 66 (1968), pp. 85-101.

1097. Lapointe, Francois H. "A Bibliography on Paul Ricoeur," Philosophy Today (Celina), vol. 16 (1972), pp. 28-33; vol. 17 (1973), pp. 176-182.

1098. Vansina, Dirk F. "Bibliographie de Paul Ricoeur," Revue Philosophique de Louvain (Louvain), vol. 72 (1974), pp. 156-181.

Semi-exhaustive bibliography of the writings of Ricoeur through 1973.

RINTELEN, FRITZ-JOACHIM VON

1099. "Veröffentlichungen von Fritz-Joachim von Rintelen (zum 70. Geburtstag des bekannten Philosophen am 16 mai des Jahres)," Zeitschrift für philosophische Forschung (Meisenheim am Glan), vol. 22 (1968), pp. 290-298.

RITTER, JOACHIM

1100. Régnier, M. "Joachim Ritter," Archives de philosophie (Paris), vol. 26 (1963), pp. 448-451.

1100. (Continued)

Contains a bibliography of his principal works.

ROBBERS, J. H.

1101. "Bibliografie van der werken van Prof. Dr. J. H. Robbers S. J.," Bijdragen (Maastricht), vol. 27 (1966), pp. 175-182.

1102. Braun, C., J. Arntz, and H. Van Luijk, eds. Philia: Wijsgerige opstellen in vriendschap aangeboden aan Prof. J. H. Robbers, S.J. [Philia: Philosophical Essays in Friendship Offered to Prof. J. H. Robbers]. Nijmegen-Utrecht: Dekker and Van de Vegt N. V., 1966. 149 pp.

Contains a bibliography of Robbers' works.

ROBERT OF HALIFAX

1103. Courtenay, William J. "Some Notes on Robert of Halifax, O.F.M.," Franciscan Studies (St. Bonaventure, N.Y.), vol. 33 (1973), pp. 135-142.

ROMAGNOSI, GIOVANNI DOMENICO

1104. Belloni, G. A. Bibliografia romagnosiana. Rome: La Bodoniana, 1934. 7 pp.

1105. Di Carlo, E. Una lettera di Vito D'Ondes Reggio a G. D. Romagnosi (con bibliografia romagnosiana). Palermo: Corselli, 1935. 36 pp.

1106. Di Carlo, E. Bibliografia romagnosiana. Palermo: Corselli, 1936. 23 pp.

ROMANO, EGIDIO

1107. Bruni, Gerardo. "Saggio bibliografico sulle opere stampate di Egidio Romano," Analecta Augustiniana (Romae), vol. 24 (1961), pp. 331-355.

ROOS, HEINRICH

1108. "Bibliographie Heinrich Roos." Cahiers de l'Institut du Moyen-age grec et latin (Copenhague), vol. 13 (1974),

1108. (Continued)

pp. 82-86.

ROSMINI-SERBATI, ANTONIO

1109. Caviglione, C. Bibliografia delle opere di A. Rosmini. Torino: G. B. Paravia, 1925. 122 pp.

1110. Castelli, Enrico. Opere edite e inedite di Antonio Rosmini Serbati (1791-1855). Roma: Anonima romana editoriale, 1934-

1111. Morando, D. "Rosmini in libri, riviste, giornali," Rivista rosminiana di filosofia et di cultura (Pallanza), vol. 28 (1934), pp. 75-80.

1112. Lopez de Oñate, F. "A proposito di una recente bibliografia rosminiana. Proposta di addizioni, rettifiche e complementi," Sophia (Padova), vol. 4 (1936), pp. 218-248, 476-504.

Additions to E. Castelli, Opere edite e inedite di Antonio Rosmini Serbati (1797-1857).

1113. "Bibliografia rosminiana degli ultimi 5 anni," Theoresi (Messina), vol. 10 (1955), pp. 443-474.

1114. "Bibliografia rosminiana," Rivista Rosminiana di filosofia e di cultura (Pallanza), vol. 49 (1955), pp. 315-316.

"Continua", vol. 50 (1956), pp. 70-79, 154-157, 239-240, 313-315.

1115. Evain, François. "Bibliographie critique des principaux oeuvres philosophiques d'Antonio Rosmini de 1816 à 1838," Rivista rosminiana de filosofia e di cultura (Milano), vol. 60 (1966), pp. 285-299.

1116. Bergamaschi, Cirillo. Bibliografia rosminiana. Vol. 1: 1814-1934; Vol. 2: 1935-1966 (Studi sul pensiero filosofico del secolè XIXe XX, 8). Milano: Marzorati, 1967.

1117. Bergamaschi, Cirillo. "Bibliografia rosminiana," Rivista rosminiana di filosofia e di cultura (Domodossola; Milano) vol. 67 (1973), pp. 44-64. See also vol. 63 (1969), pp. 308-325; vol. 65 (1971), pp. 139-159, 319-331.

1118. Bergamaschi, Cirillo. Bibliografia degli scritti editis di Antonio Rosmini Serbati. Vol. I: Opere. Vol. II: Lettere. Studi sul pensiero filosofico e religioso dei secoli XIX e XX, 17. Milano: Marzorati, 1970.

ROTHACKER, ERICH

1119. Schmandt, Jürgen. "Erich Rothacker. Schriften, Vorträge und Herausgebertätigkeit," in Konkrete Vernunft: Festschrift für Erich Rothacker. Bonn: 1958, pp. 435-444.

142 entries.

ROUSSEAU, JEAN-JACQUES

1120. Jansen, Wilhelm Albert. Zur Litteratur über Rousseau's Politik. ("Abdruck aus dem XLIX Bande der Preussischen Jahrbücher"). Berlin: G. Reimer, 1882. 40 pp.

1121. Asse, Louis Eugène Auguste. . . . Jean-Jacques Rousseau. (Bibliothèque de Bibliographies Critiques, Pub. par la Société des Etudes Historiques, 11.) Paris: A. Fontemoing, 1900. 12 pp.

Contains list of his writings and editions of his works.

1122. Paris. Bibliothèque Nationale. Départment des imprimés. . . . Catalogue des ouvrages de Jean-Jacques Rousseau conservés dans les grandes bibliothèques de Paris, par E.-G. Ledos, conservateur-adjoint. Paris: H. Champion, 1912. 60 pp.

1123. Dufour, Théophile. Recherches bibliographiques sur les oeuvres imprimées de J.-J. Rousseau. Paris: L. Giraud-Badin, 1925. 2 vols. 273, 299 pp.

Approximately 700 entries, annotated, with arrangement by subject. No index.

1124. Schinz, Albert. Bibliographie critique de Jean-Jacques Rousseau dans les cinq dernières années. Baltimore: The John Hopkins Press, 1926, pp. 423-438. From Modern Language Notes, vol. 41 (1926).

Supplementary to the author's "Le mouvement Rousseauiste du dernier quart de siècle," Modern Philology, vol. 20 (1922), pp. 149-172.

1125. Warner, J. H. "Bibliography of 18th Century English Editions of J.-J. Rousseau," Philological Quarterly (Iowa City), vol. 12 (1934), no. 2. Addenda: Vol. 19 (1940), no. 3.

1126. Sénelier, Jean. Bibliographie générale des oeuvres de J.-J. Rousseau. Paris: Presses universitaires de France, 1950. 282 pp. Also: Paris: Encyclopédie française, 1949.

1126. (Continued)

Review: B. Gagnebin in Société Jean-Jacques Rousseau. Annales, Vol. 32 (1951-1952), pp. 231-255.

1127. Spurlin, Paul M. "Jean-Jacques Rousseau [: a Bibliography]," in David C. Cabeen and Julius Brody, eds., A Critical Bibliography of French Literature. Syracuse: Syracuse University Press, 1951, vol. 4, pp. 208-251.

About 350 entries with good annotations.

1128. Beck, Leonard N. Rousseau in Russian: Additions to Sénelier. [n.p.], 1952. 247-249 pp. "Reprinted from Modern Language Notes, vol. 67 (1952)."

1129. "Recent Publications on Rousseau," Yale French Studies (New Haven, Conn.), vol. 28 (1961), pp. 136-137.

43 entries from the period 1959-1961. Helpful, but brief, annotations.

1130. Paris. Bibliothèque nationale. Jean-Jacques Rousseau, 1712-1778. (Exposition organisée pour le 250e anniversaire de sa naissance). Paris: 1962. 126 pp.

1131. Rosselet, Claire. Catalogue de la correspondance de J.-J. Rousseau conservée à la Bibliothèque de la ville de Neuchâtal, I: Lettres originales de J.-J. Rousseau. Neuchâtel: Messeiller, 1963. 111 pp.

1132. Voisine, Jacques. "Etat des travaux sur Jean-Jacques Rousseau au lendemain de son 250e anniversaire de naissance (1712-1962)," Information litteraire (Paris), vol. 16 (1964), pp. 93-107.

Useful review of the state of the literature.

1133. Rousseau, Jean-Jacques. Emile ou de l'education. Introduction, bibliographie, notes et index analytique par François et Pierre Richard (Classiques Garnier). Paris: Garnier, 1967. 669 pp.

1134. Salomon-Bayet, Claire. J.-J. Rousseau ou l'impossible unite. Presentation, choix de textes, bibliographie (Philosophes de tous les temps, 40). Paris: Seghers, 1967. 184 pp.

1135. Annales de la Société Jean-Jacques Rousseau (Geneva). 1905-

Each volume includes a bibliography.

ROUSSELOT, PIERRE

1136. "Bibliographie: écrits philosophiques et theologiques de Pierre Rousselot. Etudes principales sur la vie et l'oeuvre de Pierre Rousselot," in Memorial Pierre Rousselot 1878-1915 (Recherches de science religieuse, vol. 53 (1965), no. 3). Paris: Recherches de science religieuse, 1965, pp. 4-6.

ROYCE, JOSIAH

1137. Lowenberg, Jacob. "A Bibliography of the Unpublished Writings of Josiah Royce," The Philosophical Review (Ithaca, N.Y.), vol. 26 (1917), pp. 578-582.

1138. Rand, Benjamin. "A Bibliography of the Writings of Josiah Royce," The Philosophical Review (Ithaca, N.Y.), vol. 25 (1916), pp. 515-522.

1139. Oppenheim, Frank M. "A Critical Annotated Bibliography of the Published Works of Josiah Royce," Modern Schoolman (St. Louis, Mo.), vol. 41 (1963-1964), pp. 339-365.

1140. Devaux, André-A. "Bibliographie des traductions d'ouvrages de Royce et des études sur l'oeuvre de Royce," Revue internationale de philosophie (Bruxelles), vol. 21 (1967), pp. 159-182.

1141. Oppenheim, Frank. "Bibliography of the Published Works of Josiah Royce (Revised Edition)," Revue internationale de philosophie (Bruxelles), vol. 21 (1967), pp. 138-158.

1142. Skrupskelis, Ignos. "Annotated Bibliography of the Published Works of Josiah Royce," in vol. II of The Basic Writings of Josiah Royce, ed. and intro. by John J. McDermott. Chicago: University of Chicago Press, 1969.

RUSKIN, JOHN

1143. Wise, Thomas J., and James P. Smart. A Complete Bibliography of the Writings in Prose and Verse of John Ruskin, LL.D. London: "Printed for subscribers only," 1893. 2 vols. Reprinted: Folkestone and London: for Dawsons of Pall Mall, 1964, 1974.

About 1200 entries by and about Ruskin with notes and annotations.

RUSSELL, BERTRAND

1144. Jacob, Gertrude. "Bertrand Russell, an Essay Towards a Bibliography," Bulletin of Bibliography and Dramatic Index (Boston), vol. 13 (1929), pp. 188-189; vol. 14 (1930), pp. 28-30.

1145. Dorward, Alan. Bertrand Russell [a Bibliography]. The British Council: Bibliographical Series of Supplements: 1950. 44 pp.

150 entries.

1146. Feinberg, Barry, [et al.]. A Detailed Catalogue of the Archives of Bertrand Russell. London: Continuum 1 Ltd., 1967. 341 pp.

Contains a huge amount of material by and about Russell: Books, articles, letters, etc.; name index, Russell and Stanley family trees, autobiography, legal actions, etc., etc. A very detailed work.

1147. Blackwell, Kenneth. "The Bertrand Russell Archives," Dialogue (Kingston, Ont.), vol. 7 (1969), pp. 608-615.

Describes the Russell collection at McMaster University.

1148. Devaux, Philippe. Bertrand Russell ou la paix dans la verite. Presentation choix de textes, bio-bibliographie. (Philosophes de tous les temps, 36). Paris: Seghers, 1969. 192 pp.

1149. Dennon, Lester E. "Bibliography of the Writings of Bertrand Russell to 1951," in P. A. Schilpp, ed., The Philosophy of Bertrand Russell, 4th ed. La Salle, Ill.: Open Court, 1971, pp. 743-804.

Lists chronologically about 600 works. Also in earlier editions of Schilpp's work.

1150. ["Bibliography of Bertrand Russell"], in I. R. Willison, ed. The New Cambridge Bibliography of English Literature, vol. 4, 1900-1950. Cambridge: Cambridge University Press, 1972, cols. 1283-1291.

Lists about 220 works by and about Russell, mostly by.

1151. Ruja, Harry. "Bibliography of Russell's 'Hearst' Articles," Russell (Hamilton, Can.) (1975), pp. 18-26.

SAINT-SIMON, CLAUDE-HENRI DE ROUVROY, COMTE DE

1152. Walch, Jean. Bibliographie du Saint-Simonism e avec trois textes inédites. (Bibliotheque d'histoire de la philosophie). Paris: J. Vrin, 1967. 132 pp.

SAITSCHICH, ROBERT

1153. Saitschick, Robert. Die bibliothek Robert Saitschick, Zürich . . . vol. 3, Philosophie, Pädagogik, Theologie. Leipzig: K. F. Koehler; Stuttgart: O. Gerschel, 1925-1927.

SANCHES, FRANCISCO

1154. "Bibliografia sanchesiana," Revista portuguesa di filosofia (Lisboa), vol. 7 (1951), pp. 205-210.

SANSEVERINO, GAETANO

1155. Orlando, Pasquale. "Vita e opere di Gaetano Sanseverino secondo i documenti," Aquinas (Roma), vol. 8 (1965), pp. 221-288.

SANTAYANA, GEORGE

1156. Terzian, Shonig. "Bibliography of the Writings of G. Santayana to Oct. 1940," in P. A. Schilpp, ed., The Philosophy of George Santayana, Evanston and Chicago: Northwestern University, 1940, pp. 607-668. Also: 2nd ed.: La Salle, Ill.: Open Court, 1951, pp. 607-678, with index. Also: London: Constable, 1953.

1157. Santos Escuerda, Ceferino. "Bibliografía general de Jorge Santayana," Miscelanea Comillas (Comillas), vol. 44 (1965), pp. 155-310. Published separately: Comillas: Pontificia Universitas Comillensis, 1965. 160 pp.

SARTRE, JEAN-PAUL. See also 1679.

1158. "I. Sartre's Works in French and English," Yale French Studies, vol. 30 (1963), pp. 108-115.

37 entries on books by Sartre; 52 articles by Sartre not collected in books; 13 prefaces, introductions, Avant-propos; 22 interviews. No annotations.

1159. "II. Books and Pamphlets on Sartre," Yale French Studies, vol. 30 (1963), pp. 115-118.

73 entries. No annotations.

1160. "III. A Selection of Articles about Sartre," Yale French Studies, vol. 30 (1963), pp. 118-119.

23 entries. No annotations.

1161. Belkind, Allen. Jean-Paul Sartre: Sartre and Existentialism in English: a Bibliographical guide (The Serif Series: Bibliographies and Checklists, no. 10). Kent, Ohio: Kent State University Press, 1970. 234 pp.

527 entries. Appendix with works of Sartre. Index of authors, editors, and translators. Helpful annotations.

1162. Contat, Michel, and Michel Rybalka. Les Ecrits de Sartre: chronologie, bibliographie commentée. Paris: Gallimard, 1970. 788 pp.

Detailed descriptions of Sartre's voluminous writings, by year. Title index and name index.

1163. Suzuki, Michihiko, Takeshi Ebisaka, and Kinuko Urano. [Bibliography of Sartre [In Japanese]]. Sarutoru to sono jidai. [Also title in French:] Bibliographie synthétique Sartre et son temps. Tokyo: Jimbun Shoin, 1971. 308 pp.

1164. Lapointe, François H. "Bibliography on Jean-Paul Sartre," Man and World (Pittsburgh), vol. 5 (1972), pp. 193-246.

1165. Lapointe, François H. "The Phenomenological Psychology of Sartre and Merleau-Ponty. A Bibliographical Essay," Diálogos (Puerto Rico), vol. 8 (1972), pp. 161-182.

1166. Dunlop, Jacqueline. Sartre: a Handlist of Books by and About Jean-Paul Sartre in the [Birkbeck] College Library. (Birkbeck College Library Publication, no. 57). London: Birkbeck College Library, 1974. 10 pp.

1167. Lapointe, François A., and Claire C. Lapointe." Jean-Paul Sartre's Marxism: a Bibliographic Essay," The journal of the British Society for Phenomenology (Manchester), vol. 5 (1974), pp. 184-192.

1168. Lapointe, François H. and Claire Lapointe. Jean-Paul Sartre and his Critics: an International Bibliography (1938-1975). Bowling Green, Ohio: Philosophy Documentation Center, 1975. 447 pp.

1169. Lapointe, François H. and Claire C. Lapointe. "A Bibliography of Recent Works on Jean-Paul Sartre: 1970-1975," Philosophy Today (Celina, Ohio), vol. 19 (1975), pp. 341-357.

1170. "Bibliographie [: Jean-Paul Sartre]," in G. Deladalle and D. Huisman, eds., Les Philosophes français d'aujourd'hui [n.p., n.d.], pp. 310-313.

40 unannotated entries of works by Sartre.

SAVONAROLA

1171. Ginori Conti, Piero. Bibliografia delle opere del Savonarola. Firenze: Fondazione Ginori Conti, 1939. 165 pp.

SCHELER, MAX

1172. Kraenzlin, G. Max Schelers phänomenologische Systematik. mit einer monographischen Bibliographie Max Schelers. (Studien und Bibliographien zur Gegenwartsphilosophie, 3). Leipzig: Hirzel, 1934. 103 pp.

1173. Hartmann, Wilfried. Max Scheler; Bibliographie. Stuttgart: Fromman, 1963. 128 pp.

1031 unannotated entries arranged by topic. Most are in German. Title and name indexes.

1174. "M. Scheler: Bibliography (1963-1974) of Primary (English Translations) and Secondary Literature," in M. S. Frings, ed., Max Scheler. Centennial Essays, The Hague: Nijhoff, 1974, pp. 492-510.

1175. Ferretti, Giovanni. "Rassegna di studi scheleriani in lingua tedesca (continua)," Rivista filosofica neo-scholastica (Milano), vol. 57 (1965), pp. 483-498, 808-847.

SCHELLING, FRIEDEICH WILHELM JOSEPH VON

1176. Jost, Johannes. F. W. J. von Schelling; Bibliographie der Schriften von ihm und über ihn. Bonn: F. Cohen, 1927. 50 pp.

1177. Schröter, M. "Historische Uebersicht über die Schelling-Literatur," Idealismus (Zurich), vol. 1 (1934), pp. 219-227.

1178. Schneeberger, Guido. Friedrich Wilhelm Joseph von Schelling: eine Bibliographie. Bern: A. Francke, 1954. 190 pp.

1012 entries arranged chronologically. No annotations. Name index. Work is divided into topics: Schelling's work, work about Schelling, etc. Useful.

1179. Coreth, Emerich. "Die Ernte des Schelling-Jahres. Ein Literatur-Bericht," Zeitschrift für Katholische Theologie (Wien), vol. 78 (1956), pp. 334-351.

1180. Tilliette, Xavier. "Bulletin de l'idealisme allemand," Archives de philosophie (Paris), vol. 34 (1971), pp. 287-331.

Works on Schelling, 1965-1970.

1181. Jacobs, Wilhelm, G. "Schelling: Edition historique critique," Archives de Philosophie (Paris), vol. 38 (1975), pp. 401-408.

Covers previous editions and gives a plan for a future edition.

SCHILLER, FRIEDRICH VON. See also 775.

1182. Büchting, Adolph. Verzeichniss der zur hundertjahringer Geburtsfeier Friedrich von Schiller's erschienenen Bücher . . . Ein Beitrag zur Schiller-Literatur. Nordhausen: A. Büchting, 1860. 84 pp.

SCHILLER, FERDINAND C.S.

1183. Scarles, Herbert L., and Allan Shields. A Bibliography of F. C. S. Schiller. San Diego, Calif.: San Diego State University Press, 1974.

660 entries. [Published?]

SCHLEGEL, GUSTAAF

1184. Schlegel, Gustaaf. Liste chronologique des ouvrages et opuscules publiés par le Dr. G. Schlegel . . . 1862-1901. Leide: E. J. Brill, 1902. 24 pp.

256 entries.

SCHLEIERMACHER, FRIEDRICH DANIEL ERNST

1185. Tice, Terence N. Schleiermacher Bibliography. With Brief Introductions, Annotations and Index. (Princeton Pamphlets, 12) Princeton, N.J.: Princeton Theological Seminary, 1966. 168 pp.

SCHMAUS, MICHAEL

1186. "Bibliografia del Professor Schmaus," La Ciudad de Dios (Valladolid), vol. 176 (1963), pp. 397-408.

SCHMITT, CARL

1187. Krupa, H. Carl Schmitts Theorie des "Politischen" mit einem Verzeichnis der Schriften Carl Schmitts (Studien und Bibliographien zur Gegenwartsphilosophie, 22). Leipzig: Hirzel, 1937. 47 pp.

SCHNEIDER, HERBERT WALLACE

1188. "Herbert Wallace Schneider. A Bibliography," in Craig Walton and John P. Anton, eds., Philosophy and the Civilizing Arts. Albens, Ohio: Ohio University Press, 1974, pp. 495-504.

SCHNÜRERS, GUSTAV

1189. "Verzeichnis der Schriften Gustav Schnürers," in Gustav Schnurer. Gedächtnisschrift zum 14. December 1942. Freiburg, Switz.: Univ. Buchhandlung 1942. pp. 15-30.

SCHOPENHAUER, ARTHUR. See also 510.

1190. Laban, Ferdinand. Die Schopenhauer-Literatur. Versuch einer chronologischen Uebersicht derselben. Leipzig: F. A. Brockhaus, 1880. 124 pp. Reprinted: New York: Burt Franklin, 1970.

1350 entries.

1191. Laban, Ferdinand. . . .Beitrage zur Schopenhauer-Bibliographie. Erstes Supplement zu der Schrift: "Die Schopenhauer-literatur." Kolozsvár: Svmptibvs Editorvm

1191. (Continued)

Actorvm Comparationis Literarvm Universarvm, [Introd. 1882]. 33 pp.

Contains entries up to 1883.

1192. Grisebach, Eduard. _Edita un Inedita. Schopenhaueriana: eine Schopenhauer-Bibliographie_. Leipzig: F. J. Brockhaus, 1888. 221 pp.

1193. Zoccoli, Ettore. _Della letteratura schopenhaueriana_. Modena: 1898. 36 pp.

About 400 entries.

1194. Baer, Joseph and Co., firm, publishers, Frankfurt am Main. _Schopenhauer-Bibliothek_. _Originalhandschriften Schopenhauers, 166 Bände aus siner privat-Bibliothek, seine Schriften, Briefe und Gespräche, Literatur über ihn_. Frankfurt am Main: 1905. 47 pp.

260 entries.

1195. Wagner, Gustav Friedrich. _Encykolpädisches Register zu Schopenhauer's Werken nebst einem Anhange, der den Abdruck der Dissertation von 1813 Druckfehlerverzeichnisse u. a. m. enthält_. Karlsruhe i. B.: G. Braunsche Hofbuschdr. und Verlag, 1909. 597 pp.

1196. Pfeiffer, K. "Nachträge zur Schopenhauer Bibliographie für die Jahre 1929, 1930 und 1931," "Schopenhauer-Bibliographie für die Jahre 1932, 1933, 1934," _Jahrbuch der Schopenhauer-Gesellschaft_ (Heidelberg), vol. 22 (1935), pp. 353-376.

1197. Kalfs, G. "Schopenhauers bibliographie" in C. A. Emge and O. von Schweinichen, _Gedächtnisschrift für Arthur Schopenhauer zur 150. Wiederkehr seines Geburtstages._ (Philos. Untersuchungen, 6). Berlin: Verlag für Staatswissenschaften und Geschichte, 1938. 224 pp.

1198. Borch, Rudolf. "Nachträge zur Schopenhauer-Bibliographie für die Jahre 1910-1934," _Jahrbuch der Schopenhauer-Gesellschaft_ (Heidelberg), vol. 23 (1936), pp. 359-391.

1199. Borch, Rudolf. "I: Nachträge zur Schopenhauer-Bibliographie für die Jahre 1925-1934. II: Schopenhauer-Bibliographie für das Jahr 1935," _Jahrbuch der Schopenhauer-Geselschaft_ (Heidelberg), vol. 24 (1937), pp. 183-192.

1200. Borch, Rudolf. "Nachträge zur Schopenhauer-Bibliographie für das Jahr 1910-1935, 1936, 1937," _Jahrbuch der Schopenhauer-Geselschaft_ (Heidelberg), vol. 25 (1938), pp. 331-349.

1201. Borch, Rudolf. "Amerikanische Schopenhauer-Ausgaben," Jahrbuch der Schopenhauer-Gesellschaft (Heidelberg), vol. 27 (1940), pp. 112-114.

1202. Borch, Rudolf. "Schopenhauer-Bibliographie 1939," Jahrbuch der Schopenhauer-Gesellschaft (Heidelberg), vol. 27 (1940), pp. 216-217.

1203. Borch, Rudolf. "Nachträge zur Schopenhauer-Bibliographie für das Jahr 1910-1939," Jahrbuch der Schopenhauer-Gesellschaft (Heidelberg), vol. 28 (1941), pp. 291-300.

1204. Borch, Rudolf. "Schopenhauer-Bibliographie für das Jahr 1940," Jahrbuch der Schopenhauer-Gesellschaft (Heidelberg), vol. 28 (1941), pp. 300-302.

1205. Borch, Rudolf. "Nachträge zur Schopenhauer-Bibliographie für das Jahr 1910-40," Jahrbuch der Schopenhauer-Gesellschaft, vol. 29 (1942), pp. 285-293.

1206. Borch, Rudolf. "Schopenhauer-Bibliographie für das Jahr 1941," Jahrbuch der Schopenhauer-Gesellschaft (Heidelberg), vol. 29 (1942), pp. 294-296.

1207. "Schopenhauer-Bibliography für 1957," Schopenhauer-Jahrubch (Kiel), vol. 39 (1958), pp. 207-216.

Schopenhauer-Jahrbuch regularly carries Schopenhauer bibliographies since vol. 1 (1912).

1208. Hūbscher, Arthur. Arthur Schopenhauer und seine Verleger . . . zum 100. Todestag des Philosophen, 21. September 1960 (Bibliothek des Schweizerischen Gutenberg-Museum, Nr. 27). Bern: Schweizerisches Gutenberg Museum; im Buchhandel bei H. Lang, 1960. 30 pp.

1209. Hübscher, Arthur. "Schopenhauer-Bibliographie für 1961," Schopenhauer-Jahrbuch (Frankfurt), vol. 43 (1962), 127-132.

1210. Hübscher, Arthur. "Schopenhauer-Bibliographie für 1962," Schopenhauer-Jahrbuch (Frankfurt), vol. 44 (1963), pp. 195-202.

1211. Hübscher, Arthur. "Schopenhauer-Bibliographie," Schopenhauer-Jahrbuch (Frankfurt), vol. 48 (1967), pp. 190-200. Also: "Nachträge 1966," vol. 49 (1968), pp. 122-131; "Nachträge, 1967," vol. 50 (1969), pp. 117-126; vol. 51 (1970) pp. 165-181; vol. 52 (1971), pp. 163-177; "Nachträge, 1970, 1971," vol. 54 (1973), pp. 153-159, 159, 171.

SCHULTZ, JOHANN HEINRICH

1212. "Bibliographie Johann Heinrich Schultz," in Feestschrift für Prof. Dr. Johann Heinrich Schultz zu seinem 80. Geburstag am 20. Juni 1964. Hamburg: Anthropology Institut der Universität, 1964.

SCHULTZ, JULIUS

1213. Ditz, E. Julius Schultz' "Maschinen-Theorie des Lebens". Unter Heranziehung und mit teilweise wörthlichem Abdruck eines Briefwechsels mit Julius Schultz. Mit einer monographischen Bibliogrpahie Julius Schultz. (Studien und Bibliographien zur Gegenwartsphilosophie, 14). Leipzig: Hirzel, 1935. 120 pp.

SCHWARZ, BALDWIN

1214. "Verzeichnis der Veröffentlichung von Baldwin Schwarz," Zeitschrift für Philosophische Forschungen (Meisenheim am Glan), vol. 21 (1967), pp. 316-318.

SCHWEINICHEN, OTTO VON

1215. Klug, Ulrich. "Verzeichnis der Veröffentlichungen von Otto von Schweinichen," Archiv für Rechts- und Sozialphilosophie (Berlin), vol. 32 (1939), pp. 283-284.

SCIACCA, MICHELE FEDERICO

1216. Schiavone, Michele. L'idealismo di M. F. Sciacca come sviluppo del rosminianismo. Domodossola: S.A.L.E. "Sodolitas," 1957. 276 pp.

"Appendice bibliografica," pp. 119-246.

1217. Ottonello, Pier Paolo. Bibliografia di M. F. Sciacca (Dal 1931 al 1968). Milano: Marzorati, 1969. 552 pp.

SERGIO, ANTÓNIO

1218. "Bibliografía de António Sergio," Vértice (Coimbra), vol. 30 (1970), pp. 568-597.

SIDGWICK, HENRY

1219. "Henry Sidgwick [: a Bibliography]," in George Watson, ed. The New Cambridge Bibliography of English Literature. Cambridge: Cambridge University Press, 1969, vol. 3, cols. 1580-1582.

About 100 entries by and about him.

SIEWERTH, GUSTAV

1220. "Bibliographie Gustav Siewerth," in Innerlichkeit und Erziehung. In Memoriam Gustav Siewerth. Zum Gespräch zwischen Pädagogik, Philosophie und Theologie. Wien: Herder, 1964, pp. 345-356.

SILVA-TAROUCA, AMADEO

1221. "Bibliographie-Amadeo Silva-Tarouca," Zeitschrift für Philosophische Forschung (Meisenheim am Glan), vol. 22 (1968), pp. 459-462.

SIMARD, EMILE

1222. Bonnelly, M. Claude. "Bibliographie de Emile Simard," Laval théologique et philosophique (Quebec), vol. 25 (1969), pp. 168-170.

SIMMEL, GEORGE

1223. Gassen, Kurt. "Simmel-bibliography," in Kurt Gassen and Michael Landmann, eds., Buch des Dankes an Georg Simmel. Berlin: Dunckner und Humbolt, 1958, pp. 309-365.

1224. Wolff, Kurt. H. "Georg Simmel," Praxis (Zagreb), vol. 4 (1968), pp. 404-414.

1225. Malter, Rudolf. "Die Briefe Georg Simmels an den Grafen Hermann Keyserling," Zeitschrift für philosophische Forschung (Meisenheim am Glan), vol. 24 (1970), pp. 295-303.

SIMON, YVES RÉNE

1226. Simon, Anthony O. "Bibliographie de Yves Réne Simon (1923-1968), Revue philosophique de Louvain (Louvain), vol. 67 (1969), pp. 285-304; "Complement 1969-1974," vol. 73 (1975), pp. 362-367.

SINGH, GOBIND

1227. Jagindar Singh. Guru Gobind Singh; a Descriptive Bibliography. Chandigarh: Punjab University, 1967. 260 pp.

SJESTOW, LEO

1228. Ghuys, Walter. "Leo Sjestow, een bio-bibliografische inleiding," Dialoog, vol. 9 (1968-1969), pp. 68-90.

SKIRBEKK, GUNNAR. See 2114.

SKIRBEKK, SIGURD. See 2114.

SKJERUHEÍM, HANS. See 2114.

SMITH, ADAM

1229. Bonar, James. A Catalogue of the Library of Adam Smith. London and New York: Macmillan and Co., 1894. 126 pp. 2nd. ed.: London: Macmillan and Co., 1932; reprinted: New York: A. M. Kelley, 1966.

About 1000 entries. Aims at giving a faithful list of texts and papers known to have belonged to the library of Smith. Second edition contains additions (and portraits, not only of Smith, but also of his mother).

1230. Harvard University. Graduate School of Business Administration. Baker Library. Kress Library of Business and Economics. The Vanderblue Memorial Collection of Smithiana; an Essay by Charles Bullock . . . and a catalogue of the Collection. Boston: Baker Library. Harvard Graduate School of Business Administration, 1939. 68 pp.

Titles listed by short title, some annotations, no index.

1231. Jones, Claude Edward. "Smith's Library: Some Additions," Economic History (London), vol. 4 (1940), pp. 326-328.

1232. Franklin, Burt, and F. G. M. Cordasco. Adam Smith, a Bibliographical Checklist; an International Record of Critical Writings and Scholarship Relating to Smith and Smithian Theory 1876-1950. (Burt Franklin Bibliographical Series, 3). New York: Burt Franklin, 1950. 63 pp.

1233. Mizuta, Hiroshi. Smith's library: a Supplement to Bonar's Catalog. London: Cambridge University Press for the Royal Economic Society, 1967. 153 pp.

SOCRATES

1234. Gomperz, Heinrich. Die Deutsche Litteratur über de Sokratische, Platonische und Aristotelische Philosophie, 1899 und 1900. (Sonderabdruck aus dem Archiv für Geschichte der Philosophie, 15. Band, 4 Heft, 1902- [16. Band, 1.-2. Heft., 1903]). 3 vols. in 1.

1235. Gomperz, H. "Die Deutsche Literatur über die Sokratische, Platonische, und Aristotelische Philosophie, 1901-1904," Archiv für Geschichte der Philosophie (Bonn), vol. 19 (1906), Heft 1-4.

1236. De Magalhaes-Vilhena. Le problème de Socrate: Le Socrate historique et le Socrate de Platon. 1952. 568 pp.

Contains an extensive bibliography on Socrates.

SOLARI, GIOELE

1237. Firpo, L. "Bibliografia degli scritti di Gioele Solari," Memoria dell'Accademia delle Scienze di Torino (Torino), (1972), no. 26, 4 e serie, pp. 63-125.

SOLOMON BEN ISSAC. See RASHI.

SOREL, GEORGES

1238. Delasalle, Paul. "Bibliographie sorelienne," International review for social history (Leiden), vol. 4 (1939), pp. 463-487.

SPALDING, JOHANN JOACHIM

1239. Spalding, Johann Joachim. Catalogi Librorum Specimen. Berolini: 1790. 76 pp.

SPENCER, HERBERT

1240. Turnbull, H.G.D. "[Herbert Spencer:] Bibliography," English Illustrated Magazine (London), vol. 29 (1902), pp. 88, 90.

A checklist.

1241. "Herbert Spencer [: a Bibliography]," in George Watson, ed., The New Cambridge Bibliography of English Literature. Cambridge: Cambridge University Press, 1969, vol. 3, cols. 1583-1592.

About 350 works by and about him.

SPIEGELBERG, HERBERT

1242. "Bibliography of Herbert Spiegelberg's Published Works, 1930-1974," in P. J. Bossert, ed. Phenomenological Perspectives. The Hague: Martinus Nijhoff, 1975, pp. 276-279.

SPINOZA, BENEDICT. See also 86.

1243. Eisler, M. "Die Quellen des Spinozistischen Systems," Zeitschrift für Philosophie und philosophische Kritik (Leipzig), vol. 80 (1882), pp. 250-265.

1244. Frudenthal, Jacob. Die Lebengeschicle Spinoza's in Quellenschriften, Urkunden und nichtamtlichen Nachrichten; mit Unterstüdzung der Königl. [Preussischen Akademie der Wissenschaften]. Leipzig: Veit, 1899. 304 pp.

1245. Baer, Joseph, and Co., firm, publishers, Frankfurt am Main. Spinoza; Katalog einer Sammlung seiner Werke, der Schriften seiner Anhänger und Schüler und der Literatur über ihn, enthaltend u.a. die Spinoza-Bibliothek Herrn Geheimrat Jacob Frudenthal. Frankfurt am Main: Joseph Baer and Co., 1911. 80 pp.

1246. Meijer, Willem. Spinozana 1897-1922, bevattende uittreksels uit de jaarverslagen van den secretaris der vereeniging het Spinozahuis [W. Meijer] Benevens een

1246. (Continued)

levensbericht omtrent Dr. W. Meijer en eene lijst van diens geschriften. (Curis Societatis Spinozanae). Heildelberg: C. Winter, 1922. 143 pp.

1247. Wolf, Abraham. Spinoza; the Library of the Late Prof. Dr. A. Wolf, Head of the Department of the History and Philosophy of Science, University of London. Amsterdam: International Antiquarieat, "Catalogue No. 150," 1950. 106 pp.

1248. Van der Linde, A. Benedictus Spinoza: Bibliografie. Nieuwkoop: B. de Graaf, 1961. 113 pp. Also: 's Gravenhage: M. Nijhoff, 1871.

441 entries. Works by and about Spinoza.

1249. Oko, Adolph S. The Spinoza Bibliography, ed. by Dorothy Oko. (Published under the auspices of the Columbia University Libraries). Boston: G. K. Hall, 1964. 700 pp.

Photo reproductions of about 5,000 cards giving pre-1943 works by, about, or sometimes apparently only mentioning, Spinoza. Arranged by topic. Includes references to 80 bibliographies that somehow deal with Spinoza. A useful and extensive work, but contains much material of doubtful value. No indexes.

1250. Vereeniging "Het Spinozahuis." Bibliotheck. Catalogus van de Bibliotheck der vereeniging Het Spinozahuis te Rijnsburg. Leiden: E. J. Brill, 1965. 59 pp.

1251. Wetlesen, Jon. Spinoza-Bibliografi. Oslo, 1967. 3 v. in 1 (loose-leaf). Also published as: A Spinoza Bibliography 1940-1970. Oslo: Universitetsforlaget, 1968; New York: Humanities Press, 1970. Part I: Primarily 19th and early 20th centuries; Part II: An expansion of Part I; Part III: Influence of Spinoza on others and influences on Spinoza.

A supplement to Oko's bibliography.

1252. De Dijn, H. "Kroniek van de Spinoza-Literatur, 1960-1970" [Chronicle of the Spinoza Literature, 1960-1970] Tijdschrift voor Filosofie (Leuven), vol. 34 (1972), pp. 130-139.

1253. Preposiet, Jean. Bibliographie spinoziste. Répertoire alphabétique. Registre systematique . . . Besançon: Annales Literaries; Paris: Belles Lettres, 1973. 460 pp.

Only part of this work is a bibliography.

SPRANGER, EDUARD

1254. Bosshart, E. Die systematischen Grundlagen der Padagogik Eduard Sprangers. Mit einer monographischen Bibliographie Eduard Sprangers. (Studien und Bibliographien zur Gegenwarts-philosophie). Leipzig: Zirzel, 1935. 180 pp.

1255. Neu, Theodor. Bibliographie Eduard Spranger. Tübingen: M. Niemeyer, 1958. 117 pp.

SRI AUROBINDO. See AUROBINDO GHOSE.

STAMMLER, GERHARD

1256. "Bibliographie Gerhard Stammler," Zeitschrift für philosophische Forschung (Meisenheim am Glan), vol. 22 (1968), pp. 610-613.

STEBBING, L. SUSAN

1257. "Susan Stebbing. Publications," in Philosophical Studies. Essays in Memory of L. Susan Stebbing. London: George Allen and Unwin for the Aristotelian Society, 1948, pp. 155-156.

40 entries: her works.

STEFANINI, LUIGI

1258. Santinello, G. "Bibliografia di e su L. Stefanini," in Scritti in onore di Luigi Stefanini. Padova: Liviana, 1960, pp. 181-203.

STEGMÜLLER, FREDERICK

1259. Palacz, Ryszard. "Supplément au répertoire des Sentences de F. Stegmüller," Mediaevalia Philosophica Polonorum (Warszawa), 1961), no. 9, pp. 46-47.

STEIN, EDITH

1260. Devaux, André-A. "Introduction bibliographique à l'étude d'Edith Stein," Les Etudes philosophiques (Marseille), vol. 11 (1956), pp. 447-450.

STEINER, RUDOLF

1261. Wachsmuth, Guenther. Bibliographie der Werke Rudolf Steiners in Erlänzung zu "Die Geburt der Geisteswissenschaft." Dornach (Schweiz): Philosophisch-Anthroposophischer Verlag am Goetheanum, 1942. 64 pp.

1262. Allen, Paul Marshall. The Writings and Lectures of Rudolph Steiner. A Chronological Bibliography of his Books. New York: Whittier Books, 1956. 140 pp.

1263. Bücherverzeichnis der zur zeit erhältlichen Werke von Rudolph Steiner. Dornach: Rudolph Steiner-Nachlassverwaltung, 1957. 87 pp.

STRAUSS, LEO

1264. Cropsey, Joseph, ed. Ancients and Moderns: Essays on the Tradition of Political Philosophy in Honor of Leo Strauss. New York: Basic Books, 1964. 330 pp.

Contains a bibliography of Strauss' publications.

SUÁREZ, FRANCISCO

1265. De Scorraille, R. François Suárez de la compagnie de Jésus, d'après ses lettres, ses autres écrits inédits et un grand nombre de documents nouveaux. Paris: P. Lethielleux, 1912-1913. 2 vols.

An extensive bibliography.

1266. McCormick, J. J. A Suárezian Bibliography. Chicago: [?] 1937.

1267. Smith, Gerald. "A Suárez Bibliography," in Jesuit Thinkers of the Renaissance, ed. by Gerald Smith. Milwaukee: Marquette University Press, 1939, pp. 227-238.

1268. Iturrioz, Jesús. "Bibliographie suareziènne," Pensamiento (Madrid), vol. 4 (1948), pp. 603-638.

1269. Múgica, Placido. Bibliografía suareciana, con una introd. sobre el estado actual de los estudios por Eleuterio Elorduz. (Publicaciones de la Cátedra Francisco Suárez, 3). Granada: Universidad de Granada, Cátedra Suárez, 1948. 103 pp.

1270. Solá, Francisco de P. Suárez y las ediciones de su obras, monografía bibliografía con ocasión del IV centenario de su nacimiento, 1548-1948. (Colección Filosófica "Lux." Sección IV: Fuentes Históricas y Textes, Clásicos, no. 2.) Barcelona: Editorial Atlántida, 1948. 103 pp.

1271. "Bibliografía suarézíana," Estudios eclesiásticos (Madrid), vol. 22 (1949), pp. 603-671.

Divided according to topics. Covers about 90 works published between 1917 and 1947.

1272. De Ladana, J. A. "El IV centenario del nacimiento del P. Francisco Suárez: bibliografía," Archivo Teológico Granadino (Granada), vol. 12 (1949), pp. 333-361.

SWEDENBORG, EMANUEL

1273. Baer, Joseph, and Co. Frankfurt am Main. Bibliotheca Swedenborgiana. Frankfurt am Main, 1904. 18 pp.

TAGORE, RABINDRANATH

1274. Pinto, O. "Bibliografia tagoriana," in Centenario di Tagore: 1861-1961, (A cura dell' Istituto italiano per il medio ed estremo oriente). Roma: Tip. Julia, 1962.

TALAMO, SALVATORE

1275. Orlando, Pasquale. "Bibliografia di mons. Salvatore Talamo (Napoli 7-10-1844: Roma 12-2-1932), secondo i documenti," Aquinas (Roma), vol. 5 (1962), pp. 404-426.

TALON, OMER. See 1085.

TANDEL, NICHOLAS EMANUEL

1276. Catalogue d'une riche collection de livres spécialement sur la philosophie contemporaine, provenant de la Bibliothèque de feu Nic. Em. Tandel. Louvain: Fonteyn, 1854. 69 pp.

TASSO, TORQUATO. See 325.

TAULER, JOHANNES. See 2101.

TAYLOR, ALFRED EDWARD

1277. Ross, W. David. "A. E. Taylor: Bibliography," Proceedings of the British Academy (London), vol. 31 (1945), pp. 422-424.

His contributions to periodicals and books.

TEILHARD DE CHARDIN, PIERRE

1278. Cuénot, Claude ["Complete List of Works of Teilhard"] in his Pierre Teilhard de Chardin, les grandes étapes de son évolution. Paris: Plon, 1958. 489 pp. Also: English translation of second edition: London: Burns and Oates, 1958, and c. 1964.

Bibliography, pp. i-xli.

1279. Cuénot, Claude, and Yves Vadé. "Oeuvres, livres et principaux articles consacrés à Teilhard de Chardin," in Essais sur Teilhard de Chardin (Recherches et débats, no. 40), Paris: Arthème Fayard, 1962, pp. 97-148.

1280. Coutagne, P. "Teilhard de Chardin (Notices bibliographiques)," Revue des sciences philosophiques et théologiques (Paris), vol. 48 (1964), pp. 160-168.

1281. Cuénot, Claude. Teilhard de Chardin, a Biographical Study. London: Burns and Oates, 1965. 492 pp.

Bibliography of the works of Teilhard de Chardin, pp. 409-482.

1282. De Terra, Helmut. Bibliographie des Deutschsprachigen Schriftums von und über Pierre Teilhard de Chardin, 1955-1964. Frankfurt am Main. "Hrsg. von der Werner Reimers-Stiftung für anthropogenetische Forschung," 1965. 22 pp.

1283. Gentili, Elio. "Pierre Teilhard de Chardin in Italia: bibliografia," La Scuola cattolica (Venegono), vol. 93 (1965), pp. 247-334.

1284. Polgár, László. Internationale Teilhard bibliographie 1955-1965. Freiburg und München: Alber Verlag, 1965. 93 pp.

1285. Fragata, J. "Teilhard de Chardin noticia bibliografica," Revista portugesa de filosofia (Braga), vol. 22 (1966), pp. 287-300.

1286. Poulin, Daniel. Teilhard de Chardin: Essai de bibliographie (1955-1966). Québec: Les Presses de l'Université Laval, 1966. 157 pp.

Lists editions and commentaries and critical work. Short annotations, author index.

1287. Coutagne, Paul. "Chronique teilhardienne. Teilhard et les recherches actuelles sur la philosophie de la nature," Revue des sciences philosophiques et théologiques (Paris), vol. 52 (1968), pp. 303-343.

1288. D'Armagnac, Christian. "Notes bibliographiques: bulletin d'études teilhardiennes," Etudes (Paris), vol. 329 (1969), pp. 449-453.

1289. Almagno, Romano Stephen. Bibliografia teilhardiana. 1955-1970. Firenze: Centro di studio e di ricerca Teilhard de Chardin--Instituto Stensen, 1970. 56 pp.

1290. Coutagne, Paul. "Chronique Teilhardienne," Revue des sciences philosophiques et théologiques (Paris), vol. 54 (1970), pp. 681-715.

Covers fifteen works on "secularization" published 1967-1970.

1291. D'Armagnac, Christian. "Bulletin d'études Teilhardiennes," Etudes (Paris), vol. 332 (1970), pp. 615-622.

1292. Jarque i Jutglar, Joan E. Bibliographie génerale des oeuvres et articles sur Pierre Teilhard de Chardin parus jusqu'a fin décembre 1969. Fribourg: Editions Universitaires, 1970. 206 pp.

1293. Baudry, Gerard Henry. Pierre Teilhard de Chardin; bibliographie (1881-1972). (Mémoires et travaux des Facultés catholiques de Lille, fasc. 61). Lillie: Facultés catholiques, 1972. 113 pp.

1294. Figueiredo, Manuel Versos. "Nota bibliografica sobre Teilhard," Revista portuguesa de filosofia (Braga), vol. 28 (1972), pp. 355-369.

Evaluates recently published works on Teilhard de Chardin.

1295. Rezek, Romano. Les premières 15 années: Bibliographie française sur Teilhard de Chardin. São Paulo: Instituto Social Morumbi, 1973. 358 pp.

TEIXEIRA DE PASCOAES (i.e., PEREIRA TEIXEIRA DE VASCOACELLOS, JOAQIM)

1296. Garcia, Mario. "Teixeira de Pascoaes," Revista Portuguesa de Filosofia (Braga), vol. 29 (1973), pp. 113-122.

THÉRY

1297. Lechène, M. L. Bibliographie du T. R. P. Théry, o.p. Oran: Heintz, 1942. 95 pp.

THÉVANAZ, PIERRE

1298. Thévenaz, Pierre. L'Homme et sa raison. Neuchâtel: Baconnière, 1956. 192 pp.

Contains a complete bibliography of the works of Thévenaz.

THOMASSIN, LOUIS

1299. Clair, Pierre. Louis Thomassin (1619-1695). Etude biographique et bibliographique avec 20 lettres et 2 textes inédits. (Coll. Le Mouvement des idées au XVIIe siècle, 1). Paris: Presses universitaires de France, 1964. 156 pp.

THYSSEN, JOHANNES

1300. "Verzeichnis der Schriften Johannes Thyssen," in Klaus Hartmann, ed., Lebendiger Realismus, Festschrift für Johannes Thyssen. Bonn: H. Bouvier , 1962, pp. 249-257.

TITZE, HANS

1301. "Bibliographie von Hans Titze". Zeitschrift für philosophiche Forschung (Meisenheim am Glan), vol. 27 (1973), pp. 615-616.

TOLAND, JOHN

1302. Hinemann, F. H. "Prolegomena to a Toland Bibliography," Notes and Queries (London), vol. 185 (1943),

1302. (Continued)

pp. 182-186.

TOMMASEO, NICCOLÒ

1303. Valente, Umberto. "Bibliografia di Niccolò Tommaseo," Archivo storico per la Dalmazia (Roma), 1939, pp. 83-120, 151-160.

Review: Anon. Rivista rosminiana di filosofia et di coltura (Pallanza), vol. 34 (1940), p. 104.

TOYNBEE, ARNOLD J.

1304. Rule, J. C. and B. Steven Crosby. "Bibliography of Works on Arnold J. Toynbee, 1946-1960," History and Theory (Middletown, Conn.), vol. 4 (1965), pp. 212-233.

TRANOY, KNUT ERIK

1305. Flo, Olav. Bibliography of the Writings of Knut Erik Tranoy 1946-69 (Filosofiske bibliografier, Nr. 7). Oslo, Universitetsforlaget, 1971. 19 pp.

TREYER, HANS

1306. Willers, Dietrich. "Verzeichnis der Schriften von Hans Treyer," Darmstadt: Wissenschaftliche Buchgesellschaft, 1966. 10 pp.

TYRELL, GEORGE

1307. Loome, Thomas Michael. "A Bibliography of the Published Writings of George Tyrell (1861-1909)," Heythrop Journal (London), vol. 10 (1969), pp. 280-314. "Supplement," vol. 11 (1970), pp. 161-169.

UNAMUNO Y JUGO, MIGUEL DE

1308. Malavassi V., Guillermo. "Bibliografía de Unamuno aparecida en Costa Rica," Revista de filosofía de la universidad de Costa Rica (San José), vol. 3 (1961), pp. 219-230.

1309. Ibáñez de García Blanco, L. "Bibliografía unamuniana," *Cuadernos de la Cátedra Miguel de Unamuno* (Salamanca), vol. 19 (1969), pp. 105-107; vol. 20 (1970), pp. 133-138; vol. 21 (1971), pp. 165-171.

1310. Valdés, Mario J. and María Elena de Valdés. *An Unamuno Source Book: A Catalogue of Readings and Acquisitions with an Introductory Essay on Unamuno's Dialectical Inquiry.* Buffalo, N.Y.: University of Toronto Press, 1973. 305 pp.

Contains a catalog of the 5,700 volumes in Unamuno's library and a guide to his readings.

UVAROV, ALEKSI͡EĬ SERGI͡EEVĪCH, GRAF. See 2118, 2214.

VAIHINGER, HANS

1311. Weser, Adolf. "Bibliographie Hans Vaihingers," in Stephanie Willrodt, *Semifiktionen und Vollfiktionen in Vaihingers Philosophie des Als Ob.* (Studien und Bibliographien zur Gegenwartsphilosophie, 7). Leipzig: Hirzel, 1934. 139 pp.

VALLES, FRANCISCO

1312. Ortega, Eusebio, and Benjamín Marcos. *Francisco de Valles (el Divino). Biografía, datos, bibliograficos.* Madrid: Imprenta Clasíca Española, 1914. 189 pp.

Bibliography, pp. 87-161.

VAN DEN BERG, J. H.

1313. Van den Berg, J. H. "Bibliography of Selected Works to Date by J. H. Van den Berg," *Humanitas* (Pittsburgh), vol. 7 (1971), pp. 411-412.

VAN DEN EYNDE, DAMIANI

1314. "De Vita et Scriptis R. P. Damiani Van den Eynde O.F.M.," *Antonianum* (Roma), vol. 38 (1963), pp. 224-229.

VANDERWELDE, EMILE

1315. Van Langenhove, Fernand. "Notice sur Emile Vanderwelde, membre de l'academie," Academie Royale de Belgique. Annuaire pour 1968. Koninklijke Academie van Belgie. Jaarboek voor 1968 (Bruxelles), vol. 134, pp. 91-130.

Bibliography, pp. 124-130.

VAS FERREIRA, CARLOS

1316. Montevideo. Universidad. Facultad de numanidades y ciencias. Bibliografía de Carlos Vas Ferreira. 1962. 14 pp.

VECCHIO, GIORGIO DEL. See DEL VECCHIO, GIORGIO.

VERNEKOHL, WILHELM

1317. Wust, Peter. Gesammette Werke herausgeben von Wilhelm Vernekohl Bd. VIII. Leben und Werke. Biograph. Notizen die Philosophie, Bibliographie. Münster in Westfalen: Regensberg, 1967. 520 pp.

VIANA, AMORIM

1318. de Sá, Vítor. "Amorim Viana. Ensaio bio-bibliográfico," Miscelãnea de estudios a Joaquim de Carvalho (Figueira da Foz), no. 3 (1960), pp. 303-336.

VICO, GIAMBATTISTA

1319. Croce, Benedetto. Bibliografia Vichiana. Napoli: Riccardo Ricciardi, 1947. 2 vols. 1051 pp. Other editions: 1904, 1911. Material in the 1947 edition appeared as supplements to the earlier one. Supplements: 1 and 2: Atti della Accademia pontaniana (Napoli), vols. 37 and 40; 3: La critica, rivista di letteratura, storia e filosofia, vols. 15 (1917)-19 (1921); 4 and 5: Atti della Reale accademia di scienze morali e politiche (Napoli), vols. 51 and 55; 6: in G. F. Finetti, Difensa dell' antorità della Sacra Scrittura contro Giambattista Vico, pp. 95-108; 7: Rivista di filosofia (Milano) n.s. vol. 1 (1940).

About 1000 entries with long, long comments. Name and subject indexes.

1320. Cione, Edmondo. "Cinquant'anni di studi vichiani," Rassegna di scienze filosofiche (Napoli), vol. 14 (1961), pp. 285-304.

1321. Chaix-Ruy, Jules. J. B. Vico et les âges de l'-humanité. Presentation, choix de textes, bibliographie. (Philosophes de tous les temps, 39). Paris: Seghers, 1967. 191 pp.

1322. Gianturco, Elio. A Selective Bibliography of Vico Scholarship (1948-1968). (Published as a Supplement to Forum Italicum, 1968.) Firenze: Grafica Toscana, 1968. 104 pp.

1323. Guerrieri, Guerriera. Mostra bibliografica e documentaria [: Giambattista Vico]. Napoli: L'Arte tipografica, 1968. 79 pp. plus plates.

246 annotated entries. Supplements the Croce bibliography. Indexes.

1324. Olivier, Paul. "Eléments de bibliographie vichienne en France il centenario vichiano in America--un fascicolo del Forum italicum," Rivista di studi crociani (Napoli), vol. 5 (1968), pp. 422-437.

1325. Olivier, Paul. "Le tricentenaire de Vico en France," Rivista di studi crociani (Napoli), vol. 7 (1970), pp. 187-195.

1326. Donzelli, Maria. Contributo alla bibliografia vichiana (1948-1970) (Studi vichiani, 9). Napoli: Guida, 1973. 110 pp.

1327. Parente, Alfredo. "La bibliografia vichiana," Rivista de Studi Crociani (Napoli), vol. 10 (1973), pp. 491-493.

VISCHER, FRIEDRICH THEODOR

1328. Hensard, O. Fr.-Th. Vischer étude bibliographique. Paris: Felix Alcan, 1921. 35 pp.

References to about 200 of Vischer's works.

VIVEKĀNANDA

1329. Herbert, Jean. Swāmi Vivekānanda. Bibliographie des oeuvres parues dans les langues européennes. Paris: Maisonneuve, 1938. 29 pp.

VIVES, JUAN LUIS

1330. Bonilla y San Martín, Adolfo. Luis Vives y la filosofía del Renacimiento. Madrid: L. Rubio, 1929. 8 vols.

Contains a Vives bibliography.

1331. Barcelona. Biblioteca Central. Catalogo de la Exposición Bibliografíca celebrada con motivo del IV centenario de la muerte de Luis Vives (15 mayo-15 junio 1940). Barcelona: Casa Provincial de Caridas, Imprenta Escuela, 1940. 112 pp.

1332. Batlle y Vázquez, Manuel. Introducíon, programa y bibliografía para un curso monográfico sobre el filósofo español Juan Luis Vives, Murcia: Facultas de filosofía y letras, 1942. [n.p.].

Reviewed by González Muela, J. in Rivista Bibliografía Nacional (Madrid), Aug. 1942.

VOLLENHOVEN, D. H. THEODORE

1333. Bril, K. A. "A Selected and Annotated Bibliography of D. H. Th. Vollenhoven," Philosophia Reformata (Kampen, Neth.), vol. 38 (1973), pp. 212-228.

Complete bibliography of his works since 1961, and most important ones since 1918, also work about him.

VOLTAIRE, FRANÇOIS-MARIE AROUET DE

1334. Wallich, Paul, and Hans von Müller. Die deutsche Voltaire-Literatur des Achtzehnten Jahrhunderts, annalistisch und systemtisch Verzeichnet; bibliographische Skizze. Berlin: Liebheit und Thiesen, 1921. 78 pp.

1335. Peignot, Gabriel. Recherchés sur les ouvrages de Voltaire. Paris: Chez les Marchands de Nouveautés, 1817. 68 pp.

1336. Quérard, Joseph Marie. Bibliographie voltairienne. Paris: Firmin Didot frères, 1842. 184 pp.

250 entries.

1337. I͡Azykov, Dimitriĭ Dmitrievich. Vol'ter v russkoĭ literaturíe (Istoriko-bibliograficheskii etiud [Voltaire in

1337. (Continued)

Russian Literature (an historical-Bibliographical study) [In Russian]]. St. Petersburg: V. I. Gratsianskii, 1879. 39 pp.

1338. Bengesco, Georges. Voltaire: Bibliographie de ses oeuvres. Paris: Emile Perrin, 1882-1885. 5 vols.

About 2500 annotated entries giving editions of his works.

1339. Malcolm, Jean. Table de la bibliographie de Voltaire par Bengesco. (Publications de l'Institut et Musée Voltaire. Série d'études, 1). Genève: Institut et Musée Voltaire, 1953. 127 pp.

To accompany Bengesco's bibliography. Table of titles, and [Table des incipit].

1340. Besterman, Theodore. Quelques éditions anciennes de Voltaire inconnues à Bengesco. Genève: [n.p.], 1954. 134-204 pp.

1341. Brussels. Bibliothèque Royale de Belgique. Collection voltairienne du comte de Launoit. Bruxelles: 1955. 131 pp.

1342. Alekseev, M. P., and Tatiana N. Kopreeva. Bibliothèque de Voltaire: catalogue des livres. (Académie des Sciences de l'URSS: Institut de Littérature Russe). Moscow: Editiones de l'Academie des Sciences de l'URSS, 1961. 1171 pp.

1343. Barr, Mary Margaret Harrison. A Century of Voltaire Study; a Bibliography of Writings on Voltaire, 1825-1925. New York: B. Franklin, 1972. 123 pp. Reprint of Institute of French Studies 1929 ed. supplemented by her Quarante années d'études voltairiennes. Bibliographie analytique des livres et articles sur Voltaire, 1925-1965. Paris: Librairie Armand Colin, 1968. 212 pp.

About 2200 entries. Extensive and annotated. Index. The supplement includes additions for 1926-1940 published in Modern Language Notes, vol. 50 (1935); pp. 440-441, also 1933, 1936.

WALZER, RICHARD

1344. Kleinknecht, Angelika. "List of published works of Richard Walzer," in S. M. Stern, ed., Islamic philosophy and the Classical Tradition. Oxford: Bruns Cassirer, 1972, pp. 5-16.

WANG YANG-MING

1345. Chan, Wing-tsit. "Wang Yang-ming: Western Studies and an Annotated Bibliography," Philosophy East and West (Honolulu), vol. 22 (1972), pp. 75-92.

WARBURTON, WILLIAM

1346. Evans, A. W. ["William Warburton Bibliography"], in his Warburton and the Warburtonians. London: Oxford University Press, 1932, pp. 294-306.

WARD, JAMES

1347. Titchener, E. B. and W. S. Foster. "A List of the Writings of Ward," The Monist (London), vol. 36 (1926), pp. 170-176.

WASHBURN, M. F.

1348. Dallenbach, K. M. "A Bibliography of the Writings of M. F. Washburn," American Journal of Psychology (Ithaca, N.Y.), vol. 53 (1940), pp. 19-21.

WATSON, JOHN

1349. "Bibliography of Publications by Professor John Watson," in Philosophical Essays Presented to John Watson (Publications of the Faculty of Arts in Queen's University). Kingston, Canada: Queens University, 1922, pp. 343-346.

WEBER, MAX

1350. Mettler, A. Max Weber und die philosophische Problematik in unserer Zeit. Mit einer Bibliographie der Arbeiten über Max Weber (Studien und Bibliographien zur Gegenwartsphilosophie). Leipzig: Hirzel, 1934. 162 pp.

1351. Gerth, H., and H. I. Gerth. "Bibliography on Max Weber," Social Research (New York), vol. 16 (1949), pp. 70-89.

1352. Keller, Willy. <u>Alt Bundesrat Prof. Dr. Max Weber zum 60. Geburtstag am 2. August 1957; biographische Daten und bibliographsches Verzeichnis seiner wichtigsten Publikationen</u>. Bern: Schweizerischer Gewerkschaftsbund, 1957. 31 pp.

1353. Baba, Ako. <u>Makkusu Uēbā bunken mokuroku [Bibliography of Max Weber's writings</u> [In Japanese]]. Tokyo: Eruga, 1966. 149 pp.

1354. Amano, Keitarō. <u>Nihon Makkusu Bēbā Shoshi</u> [<u>Japanese bibliography of Max Weber's writings, 2nd ed</u>. [In Japanese]]. Tokyo: Sinsensha, 1972. 162 pp.

WEIL, ERIC

1355. Weil, Eric. "Bibliographie d'Eric Weil," <u>Archives de philosophie</u> (Paris), vol. 33 (1970), pp. 605-622.

WEIL, SIMONE

1356. Little, Janet Patricia. <u>Simone Weil: A Bibliography</u> (Research Bibliographies and Checklists, no. 5). London: Grant and Cutler, 1973. 91 pp.

WEINBERG, JULIUS R.

1357. Hay, William H. "A Bibliography of the Writings of Julius R. Weinberg," <u>Journal of the History of Philosophy</u> (San Diego, Calif.), vol. 10 (1972), pp. 82-85.

WEISCHEDEL, WILHELM

1358. Brumm, Dieter. "Bibliographie Wilhelm Weischedel (zusammengestellt für den 60. Geburtstag w. Weischelels . . ." <u>Zeitschrift für philosophische Forschung</u> (Meisenheim am Glan), vol. 19 (1965), pp. 713-720.

WEISS, AURÉLIU

1359. Weiss, Dimitri. "Auréliu Weiss, critique dramatique et esthéticien du théâtre: essai de bibliographie 1908-1970," <u>Revue de l'Universite d'Ottawa</u> (Ottawa), vol. 45 (1975), pp. 117-125.

WEISS, PAUL

1360. Getrich, Richard J. "Bibliography of Paul Weiss's Publications," Review of Metaphysics (Washington), vol. 25 (1971-1972), supp. 5-7, pp. 166-177.

WEISWEILER, HEINRICH

1361. "Verzeichnis der von Heinrich Weisweiler S. J. verfassten Aufsätze und Bücher," Scholastik (Freiburg in Bremen), vol. 40 (1965), pp. 241-243.

WENDT, DR. G.

1362. Baer, Joseph, and Co., firm, booksellers, Frankfurt am Main. Philosophie. Enthaltend einen Teil der Bibliothek des Dr. G. Wendt. Frankfurt am Main, 1913. 195 pp.

4897 titles.

WHITEHEAD, ALFRED NORTH

1363. Lowe, Victor, and R. C. Baldwin. "Bibliography of Writings of Alfred North Whitehead to Nov. 1941 (with Selected Reviews)," in P. A. Schilpp, ed., The Philosophy of Alfred North Whitehead. Evanston and Chicago: Northwestern University Press, 1941, pp. 701-725. Second edition: ". . . to January 3, 1951 . . ." New York: Open Court, 1951, pp. 745-778.

1364. Ruybinx, J. "Whitehead: Une bibliographie," Revue internationale de philosophie (Bruxelles), vol. 15 (1961), pp. 267-277.

1365. Parker, Franklin. "Alfred North Whitehead, 1861-1947, a Partial Bibliography," Bulletin of Bibliography and Dramatic Index (Boston), vol. 23 (1961), pp. 90-93.

1366. Stokes, W. E. "A Select and Annotated Bibliography of Whitehead," The Modern Schoolman (St. Louis, Mo.), vol. 39 (1961-1962), pp. 135-151.

About 225 entries with occasional annotations.

1367. Kline, George L. "Bibliography of Writings by and about Alfred North Whitehead in Languages other than English," in William Reese and Eugene Freeman, Process and Divinity. La Salle, Ill.: Open Court Publishing Co., 1964, pp. 593-609.

1368. Usai, Roberto. "Nota bibliografica [A. N. Whitehead] Aut-Aut (Milano), no. 90 (1965), pp. 85-89.

1369. Reeves, Gene, and David Griffin. Bibliography of Secondary Literature on Alfred North Whitehead (Process Studies, vol. 1 (1971), no. 4). Claremont, Calif.: Process Studies, 1971. 88 pp.

WIENER, PHILIP P.

1370. Shin, Kee Soo. "Writings of Professor Philip P. Wiener," Journal of the History of Ideas (New York), vol. 33 (1972), pp. 358-364.

WILLIAM OF AUXERRE

1371. St. Pierre, Jules A. "The Theological Thought of William of Auxerre. An Introductory Bibliography," Recherches de theologie ancienne et medievale (Louvain), vol. 33 (1966), pp. 147-155.

WILLIAM OF CONCHES

1372. Grabmann, Martin. Handschriftliche Forschungen und Mitteilungen zum Schrifttum des Wilhelm von Conches und zur Bearbeitungen seiner naturwissenschaftlichen Werke. München: Verlag der Bayerischen Akadamie der Wissenschaften, 1935. 57 pp.

WILLIAM OF OCKHAM

1373. "Bibliographische Studien über W. von stet Occam," Archivum Franciscanum Historicum (Quaraechi), vol. 6 (1913), pp. 209-233, 439-465, 654-669.

1374. Baudry, L. Guillaume d'Occam, sa vie, ses oeuvres, ses idées sociales et politiques. Vol. I. L'Homme et les oeuvres. Paris: Vrin, 1949. 317 pp.

1375. Heynck, Valens. "Ockham-literatur, 1919-1949," Franziskanische Studien (Münster), vol. 32 (1950), pp. 164-183.

1376. Reilly, James P. "Ockham Bibliography: 1950-1967," Franciscan Studies (St. Bonaventure, N.Y.), vol. 28 (1968), pp. 197-214.

1376. (Continued)

Divided according to topics. Continues Heynck's Ockham bibliography.

1377. Pernoud, Mary Anne. "Tradition and Innovation in Ockham's Theory of the Possibility of Other Worlds [Selected Bibliography]," Antonianum (Roma), vol. 48 (1973), pp. 229-233.

WILSON, JOHN COOK

1378. Wilson, John Cook. Statement and Inference, with Other Philosophical Papers . . . Edited from the Mss. . . . by A. S. L. Farquharson. Oxford: The Clarendon Press, 1926. 2 vols. Also: Corrected ed., 1969.

"List of published works and contributions to reviews," pp. lxvi-lxxii.

WIRTH, WILHELM

1379. Moede, Walter. "Schriften von Wilhelm Wirth," Archiv für die gesamte Psychologie (Leipzig), vol. 97 (1936), pp. 209-213.

WITTGENSTEIN, LUDWIG

1380. Fann, K. T. "Wittgenstein Bibliography," International Philosophical Quarterly (Bronx, N.Y.), vol. 7 (1967), pp. 311-339.

1381. Borgis, Ilona. Index zu Ludwig Wittgensteins "Tractatus-Logico-Philosophicus" und Wittgenstein-Bibliographie. Freiburg: K. Alber, 1968. 112 pp.

1382. Fann, K. T. Wittgenstein's Philosophy of Science. Oxford: Basil Blackwell; Berkeley: University of California Press, 1969.

Contains bibliography bringing the above 1967 International Philosophical Quarterly Bibliography up to date.

1383. Fann, K. T. "Supplement to the Wittgenstein Bibliography," Revue Internationale de Philosophie (Bruxelles), vol. 23 (1969), pp. 363-370.

1384. Wright, Georg Henrik von. "The Wittgenstein Papers," Philosophical Review (Ithaca, N.Y.), vol. 78 (1969), pp. 483-503.

An annotated catalogue of all the manuscripts and typescripts of Wittgenstein's philosophical works.

1385. Vera, Francisco. "Bibliography [on Wittgenstein's Tractatus Logico-Philosophicus]," in Sobre el Tractatus Logico-Philosophicus (Teorema, 1972, numero monográfico). Valencia: Universidad de Valencia, 1972, pp. 153-166.

WOLF, CHRISTIAN. See 1994.

WOLTER, ALLAN BERNARD

1386. "The Writings of Fr. Allan Bernard Wolter, O.F.M. A Bibliography," Duns Scotus philosophical association (?), vol. 28 (1964), pp. iii-v.

WOODGER, JOSEPH HENRY

1387. Woodger, Michael. "Publications by Joseph Henry Woodger," in Form and Strategy in Science. Studies Dedicated to Joseph Henry Woodger on the Occasion of his Seventieth Birthday. Dordrecht: D. Reidel, 1964, pp. 473-476.

WRIGHT, G. H. VON

1388. Flo, Olav. Bibliography of the Writings of George Henrik von Wright, 1938-1966. Helsingfors: 1967. 32 ll.

WUNDT, WILHELM

1389. Wundt, Eleonore. Wilhelm Wundts werk; ein Verzeichnis seiner sämtlichen Schriften. (Abhandlungen der Sächs. Staatl. Forschungsinstitute. Forschungsinstitut für Psychologie, no. 28). München: C. H. Beck, 1927. 77 l.

1390. Flo, Olav. Bibliografi over Egil A. Wyllers Forfatterskap 1945-1969. Bergen: Forf., Universitets-Biblioteket i Bergen, 1970. 22 l.

XENOPHON

1391. British Museum. Department of Printed Books. Cata log of Printed Books. Xenophon. London, 1883. 28 cols.

ZAMBONI, GIUSEPPE

1392. Zambonini Corona, Olga. "La Posizione di Zamboni in rapporto alla filosofia presente," in Studi sul pensiero di Giuseppe Zamboni, Milano: Marzorati, 1957, pp. 689-701.

ZELTNER, HERMANN

1393. Hossfeld, Knut. "Bibliographie Hermann Zeltner," Zeitschrift fur philosophische Forschung (Schlehdorf am Kochelsee; Meisenheim am Glan), vol. 27 (1973), pp. 453-460.

ZOCHER, RUDOLF

1394. Meyer, B. "Kurze Bibliographie Rudolf Zocher (Buchveoffentlichungen und Aufsätze)," in Wilhelm Arnold and Hermann Zeltner, eds., Tradition und Kritik. Festschrift für Rudolf Zocher zum 80. Geburtstag, Stuttgart-bad Cannstatt: Friedrich Fromann Verlag, 1967, pp. 351-352.

ZUMEL Y BUSTILLO, FRANCISCO

1395. Placer, Gumersindo. "Bibliografía del teologo mercedario Fray Francisco Zumel y Bustillo," Estudios (Madrid), vol. 21 (1965), pp. 21-68.

SUBJECT BIBLIOGRAPHIES

ABORTION. See also 2254.

1396. Clouser, K. Danner, and Arthur Zucker. Abortion and Euthanasia: an Annotated Bibliography. Philadelphia: Society for Health and Human Values, 1974. 32 pp.

About 300 entries on abortion and 135 on euthanasia. Each entry is summarized in about 100 words. Very helpful.

ADVENT MAGAZINE

1397. Manmohan Reddy, Vedre. Subject-Index to the Advent, 1944-1972. Hyderabad: Institute of Human Study [Distributors: Sri Aurobindo Books Distribution Agency, Pondicherry, 1973]. 39 pp.

Previously published in the Advent. Includes articles by Aurobindo Ghose.

AESTHETICS. See also 278, 501, 649, 908, 945, 1359, 1403, 1658, 1974, 2048, 2080, 2158.

1398. Herwig, Johann Just. Grundriss der eleganten Literatur. Würzburgh: in Verlag der Gnädiget Privilegirten Riennerischen Buchhandlung, 1774.

1399. Koller, J. Entwurf zur Geschichte und Literatur der Aesthetik (besonders in Deutschland) von Baumgarten bis auf die neueste Zeit. Regensburg: Montag und W.: 1799.

1400. Bibliothek der Schönen Wissenschaften und der freyen Künste (Leipzig), vol. 1 (1757)-12 (1806). From 1772: New bibliothek der . . . [etc.]; Successor: Briefe die neueste (Deutsche) literatur betreffend (1759-1765).

1401. Deberle, A. "Les Historiens de l'art," L'Année philosophique (Paris), vol. 2 (1868), pp. 426-468.

1402. Menard, R. J. "Les Théoriciens de l'art," L'Année philosophique (Paris), vol. 1 (1868), pp. 363-424.

1403. South Kensington Museum. London. National Art Museum. Universal Catalog of Books on Art. London, 1870. 2 vols. Reprint: New York: Burt Franklin, 1963.

1404. "Bibliography of Works Published in Germany on Aesthetics and the Philosophy of Art," in W. F. Hegel, Esthétique. Traduction française. Deuxième édition par Ch. Bénard. Paris: Germer-Baillière, 1875. 2 vols.

1405. Vinet, Ernest. Bibliographie méthodique et raisonnée des beaux-arts: esthétique et histoire de l'art. ("Pub. sous les auspices du Ministère de l'instruction publique, des cultes et des beaux-artes"). Paris: Firmin-Didot frères, fils et cie, 1874-1877. 2 vols. [No more published].

1406. Gracklauer, O. Verzeichniss der besten Schriften über Kunstliteratur, welche von 1866-1881 in deutschen Buchhandel erschienen sind. Leipzig: 1881. 16 pp.

1407. Katalog der Bibliothek des K. K. Österreichischen Museums für Kunst und Industrie. Wien: 1883. 583 pp.

1408. Gazley, Charles Mills, and F. N. Scott. A Guide to the Literature of Aesthetics. Berkeley: University of California, 1890. 116 pp. Reprinted: New York: Burt Franklin, 1974.

About 1300 entries arranged according to topic. Contains much non-philosophical work on the arts.

1409. Lipps, Theodor. "Aesthetischer Litteraturbericht," Philosophische Monatshefte (Berlin), vol. 26 (1890), pp. 17-42, 169-201, 323-346; vol. 27 (1891), pp. 161-182, 546-572.

1410. Dobbert, E., and W. Grohmann. Katalog der Bibliothek der Königlichen Akademie der Künste der Berlin. Berlin: 1893. 576 pp.

1411. Bray, L. Du Beau. Essai sur l'origine et l'evolution du sentiment esthétique. Paris: Alcan, 1902.

Contains bibliographical remarks at the beginning.

1412. Vurgey [i.e. M. Bouillot]. Bibliotheca Aesthetica. Répertoire général des travaux d'esthétique (Bibliographia Universalis). Bruxelles: Rue du Musée, 1908. 102 pp.

Arranged alphabetically by authors' names. Subject index.

1413. Turmarkin, Anna. "Berichte über die deutsche asthetische Literatur aus den Jahren 1900-1905," Archiv für Systematische Philosophie (und Soziologie) (Berlin), vol. 11 (1905), pp. 221-244; 359-386; 499-527. Also: 1905-1910: vol. 16 (1910), pp. 409-426.

1414. Schmied-Kowarzik, Walther. "Sammelbericht über das ästhetische Schrifttum der Jahre 1913 und 1914," Zeitschrift für Philosophie und philosophische Kritik (Leipzig), vol. 161 (1916), pp. 240-249.

1415. Schmied-Kowarzic, Walther. "Sammelbericht über das ästhetische Schriftum. Nachtrag 1914; 1915; erster Teil 1916," Zeitschrift für philosophie und Philosophischen Kritik (Leipzig), vol. 165 (1918), pp. 189-207.

1416. Moustoxydēs, Theodosios Mauroeidēs. Bibliographie générale de l'esthétique francaise des origines à 1914. Paris: E. Champion, 1920.

About 1400 entries.

1417. Draper, J. W. Eighteenth Century English Aesthetics; a Bibliography. Heidelberg: Winter, 1931. 140 pp. Reprinted: New York: Octagon Books, 1968. Supplement: Tempelman, W. D. "Contributions to the Bibliography of Eighteenth-Century Aesthetics," Modern Philosophy (Chicago), vol. 30 (1933), pp. 309-316.

1418. Hammond, William A. A Bibliography of Aesthetics and of the Philosophy of the Fine Arts from 1900 to 1932. Revised and Enlarged Edition. New York: Longmans, Green, and Co., 1934. 205 pp. Originally published as a supplement to the May, 1933, issue of the Philosophical Review. Reprinted: New York: Russell and Russell, 1967.

2191 entries. Annotations. Name index. By topic. Good for the period covered.

1419. Chandler, A. R. A Bibliography of Experimental Aesthetics 1865-1932. (Ohio State University, Bureau of Education Research Mineographs, no. 1). Columbus, Ohio: The Ohio State University, 1933. 25 l. Revised as: Chandler, A. R. and Edward N. Barnhart. A Bibliography of Psychological and Experimental Aesthetics, 1864-1937. London: Cambridge University Press, 1938. 190 pp.

1420. Pinilla, Norberto. Bibliografía de estética. Santiago, Chile: Edit. M. Barros Borgoño, 1939. 64 pp. Also in: Boletín de educaión fisica (Santiago), vol. 6 (1939), pp. 854-864.

About 500 entries.

1421. Barnhart, E. N. "Bibliography of Aesthetic Theory, Criticism and Psychology of Art," Journal of Aesthetics and Art Criticism (New York), vol. 1 (1941), pp. 140-148.

1422. "Schriftenverzeichnis," Zeitschrift für Aesthetik und allgemeine Kunstwissenschaft (Stuttgart), vol. 1 (1906)-37 (1943).

1423. "Bibliographie d'esthétique (1950)," Revue d'asthétique (Paris), vol. 5 (1952), pp. 71-110, 117-206.

1424. Tomas, Vincent. "Some Recent Volumes on the Arts," Philosophy and Phenomenological Research (Buffalo), vol. 11 (1950-1951), pp. 221-227.

1425. Bense, Max [et al.]. Augenblick. Aesthetica, Philosophica, Polemica. (Baden-Baden), vol. 1 (1955)-5 (1961).

1426. Gesamteuropäisches Studienwerk e. V. Bibliothek. Auswahlverzeichnis. 12: Literatur unserer Bibliothek zur Themengruppe: Bildende und darstellen de Kunst, Musik im sowjetkommunistischen Einflussbereich. Vlotho/Weser: Gesamteuropäisches Studienwerk, 1958.

1427. México (City). Universidad nacional. Instituto de investigaciones estéticas. Bibliografía de los investigadores (Supplemento núm. 2 del núm. 30 de los Anales de Instituto de investigaciones estéticas) México, 1961. 233 pp.

1428. Sakharova, Eugeniia Maihailovna. Osnovy marksistko-leninskoĭ èstetiki [The Foundations of Marxist-Leninist Aesthetics [In Russian]]. Moscow: Iskusstvo 1961. 41 pp.

1429. Hungerland, H. "Selective Current Bibliography for Aesthetics and Related Fields. January 1, 1958-December 31, 1958," Journal of Aesthetics and Art Criticism (Baltimore), vol. 17 (1958-1959), pp. 539-556. "January 1, 1959-December 31, 1959," vol. 18 (1959-1960), pp. 542-558; "January 1, 1960-December 31, 1960," vol. 19 (1960-1961), pp. 499-511; "January 1, 1961-December 31, 1961," vol. 20 (1961-1962), pp. 475-491.

1430. Apresian, Zoriĭ Grantovich. Èstetika, 1956-1960 [Aesthetics, 1956-1960 [In Russian]]. Moscow: Vseros teatral'noe ob-vo, 1963. 259 pp.

1431. Manova, Nadezhda Vasileva. Vŭprosi na marksistko-leninskata estetika i esteticheskoto vuzpitanie; bibliografski ukazatel [Questions of Marxist-Leninst Aesthetics and Aesthetic Education: A Bibliographical Index [In Bulgarian]]. Sofia: Nauka i izkustvo, 1963. 133 pp.

1432. México (City). Universidad nacional. Instituto de investigaciones estéticas. Catálogos de las exposiciones de la antiqua Academia de San Carlos de México, 1850-1898. Ed. de Manuel Romero de Terreros. México: Imprenta universitaria, 1963. 690 pp.

1433. Margolis, Joseph. "Recent Work in Aesthetics," American Philosophical Quarterly (Pittsburgh), vol. 2 (1965), pp. 182-192.

1434. Turich, Irina Mikhailovna. Èsteticheskoe vospitanie deteĭ; rekomendatel'nyĭ ukazatel' literatury [The Aesthetic Education of Children; A Guide to the Literature [In Russian]]. Moscow: Prosveshchenie, 1966. 102 pp.

1435. St. Marin, Demetrio. Bibliography of the "Essay on the Sublime" (ΠΕΡΙ ΨΟΥΣ). Leiden: E. J. Brill, 1967-1968. "Printed privately for the author."

741 entries. Arranged according to topic. Contains references to other bibliographies, which it apparently supersedes. Name Index. 101 pp.

1436. Zawadzki, Jane. "Selected Subject Bibliography (Covering the Past Ten Years)." Humanitas (Pittsburgh), vol. 4 (1968), pp. 247-256.

On "Personality and Aesthetics."

1437. Miladinova, Milka. Marksistko-Leninska estetika. Bibliografiia [Marxist-Leninst Aesthetics. A Bibliography [In Bulgarian]]. Sofia: Institut za propaganda na Marksizma-Leninizma. 1969. 119 pp.

1438. Formigari, Lia. Studi sull'estetica dell'empirismo inglese, 1931-1965. (Collana del Centro di richerche di storia della storiografia filosofica). Roma: Edizioni dell'Ateneo, 1971. 209 pp.

1439. Petrova, Galina Aleksandrovna. Kommunisticheskaia partiia Sovetskogo Soiuza i voprosy literatury i iskusstva [The Communist Party of the Soviet Union and Questions of Literature and Art [In Russian]]. Moscow: Gosudarstvennaia biblioteka SSSR imeni V. I. Lenina, 1971. 55 pp.

1440. American Home Economics Association. Textiles and Clothing Section. Aesthetics and Clothing; an Annotated Bibliography. Washington: American Home Economics Association, 1972. 159 pp.

1441. Duncan, Elmer H. "Selective Current Bibliography for Aesthetics and Related Fields. January 1, 1970-December 31, 1970," Journal of Aesthetics and Art Criticism (Baltimore), vol. 29 (1970-1971), pp. 577-614.

1442. Duncan, Elmer H. "Selective Current Bibliography for Aesthetics and Related Fields. January 1, 1971-December 31, 1971." Journal of Aesthetics and Art Criticism (Baltimore), vol. 30 (1971-1972), pp. 577-613; "January 1, 1972-December 31, 1972," vol. 31 (1972-1973), pp. 573-590.

1443. Merches, Dorina. Estetica. Ghid bibliografic [Aesthetics. Bibliographical guide [In Roumanian]]. Iasi: Biblioteca universitara Iasi, 1973. 204 pp.

1444. Bibliographische Zeitschrift für Aesthetic (Lundenberg), vol. 1 (1966)--[to date].

The volume for 1966 covers material issued 1963-1966.

AESTHETICS, AND JURISPRUDENCE

1445. Cerny, James W. Aesthetics and Jurisprudence: a Bibliographic Primer. Monticello, Ill.: Mary Vance, 11 pp.

About 90 references plus an introductory essay. Good coverage of the topic.

AFRICAN PHILOSOPHY

1446. Smet, A. J. "Bibliographie de la Pensée Africaine. Bibliography on African Thought," Cahiers Philosophiques Africains (Lubumbashi), no. 2 (1972), pp. 39-96. Also: Revised with Supplements, Kinshasa: Faculté de Théologie Catholique, Université Nationale du Zäire, 1974-1975, 239 pp.

ALCHEMY

1447. Read, J. Prelude to Chemistry: an Outline of Alchemy, its Literature and Relationships. 2nd ed. London: Bell, 1939. 328 pp. First edition: 1936.

Chapter 2, "The literature of alchemy" and pp. 295-318 contain chapter bibliographies and notes.

1448. London. Science Museum. A Hundred Alchemical Books [Its Book Exhibitions, no. 1]. London, 1952. 32 pp.

ALTDORF UNIVERSITY

1449. Apin, Sigmund Jacob. Vitae Professorum Philosophiae qui a Condita Academia Altorfina hunc usque Diem Clarverunt. Norimbergae et Altorfii: Tavberi, 1728. 346 pp.

About 1000 entries.

AMBROSIANA LIBRARY, HOLDINGS. See 2238.

AMERICAN PHILOSOPHY. See UNITED STATES PHILOSOPHY, CANADIAN PHILOSOPHY, NORTH AMERICAN PHILOSOPHY.

ANALYTIC PHILOSOPHY. See LANGUAGE, PHILOSOPHY OF.

ANALYTIC-SYNTHETIC DISTINCTION

1450. Hall, Roland. "Analytic-Synthetic: a Bibliography (Including some Items on Necessity)," Philosophical Quarterly (St. Andrews), vol. 16 (1966), pp. 178-181.

ANARCHISM

1451. Nettlau, Max. Bibliographie de l'anarchie. Brussels: 1897. 294 pp.

About 5000 entries.

1452. Woodcock, George. "Selected Bibliography," in his Anarchism: a History of Liberatarian Ideas and Movements, Cleveland and New York: The World Publishing Co., 1962, pp. 479-489.

References to about 170 selected works. No annotations.

ANCIENT PHILOSOPHY. See CLASSICAL GREEK AND ROMAN PHILOSOPHY.

ANDES, UNIVERSITY OF, LIBRARY HOLDINGS. See 2347.

ANIMAL RIGHTS. See 1747.

ANTHROPOLOGY, SOCIAL. See SOCIAL ANTHROPOLOGY, MAN.

ANTIOQUIA, UNIVERSITY OF, LIBRARY HOLDINGS

1453. Arango Betancour, Ignacio, and Carlos Cadavid Arango. Catálogo de los libros de filosofía existentes en los bibliotecas de la Universidad de Antioquia. Medellín, Col.: 1962. 125 pp. Mimeographed.

ANXIETY

1454. Romanyshyn, Robert. "Selected Subject Bibliography (Covering the Past Ten Years)," Humanitas (Pittsburgh), vol. 1 (1965), pp. 77-96.

About 230 entries on anxiety. Heavily psychological and sociological.

APPEARANCES

1455. Pouget, H.-M. Bibliographie de l'epiphanisme [par] N.-M. Pouget et Robert Vauthier. Avant propos de Henrie Perruchot. Paris: Centre Epiphaniste de Paris, 1951. 33 pp.

ARABIC PHILOSOPHY. See ISLAMIC PHILOSOPHY.

ARABIC TRANSLATIONS OF GREEK AUTHORS

1456. Ritter, H. and R. Walzer. "Arabische Uebersetzungen Griechischer Aerzte in Stambuler Bibliotheken," Sitzungberichte der Preussischen Akademie der Wissenschaften. Philosophisch-historische Klasse (Berlin), 1934 (fasc. 26), pp. 801-846.

1457. Walzer, R. "Aribsche Aristoteles-Uebersetzungen in Istanbul," Gnomon (Berlin), vol. 10 (1934), pp. 277-280.

1458. Walzer, R. "Ueber Arabische Uebersetzungen Griechischer Autoren in Stambuler Bibliotheken," Forschungen und Fortschritte (Berlin), vol. 10 (1934), pp. 391-392.

ARGENTINIAN PHILOSOPHY

1459. La Plata. Universidad Nacional. Instituto Bibliográfico. Anuario Bibliográfico; Letras, Historia, Educación, y Filosofía, vol. 1 (1926)-4 (1929).

1460. Argentina. Ministero de justicia y instrucción pública de la nación: Comisión nacional de cooperación intelectual. Bibliografía argentina de publicaciones filosóficas, años 1937 a 1943. Buenos Aires: 1943. 31 pp.

About 500 entries.

1461. Buenos Aires (Province). Instituto bibliográfico. Bibliografía argentina de filosofía y ciencias de la educación; obras y articulos publicados, 1958/1959-, no. 1-, jun. 1960- . La Plata: Ministerio de educación, Dirección de Enseñanza superior media y vocacional, 1960- .

1462. Buenos Aires (Province). Instituto bibliográfico. Bibliografía argentina de filosofía, obras y articulos publicados durante 1960, no. 2, nov. 1961. La Plata: Provincia de Buenos Aires, Ministerio de educación, Instituto bibliográfico, 1962. 230 pp.

No. 1 published under the title: Bibliografía argentina de filosofía y ciencias.

1463. Caturelli, Alberto. "Estudio critico-bibliográfico sobre la filosofía en Argentina," Documentación critica iberoamericana de filosofía y ciencias afines (Seville), vol. 2 (1965), pp. 9-42.

1464. Boletin filosofico (Resistencia, Arg.), no. 1 (1969)- .

ART, PSYCHOLOGY OF. See 1421.

ASSOCIATION OF IDEAS. See IDEAS, ASSOCIATION OF.

ASTROLOGY

1465. Sangin, M. A. F. Catalogus Codicum Astrologorum Graecorum. XII. Codices Russicos Descriptsit Mstislav Antonini F. Sangin. (Adiuvante Instituto Historiae Scientiarum et Artium Technicarum Academiae Scientiarum U.R.R.S.). Brussels: Lamertin, 1936. 268 pp.

ATHEISM

1466. Fichte, Johann Gottlieb. Die philosophischen Schriften zum Atheismusstreit. Leipzig: F. Eckardt, 1910. 142 pp.

1467. Edwards, Paul. "Atheism", in Paul Edwards, ed., The Encyclopedia of Philosophy, New York: Macmillan Publishing Co. and The Free Press; London: Collier Macmillan, 1967, vol. 1, pp. 188-189.

Mentions about 90 works with evaluative remarks.

AUTONOMY. See also FREEDOM AND DETERMINISM.

1468. Romanyshyn, Robert. "Selected Subject Bibliography (Covering Ten Years)," Humanitas (Pittsburgh), vol. 1 (1965), pp. 217-227.

About 140 entries on "Autonomy and Community." Heavily psychological and sociological in emphasis.

BABSON INSTITUTE LIBRARY, HOLDINGS. See 993.

BEING. See ONTOLOGY.

BELGIAN LIBRARIES HOLDING. See 837.

BELGIAN PHILOSOPHY. See also: 364, 1620, 1848, 1851, 1750.

1469. Henderickx, A. R. "De Wijsbegeerte in Belgie gedurende de jaren 1938-1947," Kultuurleven (Antwerpen), vol. 19 (1952), pp. 153-155.

BIBLIOTHEQUE NATIONALE (PARIS), HOLDINGS. See 68, 363, 1030, 1122, 1130, 972, 1057, 1065.

BIOLOGY. See also 54.

1470. Cole, F. J. "Bibliographical Reflections of a Biologist," Osiris (Bruges), vol. 8 (1949), pp. 289-315.

1471. Van Steenkiste, Cl. "Biologische wetenschappen," _Tijdschrift voor philosophie_ (Leuven), vol. 13 (1951), pp. 532-540.

BIRKBECK COLLEGE LIBRARY HOLDINGS. See 398.

BODY, HUMAN

1472. Gratton, Carolyn. "Selected Bibliography on the Human Body," _Humanitas_ (Pittsburgh), vol. 2 (1966), pp. 97-104.

150 entries.

BOLTON, ENGLAND, LIBRARIES, HOLDINGS

1473. Bolton, Eng. (Lancashire) Public Libraries _. . . Catalog of Books in the Central Lending and Reference Libraries_. _Philosophy and Religion_. Bolton, Eng.: The Bolton Libraries Committee, 1913. 387 pp.

BOOK REVIEWS, GENERAL. See also 1525, 1991.

1474. Arréat, Lucien. _Dix années de philosophie; études critiques sur les principaux travaux publiés de 1891 à 1900_. Paris: F. Alcan, 1901. 184 pp.

1475. _Critical Review of Theological and Philosophical Literature_. (London, Edinburgh, etc.), vol. 1 (1890)-14 (1904). Successor: _Review of Theology and Philosophy_. Predecessors: _Theological Review_ and _Free Church College Quarterly_.

Contains reviews of books in philosophy.

1476. Zampetti, Enrico. _Bibliographia regionata delle riviste filosofiche italiane dal 1900 al 1955_. Roma: Università, 1956. 136 pp.

68 entries describing Italian philosophical journals.

1477. Vicentini, José I. "Fichero de rivistas latino-americanas," _Stromata_ (San Miguel, Arg.), vol. 28 (1972), pp. 463-490.

1478. Philosophic Abstracts (New York), vol. 1 (1939)-10 (1948). [No more published.]

Abstracts in English of philosophical books published in the United States and Europe. Journal articles are listed.

1479. Bibliographie de la Philosophie. Bulletin Trimestriel/ Bulletin of Philosophy. A Quarterly Bulletin. (Paris), vol. 1 (1954)- [to date].

Notices and reviews of books only. About 1200 entries per year. Indexes. Continues Bibliographie de la Philosophie (Paris), vol. 1 (1937)-10 (1953).

1480. Philosophical Books: a Quarterly Review (Leicester), vol. 1 (1960)--[to date].

Reviews about 100 books a year.

1481. Scripta Recenter Edita. Nieuwe Uitgaven. New Publications. (Nijmegen, Metherlands), Vol. 1 (1960--[to date].

Lists new books in theology and philosophy.

1482. Indice de rivistas francesas de filosofía, historia, y literatura. (Documento 69) Montevideo: Goes, [n.d.]. 20 pp.

1483. Philosophischer Literaturanzeiger (Meisenheim am Glan), vol. 1 (1949)--[to present].

Reviews important books. About 800 per year.

BOOKS FOR LIBRARIES. See also 1758.

1484. Sears, Minnie Earl. Standard Catalog for Public Libraries: Philosophy, Religion, and General Works Section. New York: H. W. Wilson Co., 1932. 166 pp.

1000 titles. Dated and aimed at the general reader, but has good annotations, usually excerpted from published reviews. Arranged under Dewey system. With analytical index.

1485. Gutzwiller, Alois. Guide du choix des livres en philosophie pour bibliothèques de collèges. Quebec: Fédération des Collèges Classiques, 1966. 372 pp.

Covers primarily french works. Name index.

BOOKSELLER'S CATALOGS. See also 35, 1194, 1245, 1247, 1362.

1486. Hochhaufen, firm, booksellers, Jena. Verzeichniss einer Sammlung philosophischer Bücher (Antiquar. Katalog von Hochhaufen von Jena XVIII), 1850. 30 pp.

1487. Lippert, J. F., bookseller, Halle. Catalog des antiquarischen Bücherlagers von J. F. Lippert in Halle a. S. (No. VII) Philosophie. Halle: Plötz, 1853. 30 pp.

1488. Schmidt, H. W., firm, booksellets, Halle. Catalog des antiquarischen Bücherlagers von H. W. Schmidt in Halle a. S. (CXVII). Philosophie. Halle: Schmidt, 1858. 12 pp. Also: No. CLXXIII, 1861, 26 pp.

1489. Herberte, J. M., firm, printers, Köln. Bibliotheca Philosophica. Katalog philosophischer Werke. Rommerskirchen's Buchdrucherei in Köln. (Antiquar. Katalog von J. M. Herberte. LXV). Koln: 1861. 16 pp.

1490. Lempertz, Matth., firm, booksellers, Bonn. Catalog des antiquarischen Bücherlagers von Matth. Lempertz in Bonn. (No. 60) Philosophie und Pädagogik. Bonn: Krüger, 1861. 46 pp.

1491. Graeger, Ch., firm, booksellers, Halle. Verzeichniss des antiquarischen Bücherlagers von Ch. Graeger in Halle a. S. (No. 118) Philosophie. Halle: Hendel, 1863. 26 pp. Also: No. 97, 1860, 15 pp.; no. 106, 1862, 29 pp.

1492. Baer, Joseph, and Co., firm, booksellers, Frankfurt am Main. Lager-Catalog . . . IX. Theologie-Philosophie. Frankfurt am Main: A. Osterrieth, 1868. 306 pp.

1493. Charles Schribner's Sons, firm, publisher, New York. Classified and Descriptive Catalog of New and Standard Works in all Departments of Religious Literature, Including Philosophy, Published and Imported by Charles Schribner's Sons. New York: C. Schribner's Sons, 1898. 80 pp.

1494. Harrassowitz, Otto, firm, booksellers. [Katalog] 241: Philosophie. Psychologie . . ., 1899.

1495. Burgersdijk and Niermans, firm, booksellers, Leyden. Théologie, philosophie; catalogue de livres anciens et modernes aux prix marqués, No. 48 . . . Leyde: Burgersdijk and Niermans, 1900. 870 pp. 8°.

1496. Alcan, Félix, firm, publishers, Paris. . . . Bibliothèque de philosophie contemporaine. Paris: F. Alcan, 1901.

1497. Mussotter, Cos., firm, booksellers. Systematische Theologie und Philosophie . . . antiquariats-Katalog 106. (1 Abtl.: A--Patres Apostol.). Munderkingen: 1913. 66 pp.

1498. Alcan, Félix, firm, publishers, Paris. La philosophie française contemporaine (Congrès Internationale de Philosophié, 1926). Paris: Librarie Félix Alcan, 1926. 16 pp.

1499. Meiner, Felix, firm, publisher, Leipzig. Philosophischer Handkatalog, hersg. im Auftrag der Deutschen Verleger Philosophischen Schrifttums von Felix Meiner Verlag in Leipzig. Leipzig: O. Harrassowitz, 1926.

"Die systematische einteilung Werke überwacht von . . ."

1500. Cohen, Friedrich, firm, publishers. Philosphie. Antiquarists-Katalog no. 159/160. Bonn: 1927.

1501. Meiner, Felix, firm, publisher, Leipzig. Philosophischer Handkatalog. ler Nachtrag über die Jahre 1927/28. Leipzig: 1928.

1502. Meiner, Felix, firm, publisher, Leipzig. Katalog Philosophie, darin ein Gesamtverzeichnis der philosophischen Bibliothek. Leipzig: F. Meiner, 1929. 48 pp.

1503. Fock, Gustav, firm, booksellers. Philosophie. Leipzig, 1936. [n.p.]

1504. Books on Medicine, Surgery, Philosophy and Science Published during 1936. London: J. Whitaker and sons, 1937.

1505. Koehler und Volckmar, firm, booksellers, Köln. Philosophie und grenzgebiete, 1945-1964. Köln: 1964. 434 pp.

Covers German language works 1945-1964.

BRAZILIAN PHILOSOPHY. See also 2221.

1506. Toulois, Pedro. Bibliografia brasileira de filosofia. Rio de Janeiro: Instituto brasileiro de bibliografia e documentação, [no date].

BRITISH MUSEUM, HOLDINGS. See 72, 1312.

BRNO UNIVERSITY, LIBRARY HOLDINGS. See 898.

BUDDHIST PHILOSOPHY. See also 2026, 2353.

1507. Held, Hans Ludwig. Deutsche Bibliographie des Buddhismus. München-Leipzig: Hans Sachs-verlag, 1916. 190 pp.

1508. March, Arthur Charles. A Buddhist Bibliography. London: The Buddhist Lodge, 1935. 257 pp.

Mostly works in English. Subject index. Author list.

1509. De la Vallée-Poussin, L. "Notes de bibliographie bouddhique," Mélanges chinois et bouddhiques (Bruges), vol. 5 (1937), pp. 243-304.

1510. Bagchi, Prabodh Chandra. Le Canon bouddhique en Chine; les traducteurs et les traductions. (Sino-Indica: publications de l'Université de Calcutta, t. 1, 4). Paris: P. Geuthner, 1927-1938. 2 vols.

1511. Borsani, Giuseppina. Prospetti e indice del Tipitaka. (Università Cattolica del Sacro Cuore. Saggi e ricerche. Serie 12: Scienze Orientali, vol. 1). Milano: Vita e pensiero, 1942. 265 pp.

1512. Regamey, C. Buddhistische philosophie (Bibliographische Einführungen in das Studium der Philosophie, 20/21). Bern: A Francke, 1950. 86 pp.

About 800 entries. Works on oriental languages: glossaries, journals, texts, commentaries, works on most facets of Buddhist thought. Good. Interspersed with comments.

1513. Bibliographie Bouddhique (Paris), vol. 1 (1928)-32 (1958). Also: New York: International Publication Service, 1931-1958. 32 vols.

1514. Hanayama, Shinsho. Bibliography on Buddhism. Tokyo: Hokuseido Press, 1961. 869 pp. Also: New York: Perkins Oriental Books, 1962.

1515. De Jong, J. W. "Beknopte bibliografie van het boeddhisme," Wijsgerig perspectief of maatschappij en wetenschap (Amsterdam), vol. 5 (1964-1965), pp. 158-164.

1516. Yoo, Yushin. Buddism. A Subject Index to Periodical Articles in English, 1728-1971. Metuchen, N.J.: Scarecrow Press, 1973, 162 pp.

BULGARIAN PHILOSOPHY. See also 435, 886, 893, 1431, 1437.

1517. Abstracts of Bulgarian Scientific Literature. Philosophy, Psychology, and Pedagogics. (Sofia), vol. 1 (1958)--[to date].

Editions in English and Russian.

BYELORUSSIAN PHILOSOPHY. See 913.

BYZANTINE PHILOSOPHY

1518. Stéphanou, E. "Bulletin bibliographique de philosophie byzantine, 1918-1931," Echos d'Orient (Paris), vol. 35 (1932), pp. 55-74.

CALCUTTA SANSKRIT COLLEGE LIBRARY, HOLDINGS. See 2220.

CAMBRIDGE UNIVERSITY LIBRARY, HOLDINGS. See 2006.

CANADIAN PHILOSOPHY. See NORTH AMERICAN PHILOSOPHY, 2068.

CARTESIANISM. See DESCARTES, RENÉ.

CATHOLIC PHILOSOPHY. See also THEOLOGY, 1588, 1881.

1519. Korff, Heinrich. Bibliotheca Theologiae et Philosophiae Catholicae. Systematisches Verzeichniss von Deutschen Werken der Katholischen Theologie und Philosophie und einer Auswahl der Vorzüglichsten in Lateinischer sprache erschienen theol. und philos. Werke des Auslandes von 1870-1897. München: C. von Lama's Nachf (H. Korff), 1897. 196 pp.

1520. Grabmann, Martin. Die Geschichte der Katholischen Theologie seit dem Ausgang der Väterzeit. Freiburg im Breisgan: Herder, 1933. 368 pp.

Good bibliography on pp. 283-346.

1521. Nuestra bibliográfica de la filosofía católica y de su posición en la filosofía universal. (Fasc. de la Bibl. 5). San Miguel (Buenos Aires): Facutad de Filosofía y Theología, 1939, pp. 107-250.

CHANDLER, HENRY WILLIAM, COLLECTION. See 66.

CHANGE. See 1567.

CHARACTER

1522. Roback, A. A. A Bibliography of Character and Personality. Cambridge, Mass.: Sci-Art, 1927. 340 pp.

CHARLES UNIVERSITY (PRAGUE)

1523. Prague Universita Karlova [Charles University]. Filosoficko-Historická Faculta [Faculty of Philosophy and History]. Katalog publikací filosofické fakulty university Karolvy v Praze, 1954-1968 [Catalog of Publications of the Faculty of Philosophy, Charles University of Prague, 1954-1968 [In Czech]]. Praha: Universita Karlova, 1968. 122 pp.

CHICAGO PUBLIC LIBRARY, FINDING LIST. See 1749.

CHILEAN PHILOSOPHY

1524. Chile. Universidad. Facultad de filosofía y educacion. Anuario bibliográfico (Santiago), vol. 1 (1960--[to date?]

1963 issue contains 450 entries, 122 pp.

1525. De la Noi, Pedro. Repertorio de revistas teológicas y filosóficas. (Anales de la Facultad de teología, años 1965-1966, nos. 17-18. Cuaderno 5). Santiago, Chile: Ed. Universidad católica, 1966.

CHINESE LOGIC. See LOGIC, CHINESE.

CHINESE PHILOSOPHY. See also 859, 1510, 1916, 2027.

1526. Lust, John. Index Sinicus; a Catalogue of Articles Relating to China in Periodicals and other Publications, 1920-1955. Cambridge: Heffner, 1964.

1527. Cordier, H. Bibliotheca Sinica; dictionnaire bibliographique des ouvrages, relatifs a l'Empire Chinois . . . 2e ed. rev., cor. et considerablement augmentée . . . Paris: Guilmoto, 1904-08. 4 vols. Supplement et index: Paris: Geuthner, 1922-24, 4 v. in 1. Reprinted: Peking, 1938.

1528. Ch'iu, Alfred K'ai-Ming. A Classified Catalog of Chinese Books in the Chinese-Japanese Library of the Harvard-Yenching Institute at Harvard University. Vol. II. Philosophy and Religion.

Cambridge, Mas.: Harvard-Yenching Institute, 1939. 3 vols.

1529. Chan, Wing-Tsit. An Outline and a Bibliography of Chinese Philosophy. Hanover, N.H.: 1953. 62 ff. 2nd ed.: Hanover, N.H., 1955. 3rd ed.: An Outline and an Annotated Bibliography. New Haven: Yale University, Far Eastern Publications, 1959. 127 pp. 4th ed.: Revised: New Haven: (Sinological series, no. 4), 1969. 220 pp.

About 750 entries in the 1953 ed. About 1500 entries in the 1959 edition.

1530. Brière, O. Fifty Years of Chinese Philosophy, 1898-1950. London: Allen and Unwin, 1956. 159 pp. Also published as: Les Courants philosophiques en Chine depuis 50 ans, Shanghai: 1949.

A history, but with good bibliographical material.

1531. Yüan, T'ung-Li. China in Western Literature; a Continuation of Cordier's Bibliotheca Sinica. New Haven: Far Eastern Publications, Yale University, 1958. 802 pp.

More restricted than Cordier. Only monographs in English, German, French, and Portugese.

1532. Chan, Wing-Tsit. Chinese Philosophy, 1949-1963: an Annotated Bibliography of Mainland China Publications. Honolulu: East-West Center Press, 1967. 290 pp. Also: Rexdale, Ontario: Ambassador Books, 1966.

Annotated reference to 213 books and 756 articles published in mainland China, plus a few others dealing directly with Chinese philosophy. Divided by subject. Name index, chronology of dynastics and statistical tables.

1533. Berkelbach van der Sprenkel, O. "Account of a Chinese Bibliography," Abr-Nahrain (Leiden), vol. 10 (1970-1971), pp. 37-48.

1534. Reimmann, Jacob Friedrich. Historia Philosophiae Sinensis Nova Methodo Tradita, Emendata, et Aucta, et Vice

1534. (Continued)

Secunda sub Prelum ire Jussa. Brunsvigae: Schroeder, 1741. 59 pp.

An early history.

CHINESE, WORKS IN

1535. Chang, Wei-Shung. "Chinese Translations of Soviet Philosophical Works, 1949-1963, I-IV," Studies in Soviet Thought (Fribourg, Switz.; Dordrecht), vol. 11 (1971), pp. 212-225, 311-337, vol. 12 (1972), pp. 92-105, 174-189.

CHRISTIAN PHILOSOPHY. See CATHOLIC PHILOSOPHY, THEOLOGY, SCHOLASTIC PHILOSOPHY, the listings under individuals, and 1536, 1557, 1588, 1656, 2261.

CHRISTIANITY, ARABIAN

1536. Simon, I. "Répertoire des bibliothèques publiques et privées d'Europe contenant des manuscrits arabes chrétiens," Orientalia (Rome), vol. 7 (1938), pp. 239-264.

CINEMA, THEORY OF

1537. Noquez, Dominique. et al. "Choix bibliographique," Revue d'esthetique (Paris), vol. 26 (1973), pp. 383-401.

Covers french works on the theory of the cinema, 1963-1973.

CLASSICAL GREEK AND ROMAN PHILOSOPHY. See also the listings under individual philosophers and topics. Also 1456, 1457, 1458, 1823, 1825, 2167, 2168, 2200, 2351.

1538. Leisegang, H. "Bericht über die in den Jahren 1932 und 1933 erschienene deutsch Literatur zur Geschichte der antiken Philosophie," Sophia (Napoli), vol. 3 (1935), pp. 82-98, 483-509.

1539. De Corte, M. "Sur quelques livres relatifs à l'historie de la philosophie ancienne," Revue de philosophie, vol. 35 (1935), pp. 549-568.

1540. Grégoire, F. "Travaux d'historie de la philosophie ancienne," Revue néoscholastique de philosophie (Louvain), vol. 39 (1936), pp. 95-117.

1541. Keeling, S. V. "Philosophy in France. Some Recent Contributions on the Formation of Greek Thought," Philosophy (London), vol. 11 (1936), pp. 86-91.

1542. Revilla, A. Catálogo de los códices griegos de la biblioteca de El Escorial. Vol. I. Madrid: Imp. Helénica, 1936. 560 pp.

1543. De Corte, M. "Sur quelques ouvrages relatifs à l'historie de la philosophie et de la science antique," Revue de philosophie, vol. 37 (1937), pp. 450-476.

1544. Leisegang, H. "Ein Bericht über die in den Jahren 1934 und 1935 erschienne deutsche Literatur zur Geschichte de antiken Philosophie," Sophia (Napoli), vol. 5 (1937), pp. 56-63, pp. 420-432.

1545. Bréhier, Émile. Les Etudes de philosophie antique (Philosophie, Chronique Annuelle, Pub. par l'Institut International de Collaboration Philosophique. Redaction: Raymond Bayer . . ., 1). Paris: Hermann, 1939. 54 pp.

Covers works published in 1937.

1546. Kleberg, Tönnes. Catalogus Codicum Graecorum et Latinorum Bibliothecae Gotoburgensis. Göteborg: Elander, 1941. 48 pp.

1547. Rotta, Rapla. Storia della filosofia greca e romana. (Università cattolica del Saco cuore: Guide bibliografiche, vol. 2). Milano: 1944. 55 pp. Also: 1941 edition.

236 entries.

1548. Gignon, Olaf. Antike philosophie. (Bibliographische Einführungen in das Studium der Philosophie, 5). Bern: A. Francke, 1948. 52 pp.

About 520 entries arranged by subject. Some annotations. Index.

1549. Kerschensteiner, Jula. "Gli studi di storia della filosofia antica in Germania dal 1940 al 1949," Rivista di storia della filosofia (Milano), vol. 5 (1950), pp. 62-76.

1550. Lambrino, Sc. Bibliographie de l'antiquité classique (1898-1914). Paris: Belles Lettres, 1951. 650 pp.

1551. Garin, Eugenio. "Il Pensiero antico (1950)," Giornale critico della filosofia italiana (Firenze), vol. 30 (1951), pp. 395-300.

1552. Moschetti, Andrea Mario. "Bibliografia critica generale per la storia del pensiero classico," in Grande antologia filosofica, I: Il Pensiero classico. Milano: C. Marzorati, 1954, pp. xxvii-lxxi.

1553. Kristeller, Paul Oskar, ed. in chief. Catalogus Translationum et Commentariorum; Medieval and Renaissance Latin Translations and Commentaries. Annotated Lists and Guides. Washington, D. C. Catholic University of America Press, vol. I (1960); vol. II (1971).

> Lists and describes the Latin translations of ancient Greek authors and the Latin commentaries on ancient Latin and Greek authors up to the year 1600. Important for scholars interested in ancient medieval and renaissance philosophy. See preface of vol. II for list of reviews.

1554. Mondolfo, Rodolfo. Guía bibliográfica de la filosofía antigua. (Colección Filosofía). Buenos Aires: Losada, 1960. 102 pp.

1555. Nuño Montes, Juan Antonio. Filosofía antigua (Repertorios Bibliográficos de Filosofía, 1. Ediciónes de la Biblioteca, 8). Caracas: Universidad Central de Venezuela, 1962. 199 pp.

1556. Adorno, Francesco. Il Pensiero greco: Orientamenti bibliografici. (Piccola biblioteca filosofica Laterza, no. 47). Bari: Laterza, 1969. 120 pp.

1557. Adorno, Francesco. Il pensiero greco-romano e il cristianesimo. Bari: Laterza, 110 pp.

1558. Biblioteca Centrala Universitara Mihai Eminescu. Serviciul de Informare Bibliografica. Istoria filozofiei antice. Ghid bibliografic. [The History of Ancient Philosophy. Bibliographical Guide [In Roumanian]]. Iasi: 1971, 51 pp.

1559. L'Année philologique: bibliographie critique et analytique de l'antiquité gréco-latine. (Paris), vol. 1 (1924)--[to date]. Supersedes Dix années de bibliographie classique (Paris) 1914-1924.

> A yearly annotated index to all publications relative to greco-roman antiquity to the year 800 A.D., and, selectively, later years. Contains references to works on philosophy. Surveys about 800 periodicals.

CLOTHING. See AESTHETICS AND 1440.

COIMBRA, UNIVERSITY LIBRARY MANUSCRIPTS

1560. De Almeida e Sousa, Abel L. Catalogo de manuscritos. Codices 2310 a 2376. Apostilas de filosofia, II: fisica. Coimbra: Publiçaoes da Biblioteca geral da universidade, 1963. 152 pp.

COLOMBIAN PHILOSOPHY. See also 1453.

1561. Quevedo, Francisco. Mannscritos teológico-filosóficos coloniales santafereños. Bogotá: 1952. 106 pp.

1562. Giraldo Jaramillo, Gabriel. Contribucion a la bibligrafia filosofica de Colombia. (Universidad Nacional de Colombia. Facultad de Filosofia y Letras. Seccion de Historia de Colombia y de America. --Separata del Anuario colombiano de historia social y de la cultura. Vol. 1, no. 1--Fuentes bibliograficas para la historia colombiana social y de la cultura.) Bogota: 1963, pp. 107-129.

About 475 unannotated entries arranged alphabetically by author.

COMMUNIST PHILOSOPHY. See also "SOVIET PHILOSOPHY" and "MARX, KARL", ENGGUS, FRIEDRICH; LENIN, V. I., etc. See also 1654, 1655, 1756, 1856, 1922, 2102.

1563. "Les Publications communistes en France," La Vie Intellectuelle (Paris), vol. 48 (1937), pp. 250-264.

1564. Prague. Ústřední Ekonomická Knihovna. [Central Economic Library.] Bibliografie. Společenké vědy: Filosofie, politická ekonomie, dělnické a komunistické hnutí, vnitřní politika, mezinárodni vztahy a zahraniční politika. [Bibliography. Social Sciences: Philosophy, Political Economy, the Workers' and Communist Movements, Domestic Policy, International Relations and Foreign Policy [In Czech]], (Praha), vol. 1 (1956)-6 (1961).

A periodical.

1565. Tugov, Yu. M., and V. V. Misharina, comps. Chto chitat' po filosofii [What to Read on Philosophy [In Russian]]. Moscow: Gosudarstvennaia Publichnaia Biblioteka V. I. Lenina [Lenin State Public Library], 1958. 156 pp.

About 400 entries.

1566. Isachenkova, Anna Ivanova. Retrospektivnaía bibliografiía po filosofii i kommunizmu [A Retrospective Bibliography on Philosophy and Communism [In Russian]]. 1973. 57 pp.

COMMUNITY. See 1468.

COMPTE RENDU DES SÉANCES ET TRAVAUX DE L'ACADEMIE DES SCIENCES MORALES ET POLITIQUES. See Indexes.

CONFLICT

1567. Gratton, Carolyn. "Selected Subject Bibliography (Covering the Past Ten Years)," Humanitas (Pittsburgh), vol. 10 (1974), pp. 225-232.

175 entries on "Conflict and Change."

CONGRESSES, PHILOSOPHICAL

1568. Paliard, Jacques. "Bibliographie: ouvrages, principaux articles, communications aux congrès philosophiques," Les Etudes philosophiques (Marseille), vol. 6 (1951), pp. 260-261.

1569. Congresso nazionale di filosofia. Mostra internazionale del libro filosofico, 1953-1958. Firenze: 1958, 40 pp.

About 500 entries.

1570. Interamerican Congress of Philosophy. Sixth, Buenos Aires, 1959. Exposición del libro americano de filosofía, Buenos Aires. 31 de agosto/5 de septiembre/1959. Buenos Aires: 1959. 131 pp.

About 1200 entries.

CONTEMPORARY PHILOSOPHY (SINCE 1900) OR TWENTIETH CENTURY PHILOSOPHY. See also 1825.

1571. Sortais, G. "Bibliographie des principaux ouvrages de philosophie parus depuis 1900," in his Traité de philosophie, vol. II, appendix I, 4e ed. Paris: Lethielleux, 1911.

1572. Schmidkung, H. Philosophische Propädeutik in neuester Literatur. Halle: Waisenhaus, 1917. 90 pp.

1573. Schmidt, Raymund. Die Philosophie der Gegenwart in Selbstdarstellungen, mit einer Einführung hrsg. von dr. Raymund Schmidt. Leipzig: F. Meiner, 1922-1929. 7 vols.

1574. Buchenau, Artur. "Zum philosophischen Literatur der Gegenwart," Geisteskultur, vol. 33 (1924), pp. 280-286.

1575. Grau, Kurt Joachim. "Philosophie Weihnachtsrundschau 2," Preussische Jahrbücher (Berlin), vol. 198 (1924), pp. 315-322; "Literatur," pp. 303-315.

1576. Bonnet-Eymard, J. et al. "Bibliographie critique," Archives de philosophie (Paris), vol. 6 (1929), pp. 326-382.

Divided as follows: "Philosophie general," "Psychologie," "morale et sociologie," "Metaphysique," "Histoirie de la philosophie."

1577. Libreria Siglo XX, Bogotá. Catálogo general de literatura, ensayos, arte, filosofía, historia, biografías, y obras de orientación religiosa. Bogotá: Edit. El Liberal, 1946. 448 pp.

1578. García Ramos, Dagoberto, and Alberto Benavides Balbin. Bibliografía de filosofía, 1936-1948. Lima: Compañia de impresiones y publicidad, 1949. 28 pp. Reprinted from Boletín bibliográfico, Universidad. Mayor de San Marcos Lima, vol. 22 (1949) under the title "Bibliografía de religión y philosofía, 1936-1948."

1579. De Woelhens, Alphonse. "Hedendaags philosophie," Tijdschrift voor philosophie (Leuven), vol. 11 (1949), pp. 407-476.

1580. Geiger, L. B. "Bulletin de philosophie. Ouvrages généraux," Revue des sciences philosophiques et théologiques (Le Saulchoir), vol. 33 (1949), pp. 254-266.

1581. Collins, James. "Philosophers of 1950-1951 (Review of philosophy)," Thought (New York), vol. 27 (1952), pp. 101-124.

1582. Gietz, Ernesto G. et al. Bibliografía filosófica del Siglo XX. Catálogo de la Exposición bibliográfica internacional de la filosofía del Siglo XX preparado par el Instituto bibliotecologico, Universidad de Buenos Aires. Buenos Aires: Ediciones penser, 1952. 469 pp.

References to 4011 works. Three sections: I, Introduction; II, History; III, Doctrines; plus an appendix. Books only. Index. No annotations, but locates works in Argentinian libraries.

1583. Moscow. Akademiia Nauk SSSR, Fundamentalnaia biblioteka obshchestvennykh nauk. Novaia inostrannaia literatura po filosofii [New Foreign Literature on philosophy [In Russian]]. Moskva: Akademiia Nauk SSSR, 1960- . (In progress).

1584. Bianca, D. O. et al. "Rassegna di scienze filosofiche," Annali della pubblica instruzione (1961), pp. 404-409.

1585. Quinton, A. M. A Bibliography of Contemporary Philosophy, compiled for the Sub-Faculty of Philosophy. [Sanford, Calif., 1964] 76 l.

1586. Sciacca, Michele Federico, ed. Les Grands courants de la pensée mondiale contemporaine. Paris: Fischbacher, 1964. 6v.

A history: with good bibliographical references.

1587. Jahreskatalog philosophie: Jahresbibliographie der im Buchhandel erhältlichen Literatur, vorwiegend in Deutscher, Englischer und Französischer Sprache, 1966. Berlin: Elwert und Meurer, 1966. 139 pp.

1588. McLean, George F. Philosophy in the Twentieth Century: Catholic and Christian. Vol. 1: An Annotated Bibliography of Philosophy in Catholic Thought, 1900-1964; Vol. 2: A Bibliography of Christian Philosophy and Contemporary Issues. New York: Ungar, 1967.

Classified according to subjects, with indexes. Good.

1589. Klibansky, Raymond. Contemporary Philosophy/La Philosophie contemporaine. A Survey/Chroniques. Firenze: La Nuova italia editrice, 1968-1971. 4 vols.

Each volume contains about thirty articles on various topics within the broad subjects covered by each volume.

I. Logic and foundations of mathematics.
II. Philosophy of science.
III. Metaphysics, phenomenology, language and structure.
IV. Ethics, aesthetics, law, religion, politics, historical and dialectical materialism. Philosophy in eastern Europe, Asia, and Latin America.

Articles contain bibliographies of important works.

1590. Pardos Vicente, Manuel, and Andrés Ortiz Osés. Bibliografía critica de la filosofía actual. Zaragoza: Librería Pórtico, 1974. 100 pp.

CORDOVA, JESUIT LIBRARY HOLDINGS. See 1965.

COSTA RICA, UNIVERSITY OF. See 2218.

CRAKOW LIBRARY HOLDINGS. See also 57.

1591. Jelonek, Eugenius. "De quodam Manuscriptorum Catalogo Bibliothecarum Provinciae Cracoviensis O.F.M.," Collectanea Franciscana (Romae), vol. 35 (1965), pp. 383-392.

CREATIVITY. See also

1592. Romanyshyn, Robert, and Carolyn Gratton. "Selected Subject Bibliography on Creativity," Humanitas (Pittsburgh), vol. 1 (1966), pp. 357-371.

About 300 entries on Creativity.

CRITICAL PHILOSOPHY. See KANT, IMMANUAL, also 2176.

CUBAN PHILOSOPHY

1593. Vitier, M. "Los Estudios filosóficos en Cuba," Rivista cubana (La Habana), vol. 7 (1937), pp. 78-90.

CUSTOM AND TRADITION

1594. Gratton, Carolyn. "Selected Subject Bibliography (Covering the Past Ten Years)," Humanitas (Pittsburgh), vol. 7 (1971), pp. 119-128.

About 210 entries on "Creative response to Customs and Traditions."

CYBERNETICS

1595. Barrett, F. Dermot, and Herbert A. Shepard. "A Bibliographie of Cybernetics," Proceedings of the American

1595. (Continued)

Academy of Arts and Sciences, vol. 80 (1953), pp. 204-222.

CZECHOSLOVAKIAN PHILOSOPHY. See also SLOVAKIAN PHILOSOPHY, and 881, 889, 896, 898, 917, 920, 922, 1523, 1602, 1788.

1596. Pavlov, Andrei [Pawlow, Andrej] and Boris Yakovenko [Jakowenko]. Kurze Bibliographie der neuen Tschecoslowakischen Philosophie. (Internationale Bibliothek für Philosophie, vol. 1, no. 3) Prag: 1935. 58 pp.

About 3000 entries.

1597. Král, J. Bibliografia Ćsl. filosofie. Nástin vývoje podle disciplin. Praha: 1937, pp. 265-320.

1598. Prague. Státni Knihovaną společenských věd. Bibliografie státní knihovny společenských. Věd: Společenské vědy. voč 1 - (1956 -).

DANISH PHILOSOPHY

1599. Jφrgensen, Aage. Dansk litteraturhistorisk bibliografi 1974. Copenhagen: Akademisk forlag, 1975.

Many references to Kierkegaard.

DEATH, SURVIVAL OF. See IMMORTALITY.

DEATH AND DYING. See also 2254.

1600. Gratton, Carolyn. "Selected Subject Bibliography, (Covering the Past Ten Years)," Humanitas (Pittsburgh), vol. 10 (1974), pp. 95-103.

200 entries on "Death and Dying."

DEHUMANIZATION

1601. Gratton, Carolyn. "Selected Subject Bibliography (Covering the Past Ten Years)," Humanitas (Pittsburgh), vol. 2 (1966), pp. 293-299.

On the dehumanizing trends in Contemporary Culture.

DETERMINISM. See FREEDOM AND DETERMINATION.

DIALECTIC. See 1997.

DIALECTICAL MATERIALISM. See "MARX, KARL," "ENGELS, FRIEDRICH," "LENIN, V. I.", etc.

1602. Brno. University. Library. Dialekticky materialmismus [Dialectical materialism [In Czech]]. Brně: 1959. 21 pp.

1603. Baskin, N. P. Chto chitat' po dialekticheskomu materializmu [What to read on dialectical materialism [In Russian]]. Moscow: 1931. 64 pp.

DISPUTATIONS

1604. Glorieux, Palémon. La Littérature quodlibétique. Le Saulchoir: Kain (Belgique), Revue des sciences philosophiques et théologiques, 1925-1935. 2 vols.

DISSERTATIONS. See also 1816.

1605. Gründliche Auszüge aus denen neuesten theologisch-, philosophisch- und philogischen Disputationibus, welche auf denen hohen Schulen in Deutschland gehalten werden. (Leipzig), vol. 1 (1733)-13 (1745).

Successor: Vollständige nachrichten von dem theologisch- [etc.] (Leipzig), vol. 1 (1746)-15 (1760).

1606. Muller, Frederik, and Co. Amsterdam. Catalogus Dissertationum et Orationum Philosophicarum, Defensarum et Habitarum ab a. 1650 usque ad 1851 in Academiis Germaniae, etc. Praesertim Neerlandiae. Quae Venales Prostant apud Fredericum Muller. Amsterdam: 1851. 11 pp.

334 entries.

1607. Gassen, Kurt. Die Deutschen Philosophischen Universitätsschriften, 1925-1930 . . . Systematische Bibliographie. Erfurt: 1924-1930.

About 600 entries per annual issue.

1608. Madrid. Universidad, Faculdad de Filosofía y Letras. Sumarios y extractos de las tesis doctorales, leídas desde 1940 a 1950 en las secciones de filosofía y pedagogía. Madrid: C. Bernijo, 1953. 303 pp.

37 entries in philosophy, 11 in education.

1609. "Dissertatsii po filosofii zaschishchennye v 1953-1954 godakh [Dissertations in philosophy, 1953-1954 [In Russian]]," Voprosy filosofii (Moscow), no. 3 (1955), pp. 197-211.

488 entries.

1610. Gogacz, Mieczysław. Streszczenia rozpraw doktorskich magisterskich i seminaryjnych pisanych na Katolickim Uniwersytecie Lubelskim pod kierunkiem Prof. Dr. Stefana Swieżawskiego (Historia filozofi) i Prof. Dr. Alberta Krąpca (metafizyka/w wyborze) [Abstracts of Doctoral, Masters, and Seminar Dissertations Written at the Catholic University of Lublin under the Direction of Prof. Dr. Stefan Swieżawskiego (History of Philosophy) and Prof. Dr. Albert Krapca (Metaphysics) [In Polish]]. Poźnan: Pallotinum, 1956. 223 pp.

Contains 43 entries: 4 in metaphysics, 39 in the history of philosophy (medieval).

1611. Thèsis de doctorat concernant les sciences philosophiques et théologiques soutenues en France pendant l'année 1955. Paris: Presses universitaires de France, 1956. 1323 pp.

1612. Carrière, Gaston. Thèses préparées aux facultés ecclésiastiques de l'Université d'Ottawa, 1932-1963. Ottawa: 1963. 224 pp.

1613. Shanghnessy, Amy E. Dissertations in Linguistics, 1957-1964. Washington: Center for Applied Linguistics, 1965. 28 pp.

1614. Reynolds, Michael M. Guide to Theses and Dissertations: An International Annotated Bibliography of Bibliographies. Detroit: Gale Research Co., 1975. 599 pp.

Covers all fields. Is especially useful for the sections on universal and national bibliographies of dissertations. Seven works specifically on philosophy in the "philosophy" section.

1615. "Doctoral Dissertations [American: 1956-to date]," Review of Metaphysics (Washington), vol. 10 (1956/57)-to date.

List appears in September number, except for 1956, which is in December number.

1616. "Liste de thèses de doctorat concernant la philosophie médiévale," Bulletin de la Société internationale pour l'étude de la philosophie médiévale (Louvain), vol. 4 (1962), pp. 138-147; vol. 5 (1963), pp. 184-196; vol. 6 (1964), pp. 111-118.

List appears annually since vol. 2 (1960), international in scope.

1617. Walsh, Edward J. Philosophy and the History of Ideas: Dissertations in Progress, Canada and the United States (Lakewood, N.J.: Georgian Court College), 1970- .

Title varies. Irregular.

DOMINICAN LIBRARY (VIENNA) HOLDINGS. See 46.

DOMINICAN ORDER. See also 24, 35.

1618. Daley, Charles Marie. Dominican Incunabula in the Library of Congress. New York: United States Catholic Historical Society, 1932. 88 pp.

DUTCH PHILOSOPHY. See also 364, 369, 1851, 1861.

1619. Catalogus van boeken in noord-Nederland verschenen van de vroegsten tijd tot op heden. [III. Wijsbegeerte en onderwijs]. 's-Gravenhage: 1911. 42 cols.

About 500 entries.

1620. De Petter, D. M. "Wijsbegeerte in Vlaanderen en Holland," Kultuurleven (Antwerpen), vol. 5 (1934), pp. 211-215.

1621. Proost, K. F., and Jan Romein. Geestelijk Nederland 1920-1940. Onderwijs, radio, wijsbegeerte, godsdienst, kunst en letteren. Amsterdam und Antwerpen: Kosmos, 1948. 332 pp. Deel II: De Wetenschappen van natur, mens en maatschappij, ibid., 304 pp.

1622. Poortman, J. J. Repertorium der Nederlandse wijsbegeerte. Amsterdam; Antwerpen: Wereldbibliotheek, N.V., 1948. 403 pp. Supplement 1: 1958.

Arranged by concept and also by names. About 6600 entries, mostly in Dutch, through 1947. Supplement, about 2200 entries.

ECHENIQUE Y IRMÃO LIBRARY HOLDINGS. See 1797.

ECONOMICS. See 1573, 1662, 1664, 1668.

ECUADORIAN PHILOSOPHY

1623. Endara, Julio. "La Cultura filosófica en el Ecuador durante la colonia," Revista de filosofía (Buenos Aires), vol. 6 (1920), pp. 400-429.

EDUCATION, PHILOSOPHY OF

1624. Varet, Gilbert. ["Bibliography on the Philosophy of Education"], in Gaston Berger, L'Homme moderne et son éducation. Paris: Presses Universitaries de France, 1962. 368 pp.

1625. Broudy, Harry S. et al. Philosophy of Education: an Organization of Topics and Selected Sources. Urbana: University of Illinois Press, 1967. 287 pp.

Annotated.

1626. Miller, Albert Jay. A Selective Bibliography of Existentialism in Education and Related Topics. New York: Exposition Press, 1969. 39 pp.

1627. Powell, John P. Philosophy of Education: a Select Bibliography. 2nd ed. Manchester, Eng.: Manchester University Press; distr. New York: Humanities Press, 1970. 51 pp.

Listing of articles from 74 journals from 1950 to 1970. Cross referenced. Listings under 26 subjects. Author index.

EMPIRICISM. See listings under particular philosophers and 1438.

EMPIRICISM, LOGICAL. See LOGICAL POSITIVISM.

EPICUREANISM. See EPICURUS.

EPISTEMOLOGY. See also 1761, 810, 1995.

1628. Amerio, F. Epistemologia. Bresica: Morcelliana, 1948.

A good bibliography on the subject.

1629. Robert, Jean-Dominique. "Elements de bibliographie pour l'étude du problème de la connaissance," Revue Philosophique de Louvain (Louvain), vol. 56 (1958), pp. 586-604.

1630. Sanchez-Ruiz, Jóse. "Nota bibliografica di gnoseologia," (Bibliografia filosofica essenziale) Filosofia e Vita (Torino), vol. 2 (1961), pp. 94-98.

1631. Zi͡atkova, Li͡udmila Ivanova. Teori͡a poznanii͡a i sovremenni͡a nauka [The Theory of Knowledge and Present-day Science [In Russian]]. Moscow: "Kniga," Publichnai͡a Biblioteka, 1972. 76 pp.

1632. Robert, Jean-Dominique. Philosophies, épistemologies, sciences de l'homme: leurs rapports: éléments de bibliographie (Bibliothèque de la Faculté de Philosophie et Lettres de Namur; fasc. 54). Namur: Presses universitaires de Namur, 1974. 534 pp.

ESCORIAL LIBRARY HOLDINGS. See 1542.

ESOTERIC PHILOSOPHY. See 532.

ETHICS. See also SOCIAL ETHICS, 64, 65, 661, 1576, 1706, 1714, 1715, 1747, 1751, 1874, 2070, 2084, 2092, 2263, 2280, 2317.

1633. Scheurl, Heinrich Julius. Bibliographia Moralis, ad Magnificum, Nobilissimum, Amplissimum Consultissimumq; Virum, Dr. Johannem Schwartz Kopf, Serenissimi Celsissimiq; Principis ac Dn. Dn. Avgvsti Brvnsvvic. ac Lvnebvrgensivm Dvcis Sc. Cancellarivm Opt. Meritum. Auctore Henrico Ivlio Scheurl. Helmstadtii: Typis et Sumptibus Henningi Mvlleri, 1648. 224 pp. Also: 1686 edition.

1634. Boehmer, Philip Ludwig. Programma de Optimis in Philosophia Morali Scriptoribus. Helmestadii: 1691.

1635. Gottschlingio, Casparo, and Daniele Fidlero. Bibliographia Ethica, qua Nonnulli Scriptores Ethicae Praecipue Galli Recensiti et Judicati Inclutae Facultatis Philos. Benigno Indultu in Academia Lipsiensi Anno M.DCCI. Lipsiae: Lit. Gözi. [c.1700 ?]

1636. Schelle, Johann Christian. Programma de Praecipuis Moralis Philosophiae Scriptoribus. Lipsiae: 1704.

1637. Kortholt, Seb. Dissertatio de Scriptoribus, quorum Virtus Singularibus in Morum Doctrinam Meritis Illustratur. Kilonii: 1706.

1638. Mackintosh, James. "The Progress of Ethical Philosophy Chiefly During the Seventeenth and Eighteenth Centuries," in Encyclopaedia Britannica, 8th ed., vol. 1, "Dissertations," pp. 309-445.

> Not exactly a bibliography, but an overview of what was considered worthwhile during the first half of the nineteenth century. Worth looking at.

1639. Babin, A. Collection générale des ouvrages scientifiques, psychologiques, et moraux. 1879. 1,000 pp. Reprinted: Traditionnelles.

1640. Nottingham, Eng. Free Public Libraries and Museum. Mental and Moral philosophy ("Class list . . . of books in the Reference Library," no. 12). Nottingham: 1887.

1641. Hyslop, J. H. "New Text Books of Ethics in 1892," Educational Review (Fredericton), vol. 4 (1892), pp. 372-378.

1642. Dewey, John. "Review of Ethical Literature," Psychological Review (Princeton), vol. 1 (1894), pp. 109-111.

1643. Hibben, J. G. "Review of Recent Literature in Ethics," Psychological Review (Princeton), vol. 2 (1895), pp. 75-77, 320-325, 524-529, 634-637.

1644. Angot des Rotours, Bon J. "La Morale en France de 1888 à 1898," in Congrès bibliographique international tenu à Paris du 13 au 16 avril 1898. Paris: Au siège de la Sociètè Bibliographique, 1900. Vol. 1, pp. 130-136.

1645. Sheldon, W. L. "A Bird's-eye View of the Literature of Ethical Science since the Time of Charles Darwin," Transactions of the Academy of Science of St. Louis (St. Louis, Mo.), vol. 13 (1903), pp. 87-142.

1646. Whitmore, Frank Hayden. Reading List on Ethics. Submitted for Graduation by Frank Hayden Whitmore . . . New York State Library School, Class of 1901. (New York Library. Bulletin 93, April, 1905. Bibliography [v. 3] 38) Albany, New York State Education Department, 1905. 498 pp.

1647. De Labarre, A. La Morale d'après Saint Thomas d'Aquin et les théologiens scholastiques. Memento théorique et guide bibliographique. Paris: Beauchesne, 1911. 151 pp.

1648. Heyde, J. E. "Gesamtbibliographie des Wertbegriffes," Literarische Berichte aus dem Gebiete der Philosophie (Erfurt), vols. 15/16 (1928), pp. 111-119; vols. 17/18 (1928), pp. 66-75.

1649. Wigny, P. La Bibliothèque de l'honnête homme. Brussels: Goemaere, 1945. 604 pp.

1650. Victoroff, D. and B. Gilles. Nouveau guide to l'étudiant en sociologie et morale. Paris: Société d'-édition d'enseignement sepérieur (impr. de Jouve), 1949. 770 pp.

1651. New York Society for Ethical Culture. A List of Books and Pamphlets by American and British Leaders of the Societies for Ethical Culture; Compiled by the Library Committee of the New York Society for Ethical Culture, Ms. Leah Lewinson, Chairman, at the Request of the National Women's Conference of the American Ethical Union. New York: 1950.

1652. Donmeyer, Frederick C. "Recent Ethical Literature," Philosophy and Phenomenological Research (Buffalo), vol. 11 (1951), pp. 579-586.

1653. Rees, D. A. "A Survey of Literature on Ethics and the History of Ethics, 1945-1950," Philosophical Quarterly (St. Andrews), vol. 1 (1950-1951), pp. 448-459. "Part II: Ethics," vol. 2 (1952), pp. 70-81.

1654. Bochkareva, Margarita Aleksandrovna. Propaganda literatury po voprosam kommunisticheskoĭ morali. [Propaganda of literature on questions of communist morality [In Russian]]. Moscow: Gos. izd-vo kul'turno-prosvetital'noĭ lit-ry, [State Publishing House of Cultural and Educational Literature.], 1955. 86 pp.

1655. Moscow. Publichnaîa biblioteka bibliograficheskiĭ otdel. [Public library. Bibliographical division.] Chto chitat o kommunisticheskoĭ morali [What to Read on Communist Morality [In Russian]]. Moscow: 1955. 70 pp.

1656. Gustafson, R. K. "The Literature of Christian Ethics, 1932-1956." Unpublished masters thesis, Union Theological Seminary in Virginia, 1957. 307 pp.

> About 200 entries. Detailed annotations on the major works in english on christian ethics. A good survey. Works covered are rated according to their value.

1657. Schottlaender, Rudolf. "Verzeichnis der Wissenschaftlichen Schriften . . . seit 1945," in Schottlaender, Theorie des Vertrauens. Berlin: W. de Gruyter, 1957, pp. 147-148.

1658. Albert, Ethel M., Clyde Kluckhohn, et al. *A Selected Bibliography on Values, Ethics, and Esthetics in the Behavioral Sciences and Philosophy, 1920-1958*. Glencoe, Ill.: Free Press, 1959. 342 pp.

1991 annotated entries arranged by topic. Author index.

1659. Church of England. National Assembly. Joint Board of Studies. *Current Problems in the Understanding of Personal Responsibility: a Bibliography Selected from the Fields of Psychology, Sociology, Ethics, and Theology*. London: Church Information Office, 1960. 11 pp.

1660. Bastide, Georges. *Ethics and Political Philosophy* (French Bibliographical Digest, ser. II, no. 34). New York: Cultural Center of the French Embassy, 1961. 96 pp. Also: *Morale et philosophie politique: Bibliographie*. Paris: Association pour la diffusion de la pensée francaise, 1961. 91 pp.

1661. Ferreira, C. "Bibliografia filosofica essenziale: etica," *Filosofia e vita* (Torino), vol. 2 (1961), pp. 54-64.

1662. Utz, Arthur. *Bases for Social Living. A Critical Bibliography Embracing Law, Society, Economics, and Politics*. New York: Herder, 1961, 446 pp.

Also published in German.

1663. Gratton, Carolyn. "Selected Subject Bibliography (Covering the Past Ten Years)," *Humanitas* (Pittsburgh), vol. 4 (1968), pp. 383-394.

About 250 entries on the "Crisis of values in contemporary culture."

1664. Matczak, Sebastian A. *Philosophy: a Select Classified Bibliography of Ethics, Economics, Law, Politics and Sociology*. (*Philosophical questions series, no. 3*). Louvain: Editions Nauwelaerts; Paris: Béatrice-Nauwelaerts; New York: Humanities Press, 1970. 308 pp.

About 3800 entries with brief annotations. Divided into subjects. Covers more than philosophy *per se* and is at time somewhat arbitrary about the inclusion of specific works or authors. This probably results from the fact that this is a selective bibliography, but it points up the need for additional subject bibliographies in most areas of philosophy. A worthwhile book.

1665. Paulova, L. *Nravstvennye t͡sennosti nashego sovremennikal* [*The Moral Values of Contemporary Soviet Man* [In Russian]]. (At head of title: USSR Ministry of Culture. Lenin State Library of the USSR.) Moscow: "Kniga," 1971. 96 pp.

1666. Gothie, Daniel L. A Selected Bibliography of Applied Ethics in the Professions, 1950-1970; a Working Sourcebook with Annotations and Indexes. Charlottesville, Va.: University Press of Virginia, 1973. 176 pp.

1667. Walters, Le Roy. Bibliography of Bioethics, vol. 1. Detroit: Gale Research Corp. 1975. 225 pp.

Entries arranged by topic indexes.

1668. Utz, A. Bibliographie der Sozialethik. Grundsatsfragen des öffentlichen Lebens. Freiburg i. Br.: Herder. Vol. 1 (1960) Grundsatz Pragendes öffentlichen Lebens; Vol. 2 (1962) covers 1959-1961; Vol. 3 (1964) covers 1961-1963, 530 pp; Vol. 4 (1966) covers 1963-1965, 518 pp.; Vol. 5 (1968) covers 1965-1967, 521 pp.; Vol. 6 (1970) covers 1967-1969; Vol. 7 (1972) covers 1970-1971; Vol. 8 (1974) covers 1972-1973.

1669. Garber, Glenn. "A Critical Bibliography of Recent Discussions of Religion Ethics by Philosophers," Journal of Religious Ethics (Waterloo, Can.), vol. 2 (1974), pp. 53-80.

EUTHANASIA. See 1396.

EVIL, PROBLEM OF

1670. Walgrave, J. H. "Theodicee en Godsdienstphilosophie," Tijdschrift voor philosophie (Leuven), vol. 14 (1952), pp. 97-162.

1671. Gratton, Carolyn. "Selected Subject Bibliography (Covering the Past Ten Years)," Humanitas (Pittsburgh), vol. 9 (1973), pp. 129-135.

175 entries on the "human response to suffering."

EVOLUTION

1672. Klubertanz, George. "The Influence of Evolutionary Theory upon American Thought (Conspectus Bibliographicus)," Gregorianum (Romae), vol. 32 (1951), pp. 582-590.

EVORA, LIBRARY, HOLDINGS

1673. Da Costa, Manuel Gonçalves. Inéditos de filosofia da Biblioteca de Evora. Evora: 1951. 151 pp.

EXISTENTIALISM. See also 944, 1161, 1163, 1168, 1626.

1674. Bellezza, Vito A. "Bibliografia italiana sull'-esistentialismo," Archivio di filosofia (Padova), vol. 15 (1946), pp. 171-217.

1675. Jolinet, Régis. Franzosische Existenzphilosophie. (Bibliographische Einführungen in das Studium der Philosophie, 9). Bern: A. Francke, 1948. 36 pp.

Major works of existentialists and their commentators. About 360 entries. A few annotations. Index.

1676. [J. L.] "L'Existentialisme en Italie," Revue internationale de philosophie (Bruxells), vol. 3 (1949), pp. 348-359; 502-506. Also: General bibliography on Existentialism, pp. 343, 347.

1677. "Recenti pubblicazioni italiane sull'esistenzialismo," Archives de philosophie (Paris), vol. 8 (1949), pp. 124-130.

Christian existentialism.

1678. Yanitelli, Victor R. "A Bibliographical Introduction to Existentialism," Modern Schoolman (St. Louis, Mo.), vol. 26 (1949), pp. 345-363.

1679. Douglas, Kenneth. "A Critical Bibliography of Existentialism (The Paris School)," Yale French Studies (Special Monograph, no. 1 (1950)). Also: New York: Kraus Reprint, 1966. 32 pp.

1680. Geiger, L. B. "La Philosophie existentielle," Revue des sciences philosophiques et théologiques (Paris), vol. 35 (1951), pp. 61-104.

1681. Servetti de Torrano, Matilde. Aportes bibliográficos al tema: existencialismo. Fuentes, obras, crítica, etc. (Uruguay. Unidersidad. Facultad de Humanidades y Ciencias, no. 3). Montevideo: 1951. 40 pp. Mimeographed.

1682. Vander Kerken, L. "Existentie-philosophie, II," Katholiek cultureel tijdschrift streven (Amsterdam), vol. 4 (1950-1951), pp. 509-518.

"Existentie-philosophie, I," pp. 396-402.

1683. Valentini, Francesco. "Existenzialismo e marxismo. Ressegna di scritti francesi," Giornale critico della filosofia italiana (Firenze Messina), vol. 31 (1952), pp. 78-96.

1684. Bollnow, Otto Friedrich. Deutsche existenzphilosophie (Bibliographische Einführungen in das Studium der Philosophie, 23). Bern: A. Francke, 1953. 40 pp.

About 250 works by and about german existentialists. Also a nice introduction.

1685. Arce, David N. Sobre lo existencial y algunos "ismos." Ensayo de respuesta y amago bibliográfico. 2a. ed. México: Edit. Jus, 1954. 43 pp.

Originally published in the Boletín of the Biblioteca Nacional, México, D.F. 2a. ép., 5(1): 21-56 (1954).

EXPERIENCE. See 810.

EXPERIMENTATION ON HUMANS. See 2254.

FINE ARTS. See AESTHETICS.

FINNISH PHILOSOPHY. See 2232.

FLEMISH PHILOSOPHY. See 1851, 1620.

FLORENCE, PHILOSOPHICAL LIBRARY HOLDINGS.

1686. Firenze. Biblioteca filosofica. Catalogo della Biblioteca filosofica. Firenze: 1910.

Text and supplement.

1687. Garin, Eugenio. "La Biblioteca filosofica di Firenze," Filosofia (Torino), vol. 10 (1961), pp. 731-741.

FORCE, POLITICAL. See 836.

FRANCISCAN ORDER

1688. Hilarin de Milan. "La Bibliografía francescana," Collectanea Franciscana (Assisii), vol. 19 (1949), pp. 224-246.

1689. Felix a Marteo. "Bibliografía Dantesco-Francescana," Collectanea Francescana (Assisii), vol. 36 (1966), pp. 111-185.

1690. Bibliographia franciscana (Supplement to Collectanea Franciscana) (Romae). 1931-

Contains bibliographies.

FREE THOUGHT. See HUMANISM AND 2194.

FREE WILL. See FREEDOM AND DETERMINISM.

FREEDOM. See 1927.

FREEDOM AND DETERMINISM

1691. Arpe, Peter Freidrich. Theatrum Fati, sive Notitia Scriptorum de Providentia, Fortuno et Fato. Roterodami: Typis Fritch et Bohn, 1712. 101 pp.

About 150 entries. A bibliography on fate and fatalism. Reissue: 1716.

1692. Hall, Roland. "Free Will--a Short Bibliography (in Chronological Order)," Philosophical Quarterly (St. Andrews), vol. 15 (1965), pp. 179-181.

FRENCH LIBRARY (PRAGUE). See 1788.

FRENCH PHILOSOPHY

1693. Ravisson, Félix. La Philosophie en France au XIXe siècle. Paris: Ministère de l'instruction publique: Recueil de rapports sur les progrès des lettres et des sciences en France, 1868. 266 pp.

About 200 entries.

1694. Maisonneuve, [Abbe]. "La Philosophie en France de 1888 à 1898," in Comptes-rendus des travaux du [3me] Congrès bibliographique tenu à Paris du 13 au 16 avril 1898. Paris: Société bibliographique, 1900. 2 vols.

1695. Blanc, Elie. Répertoire bibliographique des auteurs et des ouvrages contemporains de langue française et latine. Paris: Aurat, 1902. 513 pp.

1696. Bibliographie de la philosophie française pour l'-année 1909-[1910]. (Bulletin de la Société Française de Philosophie, August, 1910; July/August, 1911). Paris: A.

1696. (Continued)

Colin, 1910-1911. 319 pp.

2058 entries. Name and subject indexes. Goes beyond philosophy into psychologie, economics, etc.

1697. "Bibliographie philosophique francaise de l'année," L'Année philosophique (Paris), vols. 1-24 (1890-1913).

Lists notices and gives reviews.

1698. Renoir, Edmund. Bibliography of Recent French Philosophy, 1920. [n.p., n.d.]

1699. Acton, H. B. "Philosophical Survey: Philosophy in France," Philosophy (London), vol. 14 (1939), pp. 341-344.

1700. France, Ministère de l'education nationale. Musée pédagogique de l'état . . . Catalogue de la bibliothèque circulante. 3e partie. Philosophie. Paris: Imprimerie nationale, 1942. 15 pp.

About 550 brief entries, some 180 of which are in psychology. All in French, mostly French authors.

1701. Havet, Jacques. "A Survey of some of the French Philosophical Literature since 1946," Philosophy and Phenomenological Research (Buffalo), vol. 11 (1950-1951), pp. 228-251.

1702. Acton, H. B. "Philosophy in France (Philosophical Survey)," Philosophy (London), vol. 27 (1952), pp. 66-69.

1703. Cabeen, D. C. and J. Brody, gen. eds. A Critical Bibliography of French Literature. Syracuse, N.Y.: Syracuse University Press, 1961. 4 vols.

Not restricted to philosophy, but an excellent work. Annotated. Has good sections on the major figures.

1704. Douze Mois d'Edition Religieuse, Philosophique et Pedagogique Française (Paris), vol. 1 (1960)-4 (1963).

About 2000 entries per volume.

FRIENDSHIP

1705. Gratton, Carolyn. "Selected Subject Bibliography (Covering the Past Ten Years)," Humanitas (Pittsburgh), vol. 6 (1970), pp. 249-257.

1705. (Continued)

About 200 entries on "Personal growth through Friendship."

GENERAL PHILOSOPHICAL BIBLIOGRAPHIES. Arranged chronologically and including library shelf lists of general holdings in philosophy; see also Indexes, and Student Guides; see also 1425, 1473, 1484, 1485, 1632, 1686, 1687, 1700, 1801, 1803, 1821, 1854, 1961, 1986, 2072, 2339.

1706. Schum, M. Beschreibendes Verzeichniss de Amplonianischen Handschriftensammlung zu Erfurt, im Auftrage und auf Kosten des Unterrichtsministeriums. Berlin: Unterrichts-Ministerium, 1887. 1010 pp.

Catalog of the 4000 to 5000 volumes presented by Amplonius Ratinck de Berka to the Erfurt library in 1410-1412. Logic 27 works; metaphysics 15 works; moral philosophy 35 works.

1707. Pasquali, Alberto. De Optimo Philosophorum Genere Libri Duo. Venetiis: 1532.

1708. Frisius, Johannes Jacobus [Fries, Johann Jacob]. Bibliotheca Philosophorum Classicorum Authorum Chronologica (+ Bibliotheca Patrum minor.) Tiguri: Ioannem Vvolphium, 1592. 113 pp.

Covers the period "Anno Mundi 1790. Ante Christi Natiuit 2172" to "Anno Do. 1540." Chronologically arranged. For all the entries following "Thomas Bricotus" [1496-1500?], Frisius gives only a list of philosophers' names. The work is divided into two parts: "Philosophorum series ab orbe condito ad nostra usque tempora" (pp. 1-58) and "Compendiosa Patrum . . ." (pp. 59-88). Contains references in the index to about 2000 philosophers and about 750 theologians mentioned in the text. For the period up to about 550 B.C. he mentions Daedalus, Sappho, the Druids, etc. as philosophers; after this period, he somewhat more closely follows the list of philosophers one would construct today. He gives some information on editions of works when he has it. Useful for the period up to about 1500.

1709. Gesner, Conrad. Pandectarusmsive Partitionum Universalium . . . Libri XXI. Tigri: Christophorus Froschouerus, 1548. About 1070 pp. Many editions.

1709. (Continued)

This is the second volume of Gesner's Bibliotheca Universalis and serves as an index to that work. For works on philosophy see his books 15 "De Prima Philosophia seu Metaphysica, Theologia Gentilum" and 16 "De Morali Philosophia." About 2300 titles.

1710. Gesner, Conrad. Bibliotheca Universalis, sive Catalogus omnium Scriptum in Tribus Linguis Latina, Graeca, & Hebraica. Tiguri: Christophorum Froschouerum, 1545. 631 pp. + 107 pp. appendix. Many editions: 1545, 1574, 1583.

For more important figures, he gives some detail beyond bare bio- and bibliographical sketch. More detailed than Spach. This is not a philosophical bibliography but contains much material on various philosophers. Has name index with about 2800 entries. The 1583 edition has about 9100 entries.

1711. Verderius, Antonius [Antonio Verderio]. Supplementum Epitomes Bibliothecae Gesnerianae. Quo Longè Plurimi Libri Continentur qui C. Gesnerum, I. Simlerum, & I. I. Frisium Postremum huiusce Bibliothecae Locupletatorem Latuerunt, vel Post eorum Editiones Typis Mandati sunt A. Verderio Collectore. Adiecta est . . . Bibliotheca Constantinopolitana . . . [By J. Hartung.] [etc.]. Lugduni: Bartholomeum Honorati: 1585. 70 pp.

1712. Spach, Israel. Nomenclator Scriptorum Philosophicorum atque Philologicorum. Hoc est: Succincta Recensio eorum, qui Philosophiam Omnesque eius Partes Quouis Tempore Idiomateue usq; ad Annum 1597 Descripserunt, Illustrarunt, et Exornarunt, Methodo Artificiosa Secundum Locos Communes Ipsius Philosophiae, cum Duplici Indice, Rerum uno Autorum altero. Argentinae: Antonium Bertramum, 1598. 727 pp. + indexes.

Subject index has about 410 entries. Author index has about 8200 names, some of which carry several entries. Bibliographical entries are often quite abbreviated. An amazingly large collection. Worth looking at for Renaissance material up to 1597. Contains much besides philosophy.

1713. Bolduanus, Paulus. Bibliotheca Philosophica, sive: Elenchus Scriptorum Philosophicorum at que Philologicorum Illustrium. Jena: Joannem Weidnerum, 1616. 655 pp.

About 180 subject headings, many of which do not refer to philosophical subjects. Roughly 7700 entries. "Metaphysics" has about 65 entries, "Aristotle" about 360 entries on 33 pages, "Plato" rates 3 pages. Many non-philosophers included: Homer, Heslod, Pindar. Not strictly a philosophical bibliography, but useful for certain areas.

1714. De Lesclache, Louis. La philosophie en tables, divisée en cinq parties, à sçavoir, la logique . . . la science générale . . . la physique . . . la morale . . . la théologie naturelle. 2nd ed. Béziers: Henri Martel, 1675. 188 pp. Also abridgements, 1652 etc., of the first edition.

1715. Lipenius, M. Martinus. Bibliotheca Realis Universalis Omnium Materiarum, Rerum, et Titulorum in Theologia, Jurisprudentia, Medicina, et Philosophia occurrentium, IV, Biblioteca Realis Philosophica. Francofurti ad Moenum: Johannis Friderici, 1682.

Contains much more than philosophy. Works arranged by topic. About 300 works on ethics; 600 in logic under about 50 headings; 31 on being and non-being; 170 on the soul; 850 under various "philosophia" headings. Most works cited are 17th century; a few are earlier. Index.

1716. Boyle, Robert. Catalogus Librorum Tractatumque Philosophicorum. London: 1688. Also: English edition: London: 1689.

1717. Struve, Burkhard Gotthelf. Bibliotheca Philosophica in suas Classes Distributa. Jenae: E. C. Bailliar, 1704. Also: "Recensuit et Largissimis Accessionibus Instruxit Ioannes Georgius Lotterns." Ienae: E. A. Bailliar, 1728. Also: Göttingen: 1740.

About 4200 entries.

1718. Jonsius Johannes. De Scriptoribus Historiae Philosophicae. Frankofurti: Thom. Matth. Götzii, 1659. 388 pp. Also: Franofurti: 1659. 523 pp. Also: "Nunc denvo recogniti," ed. by Io. Christophori Dornii. Ienae: 1716.

Index mentions 2000 names, most of which are from the classical period; many are of people mentioned only in passing. About 1500 entries. 1716 edition has about 2500 entries.

1719. Stolle, Gottlieb. Kurtze Anleitung zur Historie de Gelahrheit, denen, so den freyen Künsten und der Philosophie obliegen. Jena: Johann Meyers Seel. Witwe, 1718. Also: Anleitung zur historie de gelahrheit [etc.] Jena: Johann Meyers Seel. Witwe, 1724.

Contains more than philosophy. A selective guide for students. Good for 17th century. Commentaries.

1720. Heumann, Christoph Augst., ed. Acta Philosophorum, das ist: Gründlagen Nachrichten aus der Historia Philosophica, nebst beygefügten Urtheilen von denen dahin gehörigen alten und neuen Büchern. Halle im Magdeb: zu

1720. (Continued)

Finden in der Rengerischen Buchhandl. 1715-1726. 3 vols (at least 15 parts).

Broad but incomplete coverage.

1721. Conring, Hermann. [Conringius, Hermannus]. De Scriptoribus XVI. post Christum Natum Seculorum Commentarius. Wratislaviae: C. Bauchium, 1703. 130 pp. Another edition: 1727, 230 pp.

1722. Kahl [Kahlis], Ludwig Martin. Bibliothecae Philosophicae Struviane Emendate Continuatae atque Ultra Dimidiam Partem Auctae. Gottingae: Vandenhoeck et Cunonis, 1740. 2 vols. 476, 453 pp.

Expanded version of Struve's original work. Arranged in chapters according to subject. Also contains an author index (about 2100 names) and subject index (about 1000 entries). See Struve above for other editions.

1723. Fabricius, J[ohann?] A[lbert?]. Abriss einer allgemeine Historie der Gelehrsamkeit. Leipzig: 1752 ff. 3 vols.

1724. Brucker, Johann Jakob. Historia Critica Philosophiae a Mundi Incunabulis ad Nostram usque Aetatem Deducta. Lipsiae: B. C. Breitkopf, 1742-1744. 4 tomes in 5 vols. Second edition: Lipsiae: Weidemanni et Reichii, 1767. 6 vols. Summarized by William Enfield, London: C. Daily, 1840. 670 pp.

About 4000 pp. A history, but with many bibliographical notes. Index.

1725. De Bure, Guillaume-Françoise. Bibliographie instructive: ou traité de la connoissance des livres rares et singuliers. Paris: Guillaume-François De Bure le Jeune, 1763. 10 vol.

Vol. 2, "Classe troisieme: Sciences et arts," pp. 149-259, contains works on philosophy under a number of headings. About 180 works are described.

1726. Chaudon, Louis Mayeul. Bibliothèque d'un homme de goût, ou avis sur le choix des meilleurs livres écrits en notre langue sur tous les genres de sciences et de littérature. 2 vols. Avignon: A. Aubsnel, 1772.

1727. Grudé de la Croix du Maine, François. Les bibliothèques françoises de la Croix du Mainé et du Verdier . . . Paris: Saillánt et Nyon, 1773. Vol. 6, Supplementum Epitomes Bibliothecae Gesnerianae. 359, 120 pp.

About 1800 entries arranged alphabetically by author's first name. Subject and name indices. Supplements Gesner's bibliography. Contains theology and other non-philosophy.

1728. Savérien, Alexandre. Historie des philosophes modernes, avec leur portrait gravé dans le goût du crayon d'après les dessins des plus grand peintres. Paris: Brunet, 1760-1761. Vols. I-II: Historie des métaphysiciens; Vols. III-IV: Historie des restaurateurs des sciences; Other editions: Paris: Brunet, 1760-1769: 7 vols; Paris: Bluet, 1773.

1729. Hissmann, Michael. Anleitung zur Kenntniss der anserlesenen Literatur in allen Theilen der Philosophie. Göttingen: Im Verlag der Meyerschen Buchhandlung, 1778. 478 pp. Also: 1790 edition with corrections.

About 2000 entries.

1730. Heydenreich, K. Encyclopädische Einleitung in das Studium der Philosophie. Nebst Anleitungen zur philosophischen Literatur. Leipzig: Weygand, 1793.

Bibliography pp. 125 ff.

1731. Heumann, Christoph Augst. Conspectvs Reipvblicae Literariae. Hanoverae: Nicolavm Foerstervm, 1718. Other editions: 1726, 1733, 1735, 1746, 1753, 1763, 1971-97.

1732. Ortloff Johann Andreas. Handbuch der Literatur der Geschichte der Philosophie. Erlangen: Waltherschen Buchhandlung, 1798. 240 pp. Reprinted: Düsseldorf: Stern-Verlag Janssen, 1967.

Roughly 2400 entries with good coverage of 18th century. The student of that century should find it helpful.

1733. Krug, Wilhelm Traugott. Enzyklopädisch-Szientifische Literatur. Viertes Heft, die enzyklopädisch-philosophische Literatur enthaltend. Leipzig: 1805. 70 pp.

About 700 entries.

1734. Ernesti, Johann Heinrich Martin. Encyclopädisches Handbuch einer allgemeinen Geschichte der Philosophie und ihrer literatur. Nebst Beyträgen zum weiteren gebrauch der Hissmannischen Anleitung. Lemgo: Mayer [?], 1807. 656 pp.

About 3000 entries.

1735. Gumposch, Victor Philipp. Die philosophische und theologische Literatur der Deutschen von 1400 bis auf unsere Tage . . . Erster Band. Die philosophische Literatur. Regensburg: G. J. Manz, 1851. 640 pp. Reprinted: Düsseldorf: Stern-Verlag, 1967.

1736. Tübingen. Königlichen Universitätsbibliothek. Systematisch-alphabetischer Hauptkatalog der Königlichen Universitätsbibliothek zu Tübingen; erstes Heft. A. Philosophie. Tübingen: 1854. 63 pp. Also: Annual Supplements to 1880. Erstes ergunzungsheft, 1882. 60 pp. About 2500 entries.

1737. Oporto, Portugal. Biblioteca publica. Catalogo d philosophia da Bibliotheca publica municipal do Porto. Porto: Imprensa Commercial, 1883. 109 pp.

Classified; with author index.

1738. Reims. Bibliothèque. Catalogues imprimés. Sciences philosophiques et sociales. Reims: 1886. [n.p.?]

1739. Avetta, Adolfo. Abbozzo di una bibliografia critica a soggetti delle scienze filosofiche. Torino: Camilla e Bertolero, 1891.

250 annotated specimen entries to illustrate the plan of the proposed bibliography. Almost exclusively Italian works of the late nineteenth century. Contains in its preface a sketch of philosophical histories, bibliographies, and dictionaries from the work of Frisius in 1592 through 1884. Misdescribed as "Averra" in the Widener shelf-list.

1740. Cosentini, Francesco, et al. Bibliotheca Philosophica ou Guide bibliographique-critique à l'étude historique de la philosophie et des sciences analogues jusqu'a l'an 1896. Vol. 1, partie 1, Ouvrages généraux sur l'historie de la philosophie. Sassari: J. Dessi, 1895. 74 pp.

About 1200 entries. Also an 1896 edition?

1741. Sitzungsberichte der königlich-bayerischen academie der wissenschaften. Philosophisch-philologische und historische klasse. Inhaltverzeichniss. Jahrgänge 1886-1899. Munchen: Franz, 1900.

1742. Rand, Benjamin. A Philosophical Library for the American Continent. 2nd rev. ed., Cambridge, Mass. Oct. 19, 1904. [n.p.?]

1743. Rand, Benjamin. Bibliography of Philosophy, Psychology and Cognate Subjects (Vol. 3 of J. M. Baldwin, ed., Dictionary of Philosophy). New York: Macmillan, 1905. 2 vols. Reprinted: New York: Peter Smith, 1949.

1743. (Continued)

About 65,000 unannotated entries divided according to author and by topic. Covers up to 1900. A major work.

1744. Vaschide, N., and von Buschan. Index philosophique. Philosophie et sciences annexes: Biologie-neurologie-psychiatrie. (Publication of the Revue de Philosophie). Paris: Nand, 1903-1905. Vol. 1: 1902. 4623 entries. Vol. 2: 1903. 5367 entries.

Covers works in various European languages. Author index.

1745. New York City. Public Library. List of Books Relating to Philosophy. New York: 1908. 93 pp.

3250 entries.

1746. Psychological Index . . . an Annual Bibliography of the Literature of Psychology and Cognate Subjects (New York).

Philosophy notices begin in 1900 and continue through 1910. Forms a series of supplements to Rand's bibliography. Claims to cover "philosophical articles" in all languages and books in German, French, and English, but coverage is not very exhaustive.

1747. Sonnenschein, William Swan. "Philosophy," in his The Best Books: A Reader's Guide and Literary Reference Book, Being a Guide Towards Systematic Bibliography, 3rd edition. London: George Routledge and Sons, 1910, pp. 397-448. Reprinted: Detroit: Gale Research, 1969. Also appears as: A Bibliography of Philosophy. Being the Sections Relating to that Subject in The Best Books and The Reader's Guide, London: S. Sonnenschein, 1897. About 40 pp.

About 1500 entries divided by topics. References to most of the works which were thought to be important at time of publication. (A nice selection of eighteenth and nineteenth century works on animal rights.)

1748. Hilsenbeck, Adolf. Register zu den Abhandlungen denkschriften und Reden der K. Bayer Akadamie der Wissenschaften, 1807-1913. (Acadamie der Wissenschaften, München.) München: Königlich Bayerischen Akademie der Wissenschaften, 1914. 201 pp.

1749. Chicago. Chicago Public Library. Philosophy, Religion, Medicine. Finding List. Chicago: Chicago Public Library, 1916. 454 pp.

1750. Hoffmann, Jean. La Philosophie et les philosophes: ouvrages généraux. Bruxelles: Van Oest: 1920. 395 pp. Reprinted: New York: Burt Franklin, 1968.

2716 entries arranged according to a detailed list of topics. Author index. Excellent coverage up to 1920. Emphasizes European works.

1751. Newberry Library. Chicago. . . . Philosophy: Metaphysics, Psychology, Ethics. Chicago: 1922. 258 pp.

Holdings in philosophy. Indexed according to subject, title and author.

1752. Sezauer, A. Bücherverzeichnis. Fünfte Abteilung. Fachübersichten 1886-1924. C. Philosophie. Karlsruhe: Badische Landsbibliothek, 1925. 95 pp.

2750 entries.

1753. Rodenberg, Julius F. W. A. Philosophie. (Jahresberichte des Literarischen Zentralblattes, I, 7). Leipzig: Börsenvereins der Deutschen Buchhändler, 1925. 155 pp.

Philosophy covered in pp. 1-105. About 1200 entries. Name and subject indexes. Occasional annotations.

1754. Ueberweg, Friedrich. Grundriss der Geschichte der Philosophie. . . Herausgegeben von Dr. Karl Praechter. 12th ed. Berlin: E. S. Mittler, 1923-1928. 5 vols. New edition by Paul Wilpert, 1965- . 1st ed.: 1862-1866.

Covers works prior to 1923. Many thousands of entries along with text. The most important retrospective bibliography for the period 1800-1923. More useful than Rand's larger bibliography.

1755. Los Angeles. University of Southern California. School of Philosophy. Hoose Library of Philosophy. The Seeley Wintersmith Mudd Foundation Special Collection in the Hoose Library of Philosophy, School of Philosophy. Los Angeles, The University of Southern California, 1940. 39 pp.

1756. Yela, Juan Francisco. "Orientaciones bibliográficas sobre filosifía," Biblioteca hispaña (Madrid), vol. 1 (1943), pp. 175-194.

1757. Lillie, Robert. A Classified Catalogue of the Books in the Philosophical Sections of the Lending and Reference Departments of the Central Public Library. Gateshead: 1945. 35 pp.

1757. (Continued)

About 600 entries.

1758. U. S. Library of Congress, General Reference and Bibliography Division. Current Philosophical Literature Suggested for the Hebrew University in Jerusalem. Washington: Library of Congress, 1945. 15 ff.

229 entries.

1759. Bochenski, I. M., and F. Montelone. Allgemeine philosophische Bibliographie. (Bibliographische Einführungen in das Studium der Philosophie, 1). Bern: A. Francke, 1948. 42 pp.

Good for general reference works and the general bibliography of philosophy.

1760. Ferro, Carmelo. Guida storico-bibliografica allo studio della filosofia. Milano: Società Editrice Vita e pensiero, 1949. 196 pp.

About 7000 entries.

1761. Milan. Università Cattolica del Sacro curore. Guide bibliografiche. Ser. 2. Filosofia. Milano: Vita e pensiero, 194[?].

1762. Bayer, Raymond. Philosophie [bibliographie]. (Manuel de la recherche documentaire en France, t.2,1.ptie.,7. section). Beyeux: R.-P. Colas, 1950. 417 pp.

6000 entries.

1763. Bayer, Raymond. Philosophie: chronique des années de guerre 1939-1945, d'après guerre 1946-1948 (Actualitiés scientifiques et industrielles). Paris: Hermann, 1950. 5 vols.

Volumes divided by topics.

1764. Histoire de la philosophie, métaphysique, philosophie des valeurs, publication entreprise sous les auspices de la U.N.E.S.C.O. Paris: Hermann, 1950.

Vol. I: Philosophie. (Chronique des années de guerre 1939-1945), 197 pp.
Vol. II: Philosophie. (Chronique des années de d'après guerre 1946-1948), 249 pp.

1765. Ziegenfuss, Werner [et al.]. Philosophen-Lexikon. Handwörterbuch der Philosophie nach Personen. Berlin: Walter de Gruyter, 1949-1950. 2 vols. Also: Berlin: E. S. Mittler, 1937; etc.

1765. (Continued)

This work contains short bibliographies of works by and about a large number of philosophers, as well as sketches of their views. A good place to start, especially on little-known figures.

1766. Forest, Aimé. "Chronique de philosophie." Revue thomiste (St. Maximin), vol. 52 (1952), pp. 163-174.

1767. Hanover. Stadtbibliothek. Philosophie. Ein Verzeichnis von Büchern und Aufsätzen. Hanover: 1954. 169 pp.

About 4500 entries.

1768. De Brie, G. A. Bibliographia Philosophica, 1934-1945. Bruxelles: Ed. Spectrum, 1950-1954. 2 vols. Vol. 1: "Bibliographia Historiae Philosophiae," 664 pp. Vol. 2: "Bibliographia Philosophiae," 798 pp.

Attempts to cover all works published in western European languages for the period. Index of names. A great work. 48,178 entries.

1769. Tetsugaku Meicho Kaidai [Annotated Bibliography of Great Works in Philosophy [In Japanese]]. 1955. 397 pp.

1770. Varet, Gilbert. Manuel de bibliographie philosophique. Paris: Presses universitaires de France, 1956. 1058 pp. 2 vols.

Extensive coverage. Divided by topics. About 20,000 entries. Author index. An excellent work.

1771. International Association of Theological Libraries. Select List of Books on Theology and Philosophy Published in Great Britain and Ireland in 1957. London: International Association of Theological Libraries, 1958. 10 pp.

About 200 entries.

1772. Arnim, Max. Internationale Personal-Bibliographie 1800-1959. 3 vols. Stuttgart: A. Hiersemann, 1952-63. Earlier editions: Leipzig, 1936, 1944, 1952; Stuttgart, 1952; etc.

Not restricted to philosophers. Covers about 80,000 individuals, mostly European, mostly German. One or two bibliographies usually on each person. A good work for little known figures.

1773. Berg, Jan. Selektiv Bibliografi i teoretisk Filosofi. (Filosofisker Studier utgitt av Filosofiska Institut vid Stockholsm Universitet, Häfte 5), Stockholm: 1960. Supplement: 1961. 7 pp.

Classifies titles of selected books and articles under a number of headings: "Logic," "Theory of Knowledge," "History of Ideas," and so on. Selection is good. Topics in logic comprise the largest section of the book. Headings and forword in Swedish.

1774. Nuño Montes, Juan Antonio. Repertorios bibliográficos de filosofía. (Universidad Central de Venezuela. Edicions de la Biblioteca, 8. Colección Bibliografías, 2) Caracas: Universidad Central de Venezuela, 1962- .

1775. Akademii͡a nauk SSSR. Fundamental'nai͡a biblioteka obšč̌estvennykh nauk. Istoriia zarubezhnoi domarksistskoi filosofii, za 1917-1962 gody [Basic Library of Social Science. History of Foreign Pre-Marxist Philosophy, 1917-1962 [In Russian]]. Moskva: 1963. 297 pp.

1776. Totok, Wilhelm. Handbuch der Geschichte der Philosophie. Vol. 1: Alterum. Indische, chinesische, griechisch-römesche philosophie. Helmut Schröer, ed. Frankfurt am Main: V. Klosterman, 1964- .

See next entry for description.

1777. Totok, Wilhelm. Handbuch der Geschichte der Philosophie, Vol. 2: Mittelalter. Frankfurt am Main: V. Klosterman, 1964- .

Quite comprehensive. Indexes. Arranged by topics and sub-topics. Covers the period since the First World War. Attempts to bring Ueberweg's 1923 work up to date. A third volume covering modern times is in progress. First two volumes contain reference to roughly 38,000 entries. One of the more useful and important works.

1778. Zamarriego, Tomas, dir. y Juan Flors, ed. Enciclopedia de orientación bibliográfica. Vol. II ciencias religiosas, ciencias humanas. Barcelona: Raycar, 1964. 79 pp.

About 8,000 entries with annotations. Although concerned primarily with religion and theology (pp. 3-605), it contains approximately 2,400 entries in all branches of philosophy, books only, many in Spanish. Arranged according to topics.

1779. Menchaca, José A. Diccionario bio-bibliográfico de filósofos. (Publicaciónes de la Universidad de Deusto. Sección de Filosofía). Bilbao: El Mensajero del Corazón de Jesús, 1965- .

1780. Taylor, Archer. General Subject Indexes since 1548. Philadelphia: University of Pennsylvania Press, 1966. 336 pp.

Contains references to some works which deal with philosophy.

1781. Geldsetzer, Lutz. Philosophengalerie. Vol. 1: Bildnisse und Bibliographien von Philosophen aus dem 11. bis 17 Jahrhundert. Düsseldorf: Philosophia Verlag, 1967- . 240 pp.

1782. London, University. Catalog of the Warburg Institute Library. Vol. 5, "History of Philosophy." Boston: G. K. Hall and Co., 1967.

About 5400 entries. Photocopies of catalog cards.

1783. Los Angeles. University of Southern California. Hoose Library of Philosophy. Catalog. Boston: G. K. Hall, 1968. 6 vols.

1784. Richter, Richard. Hundert Jahre philosophische Bibliothek 1868-1968. Zeittafeln und gesamt-Verlagsverzeichnis 1968. (Die Zusammenstellung der Zeittafel und des Katalogs besorgte Richard Richter). Hamburg: F. Meiner, 1968. 69 pp.

1785. Walford, Albert John. Guide to Reference Material, 2d ed., vol. 2 "Philosophy and Psychology, Religion [etc.]." London: The Library Association, 1968.

Pp. 1-12 give erratic coverage of a number of works.

1786. Paris. Centre National de la Recherché Scientifique. Documentation et disciplines philosophiques. Paris: 1969. 270 pp.

1787. Plott, John C. and Paul D. Mays. Sarva-Darśana-Sangraha; a Bibliographical Guide to the Global History of Philosophy. Leiden: E. J. Brill, 1969. 305 pp.

Major emphasis on non-western works; a very unconventional book.

1788. Prague. French library. Filosofie (Seznam lit.) [Philosophy (A Collection of Literature) [In Czech]]. (Seznamy příručních knihoven, 4). Praha: St. knihovna ČSSR-francouzská, knihovna rozmn., 1969. 54 pp.

1789. Quebec (City). Université Laval. Bibliothèque. Introduction aux ouvrages de référence en philosophie. Choix d'ouvrages de la collection de la bibliothèque de l'université. Laval. Préparé per Gilles Paradis. (Guides bibliotheques, 1). Québec: Bibliothèque de l'Université Laval, 1969. 46 pp.

A selection of works from that library. About 200 annotated entries plus a name index. A good guide to introductory material.

1790. Geldsetzer, Lutz. Allgemeine Bücher-und Institutionenkunde für das Philosophiestudium; wissenschaftliche Institutionen, bibliographische Hilfsmittel, Gattungen philosophischer Publikationen. Freiburg: K. Alber, c. 1971. 209 pp.

1791. Ritter, Joachim, ed. Historisches Wörterbuch der Philosophie. Darmstate: Wissenschaftliche Buchgesellschaft, 1971. Vol. I, A-C; Vol. II, D-F; Vol. 3, G-H.

Articles on various subjects. Most have extensive bibliographies. Has name index. A good place to start when looking for bibliographies on specific subjects.

1792. Harvard University Library. Philosophy and Psychology. Volume I Classification Schedule. Classified Listing by Call Number, Chronological Listing; Volume II Author and Title Listings. (Widener Library Shelflists, 42 and 43.) Cambridge, Mass.: Harvard University Library; Distributed by Harvard University Press, 1973.

59,000 titles. Titles listed by topic, by date, by author and title. A good place to look for things. Abbreviated entries are sometimes bothersome.

1793. Bibliographic Index. A Cumulative Bibliography of Bibliographies (New York), vol. 1 (1937/1942)--[to date].

Gives bibliographies in all fields including philosophy. Especially useful for bibliographies published in monographs.

1794. Bibliographische Berichte (Frankfurt am Main), 1-(1959-)--[to date].

Each volume carries a section which reports philosophical bibliographies published over

1794. (Continued)

the preceding year. About one-third of the bibliographies are in East European languages.

1795. _Revue de l'enseignement philosophique_ (Paris), vol. 1 (1950)--[to date].

Contains bibliographies.

1796. "Selected Bibliography. Titles of New Books and Articles. Studies in Philosophy," _Philosophy and History_ (Tübingen), vol. 1 (1968)--[to date].

Philosophy and History is devoted to reviews and bibliographies of German language publications in philosophy and history. Each number carries a bibliography of roughly 90 entries.

1797. Porto Alegre. Livraria Universal de Echenique y Irmao. _Catálogo geral das obras existentes e a venta. Catálogo 6: Direito, política, philosophia_. Porto Alegre. [n.d.].

GENERAL SYSTEMS THEORY. See 195, 196.

GENETICS. See 2254.

GENEVA. See SWISS PHILOSOPHY.

GERMAN ORIENTAL SOCIETY LIBRARY, HOLDINGS. See 1937.

GERMAN PHILOSOPHY. See also 351.

1798. Adam, Melchior. _Vitae Germanorum Philosophorum: qui Seculo Superiori, et quod Excurrit, Philosophicis ac Humanioribus Literis Clari Floreurunt_. Haidelbergae[?]: Jonae Rosae, 1615. 526 pp. Also: Frankofurti: Rosae, 1663; Frankofurti ad Moenum: J. M. à Sande, 1706.

About 2000 entries.

1799. Eyring, Jeremias Nicolaus. _Litterarischer Almanach der Deutschen . . . Literatur der Philosophischen und Schönen Wissenschaften und Künste_. (Göttingen) 1775, 190 pp.

400 entries; 1776 ed., 208 pp., 415 entries; 1777 ed., 206 pp., 439 entries.

1800. La Correspondance allemande ou bibliothèque philosophique, politique . . .[etc.] (Frankfurt am Main), nos. 1-26 (1780).

1801. Ersch, Johann Samuel. Handbuch der deutschen Literatur seit der Mitte des achtzehnteu Jahr-Hunderts bis auf die neueste Zeit. Erste Abtheilung, die Literatur der Philologie, Philosophie und Padägogik enhaltend. Amsterdam: Kunst-und industrie-comptoir, 1812. 365 cols. Other editions: Leipzig: 1819, 1500 entries; Leipzig: ed. by C. A. Geissler, Bibliographishes Handbuch der Philosophischer Litteratur, 1845, 1850. Reprint of 1850 ed. Düsseldorf, 1965.

1812 edition has about 1000 entries in philosophy. 1850 ed., 2645 entries.

1802. Schaller, Karl August. Handbuch der klassischen philosophischen Literatur der Deutschen von Lessing bis auf gegenwärtige Zeit. Halle: Hemmerde und Schwetschke, 1811-1816.

This is vol. 2 of his Handbuch der neueren Deutschen klassischen Literatur.

1803. Enslin, Theodor Christian Friedrich. Bibliotheca Philosophica, oder Verzeichniss der in älterer und neuer zeit, besonders aber vom 1750 bis zu Ende vom 1823 in Deutschland erschienenen Bücher aber alle Theile der Philosophie. Berlin: Herausgeber, 1824. 82 pp.

About 2000 entries.

1804. Vierteljahrs-catalog aller neuen Erscheinungen im Felde der Literatur in Deutschland. I. Theologie und Philosophie. Leipzig: 1847-[?].

1805. Büchting, Adolph. Bibliotheca Philosophica, oder Verzeichniss der auf dem Gebeite der philosophischen Wissenschaften in den letzten X Jahren, 1857-1866, im Deutschen Buchhandel erschienenen Bücher und Zeitschriften . . . mit einen Sach-Register. Nordhausen: Büchting, 1867. 50 pp. Also 1857-1871: Büchting 1872, 43 pp.

Widener shelf list misspells his name "Buchring." 1872 edition has about 800 entries.

1806. International Congress for Philosophy, Third. Verzeichnis der vom Juli 1904 bis Juli 1908 in Deutschland erschienen philosophischen Literatur, und bedeutenderen Werke in Englisher und Französischer Sprache. Heidelberg, Weiss, 1908. 64 pp.

1807. Gesamt-katalog der Deutschen philosophischen Literatur. Leipzig: 1924. 68 pp.

1808. Spaemann, Robert. "Courants philosophiques dans l'Allemagne d'aujourd'hui," Archives de philosophie (Paris), vol. 21 (1958), pp. 274-297.

1809. Sass, Hans-Martin. Inedita Philosophica. Ein Verzeichnis von nachlässen deutschsprachinger Philosophen des 19. und 20. jahrhunderts. Düsseldorf: Philosophia Verlag, 1974. 86 pp.

Name and subject indexes. Arranged by author's name. About 1000 entries.

GNOSTICISM

1810. Jacobs, Joseph. "Bibliographical Appendix," in Charles William King, The Gnostics and Their Remains. New York: Putnam, 1887, pp. 449-456. Also: 1881.

GÖTHEBURG LIBRARY, HOLDINGS. See 1546.

GREEK PHILOSOPHY, CLASSICAL PERIOD. See CLASSICAL GREEK AND ROMAN PHILOSOPHY.

GREEK PHILOSOPHY, MODERN PERIOD

1811. Voumvlinopoulos, Georges E. Bibliographie critique de la philosophie grecque depuis la chute de Constantinople à nos jours, 1453-1953. Athens: Presses de l'Institut Français d'Athens, 1966. 236 pp.

Covers a large number of works in various languages by and about Greek authors. Arranged chronologically. Name index. The guide for the literature and period covered.

GUATEMALAN PHILOSOPHY. See 2218.

GUILT. See RESPONSIBILITY.

HANOVER STATE LIBRARY, HOLDINGS. See 1767.

HARVARD-YENCHING INSTITUTE LIBRARY, HOLDINGS. See 1528.

HEALTH CARE. See 2254.

HEBREW UNIVERSITY LIBRARY, HOLDINGS. See 1758.

HEDONISM. See 438.

HERMENEUTICS

1812. Henrichs, Norbert. *Bibliographie der Hermeneutik und ihrer Anwendungs gereiche seit Schleiermacher*. Düsseldorf: 1968. 491 cols.

HERZOG-AUGUST LIBRARY. See 774.

HINDUISM. See INDIAN PHILOSOPHY AND HINDUISM.

HINDUSTANI LANGUAGE WORKS

1813. Blumhardt, J. F. *Catalogue of Hindustani Printed Books in the Library of the British Museum*. Printed by order of the Trustees of the British Museum. London: Longman's, 1889.

Lists 8 books on philosophy and about 450 in religion.

HISTORICAL MATERIALISM. See also 899.

1814. Rozanov, J. S. *Istoričaskiǐ materializm* [*Historical materialism* [In Russian]]. *Bibliogr. knižnoj i žurnal'n literatury za 1865-1924*. [A Bibliography of Books and Journals for the Period 1865-1924.] Kiev: 1925. 153 pp.

HISTORIOGRAPHY, METHODOLOGY OF

1815. Biscione, Michele. "Metodologia e storia della storiografia. Rassegna degli studi dal 1944," *Rassegna di filosofia* (Roma), vol. 1 (1952), pp. 27-38.

HISTORY OF IDEAS. See also 1617, 1963, 2167.

1816. Flasche, Hans and Utta Warwrzinek. *Materialen zur Begriffsgeschichte; eine Bibliographie Deutscher Hoschul-Schriften von 1900-1955*. 718 pp. (Archiv für

1816. (Continued)

Begriffsgeschichte. Ed. Erich Rothacker. Band 5.) Bonn: H. Bouvier and Co., 1960. 718 pp.

9491 entries.

1817. Scholtz, Gunter. "Bibliographie begriffsgeschichtlicher Arbeiten," Archiv für begriffsgeschichte (Bonn), vol. 13 (1969), pp. 200-214.

HISTORY OF PHILOSOPHY. See also GENERAL PHILOSOPHICAL BIBLIOGRAPHIES, entries for specific periods, and 1540, 1576, 1610, 1919, 2062, 2073, 2213, 2269.

1818. Fülleborn, Georg Gustav. Beyträge zur Geschichte der Philosophie. Züllichau und Freystadt: Fromann, 1791-1796. 7 parties en 3 vol.

1819. Carus, Friedrich August. Ideen zur Geschichte der Philosophie. Leipzig: J. A. Barth, 1809. 766 pp. In his Nachgelassine Werke, 4.

Bibliography on pp. 21-90.

1820. Rand, Benjamin. "Selected Works on the History of Philosophy in the English Language," Bulletin of Books Added to the Public Library of the City of Boston, vol. 11 (1906), pp. 55-65.

1821. Tennemann, Wilhelm Gottlieb. Grundriss der Geschichte der Philosophie. Leipzig: 1812. Many editions including: Leipzig, 1829; Oxford (in English): 1832; London: 1852; Paris (in French): 1829, 1839.

1822. Saisset, E. E. "Des derniers travaux sur l'histoire de la philosophie," Revue des deux mondes (Paris), (1847), pp. 358-371.

1823. Sortais, G. Historie de la philosophie. Antiquité classique. Epoque patristique. Philosophie médiévale. Renaissance. Paris: Lethielleux, 1912. 627 pp.

Pp. 485-561 contain an extensive bibliography.

1824. Lutosławski, W. and J. Suchorzewska. "Bericht über die 1925-1930 in Polon. Sprache erschienen Schriften zur Geschichte der Philosophie," Archiv für Geschichte der Philosophie (Berlin), vol. 40 (1931), pp. 310-328.

1825. "Bollettino bibliografico. Storia della filosofia antica 1930. Storia della filosofia medievale 1928-1929-1930. Storia della filosofia moderna 1930. Storia della filosofia contemporanea 1930," Sophia (Padova), vol. 3 (1935) (Appendix), 159 pp.

1826. Saffrey, H. D., H. D. Gardeil, and Guy Leger. "Bulletin d'historie de la philosophie (1949-1951)," Revue des sciences philosophiques et théologiques (Le Saulchoir), vol. 35 (1951), pp. 645-714.

1827. Beck, Lewis White. "Introduction and Bibliography [: The Interpretation of the History of Philosophy]," Monist (La Salle, Ill.), vol. 53 (1969), pp. 523-531.

70 works since 1930.

HISTORY, PHILOSOPHY OF. See also 907, 1022, 1819, 1827.

1828. Schoeps, Hans Joachim. "Neue Literatur zur Geschichtsphilosophie," Zeitschrift für Religions-und Geistesgeschichte (Margurg), vol. 2 (1949-50), pp. 183-185.

1829. Cohen, Jonathan. "A Survey of Work in the Philosophy of History, 1946-1950," Philosophical Quarterly (St. Andrews), vol. 2 (1952), pp. 172-186.

1830. Rule, J. C. Bibliography of Works in the Philosophy of History. The Hague: Mouton and Co., 1961, pp. vii-87.

Reviewed by F. Diaz de Cerio in Gregorianum, 1963.

1831. Nowicki, M. Bibliography of Works in the Philosophy of History. I: 1958-1961 (History and Theory. Studies in the Philosophy of History, 3). The Hague: Mouton, 1964.

1832. Wurgaft, Lewis D. "A Supplement to Bibliography of Works in the Philosophy of History, 1962-1965," History and Theory (Middletown, Conn.), Beiheft 10, 1971.

1833. Wurgaft, Lewis D. "Bibliography of Works in the Philosophy of History, 1966-1968," History and Theory (Middleton, Conn.), Beiheft 10, 1970, pp. 1-46.

1834. Pruitt, Sylvia, and Astrid Witschi-Bernz. "A Supplement to Bibliography of Works in the Philosophy of History 1966-1968," History and Theory (Middletown, Conn.) Beiheft 13 (1974), pp. 105-106; "1969-1972," pp. 1-104.

1835. Witschi-Bernz, Astrid. "Bibliography of Works in the Philosophy of History, 1500-1800," History and Theory (Middletown, Conn.), vol. 12 (1972), pp. 3-50.

1836. Pruitt, Sylvia. "Bibliography of Works in the Philosophy of History (1969-1972)," History and Theory: Beiheft (Middletown, Conn.), vol. 13 (1974), pp. 1-106.

HOOSE LIBRARY. See 1755, 1783.

HUMAN DEVELOPMENT, AND SYMBOLISM. See 2326.

HUMAN EXPERIMENTATION. See 2254.

HUMANISM

1837. Henning, Max. Handbuch der freigeistigen Bewegung Deutschlands, Österreichs und der Schweiz. (Jahrbuch des Weimarer Kartells: 1914). Frankfurt am Main, 1914. 428 pp.

1838. Gollmann, Franz. Katalog freigeistiger Literatur. (Im auftrage der Reichs-Arbeitsgemeinschaft der freigeistigen Verbande der Deutschen Republik.) Dresden: J. Rudolph, 1926. 138 pp.

1839. Blackham, Harold John. A guide to Humanist Books in English. (The Plain View, supplement, no. 1). London: 1955. 84 pp.

1840. Kwee, Swan-liat. Bibliography of Humanism. Utrecht: Humanist League, 1957. 44 pp.

Has name and subject indexes.

1841. Bergier, J. F. "Bibliographie des articles relatifs à l'histoire de l'humanisme et de la Renaissance, 1960," Bibliothèque d'humanisme et renaissance (Paris), vol. 23 (1961), pp. 603-633.

1842. Bergier, J. F. "Bibliographie des articles relatifs à l'histoire de l'humanisme et de la renaissance, 1961. Supplement 1959-1960," Bibliothèque d'humanisme et renaissance (Paris), vol. 24 (1962), pp. 620-639.

1843. Becker, Karl. Freigeistige Bibliographie: ein Verzeichnis Freigeistiger, Humanistischer, und Religionskritischer Literatur. Würthemberg: Freireligionen Landesgimeinde. Württemberg. 171 pp.

About 3100 entries, occasional annotations. Name Index. Entries arranged by topic.

1844. "Bibliographie des articles relatifs à l'histoire de l'humanisme et de la Renaissance, 1962," Bibliothèque d'humanisme et Renaissance (Paris), vol. 25 (1963), pp. 588-625.

1845. Kristeller, Paul Oskar. Iter Italicum. A Finding List of Uncatalogued or Incompletely Catalogued Humanistic Manuscripts of the Renaissance in Italian and other Libraries, I: Italy. Agrigento to Novara. London: Warburg Institute; Leiden: E. J. Brill, 1963. 533 pp.

1846. Schiavone, Michele. "Bibliografia critica generale. Umanesimo e Rinascimento. La Riforma protestante. La Riforma cattolica," in Grande antologia filosofica, Milano: Marzorati, 1964, vol. 6, pp. 1-87.

1847. Bibliographie internationale de l'humanisme et de la Renaissance, I: travaux parus in 1965. Genève: Minard, 1966. 288 pp.

1848. Gerlo, Aloïs and Emile Lauf. Bibliographie de l'humanisme belge, précédée d'une bibliographie générale concernant l'humanisme européen. (Université libre de Bruxelles. Institut pour l'étude de la Renaissance et d'humanisme. Instrumenta Humanistica, 3). Bruxelles: Presses universitaires de Bruxelles, 1965. 248 pp.

Selective, not indexed. About 3000 entries arranged by subject.

1849. Cosenza, Mario Emilio. Biographical and Bibliographical Dictionary of the Italian Humanists and of the World of Classical Scholarship in Italy, 1300-1800. 2nd ed. Boston: G. K. Hall, 1962-1967. 6 vols. Supplement: A-Z, 1967.

First edition was printed in microfilm form by the Renaissance Society of America in 1954.

1850. Ronchetti, Emanuele. "Bibliografia humania dal 1937 at 1966," Rivista critica di storia della filosofia (Milano), vol. 22 (1967), pp. 495-520.

1851. Gerlo, Aloïs and Hendrik D. L. Vervliet. Bibliographie de l'humanisme des anciens Pays-Bas. Avec un répertoire bibliographique des humanistes et poètes néo-latins. (Université libre de Bruxelles. Institut pour l'étude de la Renaissance et d'Humanisme. Instrumenta Humanistica, 3). Bruxelles: Presses Universitaires de Bruxelles, 1972. 542 pp.

Over 5700 entries. Not annotated. Arranged by topics. An extensive work.

HUMANITIES

1852. American Council of Learned Societies Devoted to Humanistic Studies. Catalogue of Current Bibliographies in the Humanistic Sciences . . . Washington: American Council of Learned Societies, 1931. 73 pp.

Manuscript. Classified and annotated with index.

1853. Tokyo. Nihon Gakujutsu Kaigi. Bunkakei Bunken Mokuroku [Humanities Bibliography, part 1, 1964 [In Japanese]]. Tokyo: Nihon Kakujutsu Kaigi[?], 196[?] 250 pp.

This is volume 16 of a series begun in 1952.

HUNGARIAN PHILOSOPHY

1854. Buday. Júlia. A Magyar filozófiai irodalom bibliografiája. Magyar tudományos irodalom bibliografiája, 1901-1925. Vol. 1. Budapest: Királyi Magyar egyetemi nyomda, 1929. 248 pp.

About 5000 entries.

1855. Joó, Tibor. Magyar nyelvü filozófiai kéziratok a Széchényi könyvtárban. (Philosophische Handschriften in Ungarischer Sprache aus der sammlung der Széchényi landesbibliothek. Különlenyomat az "Athenaeum" 1940. évfolyamának 4. füzéteböl.) (Az Országos Széchenyi Könyvtár kiadványai. no. 12). Budapest: 1940. 27 pp.

1856. Laszlo, Ervin. The Communist Ideology in Hungary. Handbook for Basic Research. Dordrecht: D. Reidel, 1966. 352 pp.

IDEALISM. See also 1180, 1216.

1857. "Bibliographie der Geschichte der Idealistischen Philosophie," Idealismus: Jahrbuch für idealististischen Philosophie (Zurich), vol. 1 (1934), pp. 217-256.

About 350 entries.

1858. Ewing, Alfred Cyril, ed. The Idealist Tradition, from Berkeley to Blanshard. Glencoe, Ill.: The Free Press, 1957. 369 pp.

Bibliography, pp. 347-362.

1859. Steinkraus, Warren E. "Annual Survey of Literature," _Idealistic Studies_ (Worcester, Mass.), vol. 4 (1974), pp. 286-305.

IDEAS, ASSOCIATION OF

1860. Hiszmann, Michael. _Geschichte der Lehre von der Association den Ideen, nebst einem Anhang vom Unterschied unter Associirten und zusammengesetzten Hegriffen und an Ideenreyhen_. Göttingen: 1777.

IDEAS, HISTORY OF. See HISTORY OF IDEAS.

IDEAS, PLATONIC

1861. Brucker, Johann Jacob. _Historia Philosophica Doctrinae de Ideis qua tum Veterum Primis Graecorum, tum Recentiorum Philosophorum Placita Enarrantur_. Augustae Vindelicorum: apud D. R. Mertz et J. J. Mayer, 1723. 302 pp.

Prefex and index. A sketchy history of the Platonic doctrine of _ideas_, heavily packed with references. Probably worth seeing.

IDENTITY

1862. Göldel, Rolf W. _Die Lehre von der Identität in der Deutschen Logikwissenschaft seit Lotze; ein Beitrag zur Geschichte der modernen Logik und philosophischen Systematik, mit einer Bibliographie zur Logikwissenschaftlichen Identitäts-Lehre in Deutschland seit der Mitte des 19. Jahrhunderts_. Leipzig: S. Hirzel, 1935. 462 pp.

Literatur-Verzeichnis, pp. 445-448; Bibliographie zur Logikwissenschaftlichen Identitäts-Lehre. . . pp. 449-455.

IMMORTALITY

1863. Grässe, Johann Georg Theodor. _Bibliotheca Psychologica; oder, Verzeichniss der Wichtigsten über das Wesen der Menschen und Thierseelen, und die unstenblichketislehre handeinden Schriftsteller älterer und neuerer Zeit_. Leipzig: W. Engelmann, 1845. 60 pp.

1864. Abbot, Ezra. "Literature of the Doctrine of a Future life," in William Rounseville Alger, A Critical History of the Doctrine of a Future Life with a Complete Bibliography of the Subject. Philadelphia: G. W. Childs, 1864, pp. 677-914. Many editions: 1866, 1869, 1871, 1878, 1880, 1886, 1889. Bibliography published separately: New York: W. J. Widdleton, 1871.

Bibliography has subject and name index. A neglected work.

IMPERIALISM

1865. Akademiia nauk SSSR. Fundamental'naia biblioteka obshchestvennykh nauk. [USSR Academy of Sciences Basic Library of Social Sciences]. Kritika burzhuaznoi i reformistskoi filosofii i sotsiologii epokhi imperializma. Moskva: 1967.

INDEXES: General Philosophical indexes plus indexes to specific journals. See also 1397, 1479, 1746, 1768, 1794, 1803, 1975, 1976, 2033, 2064, 2140, 2183, 2191, 2212, 2266.

1866. Göttingische philosophische Bibliothek (Nürnberg; Hannover), vol. 1 (1749)-vol. 9 (1757). Supplement: Bemühungen der Weitseisen vom Jahr 1700-1750.

Bibliographies plus reviews.

1867. Bibliothek der Philosophie und Literatur (Frankfurt a.d. Oder), vol. 1 (1774)-2 (1775).

1868. Bibliothek der neuesten theologischen, philosophischen und schonen Literatur (Zurich), vol. 1 (1784)-3 (1786).

1869. Fortgesetzte kritische Nachrichten von kleinern theologischen, philosophischen, historischen und philologischen Schriften (Halle), vol. 1 (1785)-2 (1786). Predecessor: Kritische Nachrichten von kleinern. . . [etc.], vol. 1 (1782)-2 (1784). Successor: Neue kritische Nachrichten von kleinern theologischen, philosophischen und andern Schriften, vol. 1 (1787).

1870. Allgemeine bibliothek der meuesten philosophischen Literatur (Giessen), Stück 1, 2 (1799).

1871. Ersch, Johann Samuel. Allgemeines Repertorium der Literatur fur die Jahre 1785 bis 1790. VI. Philosophische Literatur. Jena: 1793. 34 pp. Also: 1791 bis 1795.

1871. (Continued)

Weimar: 1799. 54 pp. 1186 entries. Also: 1796 bis 1800. Weimar: 1807. 48 pp. 1008 entries. Reprint of all volumes: Bern: 1969-1970.

965 entries in the 1793 edition.

1872. Buhle, Johann Gottlieb. Lehrbuch der Geschichte der Philosophie und einer kritischen Literatur derselben (Göttingen), vol. 1 (1796)- vol. 8 (1804) [no more published].

About 4500 pp. and 2400 entries.

1873. Allgemeines Litteratur-repertorium der Philosophie . . . (Jena), Stüuck 1-12 (1842).

1874. Martin, L. A. Annuaire philosophique. Examen critique des travaux de psychologie, de métaphysique, et de morale accomplis dans l'année. Paris: Ladrange, 1864-1868. 8 vols.

1875. Picaret, François. Agrégation de philosophie en 1886. Bibliographie. Paris: P. Dupont, 1886. 15 pp.

About 3000 entries.

1876. Philosophische Monatshefte (Berlin), vol. 1 (1868)-30 (1894).

Contains an annual list of German language publications. Index to vols. 1-30 in vol. 30. From 1895-1913, appears as Archiv für systematische Philosophie.

1877. Schitlowsky, Ch. Archiv für Geschichte der Philosophie. Register zu Banden I-X (1888-1897). Berlin: Reimer, 1897. Formerly the Archiv für Philosophy (until 1888).

Critical bibliography of publications in rench, German, English, Italian.

1878. Vergé, H. and P. De Boutarel. Table alphabétique et bibliographique des matières et des auteurs figurant dans les volumes 131 à 154 (1889-1900) du Compte-rendu des Séances et Travaux de l'Academie des Sciences Morales et Politiques. Paris: Picard, 1901. 258 pp.

1879. Index philosophique (Paris), vol. 1 (1902)-2 (1903).

1880. ["Index. T. 1-30"] Vierteljahresschrift für wissenschaftliche Philosophie (Leipzig), 1906.

1881. Schreiber, Ch. Register zum Philosophisches Jahrbuch (Göerres Gezellschaft). Band I-XX. (Jahrgang 1887-1901). Fulda: 1912. 208 pp.

Systematic classification.

1882. Tables de la Revue de Philosophie (Années 1901-1913). Paris: Rivière, 1914. [n.p.]

1883. Schliebtz, Hans, and Hertha Schliebitz. Register zur Zeitschrift für Philosophie und philosophische Kritik. Band 1-150. Leipzig: J. A. Barth, 1914. 185 pp.

Author, systematic, literature, and review indexes.

1884./1885. Sommaire Idéologique des Ouvrages et des Revues de Philosophie (Louvain), vol. 1 (1895)-20 (1914). Nos. 43-50 (Feb. 1906-Nov. 1907) published as Bibliographia Philosophica, ou Sommaire idéologique des ouvrages de philosophie. Supplement to the Revue néoscholastique de philosophie (Louvain).

The major index for the period.

1886. Pansaers, J. K. Tables de la Revue neo-scholastique de philosophie (XX premières années, 1894-1913). (Collection des Tables de revues belges.) Bruxelles: Van Oest, 1914. Published as a supplement to the Revue neo-scholastique de philosophie, Feb. 1914. 67 pp.

1887. Ruge, Arnold. Die Philosophie der Gegenwart: eine internationale Jahresübersicht. Heidelberg: Weiss, 1910-1915.

Covers primarily German works for the years 1908-1913. Annotated. About 3500 works per volume. An excellent work.

1888. Review of Theology and Philosophy. (New York; Edinburgh), vol. 1 (1905)-10 (1915). [No more published].

Contains reviews, abstracts, and bibliography of the philosophical and theological literature of the period.

1889. Pimakovskiĭ, A. P. Ukazatel' stateĭ, retsenzii i zametok, nepechatannykh v zhurnale "Voprosy filosofii i psikholorii" za 1889-1918 gg. [An Index of Articles, Reviews and Remarks Printed in the Journal "Questions of philosophy and psychology" for the years 1889-1918 [In Russian]]. Moscow: Akademiia̐ nauk SSSR, 1939.

1890. Moog, Willy. Philosophie. Wissenschaftliche Forschungsberichte: Geisteswissenschaftliche Reihe 1914-1919. Vol. 5. Gotha: F. A. Perthes, 1921. 106 pp.

About 600 entries.

1891. Henrich, Norbert. Gesamtregister der Kant-studien (Philosophische dokumentation. Reihe 1: Zeitschriften bibliographien, 2) Meisenheim am Glan: A. Hain, 1969- . Vol. 1: T.1 (1897)-30 (1925).

1892. Jahrbücher der Philosophie; eine kritische Übersicht der Philosophie der Gegenwart (Berlin), vol. 1 (1913)-3 (1927). [No more published]

1893. Annalen der Philosophie und philosophischen Kritik (Leipzig), 1919- . Title varies: 1919-1923, Annalen der Philosophie; 1924- Annalen der Philosophie und philosophischen Kritik.

Includes a section, "Literatur berichte."

1894. Hoffman, Arthur. Literarische Berichte aus dem Gebiete der Philosophie. 26 nos. Erfurt: Kurt Stenger, vol. 1 (1923)-26 (1932).

First two number appeared as Literarische Berichte der Deutschen philosophischen Gesellschaft. Good coverage of all areas.

1895. Philosophische Forschungsberichte (Berlin), no. 1-6; 1930-1933. [No more published]

1896. Stäglich, Hans. Systematisch geordnetes Verzeichnis der philosophischen Zeitschriften-Literatur innerhalb der Zeitschriften für Philosophie bis 1799. Auf Grund der Bestände der Universitätsbibliothek zu Leipzig bearbeitet. Leipzig: Stäglich, 1934. 30 ll. [Typescript]

1897. "Bibliography of Philosophy," Journal of Philosophy (New York), vol. 31 (1934)-vol. 34 (1937). For 1933: vol. 31, pp. 451-503. 1244 entries. For 1934: vol. 32, pp. 450-504. 1545 entries. For 1935: vol. 33, pp. 450-504. 1543 entries. For 1936: vol. 34, pp. 422-476. 1526 entries.

Wide coverage of works primarily in English, French, German, and Italian. No annotations. Index.

1898. Bibliographie der Philosophie und Psychologie (Leipzig), vol. 1 (1920)-19 (1938).

Each annual bibliography is about 32 pp. long.

1899. _Philosophie: chronique annuelle_. (Paris), vol. 1 (1939)-8 (1946).

1900. Scott, J. W. _A Synoptic Index to the Proceedings of the Aristotelian Society, 1900-1949_. Oxford: Blackwell, 1954. 127 pp. Also: Vol. 2: 1950-1959: London: Harrison, 1961. 163 pp.

Contains summaries and index.

1901. _Decennial Index to Philosophical Literature, 1939-1950_. New York: R. F. Moore, 1952. 115 pp.

Prepared in connection with Philosophic abstracts. Lists selected works.

1902. _Bibliographie de la Phiosophie_ (Paris), vol. 1 (1937)-vol. 10 (1953).

No volumes published July 1939 - December 1945. (For these years, see De Brie.) Bibliography covering most works in Western languages. About 6000 entries per volume. Superseded by: _Bibliographie de la philosophie. Bulletin trimestrial/ Bibliography of Philosophy. A Quarterly Bulletin_. Vol. 1 (1954)-[to date], covering books only. Subject index.

1903. _The Journal of Philosophy 50-Year Index (1904-1953)_. New York: Journal of Philosophy, 1962. 442 pp.

1904. _Grundkatalog philosophie, 1966-1969: Jahreskatalog philosophie_ (Berlin), vol. 1 (1965)-

1905. _Bibliographie philosophie mit autoren und sach Register_ (East Berlin) (formerly: _Referatekartei philosophie mit bibliographischen Anhang_) 1967-

1906. _Bibliographisch Repertorium_. _Tijdschrift voor philosophie_. (Leuven; Utrecht), vol. 1 (1939)-[to date].

Dutch edition of the _Repertoire bibliographique_ de la philosophie. Continued during 1939-1945 when that publication was suspended. An important work.

1907. _Bulletin signalétique_. _Part 519: Philosophie_ (Paris), vol. 1 (1944)-[to date]. Prior to 1955 it appeared as _Bulletin analytique_. Vols. 1-14 (1947-1960), "Philosophie, sciences humaines." Vols. 15-23 (1961-1969), "Philosophie, sciences religieuses." Vol. 24 (1970)-[to date], "Philosophie."

An extensive index with worldwide coverage. Short summaries of journal articles.

1908. Humanities Index (New York), vol. 1 (1975)-[to date]. Supersedes Social Sciences and Humanities Index (New York), vol. 1 (1907)-27 (1974), which also appeared under various titles: International Index to Periodicals (1907-1955); International Index: a Guide to Periodical Literature in the Social Sciences and Humanities (1955-1965).

Contains some material on philosophy.

1909. Obshchestvennye nauka v SSSR, Seriia 3: Filosofskie nauka [Social-Sciences in the USSR, Series 3: Philosophical Sciences [In Russian]]. Moscow, Akademiia nauk SSSR. Vol. 1 (1973)-[?]. Quarterly.

A Soviet journal of the bibliography of philosophy.

1910. Répertoire bibliographique de la philosophie (Louvain), vol. 1 (1949)-[to date[. From 1934 to 1948 (with a hiatus from 1941 to 1945), the Répertoire bibliographique; from 1906 to 1914, Bibliographia Philosophica ou sommaire idéologique; from 1895 to 1905, Sommaire ideologique des ouvrages et des revues de philosophie. Revue néo-scholastique: Supplément.

About 6500 entries per volume. The most extensive bibliographical listing of current philosophical works new being published, but gives no abstracts. The coverage of The Philosopher's Index is not quite as extensive, but gives abstracts of most entries. An unfortunate duplication of much effort.

1911. Revue des sciences philosophiques et théologiques (Kain, Belg., and Paris), vol. 1 (1907)- . Suspended 1941-1946. Replaced 1941-1942 by two issues, Sciences philosophiques et théologiques. Contains "Bulletins de philosophie," "Bulletins d'historie de la philosophie," and "Bulletin bibliographique des sciences philosophiques et religieuses."

1912. The Philosopher's Index (Bowling Green, Ohio). Vol. 1 (1967)-[to date].

Entries (usually with abstracts) of major philosophical journals in English, French, German, Spanish and Italian, and selected journals in other languages and related interdisciplinary journals. Considerable overlap in coverage with the Répertoire bibliographique de la philosophie, and consequently, much duplicated effort.

INDIAN PHILOSOPHY AND HINDUISM. See also 1397, 2010, 2041, 2110, 2116, 2193, 2219, 2220, 2343, 2345, 2346.

1913. Hall, Fitzedward. A Contribution Towards an Index to the Bibliography of the Indian Philosophical Systems. Calcutta: Baptist Mission Press, 1859. 236 pp.

748 entries.

1914. Saśtrī, G-Kṛṣna and Otto Schrâder. Bibliography of Sakhya-Yoga-Samuććaẏa Works. Adyar: 1906. 18 pp.

152 entries.

1915. U. S. Library of Congress. Brief List of References on Hindu Philosophy. Washington: 1923. 5 pp.

About 50 entries.

1916. Mukherji [Mukherjee], P. K. Indian Literature in China and the Far East. Calcutta: Greater India Society, 1932. About 350 pp.

1917. Renou, L. "Travaux recents sur la philosophie indienne," Diogène (Paris), vol. 3 (1963), pp. 133-141.

1918. Riepe, Dale. "Recent Indian Philosophical Literature," Philosophy and Phenomenological Research (Buffalo), vol. 15 (1955), pp. 563-570.

1919. Frauwallner, E. Geschichte der Indischen Philosophie. Salsburg: Müller, [1953-56]. 2v. (Reihe: Wort und Antwort, Bd. 6).

First two volumes contain 50 pp. of bibliography representing references up to 1950. 10 vols. projected.

1920. Radhakrishnan, Savepalli, and C. S. Moore. A Source Book in Indian Philosophy. Princeton: Princeton University Press, 1957. 683 pp.

Pp. 643-669 contain a bibliography of about 560 entries. Listings are divided according to topic. Most works are in English.

1921. Riepe, Dale. "Indian Philosophical Literature, 1955-1967," Philosophy and Phenomenological Research (Buffalo), vol. 18 (1957-1958), pp. 384-387.

1922. C. P. Ramaswami Aiyar Research Endowment Committee. A Bibliography of Indian Philosophy. Madras: 1963. 2 vols.

1923. Potter, Karl H. Bibliography of Indian Philosophies (Encyclopedia of Indian Philosophies, vol. 1). Delhi: Published for the American Institute of Indian Studies by Motilal Banarsidass, 1970. 811 pp.

> 9222 entries of works in many languages, especially Sanskrit, Tamil, and Pali. Indexes of names, persons, and topics. Part 1: Sanskrit works and authors whose dates are known; Part 2: Sanskrit works and authors whose dates are not known; Part 3: secondary works. Very important bibliography. No annotations, but gives translations and editions.

1924. Potter, Karl H. "Bibliography of Indian Philosophies: First Supplement, I-II, II-III, IV-VI." Journal of Indian Philosophy (Toronto), vol. 2 (1972-1974), pp. 65-112, 175-209, 397-413.

INDIVIDUALISM

1925. Philosophy of Individualism: a Bibliography. London: Individualist Bookshop, 1927. 95 pp.

INFINITY

1926. Sweeney, Leo. Infinity in the Presocratics. A Bibliographical and Philosophical Study. The Hague: Martinus Nijhoff, 1972. 222 pp.

INTELLECTUAL FREEDOM

1927. Murray, J. Clayton. "A Selected Bibliography on Intellectual Freedom," Modern Schoolman (St. Louis, Mo.), vol. 31 (1954), pp. 117-124. "Addenda to 'A Selected Bibliography on Intellectual Freedom'," ibid., p. 223.

INTELLECTUAL HISTORY. See HISTORY OF IDEAS.

IRRATIONALISM. See 1952.

ISLAMIC OR ARABIAN PHILOSOPHY. See also names of individual philosophers, and 923, 924, 1968, 2317.

1928. Chauvin, V. Bibliographie des ouvrages arabes ou relatifs aux Arabes publiées dans l'Europe chrétienne de

1928. (Continued)

1810 à 1855. Liège: H. Vaillant-Charmanne, 1892-1922. 12 vols.

Contains works on a wise variety of topics.

1929. Horten, Max Joseph Heinrich. Jahresbericht ueber Neuerscheinugen aus Berichte der Arabischen Philosophie (Reprinted from Archiv für Geschichte der Philosophie. Bd. 19, Heft 2, pp. 288-291). Berlin: Georg Reimer, [1905?]. 4 pp.

1930. Horten, Max Joseph Heinrich. Berichte ueber Neuerscheinungen auf dem Gebiete der Geschichte der Arabischen Philosophie. (Reprinted from Archiv für Geschichte der Philosophie, Bd. 19, Heft. 3, pp. 426-446). Berlin: Georg Reimer, 1906. About 20 pp.

1931. Horten, Max Joseph Heinrich. Berichte ueber Neuerscheinungen auf dem Gebiete der Geschichte der Arabischen Philosophie (Reprinted from Archiv für Geschichte der Philosophie. Bd. 20, Heft. 3, pp. 403-426). Berlin: Georg Reimer, 1907. About 23 pp.

1932. Pfannmüller, Gustav. Handbuch der Islam-Literatur. Berlin: 1923.

1933. "Studien über Islamische Philosophie im Deutschen Sprachgebiet. Sammelbericht 1928-1934," Sophia (Napoli; Palermo), vol. 3 (1935), pp. 238-240.

1934. Della Vida, G. L. Elenco dei manoscritti arabi islamici della Biblioteca Vaticana: Vaticani, Barberiani, Borgiani, Rossiani. (Studi e Testi, 67), Città del Vaticano, 1935. 347 pp.

1935. "Sammelbericht über Islamische Philosophie für 1935," Sophia (Napoli, Palermo), vol. 4 (1936), pp. 505-506.

1936. Quadri, G. La Filosofia degli Arabi nel suo fiore. 1. Dalle origini fino ad Averroe; 2. Il pensiero filosofico di Averroe. Firenze: 1939.

1937. Wehr, H. Verzeichnis der Arabischen Handschriften in der Bibliothek der Deutschen Morganländischen Gesellschaft. Leipzig: Brockhaus, 1940. 62 pp.

1938. Calverley, E. "A Brief Bibliography of Arabic Philosophy," The Moslem World (Hartford, Conn.), vol. 32 (1942), pp. 60-68.

1939. Sauvaget, Jean. Introduction à l'histoire de l'Orient musulman; éléments de bibliographie. Paris: Adrien-Maisonneuve, 1943. 202 pp. Also: 1961 edition. Corrections et supplément, 1946.

1940. De Menasce, P. J. Aribische Philosophie (Bibliographische Einführungen in das Studium der Philosophie, 6). Bern: A. Francke, 1948. 48 pp.

About 420 entries arranged by topic. Has a few annotations. Helpful. Index.

1941. Sola, José. "Obras en curso sobre filosofía arabe medieval," Crisis (Madrid?), vol. 13 (1966), pp. 357-367.

1942. Anawati, Georges-C. "Philosophie arabe ou philosophie musulmane? Plan pour une bibliographie de philosophie médiévale en terre d'Islam," in Mélanges offerts à m.-D. Chenu, maître en théologie (Bibliothèque thomiste, 37), Paris: J. Vrin, 1967, pp. 51-71. Also in S. M. Stern, et al. eds., Islamic Philosophy and the Classical Tradition. Essays presented . . . to Richard Walzer . . . Oxford: Bruno Cassirer, 1972, pp. 69-89.

ISTANBUL LIBRARIES, HOLDINGS. See 1456, 1457, 1458.

ITALIAN PHILOSOPHY. See also 355, 617.

1943. Pompa, Raffaele. L'Italia filosofica contemporanea o cenni bibliografico-critici intorno filosofi italiani viventi. Salerno: Tip. Nazionale, 1877. 4 vols.

1944. Pompa, Raffaele. L'Italia filosofica e cenni bibliografico-critici. Salerno: 1879. 2 vols.

1945. Levi, Allesandro, and Bernardino Varisco. Saggio di una bibliografia filosofica italiana dal 1° gennaio 1901 al 30 giugno 1908. Bologna; Modena: A. F. Formiggini, 1908. 145 pp.

About 3000 entries.

1946. Levi, Allesandro. Bibliografia filosofica italiana (Opuscoli di Filosofia e de pedagogia, nos. 7, 14, 19, 22, 25, 28). Modena: 1908-1916. 1908-1909: (no. 7), 56 pp. 875 entries; 1910: (no. 14), 38 pp. 468 entries; 1911: (no. 19), 47 pp. 547 entries; 1912: (no. 22), 55 pp. 637 entries; 1913: (no. 25), pp. 57. 598 entries; 1914-1915: (no. 28), pp. 92. 1012 entries.

Continues Levi's Saggio di una bibliografia filosofica italiana.

1947. Istituto nazionale per le relazioni culturali con l'estero. . . . Scienze religiose, filosofia, pedagogia. Roma, I.R.C.E., 1941 (on cover, "Bibliografie del rentennio"), 173 pp.

1947. (Continued)

Covers Italian works, 1920-1941.

1948. Dal Pra, Mario. "Rassegna della filosofia italiana nel 1942. (Storia della filosofia)," Sophia (Roma), vol. 11 (1943), pp. 13-25.

1949. Sciacca, Michele Federico. Italianische Philosophie der Gegenwart (Bibliographische Einführungen in das Studium der Philosophie, 7). Bern: A. Francke, 1948. 36 pp.

About 330 entries with occasional annotations. Index.

1950. Caponigri, A. Robert. "Italian Philosophy, 1943-1950," Philosophy and Phenomenological Research (Buffalo), vol. 11 (1951), pp. 489-509.

1951. Ferro, Carmelo. "Rassegna della filosofia italiana nel 1950 (Storia della filosofia)," Sophia (Padova), vol. 19 (1951), pp. 201-208.

1952. Garin, Eugenio. "Cronache di cinquant' anni di filosofia italiana. II: Gli albori del Novecento: irrazionalisti, pragmatisti, mistici," Giornale critico della filosofia italiana (Firenze), vol. 30 (1951), pp. 382-394.

1953. Istituto di studi filosofici. Bibliografia filosofica italiana dal 1900 a 1950. (A cura dell' Instituto di studi filosofici e del Centro nazionale di informazioni bibliografiche [etc.]). Roma: Delfino, 1950-1956. 4 vols. Vol. 1: A-D, 1950, 398 pp., 10,000 entries; Vol. 2: E-M, 1952, 414 pp., 12,000 entries; Vol. 3: N-T, 1953, 380 pp., 9,000 entries; Vol. 4: W-Z, 1956, 499 pp., 9,000 entries.

Attempts complete coverage of Italian works. Index. Last volume contains additions and corrections. Last volume also contains Bibliografia ragionata dell e reviste filosofiche italiana dal 1900 al 1955.

The above bibliography is continued by Bibliografia filosofica italiana (Milano), vol. 1 (1949) - vol. 18 (1966).

1954. Istituto di studi filosofici (Roma). Bibliografia ragionata delle riviste filosofiche italiane dal 1900 al 1955. Roma: 1956. 136 pp.

1955. Bibliografia filosofica italiana (Milano). Vol. 1-18. Continues the Bibliografia filosofia italiana dal 1900 al 1950.

Covers the years 1949-1966. Each volume contains from 1600 to 4000 entries.

1956. Istituto di studi filosofici (Roma). Bibliografia filosofica italiana, 1850-1900. Roma: Edizione Abete, 1969. 644 pp.

Arranged by topics and authors. About 19,000 entries. Aims at completeness. Works published in Italy by Italians. Seeing this huge number of references covering only the work in one country for one 50-year period raises questions about the amount of material that is published.

JAIN BHANDARS LIBRARY HOLDINGS. See 1958.

JAINISM

1957. Guérinot, Armand Albert. Essai de bibliographie jaina; répertoire analytique et méthodique des travaux relatifs au jainisme. (Ministère de l'instruction publique. Annales du Musée Guimet. Bibliothèque d'études. t.22) Paris: E. Leroux, 1906. 568 pp.

Indexes of authors and works, of jain authors, of jain works, geographical index, index of periodicals, general index.

1958. Gandhi, L. B. Descriptive Catalogue of Mss in the Jain Bhandars at Pattan. Baroda: Oriental Institute, 1937. 498 pp.

1959. Berlin. Preussische Staatsbibliothek. Die Jaina-Handschriften der Preussischen Staatsbibliothek; Neuerwerbungen seit 1891. (Verzeichnis der Handschriften im Deutschen Reich, T.3, Reihe 1, Bd. 1). Leipzig: O. Harrassowitz, 1944. 647 pp.

JANSENISM. See JANSEN, CORNELIUS.

JAPANESE PHILOSOPHY

1960. Holzman, Donald, et al. Japanese Religion and Philosophy. A Guide to Japanese Reference and Research Materials (University of Michigan Center for Japanese Studies. Bibliographical Series, no. 7). Ann Arbor; University of Michigan Press, 1959. 102 pp.

992 entries.

1961. Kuno, Osamu. Tetsugaku no Meicho [Great Works in Philosophy [In Japanese]]. 1964. 329 pp.

1962. Kanazawa Bunko. Kanazawa Bunko Zōsho Mokuroku [List of Kanazawa Bunko Collections [In Japanese]]. Yokohama: Kenritsu Kanazawa Bunko[?], 1971. 382 pp.

1963. Yokohama. Okuma seishin bunka kenykyusho. Nohon shisō shi bunken kaidai (Annotated Bibliography of Writings in Japanese Intellectual History [In Japanese]]. 432 pp.

JESUIT ORDER

1964. De Backer, Augustin and Victor van Tricht. Bibliothèque des écrivains de la Compagnie de Jésus. Bruxelles: O. Schepens; Paris: A. Picard, 1890-1932. 10 vols.

In many editions. Covers writings by Jesuits since this founding of the order.

1965. Córdoba, Arg. Universidad Nacional. Biblioteca Mayor. Catálogo de la Libererîa jesuitica. (Publicaciónes de la nueva serie, 4). Córdoba: Universidad Nacional de Córdoba, 1942. 311 pp.

Author list through "F" of pre-1767 works mostly in philosophy and theology.

1966. Orellá, José L. "Manuscritos de filósofos jesuitas españoles conservados en el Archivo de Loyola [17e y 18e Siglos]," Pensamiento (Madrid), vol. 17 (1961), pp. 333-348.

JEWISH PHILOSOPHY. See also 2096, 2099.

1967. Vajda, Georges. Jüdische Philosophie (Bibliographische Einführungen in das Studium der Philosophie, 19). Bern: A. Francke, 1950. 40 pp.

General works on Judaism, works on rabbinical thought, Jewish philosophy in the Middle Ages, and Jewish mysticism. About 300 entries.

JOURNAL OF PHILOSOPHY. See INDEXES.

JURISPRUDENCE. See LAW, POSITED, AND 1445, 2028.

JURISPRUDENCE AND AESTHETICS. See 1445.

KABBALA. See MYSTICISM.

KALAM

1968. Nader, Albert. "Bibliographie d'ouvrages en langues européens concernant le Kalam," Bulletin de philosophie médiévale (Louvain), vol. 15 (1973), pp. 191-209.

KANAZAWA BUNKO COLLECTIONS. See 1962.

KNOWLEDGE. See EPISTEMOLOGY.

KNOWLEDGE, SOCIOLOGY OF

1969. "Bibliographie de la sociologie de la connaissance. Oeuvre collective du Groupe de la sociologie de la connaissance et de la vie morale," Cahiers internationaux de sociologie (Paris), vol. 32 (1962), pp. 135-176.

KOREAN PHILOSOPHY. See also 2132.

1970. Chung-Hun, Lee. ["Bibliography"] in his The Outline of Philosophy. Seoul: Mun Yang Sa, 1974. 427 pp.

130 entries.

1971. In-Jae, Jeun. ["Bibliography"] in his Philosopher: Seoul: Sam Ill Gak, 1974. 342 pp.

1972. Min-Hong, Choi. ["Bibliography"] in his The History of Korean Philosophy. Seoul: Seng Moon Sa, 1974. 323 pp.

109 entries.

LANGUAGE, PHILOSOPHY OF, AND LINGUISTICS. See also 1613, 2020, 2045, 1995.

1973. Rice, Frank A., and Allene Guss. Information Sources in Linguistics. A Bibliographical Handbook. Washington: Center for Applied Linguistics, 1965. 42 pp.

1974. Neu, Jerome, and Richard Rorty. "A Bibliography of Writings in English on Linguistic Method in Philosophy and Related Issues, 1930-1965," in Richard Rorty, ed., The Linguistic Turn. Chicago and London: University of Chicago Press, 1967, pp. 361-393.

About 850 entries.

1975. Bibliographie linguistique/Linguistic Bibliography (Utrecht), vol. 1 (1939)-[to date].

Reviews about 900 worldwide periodicals for articles on and related to language. Analytical table of contents and occasional short annotations. Author index. Some articles of interest to philosophers. About 13,000 entries per year (1971).

1976. Language and Language Behavior Abstracts (Ann Arbor, Mich.), vol. 1 (1967)-[to date].

Clear abstracts of articles from more than 600 journals. Good for works in the philosophy of language.

LATIN AMERICAN PHILOSOPHY. See also 175, 1477, 1570, 2218, 2269, 2271, 2272.

1977. Barreda y Laos, Felipe. Vida intelectual de la Colonia (educación, filosifía, y ciencias). Ensayo histórico crítico. Lima: Impr. "La Industria," 1909. 422 pp. Another edition: Buenos Aires: Tall. Graf. Argentinos.

L. J. Rosso, 1937. 391 pp.

1978. Frondizi, Risieri. Publications in Philosophy in Latin America in 1940 (Reprinted from Handbook of Latin American Studies, 1940. Boston: Harvard University Press.

1979. La Salle, Edmundo. Philosophic Thought in Latin America; a Partial Bibliography. Washington, D. C.: Division of Intellectual Cooperation, Pan American Union, 1941. 17 pp.

1980. Grismer, Raymond Leonard, Joseph E. Lepine, and Richard H. Olmsted. A New Bibliography of the Literature of Spain and Spanish America, Including many Studies on . . . Philosophy, and Other Subjects. Minneapolis: Perine Book Co., 1941-1944. Vols. 1-7. Apparently incomplete.

1981. Vásquez, Juan Adolpho. "Fifty Years of Philosophy in Latin America," Hibbert Journal (London), vol. 49 (1951), pp. 291-296.

1982. Sevilla. Centro de estudios de filosofía. Documentación critica iberoamericana de filosofía y ciencias afines. Vol. 1 (1964)--[to date?].

Bibliography with abstracts.

1983. Pan American Union. Division of Philosophy and Letters. Fuentes de la filosofía latinoamericana. (Bibliografías básicas, 4). Washington: Union panamericana, 1967. 100 pp.

About 600 entries arranged by topic. Index.

1984. Redmond, Walter Bernard. Bibliography of the Philosophy in the Iberian Colonies of America. (International Archives of the History of Ideas, 51) The Hague: Nijhoff, 1972. XIV. 175 pp.

1985. Donoso, Anton. "Philosophy in Latin America: a Bibliographical Introduction to Works in English," Philosophy Today (Celina, Ohio), vol. 17 (1973), pp. 220-231.

1986. Medellín, Colombia. Escuela Interamericana de Bibliotecología. Bibliografía B-2: Filosofia, psicología, y religión. Medellín: [no date]. 2 pp. Mimeographed.

LATIN LANGUAGE WORKS. See also 53, 54, 71, 75, 1553, 1695, 2088.

1987. Kristeller, Paul Oskar. Latin Manuscript Books before 1600; a List of Printed Catalogues and Unpublished Inventories of Extant Collections. Revised ed. New York: Fordham University Press, 1960. 234 pp.

LATVIAN PHILOSOPHY. See also 916.

1988. Egle, L. Mans laikabiedrs. Ieteicamās literaturas rāditājs. (Vila lāča Latvijas PSR valsts biblioteka. Zinātniski methodiskā un bibliogrāfiskā darba nodala). Rīga: 1972: 1972. 32 pp.

LAW, NATURAL

1989. Meister, Christian Freidrich Georg. Bibliotheca Juris Naturae et Gentium. Gottingae: A. Vanderhoeck, 1749-1757. 3 vols in 1.

Vol. 3: "Accedit Index Auctorum Locuples."

LAW, POSITED. See also 951, 1662, 1664, 1668, 1989, 2028.

1990. Cosentini, Francesco. Filosofia del diritto. Nozioni ad uso degli studenti universitari, con una guida

1990. (Continued)

bibliografica allo studio della filosofia giuridica. Torino e Roma: Paravia, 1914. 611 pp.

With an alphabetical table of contents.

1991. "Rivista delle rivista," Rivista internazionale di filosofia del dritto (Milano), vol. 42 (1965), pp. 207-216, 604-612.

1992. Annuario bibliografico di filosofia del dritto. (Centro di documentazione per la filosofia del dritto, I. Bibliografia 1965. Rassegne Internazionali.) Milano: A. Giuffrè, 1967. 459 pp.

1993. Saavedra, Modesto. "Bibliografía de la filosofía del derecho en España (1961-1971)," Anales de la Cátedra Francisco Suárez (Banco de Vizcaya), vol. 12 (1972), pp. 161-200.

LAW, SCIENTIFIC. See SCIENCE, PHILOSOPHY OF.

LEISURE. See PLAY, RECREATION, AND LEISURE.

LENINISM. See LENIN, V. I.

LIBRARY OF CONGRESS, HOLDINGS. See 6, 427, 1618.

LITERATURE, PHILOSOPHY AND. See 2235.

ŁÓDŹ PUBLIC LIBRARY (HOLDINGS). See 314.

LOGIC. See also 1706, 1714, 1715, 1747, 1773, 1862, 2026-2032, 2047, 2109, 2311.

1994. Frobes, Johann Nikolaus. C. Wolfii Logica in Compendium et Tab. Redacta a J. N. Frobesio. Helmes-tadii: 1746.

Contains a "Bibliographia logica." An edition of Christian Wolff's Philosophia Rationalis sive Logica [etc.]

1995. Alston, R. C. Logic, Philosophy, Epistemology, Universal language. (A Bibliography of the English Language From the Invention of Printing to the Year 1800, vol. 7).

1995. (Continued)

Bradford: Printed for the author by E. Cummins, 1967. 111 pp.

1996. Schüling, Herman. Bibliographie der im 17. Jahrhundert in Deutschland erschienenen logischen Schriften. (Berichte und Arbiten aus der Univesitätsbibliothek Giessen, 3). Giessen: Universitätsbibliothek, 1963. 143 pp.

Not as broad as Risse.

1997. Calker, Johann Friedrich August van. Denklehre, oder Logik und Dialektik nebst einem Abriss der Geschichte und Literatur derselben. Bonn: Weber, 1822. 554 pp.

1998. Denziger, Ig. "Bibliographica Logica," Institutiones Logicae (Leodii), vol. 3 (1824), pp. 737-757.

1999. "Recent Publications on Logical Science," Edinburgh Review, or Critical Journal (Edinburgh; London), vol. 57 (1833), pp. 194-239.

2000. Reiffenberg, Frédéric Auguste Ferdinand Thomas, Baron de. Principles de logique, suivis de l'historie et de la bibliographie de cette science. Bruxelles: L. Hauman et Comp., 1833. 419 pp.

Pp. 350-406 contain an extensive bibliography of works published up to the time.

2001. Porter, H. "Recent English Works on Logic and Meta physics." Bibliotheca Sacra (Andover, Mass.; Oberlin, Ohio), vol. 4 (1849), pp. 596-603.

2002. Blakey, Robert. Historical Sketch of Logic, Earliest Times to the Present Day. London: H. Baillière; Edinburgh: J. Nichol; [etc.], 1851. 524 pp.

Contains a list of works on logic. Alphabetically arranged, pp. 493-524.

2003. Rabus, Leonhard. Logik und Metaphysic. Frlangen: 1868.

Bibliography, pp. 453-508.

2004. Prantl, Carl von. Geschichte der Logik im Abenlande. Leipzig: S. Hirzel, 1855-70. 4 vols. in 2, pp. 733, 399, 426, 305.

2005. Rabus, Leonhard. Die neuesten Bestrebungen auf dem Gebiete der Logik bei den Deutschen. Erlangen: 1880. 204 pp.

2006. Cambridge University. Library. Venn Collection. . . .Catalogue of a Collection of Books on Logic Presented to the Library by John Venn . . . (University Library Bulletin. Extra Series.). Cambridge: Cambridge University Press, 1889. 125 pp.

Contains about 1040 entries, plus a name index. No apparent organization to the listing. Covers a wide variety of books bearing on logic. Contains a surprising number of references to works on logic and the philosophy of logic from the 15th century onwards. Has a name index. Now largely superseded by Risse's book.

2007. Rabus, Leonhard. Lehrbuch zur Einleitung in die Philosophie, Bd. 2, Logik und System der Wissenschaften. Erlangen; Leipzig: 1895. 360 pp.

2008. Schröder, Ernst. Vorlesungen über die Algebra der Logik. Leipzig, 1870-1895. 3 vols.

"Literatur-verzeichniss," vol. 1, pp. 700-715.

2009. Berry, G. G. Catalogue of Books Bequeathed by Thomas Fowler . . . to the Wykeham Chair of Logic. Oxford: 1906. 36 pp.

About 500 entries.

2010. Church, Alonzo. "A Bibliography of Symbolic Logic," Journal of Symbolic Logic (Menasha, Wisc.), vol. 1 (1936), pp. 121-128. "Additions and Corrections to A Bibliography of Symbolic Logic," vol. 3 (1938), pp. 178-212. Both works also published separately, 1939.

Covers the period 1666-1935 with about 1750 entries. "Additions" contains about 150 entries.

2011. Grabmann, Martin. Bearbeitungen und Auslegungen der Aristotelischen Logik aus der Zeit von Peter Abaelard bis Petrus Hispanus. Mitteilungen aus Handschriften Deutscher Bibliotheken. Berlin: Adademie der Wissenschaften, in Kommission bei W. de Gruyter, 1937. 58 pp.

2012. Beth, E. W. Symbolishce Logik und Grundlegung der exakten Wissenschaften (Bibliographische Einführungen in das Studium der Philosophie, 3). Bern: A. Francke, 1948. 28 pp.

An unannotated list divided by subject. About 300 entries. Broad scope, useful.

2013. Korcik, A. "Publikacje autorow polskich z zakresu logiki w Polsce i zagrancia w ostatnich trzech latach [Publications of Polish authors on logic [In Polish]]," Roczniki Filozoficzne (Lubin), vols. 2-3 (1949-1950), pp. 414-422.

2014. Feys, Robert. "Logica en Wijsbegeerte van de wiskunde," Tijdschrift voor Philosophie (Leuven), vol. 13 (1951), pp. 303-314.

2015. Church, Alonzo. "Brief Bibliography of Formal Logic," Proceedings of the American Academy of Arts and Sciences (Boston), vol. 80 (1952).

2016. Primakovskii, A. P. Bibliografiia po logike; khronologicheskiĭ ukazatel' proizvedenii po voprosam logiki, izdannykh na russkom iazyke v SSSR, XVIII-XX vv. [A Bibliography on Logic: a Chronological List of Works on Questions of Logic Published in Russian in the USSR, 18th-20th cc. [In Russian]]. Moscow: Iza-vo Akademii nauk SSSR, 1955.

About 1000 entries.

2017. Bochenski, I. M. Formale Logik. 2. erweiterte Aufl. Freiburg: K. Alber, 1956. 639 pp. Also: 1962 edition.

Has a large bibliography.

2018. D'Ainville, Varin. Logic and the Philosophy of Science (French Bibliographical Digest, no. 29). New York: Cultural Center of the French Embassy, 1959. 60 pp.

2019. Küng, Guido. "Bibliography of Soviet Work in the Field of Mathematical Logic and the Foundations of Mathematics, 1917-1957," Notre Dame Journal of Formal Logic (Notre Dame, Ind.), vol. 3 (1962), pp. 1-40.

2020. "Bibliographie [logique et linguistique]," Languages (Paris), no. 2 (1966), pp. 124-136.

2021. Laugwitz, Detlef. "Auswahl-Bibliographie [: Allgemeine Functionentheorie]," in Paul DuBois-Reymond, Die Allgemeine Functionentheorie. Darmstadt: Wissenschlaftliche Buchges, 1968.

2022. Muñoz-Delgado, Vincente. "Lógica Hispano-Portuguesa hasta 1600 (Notas bibliografico-doctrinales)," in Repertorio de historia de las ciencias eclesíasticas en España, IV: Siglos I-XVI, (Corpus Scriptorum Sacrorum Hispaniae. Estudios, 4), Salamanca: Instituto de Historia de la teologica española, 1972, pp. 9-122.

2023. Ashworth, E. J. "Some Additions to Risse's 'Bibliographia Logica'," Journal of the History of Philosophy (St. Louis, Mo.), vol. 12 (1974), pp. 361-365.

2023. (Continued)

Lists works published during the period 1472-1800 that do not appear in Risse.

2024. Lifshits, I. and G. E. Mints. Matematicheskaia logika: Katalog zarubezhnykh knig [Mathematical Logic: a Catalogue of Foreign Books [In Russian]]. Leningrad: Biblioteka akademii nauk SSSR [USSR Academy of Sciences Library], 1974. 173 pp.

About 400 entries of works in various languages. Name index.

2025. Risse, W. Bibliographica Logica; Verzeichnis der Druckschriften zur Logik mit Angabe der Fundarte. (Studien und Materialien zur Geschichte der Philosophie). Hildesheim: Olms, vol. 1, 1965; vol. 2, 1973; [vol. 3, 1975, in preparation].

About 24,000 entries. Vol. 1, covers the years 1472-1800; vol. 2, 1801-1969. An excellent work.

LOGIC, ARISTOTELIAN. See LOGIC.

LOGIC, BUDDHIST

2026. Sacki, Ryōken. Immyō Sahō Hnsen to Chojutsu [The Changes in Immyo Saho and the Writings [In Japanese]]. 1969. 182 pp.

LOGIC, CHINESE

2027. Ching, Chung-ying. "Inquiries into Classical Chinese Logic," Philosophy East and West (Honolulu). Vol. 15 (1965).

Bibliography on pp. 204-215.

LOGIC, JURIDICAL

2028. Conte, A. G. "Bibliografia di logica giuridica (1936-1960)," Revista internazaionale di filosofia del diritto, vol. 38 (1961), pp. 120-144. "Addenda," vol. 39 (1962), pp. 45-46.

LOGIC, LATE SCHOLASTIC

2029. Hickman, Larry. "Late Scholastic Logics: Another Look," Journal of the History of Philosophy (Berkeley, Calif.), vol. 9 (1971), pp. 226-234.

83 additions from Mexican libraries to Risse's bibliography of late (1775-1800) scholastic logic.

LOGIC, MANY-VALUED

2030. Rescher, Nicholas. "A Bibliography of Many-Valued Logic (to 1965)," in his Many-Valued Logic. New York [etc.]: McGraw-Hill, 1969, pp. 236-331.

Extensive. About 1500 entries divided by topics.

LOGIC, MODAL

2031. Feys, Robert. Modal logics. Edited with some Complements by Joseph Dopp. Louvain: E. Nauwelaerts; Paris: Gauthier-Villars, 1965. 219 pp.

Bibliography, pp. 187-215, with about 300 entries.

LOGICAL ALGEBRA

2032. Holst, P. A. "Bibliography on Switching Circuits and Logical Algebra," Institute of Radio Engineers. Transactions on Electronic Computers (New York), vol. 10 (1961), pp. 638-661.

LOGICAL EMPIRICISM. See LOGICAL POSITIVISM.

LOGICAL POSITIVISM

2033. Belke, Felicitas. Gesamtregister der Annalen der Philosophie. (U. Philos. Kritik), 1-8 (1919-1929). Erkenntnis, 1-7 (1930/31-1937/38). The Journal of Unified Science (Erkenntnis), 8 (1939/40). Forum Philosophicum, 1 (1930/31). Meisenheim am Glan: Hain, 1971. 394 pp.

2034. Dürr, Karl. Der logische Positivmns (Bibliographische Einführungen in das Studium der Philosophie, 11). Bern: A. Francke, 1948. 24 pp.

About 80 entries, but good annotations on most works mentioned. Sticks primarily to the Vienna Circle group.

2035. Feigl, Herbert. "Bibliography of Logical Empiricism," Revue Internationale de Philosophie (Bruxelles), vol. 4 (1950), pp. 64-83.

2036. Ayer, A. J. "Bibliography of Logical Positivism," in his Logical Positivism, Glencoe, Ill.: The Free Press, 1959, pp. 381-446.

Very extensive bibliography. Goes beyond logical positivism to cover "every form of modern analytical" philosophy. About 1500 entries.

LONELINESS AND SOLITUDE

2037. Gratton, Carolyn. "Summaries of Selected Works on Loneliness and Solitude," Humanitas (Pittsburgh), vol. 10 (1974), pp. 329-334.

LOUVAIN, UNIVERSITY OF. See also 581.

2038. Bibliographie [des membres du corps académique de l'Université de Louvain attachés à l'Institut de philosophie]. Louvain: (Prof. A. Wylleman, Tienesestraat 112 - CCP Bruxelles 48.07.57), 1963. 104 pp.

LOVE

2039. Gratton, Carolyn. "Selected Subject Bibliography, (Covering the Past Ten Years)," Humanitas (Pittsburgh), vol. 2 (1966), pp. 215-221.

150 entries.

LOVELACE COLLECTION. See 792.

LOW COUNTRIES. See specific countries and 364, 1851.

LYMINGTON COLLECTION. See 991.

MADRID UNIVERSITY. See 1608.

MAGIC. See also 2187.

2040. Bibliotheca Magica. Bibliographie und Besprechugen. Eine Auswahl Deutschsprachiger Neuerscheinungen. Köln: 1961. 62 pp.

About 50 entries.

MAHABHARATA

2041. Lal, P. Annotated Mahabharata Bibliography. Calcutta: Writers Workshop, 1967. 111 pp.

MAN. See also SOCIAL ANTHROPOLOGY, 906, 1632, 2259.

2042. Landmann, Michael. De Homine. Freiburg: K. Alber, 1962.

Pp. 543-614 contain a long bibliography.

2043. Zawadzki, Jane. "Selected Subject Bibliography (Covering the Past Ten Years)," Humanitas (Pittsburgh), vol. 4 (1968), pp. 117-127.

On "The Changing Nature of Man." About 230 entries.

2044. Holbrook, David. Changing Attitudes to the Nature of Man: a Working Bibliography . . . with Addenda by Masud Khan, Andrew Brink and David Boadella. Hatfield, Eng.: Hertis, 1973. 1325 pp.

MANUSCRIPTS. See 46, 51, 1465, 1542, 1560, 1591, 1673, 1809, 1855, 1934, 1937, 1958, 1966, 2063, 2214, 2219, 2220, 2238, 2247, 2250.

MARXISM. See MARX, KARL.

MARXISM-LENINISM. See MARX, KARL and LENIN, V. I.

MASS TERMS

2045. Pelletier, Francis Jeffery. "A Bibliography of Recent Work on Mass Terms," Synthese (Dordrecht), vol. 31 (1975), pp. 523-526.

MATERIALISM. See 1814.

MATHEMATICS, PHILOSOPHY OF

2046. Grünbaum, Adolph. "Some Recent Writings in the Philosophy of Mathematics," Review of Metaphysics (Washington), vol. 5 (1951-1952), pp. 281-292.

2047. Mostowski, Andrezej. Thirty Years of Foundational Studies; Lectures on the Development of Mathematical Logic and the Study of the Foundations of Mathematics 1930-1964 (Acta Philosophica Fennica, no. 17) New York: Barnes and Noble, 1966. 180 pp.

Pp. 151-171 contain a bibliography.

2048. Rozenfeld, Boris. "Traductions et publications sobiétiques d'oeuvres mathématiques médiévales [XIIe Congrès international d'histoire des sciences, Paris, 1968]." Revue de synthèse (Paris), vol. 89 (1968), pp. 95-100.

MEDICAL ETHICS. See 2254.

MEDIEVAL PHILOSOPHY. See also 1520, 1553, 1616, 1823, 1825, 2011, 2048.

2049. Thomasius, Jacobus. De Doctoribus Scholasticis. Lipsiae: 1676.

2050. De Wulf, M. Histoire de la philosophie médiéval-Quatrième édition revue et mise à jour. (Cours de philosophie de l'Institut supérieur de philosophie, vol. 6). Louvain: Institut supérieur de philosophie; Paris: Alcan, 1912. Also: In English: London and New York, 1909; Italian: Firenze: 1913; German: Tübingen, 1913.

Excellent bibliography for the period prior to about 1912.

2051. Chenu, Marie Dominique. Les Etudes de philosophie médiévale. Paris: Hermann, 1939. 87 pp.

2052. Giacon, Carlo. Il Pensiero cristiano con particolare riguardo alla scholastica medievale. (Guide Bibliografiche, 2nd ser. Filosofia. 3. Università cattolica del Sacre cuore). Milano: Società editrice Vita e pensiero, 1943. 265 pp.

Good coverage.

2053. Farrar, C. P., and A. P. Evans. Bibliography of English Translations from Medieval Sources. New York: Columbia University Press, 1946. 534 pp.

Annotated.

2054. Van Steenberghen, Fernand. Philosophie des Mittelalters (Bibliographische Einführungen in das Studium der Philosophie, 17). Bern: A. Francke, 1950. 52 pp.

About 400 entries with subject headings, annotations, and index. Good

2055. Callus, Daniel. "Ten Years of Research in the Medieval Field (1940-1950) I: Editions of Texts (to be Concluded)," Dominican Studies (Oxford), vol. 4 (1951), pp. 1-13.

2056. Garin, Eugenio. "Il Pensiero medievale (1950)," Giornale critico della filosofia italiana (Firenze), vol. 30 (1951), pp. 546-551.

2057. Williams, Harry. An Index of Mediaeval Studies Published in Festschriften, 1865-1946. Berkeley: University of California Press, 1951. 165 pp.

2058. Burch, George Bosworth. "Medieval Philosophy," Review of Metaphysics (Buffalo), vol. 5 (1952), pp. 455-464.

Discusses some recent works.

2059. Bataillon, L.-J. "Bulletin d'histoire des doctrines médiévales, IV: Le Douzième siècle. V: Le Début du treizième siècle (à suivre)," Revue des sciences philosophiques et théologiques (Le Saulchoir), vol. 46 (1962), pp. 499-543.

2060. Van Steenberghen, Fernand. "Travaux de synthèse et recueils d'études sur la pensée médiévale," Revue philosophique de Louvain (Louvain), vol. 20 (1962), pp. 665-694.

2061. Beaujouan, Guy. Manuscrits scientifiques médiévaux de l'Université de Salamanque et des ses <<Colegois mayores>>. (Bibliothèque de l'Ecole des hautes études hispaniques, 32). Bordeaux: Féret et Fils, 1962. 232 pp.

2062. Swiezawski, Stefan. "Aperçu sur les recherches des médiévistes polonais dans le domain de l'histoire de la philosophie," in Die Metaphysik im Mittelalter, ihr Ursprung und ihre Bedeutung. Berlin: Walter de Gruyter, 1963, pp. 110-125.

2063. Wlodek, Sophie. "L'Enregistrement des manuscrits médiévaux philosophiques en Pologne," Rivista critica di storia della filosofia (Milano), vol. 21 (1966), pp. 115-120.

2064. Rouse, Richard H. Serial Bibliographies for Medieval Studies. Berkeley and Los Angeles: University of California Press, 1969. 150 pp.

Annotated references to about 270 periodicals. Probably of interest to the advanced student of medieval philosophy.

2065. Vasoli, Cesare. Il Pensiero medievale: Orientamenti bibliografici (Piccola Biblioteca Filosofica Laterza, 70). Bari: Casa editrice Gius. Laterza e Figli, 1971. 302 pp.

Divided by topics from "Boethius" to "Gerson". Works in many languages. At least 4000 entries. A good work.

2066. Van Steenberghen, Fernand. La Bibliothèque du philosophe médiéviste. "Complément au tome 18: Introduction à l'étude de la philosophie médiévale." Louvain: Publications universitaires, 1974. 540 pp.

2067. Bulletin de théologie ancienne et médiévale (Supplement to Recherches de théologie ancienne et médiévale) (Louvain), 1929-

Covers new literature on patristic, medieval, and scholastic theology and philosophy.

2068. Landry, A. M. "La pensée philosophique médiévale: contribution canadienne (1960-1973)," Philosophiques (Montreal), vol. 1 (1974), pp. 111-139.

METABLETICS

2069. Van den Berg, J. H. "Selected Subject Bibliography," Humanitas (Pittsburgh), vol. 7 (1971), p. 411.

On "Metabletics and phenomenology."

<u>METAPHYSICS</u>. See also 334, 1576, 1610, 1706, 1728, 1747, 1751, 1874, 2001, 2003, 2277, 2278, 2351.

2070. Stewart, Dugald. "Progress of Metaphysical, Ethical, and Political Philosophy," in <u>Supplement to the Fourth, Fifth, and Sixth Editions of the Encyclopaedia Britannica</u>. Vol. 1 (MacVey Napier, ed.), Edinburgh, 1824, pp. 19-166. Reprinted: <u>Encyclopedia Britannica,</u> 8th ed., vol. 1.

Not exactly a bibliography, but an interesting account of what the early nineteenth century philosopher took to be important. Stewart's essay is modelled after D'Alembert's "Preliminary Discourse" in the French encyclopaedia.

2071. Belfast. Queen's College Library. <u>Catalogue of Books in the Department of Logic and Metaphysics and on Kindred Subjects</u>. Belfast: 1856. 23 pp.

About 450 entries.

2072. De'Paoli, Stefano Lorenzo. "Filosofia generale e metafisica (1946-1948)," <u>Humanitas</u> (Bresica), vol. 4 (1949), pp. 937-943.

<u>METHODOLOGY</u>. See also 1815.

2073. Tonelli, Giorgio. "A Contribution Towards a Bibliography on the Methodology of the History of Philosophy," <u>Journal of the History of Philosophy</u> (Berkeley), vol. 10 (1972), pp. 456-458.

2074. Kwee, Swan-Liat. "Bibliografische kanttekeningen [over techniek en wijsbegeerte]," <u>Wijsgerig perspectief of maatschappij en wetenschap</u> (Amsterdam), vol. 6 (1965-1966), pp. 132-140.

<u>MÉXICAN PHILOSOPHY</u>. See also 1427, 1432, 2082.

2075. Valverde Téllez, Emeterio. <u>Apuntaciónes históricas sobre la filosifía en México</u>. México, D. F.: Herrero Hermanos, 1896. 477 pp.

2076. Valverde Téllez, Emeterio. <u>Crítica filosófica; ó, Estudio bibliográfico y crítico de las obras de filosofía, escritas, traducidas ó publicadas en México desde el Siglio XVI hasta nuestros días. Concluyen las "Apuntaciones historicas sobre la filosofía en México</u>," México, Tip. de los Sucesores de Francisco Díaz de León, 1904. 496 pp.

2077. Valverde Téllez, Emeterio. Bibliografía filosófica méxicana. (Obras de Don Emeterio Valverde Téllez, III). México: Tip. de la Viuda de F. Diaz de Leon, 1907. 218 pp. Also: 2nd enlarged ed.: León: Imprenta de J. Rodríquez, 1913. 2 vols.

About 1000 entries. About 2000 entries in the 2nd edition.

2078. Zea, Leopoldo. "La Producción filosófica méxicana en 1941," Letras de México (México), vol. 3, no. 13.

2079. México (City). Universidad nacional autónoma. Centro de estudios filosóficos. Boletín bibliográfico. Mexico: Vol. 1 (1940)-6 (1945).

Vols. 1-3 (1940-1943). 117 entries.
Vol. 4 (1943-1944). 31 entries.
Vol.s 5-6 (1945). 34 entries.

2080. México (City). Universidad nacional. Instituto de investigaciones estéticas. Ongay Muza, D., ed. Bibliografía del instituto de investigaciones estéticas, 1935-1965, por Danilo Orgay Muza. México: Universidad nacional autónoma de México, 1966. 149 pp.

2081. México (City). Universidad Nacional. Instituto de investigaciónes bibliográficas. Bibliografía filosófica méxicana. Año 1 (1970)-

Devoted to Mexican philosophy. Divided by topics. Index.

MÉXICO, NATIONAL LIBERTY (HOLDINGS)

2082. Vigil, José María. Catálogos de la biblioteca nacional de México. Tercera división. Filosofía y pedagogía. México: 1889. 83 pp.

About 1500 entries.

MIND. See also EPISTEMOLOGY: PSYCHOLOGY: 1640, 1995.

2083. Blakey, Robert. History of the Philosophy of Mind. London: 1850. 4 vols. Also 1848 edition.

Bibliographies: vol. 1, pp. 439-444; vol. 4, pp. 209-645. Indexes of names and subjects. Vol. 4 contains a survey of European and American philosophy, 1800-1848.

2084. Briscoe, John Potter. _Mental and Moral Philosophy_. (Public Libraries: Class List, no. 12). Nottingham: 1887. 12 pp.

About 400 entries.

MODALITIES. See LOGIC, MODAL, AND 1450.

MODERN PHILOSOPHY. See especially GENERAL PHILOSOPHICAL LIOGRAPHIES, INDEXES and the names of specific philosophers. See also 1825.

2085. Chevalier, Cyr Ulysse Joseph. _Répertoire des sources historiques du moyen âge . . . Bio-bibliographie_. Nouv. ed. Paris: A. Picard et fils, 1905-1907. 2 vols.

2086. Aster, E. von. "Bericht über die Deutschen Schriften der Jahre 1932-1934 zur Geschichte der neueren Philosophie von Bacon bis Kant," _Sophia_ (Roma), vol. 3 (1935), pp. 226-237.

2087. De Vos, A. "De moderne wijsbegeerte," _Tijdschrift voor Philosophie_ (Leuven), vol. 11 (1949), pp. 447-466.

2088. Pelzer, Auguste. _Répertoires d'incipit pour la littérature latine philosophique et theologique du Moyen âge. Edition augmentée_. (Sussidi eruditi, 2). Roma: 1951. 33 pp. Originally appeared in the _Revue d'Histoire Ecclésiastique_, vol. 43 (1948), pp. 495-512.

About 100 entries.

2089. Garin, Eugenio. "Il pensiero moderno," _Giornale critico della filosofia italiana_ (Firenze), vol. 31 (1952), pp. 241-249.

2090. Parkinson, G. H. R. "From Descartes to Collingwood: Recent Work on the History of Philosophy," _Philosophy_ (London), vol. 50 (1975), pp. 205-220.

A survey of the literature.

2091. [Southern Illinois University Library, Carbondale, Philosophy Collection.] "Archives of Paul Carus and Open Court Publishing Co.," _College and Research Libraries News_, no. 3 (March, 1969).

Describes 60,000 pages relating to modern philosophy received by that library.

MODERN SOCIETY. See SOCIETY, MODERN.

MORAL LIFE, SOCIOLOGY OF

2092. "Bibliographie de la sociologie de la vie morale. Oeuvre collective de la Section de sociologie de la connaisance et de la vie morale," Cahiers Internationaux de Sociologie (Paris), vol. 36 (1964), pp. 133-184.

MOTIVATION

2093. Zawadzki, Jane. "Selected Subject Bibliography (Covering the Past Ten Years)," Humanitas (Pittsburgh), vol. 3 (1968), pp. 357-366.

About 175 entries on "motivation and human need."

MUDD, SEELEY WINTERSMITH, COLLECTION. See 1755.

MUSÉE PEDAGOGIQUE DE L'ÉTAT (PARIS) HOLDINGS. See 1700.

MYSTICISM. See also 2087, 978, 1952, 2199.

2094. Naudé, Gabriel. Bibliothecae Mystica Clarissimi Viri Ludovici Servini. [n.p.]: 1626.

2095. Du Saussay, André. De Mysticis Galliae Scriptoribus. Parisiis: 1639.

2096. Scholem, Gershom Gerhard. Bibliographia Kabbalistica. Verzeichnis der Gedruckten die Jüdische Mystik (Gnosis, Kabbala, Sabbatianismus, Frankismus, Chassidismus) behandelnden Bücher und Aufsätze von Reuchlin bis zur Gegenwart. Mit einen Anhang: Bibliographie des Zohar und seiner Kommentare. Leipzig: W. Drugulin, 1927. 230 pp. Also: 1933 edition.

2097. National Book Council. Christian Mysticism. A Representative Selection of Works. 2nd ed. (Bibliography, no. 90). 1929. 4 pp.

About 100 works.

2098. Sankey-Jones, Nancy E. Bibliography of Theodore Schroeder on the Psychology of Religion and the Erotogenetic Interpretation of Mysticism. Cos Cob, Conn.: [Privately rpinted]. 1934. 24 pp.

2099. Scholem, Gersholm Gerhard. [Translated title]. Desiderata in Kabbala and Jewish Mysticism. Jerusalem:

2099. (Continued)

1937. 5 ff.

111 entries.

2100. Dagens, Jean. Bibliographie chronologique de la littérature de spiritualité et de ses sources (1501-1610). 1952. 229 pp.

About 3000 entries.

2101. Dagens, Jean. La Mystique rhénane. VIe centenaire de la morte de Tauler. Exposition. Strasbourg: 1961. 24 pp.

About 100 entries.

NATURAL DEVELOPMENT

2102. Levin, M. I. Ob"ektivnyi kharakter zakonov razvitiia, pirody i obshchestva. Rekomendatel'nyi ukazatel' literatury. [The Objective Character of the Laws of Natural and Social Development. A Guide to the Literature [In Russian]]. Leningrad: Gosudarstvennaiia biblioteka imeni M. E. Saltykova-Shchedrina [Saltykov-Shchadtin state library], 1954. 31 pp.

NATURAL THEOLOGY. See THEOLOGY.

NECESSITY. See 1450.

NEED, HUMAN. See 2093.

NEO-PLATONISM

2103. Beierwaltes, Werner. "Neoplatonica," Philosophische Rundschau (Tübingen), vol. 16 (1969), pp. 130-151.

NEO-POSITIVISM

2104. Drudis-Baldrich, Raimundo. "Repertorio bibliográfico de filosofía de las ciencias: la filosofía neopositivista," Theoria (Madrid), no. 9 (1955), pp. 170-178.

NEO-SCHOLASTICISM. See also 1392.

2105. Picaret, François. "Travaux récents sur le néo-thomisme et la scholastique," Revue philosophique de la France et de l'étranger (Paris), vol. 35 (1893), pp. 394-421.

A survey of the literature.

2106. Ryan, James Hugh. A Student's Library of Neo-Scholastic Philosophy. Philadelphia, Pa.: American Ecclesiastical Review, 1928. 12 pp. Reprinted from the Ecclesiastical Review, Jan. 1928.

2107. Beschin, G. "Revista di filosofia neo-scholastica," Filosofia e vita, (1961), no. 5, pp. 90-92.

NETHERLANDS PHILOSOPHY. See DUTCH PHILOSOPHY.

NEUCHÂTEL LIBRARY. See 1131.

NEW YORK PUBLIC LIBRARY (HOLDINGS). See 1745.

NEWBERRY LIBRARY (HOLDINGS). See 1751.

NIHILISM

2108. Neinemann, F. H. "Nihilism in Germany," Philosophy (London), vol. 15 (1940), pp. 80-84.

A survey.

NOMINALISM

2109. Muñoz-Delgado, Vincente. La Lógica nominalista en la Universidad de Salamanca, 1510-1530; ambiente, literatura, doctrinas. (Publicaciones del Monasterio de Poyo, 11). Madrid: Revista estudios, 1964. 448 pp.

With bibliography, pp. 371-382.

NON-VIOLENCE

2110. Gandhian Institute of Studies (Varanasi). Bibliography on Non-violence and Satyagrah. Varanasi: 312 pp.

NORTH AMERICAN PHILOSOPHY

2111. Caponigri, A. Robert. "Recenti pubblicazioni filosofiche nord-americane," Giornale di metafisica (Torino), vol. 6 (1951), pp. 639-646.

2112. "Bibliography of Current Philosophical Works Published in North America," The Modern Schoolman (St. Louis, Mo.), vol. 25 (1947/1948)-vol. 37 (1959/1960).

An annual supplement to this journal for the above mentioned years. About 400 entries per issue.

NORWEGIAN PHILOSOPHY

2113. Flo, Olav. Bibliografisk nøkkel til "Bergens-filosofene." Selektiv bibliografi for arene 1943-1970. Bergen: Universitetsforlaget, 1971. 36 pp.

2114. Flo, Olav. Bibliografi over forflatterskapet til Jon Heilesnes, Knut Midgaard, Tore Nordenstam, Gunnar og Sigurd, Skivbekk og Hans Skjeruneím, 1948-1970. (Filosofiske bibliografiker, no. 11). Oslo: Universitetsforlaget, 1971. 47 pp.

2115. Flo, Olav. Bibliography of the Philosophical and Other Writings of Jens Erik Fenstad, Guttorn Fløistad, Dagfinn Føllesdal, Finngeir Hiorth and Dag Prawitz 1953-1970. (Filosofiske bibliografiker, 10). Bergen: Universitetsforlaget, 1972. 37 pp.

NOTTINGHAM LIBRARIES HOLDINGS. See 1640.

NYAYA-VAISESIKA

2116. Gopinath, Kaviraj. Gleanings from the History and Bibliography of the Nyaya-Vaisesika Litterature. Calcutta: Indian Studies Past and Present, 1961. 86 pp.

OCCULT PHILOSOPHY. See also PSYCHICAL RESEARCH.

2117. Steinschneider, Moritz. Zur pseudepigraphischen Literatur, insbesondere der geheimen Wissenschaften des Mittlalters. Veitel Heine Ephraim'sche Lehranstalt: wissenschaftliche Blätter (1st ser., no. 3). Berlin: 1862. 97 pp.

8 entries.

2118. Ladragne, A. Bibliothèque ouvaroff catalogue spécimen. Moscow: Imprimerie W. Gautier, 1870. 217 pp.

1883 entries of works from A. S. Uvarov's library.

2119. Encausse, Gérard. Bibliographie méthodique de la science occulte (livres modernes). Etude critique des principaux ouvrages, par un groupe d'occultistes sous la direction de Papus. [n.p.]: 1892. 112 pp.

350 entries.

2120. Durville, Hector. Bibliographie du magnétisme et des sciences occultes. 1895. 36 pp.

26 entries.

2121. Gardner, Frederick Leigh. A Catalogue Raisonné of Works on the Occult Sciences, 1903-1912. 2nd ed. Vol. 1. Leipzig: [privately printed], 1923. 101 pp. Also: London: [privately printed], 1903-1912. 3 vols.

About 2200 entries.

2122. U. S. Library of Congress. List of References on Occultism and Theosophy. 1923. 4 pp. Supplements: 1923-1935; 1936.

2123. Theosophical Society in England. Lending Library Catalogue. 1929. 158 pp.

About 3500 entries.

2124. Santoro, Caterina. Mostra di libri di profezie, astrologia, chiromanzia, alchimia. Milano: 1953. 48 pp.

112 entries.

2125. Abbot, A. E. A Guide to Occult and Sacred Writings. 1963? 66 pp.

About 1500 entries.

ONTOLOGY. See also METAPHYSICS, 1065, 1392.

2126. Nacke, Gabriele. "Zum begriff "Lebensbedingungen," *Deutsche Zeitschrift für Philosophie* (Berlin), vol. 17 (1969), pp. 1489-1499.

ORIENTAL PHILOSOPHY. See also entries for individual philosophers and countries, also 1853.

2127. "Catalogus Scriptorum de Philosophia Veterum in Oriente Barbaroum," in Christoph A. Heumann, ed., *Acta philosophorum. Stück 8*. Halle im Magdeb.: Kenger, 1717, pp. 173-204; Also: *Stück 15*: 1724, pp. 485-494.

2128. Masson-Oursel, P. *Les Philosophies orientales* (Actualités scientifiques et industrielles, 874. Philosophie chronique annuelle, 8). Paris: Hermann, 1940.

2129. Herbert, Jean. *Wat kan het westen van het oosten leren?* [?]: Deventer, 1949. 34 pp.

About 150 entries.

2130. Moore, Russell Franklin. *Bibliography for Oriental Philosophies*. New York: Russell F. Moore Co., 1951. 13 pp.

2131. De Bary, Theodore, and Ainslee T. Embree. *A Guide to Oriental Classics*. New York: Columbia University Press, 1964. 199 pp.

References to works in European languages. Annotated.

2132. Un-Aham, Han. ["Bibliography"] in his *The Outline of Oriental Philosophy*. Seoul: Won Gak Sa, 1974. 335 pp.

103 entries.

OTTOWA, UNIVERSITY OF, THESES. See 1612.

OXFORD UNIVERSITY HONOR SCHOOL

2133. Ryle, Gilbert, J. E. Meade and K. C. Wheare. *Bibliography for the Honor School of Philosophy, Politics, and Economics*. Oxford: Blackwell, 1937. 36 pp. Also: 1935 edition.

PAIN. See EVIL, PROBLEM OF.

PALMA LIBRARY, HOLDINGS. See 824, 826.

PARAPSYCHOLOGY

2134. Zorab, George. Bibliography of Parapsychology. New York: Parapsychology Foundation, 1957. 127 pp.

PARIS LIBRARIES, HOLDINGS. See 735.

PATRISTIC PHILOSOPHY. See also 1414, 1497, 1823, 2067.

2135. Geyer, B. "Die patristische und scholastische Philosophie," in Fredrich Überweg, Grundriss der Geschichte der Philosophie, 2 Teil, 11.A. Berlin: E. S. Mittler & Sohn, 1922.

2136. Madoz, J. Segundo decenio de estudios sobre patrística española, 1941-1950. (Estudios onienses. Serie I, vol. v). Madrid: Ed. Fax, 1951. 212 pp.

2137. Perler, Othmar. Patristische Philosophie (Bibliographische Einführungen in das Studien der Philosophie, 18). Bern: A. Francke, 1950. 44 pp.

About 400 entries with subject headings. A few annotations. Index.

2138. Schneemelcher, W. Bibliographia Patristica: International Patristic Bibliography. Patrist. Komm. d. Akad. d. Wiss. in d. Bundesrepublik Deutschland. Bd. XII-XIII: 1967/1968. Die Erscheinungen der Jahre 1967 und 1968. Berlin: de Gruyter, 1975. 253 pp.

2139. Centre De Wulf-Mansion. Liste des reproductions photographiques de manuscrits. 1 er octobre 1962. Louvain: Centre De Wulf-Mansion, 1962. 200 pp.

2140. Schneemelcher, Wilhelm et al. Bibliographia Patristica. Internationale patristische Bibliographie. (Berlin), vol. 1 (1956)-

PEDAGOGY. See also EDUCATION, PHILOSOPHY OF, and 46, 1603.

2141. Collière, H. "Note bibliographique de pédagogie," Bulletin de Littérature Ecclésiastique (Toulouse), vol. 51

2141. (Continued)

(1950), pp. 267-269.

"IIe Rencontre des Professeurs de Philosophie."

PENNSYLVANIA, UNIVERSITY OF, LIBRARY HOLDINGS. See 62.

PERIODICALS IN PHILOSOPHY. See also INDEXES, 1476, 2338.

2142. Caramella, S. "Le Reviste filosofiche italiane nell'ultimo quarto di seculo," La Cultura (Roma), vol. 3 (1923-1924), pp. 508-516, 550-556.

2143. Caron, Pierre, and Marc Jaryc. Répertoire des périodiques de langue français, philosophiques, historiques, philologiques, et juridiques. Paris: Fédération des sociétés françaises de sciences philosophiques, historiques, philologiques, et juridiques, 1935. Supplement: 1937, 19 entries. Supplement: 1939, 62 pp.

2144. Baumgardt, David. Philosophical Periodicals. An Annotated World List. Washington: Library of Congress, 1952. 89 pp.

489 entries.

2145. Paris. Maison des sciences de l'homme. Philosophie. Liste mondiale des périodiques spécialises Philosophy. World List of Specialized Periodicals. 's-Gravenhage: Mouton, 1967. 124 pp.

An extensive listing and description of journals, most of which are in philosophy.

2146. Syracuse University Libraries. Philosophy Serials in Syracuse University Libraries. Compiled by Savita Sharma and Janet Graham. Syracuse, N.Y.: 1971. 15 l.

2147. Hogrebe, Wolfram, Rudolf Kamp, and Gert König. Periodica Philosophica: Eine internationale Bibliographie philosophischer Zeitschriften von den Anfängen bis zur Gegenwart. (Kleine Philosophische Bibliographien aus dem Philosophischen Institut der Universität Düsseldorf, Bd. 2). Düsseldorf: Philosophia Verlag, 1972. 728 cols.

Excellent coverage of about 1800 philosophy journals. Topic index, national index, charts of relationships.

PERSONALITY. See 1357, 1522, 1705, 2156, 2254, 2322, 2350.

2148. Gratton, Carolyn. "Selected Subject Bibliography (Covering the Past Ten Years)," Humanitas (Pittsburgh), vol. 3 (1967), pp. 227-235.

About 175 entries on "Neuroses and Personal Growth."

PESSIMISM

2149. Sully, James. Pessimism, a History and a Criticism. New York: D. Appleton and Co., 1891. 477 pp.

2150. Stäglich, Hans. Bibliographie des pessimistischen Schrifttums, 1871-1900. Leipzig: [Typescript], 1932. 2 pp.

2151. Stäglich, Hans. "Chronologisch geordnete wissenschaftliche Bibliographie des selbständigen Schrifttums zum Thema Pessimismus." Leipzig: [Typescript], 1933. 102 l.

2152. Stäglich, Hans. "Chronologisch geordnete wissenschaftliche Bibliographie der Zeitschriften- und Zeitungsaufsätze zum Thema Pessimismus." Leipzig: [Typescript], 1933. 53 l.

2153. Stäglich, Hans. Standortverzeichnis des selbständigen Schrifttums zum Thema Pessimismus. Leipzig: [Typescript], 1933. 8 l.

2154. Stäglich, Hans. Verzeichnis der schriften zum Thema Pessimismus für die Jahre 1872-1931. 2. auflag. Leipzig: [Typescript], 1933. 26 l.

PERSUASION

2155. Warnotte, D. "Bibliographie sélectionnée d'ouvrages et articles relatifs à l'art de persuader," Revue de l'institut de sociologie (Brussels), vol. 18 (1938), pp. 831-851.

PHENOMENOLOGY. See HUSSERL, EDMUND, AND 863, 944, 959, 1242, 2069, 2198.

PHILOSOPHY OF HISTORY. See HISTORY, PHILOSOPHY OF.

PLAY, RECREATION, AND LEISURE

2156. Gratton, Carolyn. "Selected Subject Bibliography (Covering the Past Ten Years)," Humanitas (Pittsburgh), vol. 5 (1969), pp. 107-119.

About 175 entries. Interdisciplinary. On personality and play.

2157. Gratton, Carolyn. "Selected Subject Bibliography (Covering the Past Ten Years)," Humanitas (Pittsburgh), vol. 8 (1972), pp. 397-404.

175 entries.

POETRY

2158. Belknap, George Nicholas. A Guide to Reading in Aesthetics and Theory of Poetry (Oregon University Studies in College Teaching, vol. 1, no. 5) (University of Oregon Publication, vol. 4, no. 9, July 1934). Eugene, Oregon: University of Oregon Press, 1934.

POLEMICS. See 1425.

POLISH PHILOSOPHY.

See also 57, 361, 368, 393, 888, 903, 2352.

2159. Bibliografia filozofii polskiej, 1750-1830 [Bibliography of Polish Philosophy, 1750-1830 [In Polish]]. Warszawa: Państwowe wydawnictwo naukowe, 1955. 264 pp.

About 1200 entries. Annotations. Works written or published in Poland.

2160. Bibliografia filozofii polskiej 1831-1864 [Bibliography of Polish Philosophy, 1831-1854 [In Polish]]. Élaborie à l'aide des materiaux rassemblés par Adam Bar, Alicja Kadler et Irena Raczyńska, en coopération avec Barbara Skarga et Alicja Sawicka. Warszawa: Pańistowe wydawnictwo naukowe, 1960. 409 pp.

A continuation of the earlier volume (to 1830). About 3800 entries.

2161. Grzegorczyk, Andrzeij, and Ludwik Kasiński. Bibliografia filozofii w Polsce 1945-1946 [Bibliography of Philosophy in Poland, 1945-1946 [In Polish]]. (Odbitka z Przegladu filozoficznego, no. 1-4, 1947). Kraków: Duk. narodowa, 1947.

2161. (Continued)

About 300 entries.

2162. Sobociński, B. "Polskie wydawniclwa filozoficzne 1918-1936," Nowa Ksiazka, vol. 3 (1936), pp. 114-121.

2163. Pisarzy, Słownik. Filozofia w Polsce [Philosophy in Poland [In Polish]]. (Instytut filozofii i socjologii polskiej akademii nauk). Wrocław, [etc.]: Zakład narodowy imienia ossolińskich wydawnictwo polskiej akademii nauk, 1971. 462 pp.

Brief articles on polish philosophers with some bibliographical material in each. Name index.

2164. Warszawa. Polska akademia nauk. Komitet filozoficzny--filozoficzny--Monografie bibliograficzne. Warszawa: 1958-

POLITICAL ECONOMY. See 771.

POLITICAL PHILOSOPHY AND POLITICS. See also POLITICAL PHILOSOPHY, ANCIENT, and 951, 1120, 1660, 1662, 1664, 1668, 2070, 2258.

2165. Mühlbrecht, O. Wegweiser durch die neuere Literature der Rechtsund Staatswissenschaft für die Praxis bearbeitet, 2nd ed. Berlin: Puttkamer und Mühlbrecht, 1893-1901. 2 vols. 764, 651 pp.

2166. Warrender, J. H. "A Survey of Publications in Political Philosophy, 1945-1950," Philosophical Quarterly (St. Andrews), vol. 1 (1950-1951), pp. 356-366.

2167. Montenegro, A. "Bibliografía de theoría política e historia de las ideas políticas en la edád antigua," Revista de estudios políticos (Madrid), vol. 13 (1953), pp. 193-200.

2168. Ilari, R. and S. Di Fiore. "Bene comune e persona nello stato contemporaneo. Bibliografia," in Orientamenti sociali, 1964, pp. 193-209.

POLITICAL PHILOSOPHY, ANCIENT

2169. Hadas, Moses. "Recent Work in Ancient Politics," Journal of the History of Ideas (New York), vol. 13 (1952), pp. 110-118.

<u>POPULATION</u>. See 2254.

<u>PORTO MUNICIPAL PUBLIC LIBRARY HOLDINGS</u>. See 1737.

<u>PORTUGUESE PHILOSOPHY</u>. See also 1737, 2022, 2247, 2270.

2170. De Figueiredo, Fidelino. <u>Para a historia da filosofia em Portugal</u> (Subsidio bibliografico) Porto: 1922. 33 pp. 200 copies printed.

550 entries.

2171. Da Costa, Manuel Gonçalves. <u>Inéditos de filosofia em Portugal [1500-1800]</u> (Filosofia; Estudos publicados pela Faculdade de Filosofia de Braga). Porto: Tavares Martins, 1949. 143 pp.

2172. Da Silva, Augusto and José Barbosa Pinto. <u>Revistas de filosofia.</u> Braga: Faculdade pontificia de Filosofia, 1955. 43 <u>ll</u>.

2173. De Gama Caeiro, Francisco. "História da filosofia em Portugal (Roteiro de matérial e guia bibliografico)," <u>Revista da Faculdade de letras</u> (Lisbon), 2a ser., no. 7 (1963), pp. 102-132.

2174. <u>Revista Portugesa de Filosofia</u> (Braga). (Faculdade Pontifica de Filosofia.) Vol. 1 (1945)-[to date].

Has bibliographical supplements.

<u>POSITIVISM</u>. See also COMTE, AUGUSTE, and LOGICAL POSITIVISM, also 2104.

2175. Comte, Auguste. <u>Bibliothèque du prolétaire au dix-neuvième siècle.</u> 1851. 5 pp.

About 150 entries.

2176. Poëy, André. "Bibliographie positive et critique," <u>La Philosophie Positive</u> (Paris), vol. 7 (1870-1871), pp. 500-501.

2177. Ducassé, Pierre. <u>La Méthode positive et l'intuition comtienne: Bibliographie</u>. 1939. 175 pp. Also: a 1940 edition.

About 1000 entries.

PRAGMATISM. See also 1952.

2178. Leroux, E. Bibliographie méthodique du pragmatisme américain. (Thése) Paris: F. Alcan, 1922. 99 pp. Also published, 1923, in the author's Le Pragmatisme américain et anglais, étude historique et critique, 419 pp.

PRE-SOCRATIC PHILOSOPHY. See also 1926.

2179. Howald, E. "Bericht über die Vorsokratiker (einschliesslich Sophistik). 1923 bis 1926," Jahresbericht über die Fortschritte der klassischen Alterumswissenschaft (Berlin), vol. 216 (1928), pp. 111-129.

2180. "Selective Bibliography [on the Pre-Socratics]," in A. P. D. Mourelatos, ed., The Pre-Socratics. A Collection of Critical Essays. Garden City, N.Y., Anchor Press, Doubleday Books, 1974, pp. 527-542.

PROCESS PHILOSOPHY. See 171.

PRUSSIAN STATE LIBRARY HOLDINGS. See 1959.

PSYCHICAL RESEARCH. See also OCCULT PHILOSOPHY.

2181. The bibliography of Progressive Literature. Descriptive Catalogue Comprising a Complete and Classified List of Works Relating to . . . Psychical Science . . . [etc., etc.]. New York: 1899. 96 pp.

About 4000 entries.

2182. Catalogue de la bibliotheque. Société d'études psychiques de Nancy. Nancy: 1900. 16 pp.

About 200 entries.

2183. Society for psychical research, London. Combined index to 'Phantasms of the Living,' vols. I and II. 'The Proceedings,' vols. I-XV. 'The Journal,' vols. I-IX, and 'The Proceedings of the American Society for Psychical Research.' With Table of Contents of 'The Proceedings,' London: R. B. Johnson, 1904. 239 pp.

2184. Caillet, A. L. Manuel bibliographique des sciences psychiques ou occultes. Paris: Dorbon, 1912-1913. 3 vols. Reprinted: Nieuwkoop: de Graaf, 1964.

Detailed and annotated, 11,648 entries.

2185. Lovi, Henrietta. Best Books on Spirit Phenomena, 1847-1925. Boston: Richard G. Badger (The Gorham Press), [n.d.]. 94 pp.

A survey of about 150 titles. Index.

2186. Besterman, Theodore. Library Catalogue of the Society for Psychical Research. Glasgow: Printed for the Society by R. Meclehose and Co., 1927. n.p.

Supplements: 1927-1928; 1928-1929; 1929-1930; 1931-1933. 9350 entries in all.

2187. Price, Harry. Short-title Catalogue of Works on Psychical Research, Spiritualism, Magic, Psychology, Legerdemain and other Methods of Deception, Charlatanism, Witchcraft, and Technical works for the Scientific Investigation of Alleged Abnormal Phenomena from Circa 1450 A.D. to 1929 A.D. (Proceedings of the National Laboratory of Psychical Research, vol. I, part 2, April 1929). 422 pp. Supplement: Short-title Catalogue of the Research Library. University of London council for psychical investigations. 1935. 112 pp.

About 8500 entries. With interesting illustrations. About 2500 entries in the supplement.

2188. Exhibition of Rare Works from the Research Library of the University of London Council for Psychical Investigation. London: 1934. 48 pp.

About 500 entries.

2189. Moine, Michel. La Bibliographie et l'annuaire international des sciences psycho-physiques et occultes. Paris: L'Ernite, 1949. 216 pp.

2190. Society for psychical research, London. Psychical Research: A Guide to Publications in English [London: ?], 1949. 11 pp.

2191. Morgan, S. R. Index to Psychic Science. Swarthmore, Penn.: 1950. 117 pp.

Subject index, author index, glossary. 513 entries, nicely cross indexed. With photographs of investigators into psychic science and their subjects.

2192. A Bibliography and Index of Psychic Research and Related Topics. Chicago: 1962-1964.

PSYCHOLOGY. See 121, 863, 944, 1659, 1898.

PSYCHOLOGY OF ART. See ART, PSYCHOLOGY OF.

QUEENS COLLEGE LIBRARY (BELFAST) HOLDINGS. See 2071.

RAMAYANA

2193. Gore, N. A. Bibliography of the Ramayana. Poona: Gore, 1943. 99 pp.

RATIONALISM

2194. Verlière, A. Publication rationaliste. Guide du libre penseur, ou catalogue de tous les ouvrages philosophiques et scientifiques basé sur le libre examen. Bruxelles: 1872. 48 pp.

2195. A Rationalist Bibliography. Preliminary List. London: Watts, 1896. 20 pp.

2196. Librairie rationaliste. Essai de bibliographie contemporaine sur le résumé de nos connaissances depuis l'antiquité jusqu'à nos jours. Paris: Reinwald-Schleicher, [n.d.]

REALISM. See also 907.

2197. Harlow, Victor Emmanuel. Bibliography and Genetic Study of American Realism. Oklahoma City: Harlow Publishing Co., 1931. 132 pp. Reprinted: New York: Kraus reprint, 1970.

About 700 entries.

2198. Chisholm, R. M. Realism and the Background of Phenomenology. Glencoe, Ill.: The Free Press, 1960. 308 pp.

Bibliography on pp. 283-304.

RECREATION. See PLAY, RECREATION, AND LEISURE.

REIMS LIBRARY HOLDINGS. See 1738.

RELATIVISM. See 2344.

RELIGION, PHILOSOPHY OF. See also 532, 1704, 1778.

2199. Cavallera, Ferdinand. "Bibliographie d'études concernant les idées religieuses (1940-1945)," Revue d'ascetique et de mystique (Toulouse), vol. [?] (1947), pp. 349-387.

2200. Des Places, Edouard. "Bulletin de la philosophie religieuse des Grecs. Bibliographie critique," Recherches de Science Religieuse (Paris), vol. 36 (1949), pp. 147-160; vol. 37 (1950), pp. 300-320.

2201. Millard, Richard M. "Some Recent Literature in Philosophy of Religion," Philosophy and Phenomenological Research (Buffalo), vol. 12 (1951-1952), pp. 422-430.

2202. Berkowitz, Morris I., and Edmund J. Johnson. Social Scientific Studies of Religion: a Bibliography. Pittsburgh: Pittsburgh University Press, 1967. 258 pp.

RELIGION AND SCIENCE. See SCIENCE AND RELIGION.

RENAISSANCE PHILOSOPHY. See also 60, 83, 483, 1553, 1742, 1823, 1841, 1842, 1844, 1845, 1846, 1847.

2203. Taylor, Archer. Renaissance Guides to Books. Berkeley: University of California Press, 1945.

Most books discussed are non-philosophical, but the work should nevertheless be useful to students of the philosophies of the period.

2204. Craig, Hardin. "Recent Literature of the Renaissance," Studies in Philosophy (Chapel Hill, N. C.), vol. 46 (1949), pp. 204-386.

2205. Mommsen, Theodor E. "A Bibliography of Books and Articles on Italian Renaissance Thought," Philosophical Review (Ithaca, N.Y.), vol. 59 (1950), pp. 237-239.

2206. Rummens, Jean. "Bibliographie des principaux ouvrages concernant la philosophie de la renaissance italienne (1930-1950)," Revue internationale de philosophie (Bruxelles), vol. 5 (1951), pp. 200-228.

2207. Garin, Eugenio. "Il Rinascimento," Giornale critico della filosofia italiana (Firenze), vol. 31 (1952), pp. 97-105.

2208. Riedl, John O., ed. A Catalog of Renaissance Philosophers (1350-1650) Compiled by Robert A. Baker, et al. Under the Direction of John O. Riedl. Milwaukee: Marquette University Press, 1940. 179 pp. Reprint: Hildesheim, New York, G. Olms, 1973.

"Compiled by a group of 17 undergraduate students." About 2000 entries.

RESPONSIBILITY. See FREEDOM AND DETERMINISM, also 1659.

2209. Gratton, Carolyn. "Selected Subject Bibliography (Covering the Past Ten Years)," Humanitas (Pittsburgh), vol. 9 (1973), pp. 225-232.

175 entries on "Responsibility and guilt."

2210. Gratton, Carolyn. "Selected Subject Bibliography (Covering the Past Ten Years)," Humanitas (Pittsburgh), vol. 5 (1969), pp. 242-250.

About 200 entries on "Guilt and self renewal."

REVELATION. See 1022.

RHETORIC. See ARISTOTLE.

RISORGIMENTO

2211. De Campos Ferreiora Lima, Henrique. "Bibliografia portoghese del Risorgimento," Rivista di storia del Risorgimento, vol. 27 (1940), pp. 451-462.

ROMAN PHILOSOPHY. See CLASSICAL GREEK AND ROMAN PHILOSOPHY.

ROTTERDAM LIBRARY, HOLDINGS. See 440.

ROUMANIAN PHILOSOPHY. See also 891, 1443, 1558.

2212. Revista de referate si recenzii (Bukarest), vol. 1 (1964)-

Bibliographies and abstracts.

ROYAL ACADEMY OF ART (BERLIN), HOLDINGS. See 1410.

ROYAL AUSTRIAN MUSEUM FOR ART AND INDUSTRY, HOLDINGS. See 1407.

ROYAL BAVARIAN ACADEMY OF SCIENCE, HOLDINGS. See 1748.

RUSSIAN PHILOSOPHY. See also SOVIET PHILOSOPHY, COMMUNIST PHILOSOPHY, MARX, KARL, etc., also 481, 1337, 1889.

2213. Besobrasof, Marie. Handschriftliche Materialien zur Geschichte der Philosophie in Russland. Leipzig: G. Foch, 1892. 34 pp.

About 100 entries.

2214. Uvarov, Aleksiei Sergieevich. count. Sistematicheskoe opisanie slaviano-rossiiskikh rukopisei sobraniia grafa A. S. Uvarova . . . Sostavil arkhimandrit Leonid. [A systematic description of Slavo-Russian manuscripts in the collection of Count A. S. Uvarov. Compiled by Archimandrite Leonid [In Russian]]. Moscow: A. I. Mamontov, 1893-1894. 4 vols.

Primarily works in religion, some in ethics.

2215. Sergius. "Obzor russkoj filosofskoj literatury za vremia revoljucii (1917-1924) [Survey of Russian Philosophical Literature during the Revolution (1917-1924)]," [New Russian Book], (1923), 3/4, pp. 3-7.

2216. Jakovenko, B. V. "Desjat' let russkoi filosofii (1914-1924) [Ten Years of Russian Philosophy--1914-1924 [In Russian]]," Logos (Prague), vol. 1 (1925), pp. 195-206.

SACRO COURE, UNIVERSITY OF (ROME) HOLDINGS. See 357.

SAKHYA. See 1811.

SALAMANCA, UNIVERSITY OF, AND LIBRARY. See also 2061, 2109.

2217. Otílio del Niño Jesús. "Para una bibliografía de los salmanticenses," El Monte carmelo (Burgos), vol. 41 (1938), pp. 145-152.

SAMUĆĆAYA. See 1914.

SAN CARLOS (GUATEMALA), UNIVERSITY OF, HOLDINGS.

2218. Bendfelt Rojas, Lourdes, and Alba Rosa Calderón de Muñoz. Bibliografía filosófica de publicaciones de las Universidades de Costa Rica y San Carlos de Guatemala y de autores guatemaltecos que exhibió la Biblioteca national. Primer coloquio de filosofía, septiembre 30-octubre 3, 1964. Guatemala: 1964. 26 l.

SANSKRIT LANGUAGE WORKS

2219. Burnell, Arthur Coke. A Classified Index to the Sanskrit Mss. in the Palace of Tanjore. Part II. Philosophy and Law. Madras: Madras Government, 1879, pp. 81-151.

About 1000 entries.

2220. Śástrí, Hrisgúkeśa and Śiva Chandra Gui. A Descriptive Catalogue of Sanskrit Manuscripts in the Library of the Calcutta Sanskrit College. Volume III. Philosophy Manuscripts. Calcutta: 1899-1900. 327 pp.

583 entries.

SÃO PAULO UNIVERSITY, PUBLICATIONS

2221. São Paulo. Universidade. Indice bibliográfico das publicações da Universidade de São Paulo. Vol. 1. fasc. 4: Fasculdade de filosofia, ciências e Letras. São Paulo, 1951-

SATYAGRAH. See NON-VIOLENCE.

SCANDINAVIAN PHILOSOPHY. See also names of individual philosophers, and countries, also 2232.

2222. Theoria (Lund), vol. 7 (1941-[to date].

Useful bibliographies of current philosophical works from the Scandinavian countries. Bibliography appears irregularly.

SCHOLASTIC PHILOSOPHY. See also 1604, 1647, 2067, 2105, 2135.

2223. Carbone de Costacciaro, Lodovico. Catalogus Scholasticorum Theologorum. Coloniae Agrippinae: 1618.

2224. Blanc, Élie. Manuale Philosophiae Scholasticae . . . Quibus Accedit Opusculum. Lugduni: 2. Vitte, 1901. 2 vols.

SCIENCE. See 483, 509, 2007, 2061, 2104.

SCIENCE, ANCIENT. See 54, 1543.

SCIENCE, FOUNDATIONS OF. See 2012.

SCIENCE, HISTORY OF

2225. Fischer, Hans. "Schweizerische Bibliographie der Gesichte des Naturwissenschaften und der Medizin," Gesnerus (Zollikon, Switz.), vol. 1-2 (August, 1948), pp. 43-52.

2226. Millás-Vallicrosa, J. M. "Las Primeras traducciones científicas de origen oriental hasta mediados del Siglo XII," in Actes IXe Congrès International d'Histoire des Sciences, Barcelona: Asociación para la historia de la ciencia española; Paris: Hermann, 1960, pp. 33-68.

SCIENCE, PHILOSOPHY OF. See also 464, 1631,

2227. Guérard des Lauriers, M. L. "Bulletin de philosophie des sciences," Revue des sciences philosophiques et théologiques (Le Saulchoir), vol. 35 (1951), pp. 431-469.

2228. Filiasi, Carcano. "Rassegna di filosofia della scienza," Rassegna de filosofia (Roma), vol. 1 (1952), pp. 14-26.

2229. Lalande, André. "Principal Publications on the Philosophy of the Sciences Brought out in France since 1900," in Marvin Farber, ed., Philosophic Thought in France and the United States, 2nd ed. Albany: State University of New York Press, 1968, pp. 169-180.

2230. Robert, Jean-Dominique. Philosophie et science. Philosophy and Science. Eléments de bibliography. Elements of Bibliography. (Bibliothèque Archives de Philosophie, nouv. sér., 8). Paris: Chez Beauchesne, 1968. 384 pp. Supplement for 1968 and 1969: Archives de philosophie (Paris), vol. 33 (1970), pp. 110-112, 295-324.

About 5300 entries. Annotations, abbreviated subject keys for entries.

2231. Feigl, Herbert, and Charles Morris. "Bibliography and Index," International Encyclopedia of Unified Science, vol. 2, no. 10. Chicago: University of Chicago Press, 1969. 108 pp.

About 675 unannotated entries divided according to topic.

2232. Hintikka, Jaakko. "Philosophy of Science (Wissenschaftstheorie) in Finland," Zeitschrift für allgemeine Wissenschaftstheorie (Wiesbaden), vol. 1 (1970), pp. 119-132.

Surveys the recent work in the philosophy of science in Finland.

2233. Bona, E., and J. Farkas. "Bibliographie: Veroeffentlichungen Ungarischer Wissenschaftstheoretiker," Zeitschrift für allgemeine Wissenschaftstheorie (Wiesbaden), vol. 4 (1973), pp. 188-193.

2234. Isis (Washington), vol. 1 (1931)-[to date].

Each volume contains one, sometimes two, bibliographies, now entitled "Critical Bibliography of the History of Sciences and its Cultural Influences." Bibliographies are extensive and important.

2235. Schatzberg, Walter. "Relations of Literature and Science: a Bibliography of Scholarship, 1973-1974," Clio (Kenosha, Wisc.), vol. 5 (1975), pp. 97-122.

SCIENCE, SOCIOLOGY OF

2236. Barber, Bernard, and Robert K. Merton. "Brief Bibliography for the Sociology of Science," Proceedings of the American Academy of Arts and Sciences, vol. 80 (1952), pp. 140-154.

SCIENCE AND RELIGION

2237. Répertoire de la collection "Science et religion" publiée à Paris chez Blond. Bruxelles: A. Dewit, 1912. 80 pp.

About 700 entries from that collection. Indexes.

SCIENTIFIC MANUSCRIPTS

2238. Gabriel, Astrik L. A Summary Catalogue of Microfilms of One Thousand Scientific Manuscripts in the Ambrosiana Library, Milan. Notre Dame, Ind.: The Medieval Institute, University of Notre Dame, 1968. 440 pp.

SCIENTIFIC PHILOSOPHY

2239. Faber, F. Register zum Vierteljahresschrift für wissenschaftlichen Philosophie (1876-1906). Leipzig: Reisland, 1908.

SCOTTISH PHILOSOPHY. See also 604.

2240. MacCosh, J. Scottish Philosophy; Bibliographical, Expository, Critical, from Hutcheson to Hamilton. New York: B. Carter, 1874. 481 pp. Also: London: Macmillan, 1875; New York: Carter, 1875, 1880 [1883?], 1890. Reprint of 1875 edition, 1966.

SELF. See 2322.

SEMIOTICS

2241. Pelc, Jerzy. "The Development of Polish Semiotics in the Post-War Years," Dialectics and Humanism (Warsaw), (Autumn, 1973), pp. 225-235.

SET THEORY

2242. Fraenkel, Abraham A. Abstract Set Theory. Amsterdam: North Holland, 1953.

Bibliography, pp. 343-479.

SEVENTEENTH CENTURY PHILOSOPHY. See also GENERAL PHILOSOPHICAL BIBLIOGRAPHIES.

2243. Beyer, Charles J. et al. "Philosophical and Scientific Literature [: France: the Seventeenth Century]," in D. C. Cabeen and J. Brody, gen. eds. A Critical Bibliography of French Literature, Syracuse, N.Y.: Syracuse University Press, 1961, vol. 3, pp. 457-503.

About 440 entries by a number of scholars. Covers a number of 20th century studies of 17th century authors.

2244. Curley, Edwin. "Recent Work on 17th century Continental Philosophy," American Philosophical Quarterly (Pittsburgh), vol. 11 (1974), pp. 235-255.

Covers the period 1960-1972. A survey of the literature on Descartes, Malebranche, Spinoza, and Leibniz. Bibliography.

SICILIAN PHILOSOPHY

2245. Di Giovanni, Vincenzo. ["Bibliography of Sicilian Philosophy from the XV until the XIX Century"], in his Storia della filosofia in Sicilia da' tempi antichi al Secolo XIX. Palermo: Lauriel, 1873, vol. 2, pp. 562-615.

Also contains a "Catalogo di mss. di filosofia esistente nelle biblioteche di Sicilia."

SIKH PHILOSOPHY

2246. Barrier, N. Gerold. Sikhs and Their Literature; a Guide to Tracts, Books, and Periodicals, 1849-1919. Delhi: Manohar Book Service, 1970. 153 pp.

SIXTEENTH CENTURY PHILOSOPHY. See also GENERAL PHILOSOPHICAL BIBLIOGRAPHIES.

2247. Machado dos Santos, Mariana Amélia. "Manuscritos de filosofia do Século XVI existentes em Lisboa," Boletin da Biblioteca da Univ. de Coimbra (Coimbra), vol. 19 (1950), pp. 241-382. Also: Coimbra: 1951, 384 pp.

135 entries.

SLOVAKIAN PHILOSOPHY. See also CZECHOSLOVAKIAN PHILOSOPHY, and 896, 900, 917, 2307.

2248. Slosiar, Dezider. Bibliografia filozofíckéj knižnej Tvorby na Slovensku za roky 1945-1960 [Bibliography of Philosophical Literature in Slovakia for the Years 1945-1960 [In Slovak]]. (Séria: Bibliografické Materiály a Pomočky, č. 8). Martin: Matica slovenska, 1965. 151 pp.

2249. Verbinc, Franc. Filozofski tokovi na Slovenskem (Slovenska filozofska bibliografija (1800-1945)) [Philosophical Currents in Slovenia (Slovenian Philosophical Bibliography (1800-1945)) [In Slovenian]]. Ljubljana: Inštitut za Sociologijo in Filozofijo pri Univerzi, 1967. 452 pp.

Also: #1970.

2250. Simoniti, Primož. Bibliografija filozofskih tekstov (rokopisov in tiskov) na Slovenskem do leta 1800 [A Bibliography of Philosophical Texts (Handwritten and Printed) in Slovenian before the Year 1800 [In Slovenian]]. Ljubljana: Inštitut za Sociologijo in Filozofijo pri Univerzi, 1971. 70 pp.

SOCIAL ANTHROPOLOGY

2251. "Bibliographie d'initiaton à l'anthropoligie sociale," Cahiers de Philosophie (Paris), (1966), pp. 105-110.

SOCIAL DEVELOPMENT. See 2102.

SOCIAL ETHICS

2252. Harvard University. A Guide to Reading in Social Ethics and Allied Subjects: List of Books and Articles Selected and Described for the Use of General Readers. By Teachers in Harvard University. (Publications of the Department of Social Ethics in Harvard University, no. 3). Cambridge, Mass.: Harvard University Press, 1910. 265 pp. Reprinted: Ann Arbor, Michigan: Gryphon Books, 265 pp.

Selectively covers various specific topics in social ethics (really sociology). Dated, and for the general reader, but does introduce one to some ethical issues. Annotated; e.g., "A mass of descriptive material concerning state, municipal and private bath-houses in the United States. Illustrated by photographs and plans."

2252. (Continued)

The historian of ideas should find it fun. About 800 entries. Index.

2253. Freiburg, Schweiz. Internationalen Institut für Sozialwissenschaft und Politik. Bibliographie der Sozialethik. Freiburg, Schweiz: Heider, 1961-1963. 530 pp.

2254. Bibliography of Society, Ethics and the Life Sciences (Hastings-on-Hudson, N.Y.) Annual. 1973?-

About 1100 entries per issue. Some annotations. Divided according to topic. Extensive and valuable for information on abortion, euthanasia, genetics, population, health care, experimentation, etc.

SOCIAL LIVING. See 1662, 1668.

SOCIAL PHILOSOPHY. See also 334, 929, 2259.

2255. Gratton, Carolyn. "Selected Subject Bibliography (Covering the Past Ten Years)," Humanitas (Pittsburgh), vol. 5 (1970), pp. 369-377.

About 200 entries on "Society and self emergence."

SOCIALISM. See also entries under MARX, KARL; ENGELS, FRIEDRICH, COMMUNISM, etc., and 1018.

2256. Stammhammer, Josef. Bibliographie des Socialismus und Communismus. Neudr. Bd. 1: Neudr. d. ausg. 1893. Bd. 2: Nachträge und Ergänzungen bis Ende des Jahres 1898. Neudr. d. ausg. 1900. Aalen: Zeller, 1963. Vol. 1, 303 pp.; vol. 2, 403 pp.

2257. Silvin, E. Index to Periodical Literature on Socialism. Santa Barbara: Roger and Morley, 1909. 153 pp.

2258. "Bibliographie [: Der Mensch und die objektive Gesetzmässigkeit der soziolistischen Gesellschaft, 1963-1964] in Der Mensch und die objektive Gesetzmässigkeit in der sozialistischen Gesellschaft, Berlin: VEB Deutsche Verlag der Wissenschaften, 1964, pp. 116-124.

SOCIETY, MODERN. See also 1601.

2259. Mannheim, Karl. Man and Society in an Age of Reconstruction . . . with a Bibliographic Guide to the Study of Modern Society. New York: Harcourt, Brace, and World, 1967. 469 pp.

SOCIETY OF PSYCHICAL STUDIES (NANCY). See 2182.

SOCIOLOGY. See also 1650, 1659, 1664, 2092.

2260. Paumen, Jean. "Sociologie et philosophie: Essai de bibliographie succincte," Revue internationale de philosophie (Bruxelles), vol. 4 (1950), pp. 335-340.

SOCIOLOGY OF CHRISTIANITY

2261. Carrier, Hervé and Émile Pin. Sociology du christianisme-bibliographie internationale. Sociology of Christianity. International Bibliographie (Studia Socialia, vol. 8). Rome: Presses de l'Université grégorienne, 1964. 316 pp.

3,200 entries on history, psychology, and sociology of religion. Arranged by author, by subject (400), by country.

SOCIOLOGY OF KNOWLEDGE. See KNOWLEDGE, SOCIOLOGY OF.

SOCIOLOGY OF SCIENCE. See SCIENCE, SOCIOLOGY OF.

SOCIOLOGY OF THE MORAL LIFE. See MORAL LIFE, SOCIOLOGY OF.

SOLITUDE. See LONLINESS AND SOLITUDE.

SOUTH AFRICAN PHILOSOPHY. See also 490.

2262. Dawe, H. Philosophy in South Africa, 1950-1962; a Bibliography. (University of Cape Town. School of Librarianship. Bibliographical Series). Cape Town: University of Cape Town, School of Librarianship, 1964. 32 pp.

Index. About 219 entries with brief annotations.

SOVIET PHILOSOPHY. See also MARX, KARL; ENGELS, FRIEDRICH; LENIN, V. I.; COMMUNIST PHILOSOPHY, and 1665, 2019.

2263. Semenova, V. A. and V. T. Chernysheva. Chto chitat' o moral'nom oblike sovetskogo cheloveka [What to Read About the Moral Profile of Soviet Man [In Russian]]. Moscow: Publichnaîà Biblioteka, 1951. 38 pp.

2264. Bochenski, I. M. et al. Bibliographie der Sowjetischen Philosophie (Sovietica Series). Freiburg/Schweiz: Ost-Europa Instituts, Universität Freiburg/Schweiz, 1959-1968.

Vol. 1: De "Voprosy filosofii," 906 entries.
Vol. 2: Bücher, 1947-1956. Bücher und Aufsätze, 1957-1958. 1303 entries.
Vol. 3: Bücher und Aufsätze, 1959-1960. 1309 entries.
Vol. 4: Ergänzungen/Supplement, 1947-1960. 2217 entries.
Vol. 5: Register/Indices, 1947-1960. 144 pp.
Vol. 6: Bücher und Aufsätze, 1961-1963. 2039 entries.
Vol. 7: Bücher und Aufsätze, 1964-1966. 2823 entries. Index, 1961-1966.

Works published in the Soviet Union 1947-1966. Continued by "Bibliography of Soviet philosophy" in Studies in Soviet Thought (Dordrecht).

2265. Akademiîà Nauk SSSR. Fundamental'naîà Biblioteka Obšč̌estvennykh Nauk [USSR Academy of Science. Basic Library of Social Sciences]. Novaîà sovetskaîà literatura po filosofiĭ [New Soviet Literature on Philosophy [In Russian]]. 1954 - . In progress.

About 7000 items per volume.

2266. "Bibliography of Soviet Philosophy," Studies in Soviet Thought (Dordrecht), vol. 7 (1967)-[to date].

Continues Bibliographie der Sowjetischen Philosophie.

2267. Novaîà sovetskaîà literaura po filosofii [New Soviet Literature on Philosophy [In Russian]]. (Moskva), 1965- .

SOVIET STRUCTURE. See STRUCTURE, SOVIET.

SPANISH PHILOSOPHY. See also 175, 705, 962, 1966, 1980, 1993, 2022, 2136.

2268. Vidart, Luis. La Filosofía española; indicaciones bibliográficas. Madrid: 1866. 406 pp.

About 250 entries.

2269. Ysart, F. X. "Resena de trabajos sobre historia de la filosofía de España y América latina (1930-1933)," Sophia (Napoli; Palermo), vol. 4 (1936), pp. 99-101.

2270. Spain. Junta del centenario de Suarez. Filosofía española y portuguesa de 1500 a 1650. Madrid: Ministerio de educación nacional, 1948. 173 pp.

1243 entries.

2271. Martínez Gómez, Louis. "Literature filosófica española e hispano-americana. Año 1949," Pensamiento (Madrid), vol. 7 (1951), pp. 419-444.

2272. Martinez Gomez, Luis. Bibliografía filosófica española hispano-americana (1940-1958). (Pensamiento; Ser. Difusión, vol. 1). Barcelona: Juan Flores, 1961. 500 pp.

10,166 entires divided by subject and period. Name index. Good for Spain, major figures in the history of philosophy, and subject bibliographies.

2273. Arostequi, Antonio. "Notas para una bibliografía de la historia de la filosofía española," Aporia (?), vol. 2 (1966), pp. 89-103.

2274. Martinez Gomez, Luis. "Bibliografía filosófica española, elenco 1973," Pensamiento (Madrid), vol. 29 (1973), pp. 465-494.

711 entries.

2275. Bibliotheca Hispana: revista de información y orientación bibliográficas. (Madrid). Vol. 1 (1943)- [to present].

Contains a section on philosophical works divided into topics: "Generaladades y Historia," "Lógica," "Psico-logía," "Metafísica," "Ethica." Only works published in Spain. Annotated.

SPANISH LANGUAGE WORKS. See also 672, 673.

2276. Schmidt-Koch, Ria. Filosofía alemana traducída al Español. Repertorio bibliográfico. Berlin: Sociedad Kantiana de Buenos Aires, 1935. 88 pp. Second edition: "A cargo de Ilse de Brugger,". Buenos Aires: Universidad de Buenos Aires: Instituto de estudios germánicos, 1942. 199 pp. Premier Supplemento: Buenos Aires: Coni, 1954. 88 pp.

About 600 entries in 1935 edition. About 1000 entries in 1942 edition.

SPECULATIVE PHILOSOPHY

2277. Morell, John Daniel. An Historical and Critical View of Speculative Philosophy in Europe in the Nineteenth Century. London: W. Pickering, 1846. 2 vols.

This work has been published in at least fifteen editions.

2278. Nicolas, Jean-Hervé. "Chronique de philosophie spéculative. Revue thomiste (St. Maximin), vol. 48 (1948), pp. 538-591.

SPIRIT. See 697.

SPIRITUALISM. See PSYCHICAL RESEARCH.

SPIRITUALITY

2279. Dagens, Jean. Bibliographie chronologique de la littérature de spiritualité et de ses sources (1501-1610). Paris: Desclée de Brouwer, 1952. 208 pp.

Covers French works of the 16th century.

STOICISM

2280. D'Angers, Julien Eymard. "Le Renouveau du stoïcisme en France au XVIe siècle et au début du XVIIe," Bulletin de l'Association Guillaume Budé (Paris), no. 1 (1964), pp. 122-147.

STRUCTURALISM

2281. Harari, Jeané V. Structuralists and Structuralisms; a Selected Bibliography of French Contemporary Thought (1960-1970). Ithaca, N.Y.: Diacritics, 1971. 82 pp.

1275 entries, of which 288 are in philosophy. Contains bibliographies on Louis Althasser, Gilles Deleuze, Jacques Derrida, and Michel Foucault.

STRUCTURE, SOVIET

2282. Moscow. Publichnaîà biblioteka. Chto chitat' o sovetskom stroe [What to Read on Soviet Structure [In Russian]] pod obshcheĭ red. Moskva: 1947. 48 pp.

STUDENT GUIDES. See also 2133.

2283. Stockhausen, Johann Christoph. Critischer Entwarf einer auserlesenen Bibliothek für den Liebhaber der Philosophie und schönen Wissenschaften. In einigen Sendschreiben an einen Freund. Berlin: Ambrosius Hande und Joh. Carl. Spener, 1752. Also: Berlin: 1764. 408 pp.

A student's manual. Most of the material is non-philosophical. About 300 references of little value.

2284. Brieglebs, Johann Christian. Einleitung in die philosophischen Wissenschaften nebst einem Abriss der Geschichte derselben und einem Verzeichniss der vornehmsten philosophischen Schriftten. Coburg: Ahl, 1789. 206 pp.

About 750 entries.

2285. Krug, Wilhelm Traugott. Handbuch der Philosophie und der philosophischen Literatur. Leipzig: F. A. Brockhaus, 1820-1821. 2 vols. in 1. Also: Stockholm: Z. Häggström, 1831 [In Swedish]; Leipzig: 1822, 1828, 1836.

About 2500 entries, analytic index.

2286. Freude, C. G. A. Wegweiser alter und neuer gemeinnützinger Schriften aus verschiedenen Wissenschaften. 3 vols. Ebersbach, 1858-1860. Volume II: Philosophie, 440 pp. Volume III: Pédagogie. 384 pp. Also: 1860-1861.

2287. Krug, Wilhelm Traugott. Allgemeines Handwörterbuch der philosophischen Wissenschaften, nebst ihrer Literatur und Geschichte. Leipzig: F. A. Brockhaus, 1927-1834. 5 vols. Also: 1832-33, 1838.

2288. Dr. Buttners literaturführer. Abteilung IV, enthält sämtliche literarische Erscheinungen auf dem Gebiete der Philosophie aus den Jahren 1884-1889. Leipzig: 1890. 31 pp.

About 600 entries.

2289. Wolf, Gustav. Philosophisches Vade-Mecum und systematisches Zusammenstellung der litterarischen Erscheinungen auf dem Gebiete der Philosophie. I. Litteratur von 1882-86, 47 pp.; II. Litteratur von 1886-90, 51 pp. Leipzig: Levien, 1889-1890.

2290. Eisler, Rudolf. Wörterbuch der philosophischen Begriffe und Ausdrücke. Berlin: E. S. Mittler und Sohn, 1899, 1904. 956 pp. Revised as: Wörterbuch der philosophischen Begriffe, Historisch-Quellenmässig. Berlin: E. S. Mittler und Sohn, 1910. 3 vols. Reprinted: 1927-1930.

Third volume contains bibliography, pp. 1980-2076.

2291. Herbertz, Richard. Die philosophische Literatur; ein Studienführer. Stuttgart: W. Spemann, 1912. 222 pp.

Contains references only to works in German. Divided according to subject areas, "Ethik," "Logik," etc. A students' guide, now somewhat dated but, nevertheless, helpful. Annotated. Name index.

2292. Burns, Cecil Delisle. What to Read on Philosophy. Leeds: Public Libraries, 1930. 28 pp. Also a 1939 edition.

125 entries.

2293. National Book Council, London. British Institute of Philosophical Studies. Philosophy. London: 1930. 11 pp.

About 300 entries.

2294. Gunn, J. Alexander. Psyche and Minerva. What to Read in Psychology and Philosophy. A Select Bibliography. 2nd ed. Melbourne: Melbourne University Press, 1933. 31 pp.

300 entries in philosophy.

2295. National Book League, London (Formerly, National Book Council). *Philosophy*. ("The Reader's Guides," no. 2). 20 pts. London: September, 1928-May, 1934.

2296. Eisler, Rudolf. *Philosophen-Lexikon. Lebenwerke und Lehren der Denker*. Berlin: E. S. Mittler, 1912. pp. v-890. See also: *Philosophen Lexikon. Bearbeitet von Eugen Hauer, Werner Ziegenfuss, Gertrud Jung*. 1937. pp. iv.480. A-J only; no more published.

20,000 entries in 1912 edition. 10,000 entries in 1937 edition.

2297. De Raeymaker, Louis. *Introduction à la philosophie, 3e éd*. Louvain: Institut supérieur de philosophie, 1938. 278 pp. Also a German edition.

Good survey of the important works. About 1000 entries.

2298. Hope, Richard. *A Guide to Readings in Philosophy*. Ann Arbor, Mich.: Edwards Brothers, Inc., 1939. 173 pp.

2299. Vloemans, Antoon. *Voor bereiding tot de wijsbegeerte. 3., herz. druk*. 's-Gravenhage: H. P. Leopold, 1943. 306 pp.

2300. U. S. Library of Congress. General Reference and Bibliography Division. *A List of One Hundred Philosophical Source Books from the Early 20th Century Back to the Pre-Socratic Period*. Washington: Library of Congress, 1945. 9 pp.

2301. Carlini, Armando. *Avviamento alla filosofia, con una piccola guida storico-bibliografica*. (Biblioteca enciclopedica sansoniana, 14). Firenze: Sansoni, 1950. 228 pp. In several editions.

2302. Huisman, Denis. *Guide de l'étudiant en philosophie*. Paris: Presses universitaires de France, 1956. 180 pp.

2303. Library Association, County Libraries Section. *Readers' Guide to Books on Philosophy*. ("Readers' Guide," new ser., no. 38.) London: Library Association, 1957. 31 pp. Also: No. 33 (1940), 20 pp.

About 500 entries.

2304. Le Senne, René. *Introduction à la philosophie, 4e éd*. Paris: Presses universitaires de France, 1958. 480 pp.

A student's guide, but the last 40 pp. contain a very good bibliography of the standard works. Some annotations.

2305. Edmunds, Heinz. Zugänge zur Philosophie; ein besprechendes Auswahlverzeichnis für Leser. (Veröffentlichung des Bibliothekar-Lehrinstituts des Landes Nordrhein-Westfalen). Köln: Greven Verlag, 1959. 40 pp.

About 200 entries.

2306. Totok, Wilhelm. Bibliographischer Wegweiser der philosophischen Literatur. Frankfurt am Main: Klostermann, 1959. 35 pp.

2307. Matica slovenská, Turčiansky sv. Martin. Bibliografia filozofie; výber základnej knižnej tvorby z oblasti filozofie a metodické pokyny k štúdiu [Philosophical Bibliography: a Selection of Basic Literature from the Field of Philosophy with Methodological Suggestions for Study [In Slovak]]. Martin: 1964. 115 pp.

2308. Higgins, Charles L. The Bibliography of Philosophy; a Descriptive Account. (University of Michigan. Department of Library Science. Studies, 7). Ann Arbor: Campus Publishers, 1965. 29 pp.

A rather short but good discussion of the major philosophical bibliographies. Perhaps more useful to the reference librarian than the philosopher.

2309. Koren, Henry J. Research in Philosophy, a Bibliographical Introduction to Philosophy and a few Suggestions for Dissertations. Pittsburgh: Duquesne University Press, 1966. 203 pp.

A good guide with much useful information. Bibliographies.

2310. Otto, Anneliese. Philosophie. Eine Literaturzusammenstellung der wichtigsten philosophischen Literatur einschliesslich der Literatur zu Fragen der Religion. Suhl: Stadt-und Bezirksbibliothek, 1966. 111 pp.

About 880 entries with special section on Marxism-Leninism. Annotated. A student's guide to the standard important works.

2311. Bräuner, Wilém. Psychologie, Logika, Filosofie; na pomoc vyučujícím na SVVŠ. Výberová bibliografic. [Psychology, Logic, Philosophy: an Aid to Students at the SVVS (State School of Higher Scientific Studies[?]) [In Czech]]. Brno: 1967. 52 pp.

2312. Borchardt, Dietrich Hans. How to Find Out in Philosophy and Psychology. Oxford; New York: Pergamon Press, 1968. 97 pp.

2312. (Continued)

A research guide intended for the beginning student. Quite solid. Contains most of the basics.

2313. Matczak, Sebastian A. Research and Composition in Philosophy. New York: Humanities Press, 1968. 88 pp.

Aimed at the beginning undergraduate student. Has sections on how to do scholarly writing and some remarks on bibliographical sources in philosophy.

2314. De George, Richard T. Guide to Philosophical Bibliography and Research. New York: Appleton-Century-Crofts, 1971. 141 pp.

An excellent up-to-date guide. Contains references to major bibliographies and standard editions, dictionaries, encyclopedias, journals, and biographies of use to the philosopher. Anyone with a serious interest in philosophy should find it helpful.

2315. McGill University, Montreal, Library Reference Department. A Student's Guide to Reference Resources in Philosophy. Montreal: 1971. 17 l.

2316. Ziat'kova, Liudmila Ivanova. Molodezhi o filosofii [To Youth on Philosophy [In Russian]]. Moscow: "Kniga," Publichnaia Bibliteka, 1971. 93 pp.

SUFFERING. See EVIL, PROBLEM OF.

SUFI PHILOSOPHY

2317. Arberry, A. J. Catalog of the Arabic Mss. in the Library of the India Office. Vol. II, "Sufism and Ethics." London: Oxford University Press, 1936.

SUICIDE

2318. Oettinger, E. M. "Bibliographie da suicide," Bulletin de bibliophile belge (Bruxelles), 2nd ser., vol. 4 (1857), pp. 107-114, 358-359.

115 entries.

2319. Motta, E. Bibliografia del suicidio. Bellinzona: Tip. di C. Salvioni, 1890. 102 pp.

2320. Boehn, Max von. Selbstmord und Selbstmörder. Verzeichniss der Buchersammlung von Max V. Boehn. Zugleich eine Ergänzung zu: Motta: Bibliografia del Suicido. Charlottenburg: [n.p.], 1907. 64 pp.

2321. Rost, Hans. Bibliographie des Selbstmords. Augsburg: 1927.

2322. Gratton, Carolyn. "Selected Subject Bibliography (Covering the Past Ten Years)," Humanitas (Pittsburgh), vol. 6 (1970), pp. 125-134.

About 230 entries on "self destruction and self creation."

SURVIVAL OF DEATH. See IMMORTALITY.

SWEDISH PHILOSOPHY. See also 1773.

2323. Vannérus, A. Svensk filosofi: Bibliografisk förteckning omfattende tiden till och med ar 1900 [Swedish Philosophy: Bibliographical Outline Comprising the Years up to and Including 1900 [In Swedish]]. Stockholm: 1930. 262 pp.

SWISS PHILOSOPHY. See also 2225.

2324. Heyer, Henri. Vingt-huitième rapport, . . . avec an appendice bibliographique relatif aux publications théologiques et philosophiques d'auteurs genevois de 1887-1903. Genìve: Societe des sciences théologiques, 1904. 37 pp.

650 entries.

2325. Heuss, Eugen et al. [Schweizerische Philosophische Gesellschaft]. Bibliographie der Philosophischen, Psycologoischen und Pädagogischen Literatur in der Deutschsprachigen Schweiz 1900-1940. Basel: Verlag für Recht und Gesellschaft, 1944. 207 pp.

Supplement: 1941-1944, by Hans Zantop, Jahrbuch der Schweizerische philosophische Gesellschaft, vol. 5, pp. 218-278. This is now an annual supplement.

SWITCHING CIRCUITS. See LOGICAL ALGEBRA.

SYMBOLISM, AND HUMAN DEVELOPMENT

2326. Gratton, Carolyn. "Selected Subject Bibliography (Covering the Past Ten Years)," Humanitas (Pittsburgh), vol. 8 (1972), pp. 267-274.

175 entries.

SYRACUSE UNIVERSITY LIBRARIES HOLDINGS. See 2146.

SYSTEMATIC PHILOSOPHY

2327. Royce, Josiah. "Systematic Philosophy in America in 1893, '94, '95," Archiv fur systmatischer philosophie (Berlin), vol. 3 (1897), pp. 245-266.

SZÉCHENYI LIBRARY MANUSCRIPTS. See 1855.

TANJORE PALACE, LIBRARY HOLDINGS. See 2219.

TECHNOLOGY

2328. Gratton, Carolyn. "Selected Subject Bibliography (Covering the Past Ten Years)," Humanitas (Pittsburgh), vol. 3 (1967), pp. 101-107.

About 175 entries on "Automation and leisure."

2329. Gratton, Carolyn. "Selected Subject Bibliography (Covering the Past Ten Years)," Humanitas (Pittsburgh), vol. 6 (1971), pp. 371-377.

About 150 works on "Human response to a functional world."

2330. Mitcham, C. and R. Mackey. Bibliography of the Philosophy of Technology. Chicago: University of Chicago Press, 1973.

2331. "Select Bibliography on the Philosophy of Technology," in Friedrich Rapp, ed., Contributions to a Philosophy of Technology (Theory and Decision Library, 5). Dordrecht, Boston: D. Reidel, 1974, pp. 210-228.

TER DOEST ABBEY

2332. Pelzer, Auguste. "Livres de philosophie et de théologie de l'Abbaye de Ter Doest à l'usage du maître cistercien Jean Sindewint de 1311 à 1319," in Etudes d'histoire littéraire sur la scholastique médiévale. Louvain: Publications universitaires: Paris: Béatrice-Nauwelaerts, 1964, pp. 70-96.

THEATER, AESTHETICS OF. See 1359.

THEODICY. See LEIBNIZ, G. W.

THEOLOGY. See also 546, 1475, 1492, 1495, 1519, 1525, 1659, 1714, 1735, 1771, 1778, 1787, 2223.

2333. Tritheim, Johann. Liber de Scriptoribus Ecclesiasticus. Basel: Johann Amerbach, 1494.

About 300 pp. and 7000 entries. Deals primarily with theologians.

2334. Buddeus, Joannes Franciscus. Isagoge Historico-Theologica ad Theologiam Universam Singulasque Partes. Leipzig: Thomae Fritschii, 1727. 730 pp. Also: 1730, edition.

2335. Federn, R. Répertoire bibliographique de la littérature française des origines à nos jours. Théologie. Philosophie. Littérature. Paris: Federn, 1913. Vol. I: Liste alphabétique. 413 pp.; vol. II: Index méthodique, pp. 414-612.

2336. Elenchus Bibliographicus. Ephemerides Theologicae Louvanienses (Louvanii), vol. 27 (1951), pp. 558-676.

THEOSOPHY. See OCCULT PHILOSOPHY.

THIRTEENTH CENTURY PHILOSOPHY

2337. Glorieux, Palémon. Répertoire des maitres en théologies de Paris au XIIIe siècle. (Etudes de philosophie médiévales, 17-18). Paris: J. Vrin, 1933-1934. 2 vols.

THOMISM. See AQUINAS, THOMAS.

THOUGHT, FREEDOM OF. See INTELLECTUAL FREEDOM.

TRADITION. See CUSTOM AND TRADITION.

TRANSCENDENTALISM

2338. Gohdes, Clarence, L. F. The Periodicals of the American Transcendentalists. Durham: Duke University Press, 1931. 264 pp.

Discusses about 11 periodicals.

TÜGINGEN LIBRARY HOLDINGS. See 1736.

TURIN, PHILOSOPHICAL LIBRARY HOLDINGS

2339. Guzzo, A. "La Biblioteca filosofica di Torino," Filosofia (Torino), vol. 12 (1961), pp. 753-764.

TWENTIETH CENTURY PHILOSOPHY. See CONTEMPORARY.

UKRANIAN PHILOSOPHY. See also 914.

2340. Mircuk, J. "Ukrainische philosophische Bibliographie der letzten Jahre (1921- bis 1926)," Mitteilungen des Ukrainische Wissenschaft Instituts in Berlin (Berlin), vol. 1 (1927), pp. 60-69; vol. 2 (1928), pp. 69-74.

UNITED STATES PHILOSOPHY. See also NORTH AMERICAN PHILOSOPHY, and 1672, 2197, 2327, 2338.

2341. Winn, Ralph B. Americanische Philosophie (Bibliographische Einführengen in das Studium der Philosophie, 2). Bern: A. Francke, 1948. 32 pp.

About 30 entries.

2342. Balz, A. G. A. Southern Teachers of Philosophy (University of Kentucky Library. Occasional Contribution, no. 65). Lexington: University of Kentucky Press, 1954. 124 pp.

About 1500 entries. Bibliographies and chronicles of southern (U.S.A.) teachers of philosophy. For the student of southern intellectual history.

UNIVERSAL LANGUAGE. See 1995.

UPANISHADS. See also INDIAN PHILOSOPHY AND HINDUISM.

2343. Hume, Robert Ernest. The Thirteen Principal Upanishads, Translated from the Sanskrit, with an Outline of the Philosophy of the Upanishads and with an Annotated Bibliography. 2nd ed. Madras: Indian Branch, Oxford University Press, 1949.

UTOPIAS. See also 972.

2344. Leemans, Victor. "Tussen relativisme en utopisme," Tijdschrift voor Philosophie (Leuven), vol. 13 (1951), pp. 541-560.

UVAROV, A. S., LIBRARY OF. See 2118, 2214.

VALUES. See ETHICS.

VANDERBLUE MEMORIAL COLLECTION. See 1230.

VATICAN LIBRARY HOLDINGS. See 226, 1934.

VEDAS. See also INDIAN PHILOSOPHY AND HINDUISM.

2345. Renou, L. Bibliographie védique. Paris: Maisonneuve, 1931. 339 pp.

2346. Dandekar, Ramchandra Narayan. Vedic Bibliography; an Up-to-date Comprehensive and Analytically Arranged Register of all Important Work Done Since 1930 in the Field of the Veda and Allied Antiquities. Bombay: Karnatak, 1946. 395 pp. Vol. 2: Poona, India: University of Poona, Ganeshkhind, 1961. 760 pp.

VENEZUELAN PHILOSOPHY

2347. Mérida, Venezuela. Universidad de los Andes. Facultad de Humanidades y Educación. Biblioteca. Catálogo bibliográfico de filosofía, psicología, arte, historia de Venezuela. Mérida; 1960. 97 pp.

2347. (Continued)

Pt. 1 of the Cátalogo bibliográfico general of the above library.

2348. Parra, Caracciolo. Filosofía universitaria venezolana, 1788-1821. Caracas: Parra León Hermanos, 1933. 280 pp. Also: Second edition, 1934.

Contains a long bibliography, pp. 243-278.

VENN, JOHN, COLLECTION. See 2006.

VIOLENCE. See SOREL, GEORGE, and 2039.

WARBURG INSTITUTE LIBRARY HOLDINGS. See 1782.

WIDENER LIBRARY HOLDINGS. See 1792.

WOLFF, ABRAHAM, COLLECTION. See 1247.

WOMEN

2349. Menaguis, Aegidius [Menage, Gilles]. Historia Mulierum Philosopharum. Lugduni: apud Anissonios, Joan. Poseul, et Claudium Rigaud, 1690. About 250 pp. Also: Amstelodami: H. Wetstenium, 1692, 72 pp.; and Abregé de l'historie de la vie des femmes philosophes de l'antiquité. Amsterdam: 1761; London [In English], 1702, in The Lives of the Ancient Philosophers, pp. 535-564.

WORK

2350. Gratton, Carolyn. "Selected Subject Bibliography (Covering the Past Ten Years)," Humanitas (Pittsburgh), vol. 7 (1971), pp. 255-264.

225 entries on "Work and human development."

WORLD VIEWS

2351. Prümm, Karl. Die Fortschritte des Jahrzehnts 1941-1951 in der Erarbeitung der weltanschaulichen Gehalte der antiken Philosophie. Roma: Pontifico istituto biblico,

2351. (Continued)

1950. 50 pp.

About 500 entries.

YOGA. See 1914.

YUGOSLAVIAN PHILOSOPHY. See also 921.

2352. Tvrdy, A. "Bibliogr. polské a jihoslav. filosofie [A Bibliography of Polish and South Slavic Philosophy [In Czech]]," Současná Filosofie a Slovanů (1932), pp. 161-173.

ZEN BUDDHISM. See also BUDDHIST PHILOSOPHY.

2353. Beautrix, Pierre. Bibliographie du bouddhisme Zen. (Publications de l'Institut belge des hautes études bouddhiques. Série Bibliographie, 1.) Bruxelles: Institut belge des hautes études bouddhiques, 1969, 114 pp.

INDEX

[THE NUMBERS GIVEN BELOW ARE ENTRY NUMBERS, NOT PAGE NUMBERS.]

Abbot, A. E., 2125
Abbot, Ezra, 1864
Academia republicii populare Romîne, 891
Acton, H. B., 1699, 1702
Adam, Carlos, 1016
Adam, Melchior, 1798
Adams, E. M., 780
Adickes, Erich, 653
Adorno, Francesco, 1556, 1557
Akademiīa nauk SSSR, 1583, 1775, 1865, 2265
al-Alwajī, 'Abd al-Hamīd, 622
Albert, Ethel M., 1658
Alcan, Félix, 1496, 1498
Alcinous, 1053
Alekseev, M. P., 1342
Alessio, F., 142
Alexander, Henry A., 649
Alexander, Samuel, 14
Allen, Paul Marshall, 1262
Allihn, F. H. Th., 582
Almagno, Romano Stephen, 1289
Alston, R. C., 1995
Amano, Kazuo, 954
Amano, Keitarō, 1354
Amedeus a Zedelgem, 410
American Council of Learned Societies, 1852
American home economics association, 1440
Amerio, F., 1628
Amerio, Romano, 263
Anawati, Georges C., 124, 1942
Anderson, John, 23
Andressen, Carl, 107, 109, 113
Angelelli, I., 3
Angot des Rotours, Bon J., 1644
Anthony, R., 1046
Apresíàn, Zoriĭ Grantovich, 1430
Arango Betancour, Ignacio, 1453
Arberry, A. J., 2317
Arce, David N., 1685
Archibald, R. C., 183
Armani, Giuseppe, 288
Arnim, Max, 1772
Arntz, J., 1102
Aron, Raymond, 131
Arostequi, Antonio, 2273
Arpe, Peter Freidrich, 1691
Arréat, Lucien, 1474
Arvon, Henri, 812
Ashcraft, R., 795
Ashworth, E. J., 2023
Aspelin, Inga-Lill, 89
Asse, Louis Eugène Auguste, 1121
Aster, E. von., 2086
Astruc, Charles, 505
Avetta, Adolfo, 1739
Avinyó, Joan, 819
Ayer, A. J., 2036

Baba, Akio, 1353
Babin, A., 1639
Babson institute Library, 993

Badawī, 'Abd al-Rahmān, 18, 623
Baege, Dr., 731
Baer, Joseph and Co., 657, 1194, 1245, 1273, 1362, 1492
Bagchi, Prabodh Chandra, 1510
Balbo, P., 158
Baldassari, Mariano, 634
Baldwin, R. C., 1363
Balluf, Theodor, 534
Balz, A. G. A., 2342
Bar. A., 368
Baranowski, Henry K., 313
Barber, Bernard, 2236
Barboza, Enrique, 382
Barcani, N., 423
Barcelona. Biblioteca Central, 1331
Barnabas, Hechich, 145
Barnhart, Edward N., 1419, 1921
Barr, Mary Margaret Harrison, 1343
Barreda y Laos, Felipe., 1977
Barrett, F. Dermot, 1595
Barrier, N. Gerold, 2246
Barthélemy-Madaule, Madeleine, 664
Baskin, M. P., 1603
Basse, J. H., 1025
Bastide, Georges, 1660
Bataillon, L. J., 1002, 2059
Batista y Roca, Joseph M., 815
Batlle y Vázquez, Manuel, 1332
Batllori, Miguel, 820
Baudry, Gerard Henry, 1293
Baudry, L., 1374
Baumanns, Peter, 150
Baumgardt, David, 2144
Baumgartner, Hans M., 456
Bauschenplat, Hellmut, 987
Baxandall, Lee, 908
Bayen, Maurice, 169
Bayer, Raymond, 1762, 1763
Beaujouan, Guy, 2061
Beautrix, Pierre, 2353
Beck, Leonard N., 1128
Becke, Louis White, 661, 1827
Becker, W., 988
Beirwaltes, Werner, 2103
Belin, Leonid A., 771
Belke, Felicitas, 2033
Belkind, Allen, 1161
Belknap, George Nicholas, 2158
Bellezza, Vito, 500, 501, 743, 1674
Belloni, G. A., 1104
Benavides Balbin, Alberto, 1578
Bendfeldt Rojas, Lourdes, 2218
Bengesco, Georges, 1338, 1339
Bense, Max, [et al.], 1425
Benson, Arthur, 280
Bentoz, Hans W., 647
Berg, Jan, 1773
Bergamaschi, Cirillo, 1084, 1116
Bergier, J. F., 1841, 1842
Bergmann, E., 351
Berkelbach van der Sprenkel, O., 1533
Berkowitz, Morris I., 2202
Berlin. Stadtbibliothek, 909
Berry, G. G., 2009
Beschin, G., 2107
Besobrasof, Marie, 2213
Besterman, Theodore, 1340, 2186
Beth, E. W., 2012
Bettoni, Efrem, 416
Beyer, Charles J., 2243
Bianca, D. O. [et al.], 1584
Biblioteka narodowa (Warsaw), 888
Biblioteca Centrală Universitară Mihai Eminescu, 1558
Bibliothèque nationale (France), 68, 177, 1030, 1122, 1130
Bibliothèque royale de Belgique, 1341
Bigaev, I͡Usuf Kurbanovich, 915
Biscione, Michele, 1815
Bishop, Morris, 1033
Biskup, Marian, 315
Blackham, Harold John, 1839
Blackwell, Kenneth, 1147
Blakey, Robert, 2002, 2083
Blampignon, Emile Antoine, 847
Blanc, Élie, 1695, 2224
Blanco Soto, Pedro, 816

Bloch, (Ernst), 201
Blumhardt, J. F., 1813
Boccassino, R., 1073
Bochenski, I. M., 1759, 2017, 2264
Bockrareva, Margarita Aleksandrovna, 1654
Bodemann, Eduard, 728, 729
Boehlich, Walter, 330
Boehmer, Philip Ludwig, 1634
Boehn, Max von., 2320
Boffito, Giuseppe, 477
Bogliolo, Luigi, 750
Bolduanus, Paulus, 1713
Bolin, W., 455
Bollnow, Otto Friedrich, 1684
Bolton, Eng., 1473
Bona, E., 2233
Bona, Ida, 616
Bonar, James, 1229
Bondi, G., 502
Boni, Nell, 431
Bonilla y San Martín, Adolfo, 934, 935, 1330
Bonnelly, M. Claude, 1222
Bonnet-Eymard, J. [et al], 1576
Bontadini, G., 352, 353
Boorsch, Jean, 354
Borch, Rudolf, 1198, 1199, 1200, 1201, 1202, 1203, 1204, 1205, 1206
Borchardt, Dietrich Hans, 2312
Borgis, Ilona, 1381
Borne, Petro, 515
Borsani, Giuseppina, 1511
Borsari, Silvano, 321
Bosshart, E., 1254
Bougerol, J. Guy, 224
Bourke, Vernon J., 37
Bousquet, Georges Henri, 1024
Boutarel, P. de, 1878
Bouton, Jean de la Croix, 193
Bouyges, Maurice, 17, 117
Boyancé, Pierre, 809
Boydston, Jo Ann, 387, 388, 389
Boyer, Charles, 104
Boyle, Robert, 1716
Bräuner, Vilém, 2311
Bratislava. Univerzita. Kniżnica, 896
Braun, C., 1102
Bravo, Gian Maria, 897
Bray, L. Du Beau, 1411
Bredenfeld, Hermann, 555
Bréhier, Emile, 178, 1545
Breitholz, Paul, 1050
Brescia, Giuseppe, 324, 325
Brieglebs, Johann Christian, 2284
Brière, O., 1530
Bril, K. A., 1333
Briscoe, John Potter, 2084
British Museum, 73, 133, 214, 1391
Brno University Library, 898, 1602
Broudy, Harry S. [et al], 1625
Brounts, Simon, 10
Brucker, Johann Jakob, 1724, 1861
Brumbaugh, Robert S., 1063, 1064
Brumm, Dieter, 1358
Bruni, Gerardo, 1107
Buchanan, Emerson, 969
Buchenau, Artur, 1574
Buchicchio, Fausto Maria, 668
Buday, Júlia, 1854
Buddecke, W., 215, 217
Buddeus, Joannes Franciscus, 2334
Budge, Edwin S., 807
Büchting, Adolph, 1182, 1805
Bütow, Hellmuth G., 899, 904
Buhle, Johann Gottlieb Gerhard, 63, 1872
Bulgakova, Lidii͡a V., 760
Burch, George Bosworth, 2058
Burgersdijk and Niermans, (firm), 521, 1495
Burnell, Arthur Coke, 2219
Burns, Cecil Delisle, 2292
Byrns, Ruth, 868
Buschan, von, 1744

C. P. Ramaswami Aiyar Research Endowment Committee, 1922
Cabeen, David Clark, 967, 1703
Cadavid Arango, Carlos, 1453
Caillet, A. L., 2184

Calderon de Muños, Alba Rosa, 2218
Calker, Johann Friedrich August van., 1997
Callus, Daniel, 2055
Calverley, E., 1938
Cambridge University Library, 2006
Camto, Frederico, 941
Capánaga, Victorino, 111
Caponigri, A. Robert, 1950, 2111
Cappelletti, M., 257
Cappuyns, M., 448
Caramella, S., 2142
Carballal de Torres, Maria Teresa, 631
Carbone de Costacciaro, Lodovico, 2223
Caron, Pierre, 2143
Carli, Alarico, 472, 474
Carlini, Armando, 2301
Carrier, Hervé, 2261
Carrière, Gaston, 1612
Carus, Friedrich August, 1819
Carus, Paul, 284
Caruso, Paolo, 777
Casas, M. G., 175
Caserta, Ernesto G., 326
Caspar, Max, 679
Cassirer, Ernst, 367
Castagnino, Franco, 695
Castellano, G., 317
Castelli, Enrico, 1110
Catania, Francis J., 11
Catanne, Moshe, 244
Caturelli, Alberto, 1463
Cavallera, Ferdinand, 2199
Caviglione, C., 1109
Centre De Wulf-Mansion, 2139
Centre national de la recherche scientifique (Paris), 1786
Centro de estudios de filosofía (Sevilla), 1982
Centro di documentazione per la filosofia del dritto, 1992
Cerny, James W., 1445
Chaix-Ruy, Jules, 1321
Chan, Wing-tsit, 1345, 1529, 1532
Chandler, A. R., 1419
Chandler, Henry William, 64, 65
Chang, Wei-Shung, 1535
Charles University (Prague), 889, 1523
Chauden, Louis Mayeul, 1726
Chauvin, V., 1928
Cheng, Chung-ying, 2027
Chenu, Marie Dominique, 2051
Cherniss, H. F., 1062
Chernyshevz, V. T., 2263
Chevolier, Cyr Ulysse Joseph, 25, 2085
Chicago Public Library, 1749
Chile. Universidad, 1524
Chiriotti, E., 355
Chisholm, R. M., 2198
Ch'iu, Alfred K'ai-Ming, 1528
Christopherson, Halfdan Olaus, 784
Chung-Hun, Lee, 1970
Church, Alonzo, 2010, 2015
Church of England, 1659
Cione, Edmondo, 322, 1320
Clair, Pierre, 335, 1299
Clark, Harry Hayden, 1021
Clouser, K. Danner, 1396
Cogni, G., 544, 548, 552
Cohen, Friedrich (firm), 1500
Cohen, Jonathan, 1829
Cole, F. J., 1470
Colette, Jacques, 691
Collière, H., 2141
Collins, James, 1581
Colombo, C., 365
Colomer, Eusebi, 827
Columbia University Libraries, 170
Comisión nacional de cooperación intelectual (Argentina), 1460
Comte, Auguste, 2175
Conche, Marcel, 810
Congar, M.-J., 254
Congresso nazionale di filosofia, 1569
Conrieri, Davide, 327
Conring, Hermann, 1721
Contat, Michel, 1162
Conte, A. G., 2028
Contri, S., 553
Cooke, George Willis, 433
Cooper, Lane, 72
Copeland, Thomas Wellsted, 249

Cordasco, F. G. M., 247, 1232
Cordier, H., 1527
Coreth, Emerich, 1179
Cortese, M. Allessandro, 690
Cosentini, Francesco [et al], 1740, 1990
Cosenza, Mario Emilio, 1849
Cosenza, Paolo, 84
Costa, Antonina, 210, 211
Courtenay, William J., 1103
Coutagne, Paul, 1280, 1287, 1290
Coviello, Alfredo, 171
Craig, Hardin, 2204
Cranston, Maurice, 791, 953
Cranz, F. Edward, 60
Crepin, Simone, 269
Cresson, André, 1090
Crippa, Romeo, 206, 209
Croce, Benedetto, 540, 1319
Croissant, Jeanne, 375
Crook, Ronald Edward, 1075
Cropsey, Joseph, ed., 1264
Crosby, B. Steven, 1304
Crowe, Michael J., 483
Crowley, John Dennis, 599
Cuellar-Bassoes, Luis, 282
Cuenot, Claude, 1278, 1279, 1281
Cunbur, Müjgân, 16

Da Costa, Manuel Gonçalves, 1673, 2171
Da Gama Caeiro, Francisco, 2173
Dagens, Jean, 2100, 2101, 2279
Dagognet, François, 132
D'Ainville, Varin, 2018
Daley, Charles Marie, 6, 1618
Dallenbach, K. M., 1348
Dal Pra, Mario, 1948
D'Alverny, Marie Thérèse, 356
Dandekar, Ramchandra Narayan, 2346
Dangeau, Louis [Louis Vian], 966
D,Angers, Julien Eymard, 2280
Danzer, R., 1000
D'Armagnac, Christian, 1288, 1291
Da Silva, Augusto, 2172
Dawe, H., 2262
De Aldana, J. A., 1272
De Almeida e Sousa, Abel L., 1560
De Backer, Augustin, 1964
De Bary, Theodore, 2131
Deberle, A., 1401
De Brie, G. A., 1768
De Bure, Guillanme-François, 1725
De Campos Ferreiora Lima, Henrique, 2211
De Cerio, Franco Diaz, 401
De Corte, M., 1539, 15
De Dijn, H., 1252
De Dios Mendoza, Juan, 147
De Figueiredo, Fidelino, 2170
De George, Richard T., 2314
De Giuli, G., 345, 347
De Guaita, Stanislas, 337
De Jaucourt, Louis, 724
De Jong, J. W., 1515
De Labarre, A., 1647
De Lacy, Phillip, 438
Dela Noi, Pedro, 1525
Delasalle, Paul, 1238
De la Vallée-Poussin, L., 1509
De Lellis, Enzo, 617
De Lesclache, Louis, 1714
Delfgaauw, Bernard, 686, 693
Della Vida, G. L., 1934
Delle Piano, Mario, 976
Del Noci, Augusto, 848
De Magalhaes-Vilhena, 1236
Demattei, Rodolfo, 267
De Mattos, Carlos Lopes, 240
De Menasce, P. J., 1940
De Mendosa, Juan, 146
De Meyer, A., 255
De Montpellier, Gerard, 950
Demortier, Roger, 336
Dempf, A., 309
De Mullewie, M., 747
Dennon, Lester E., 1149
Denziger, Ig., 1998
De' Paoli, Stefano Lorenzo, 2072
De Petter, D. M., 1620
De Pourtalès, Guy, 1026
De Raedemaeker, F., 41, 44
De Raedemaeker, Jozef, 58, 59

De Raeymaeker, Louis, 2297
De Ruggiero, G., 737
de Sá, Vítor, 1318
Deschamps, Pierre Charles Ernest, 294
De Scorraille, R., 1265
Desgraves, Louis, 968
Deshpande, P. G., 487
Des Places, Edouard, 2200
Destrez, J., 32
De Strycker, E., 1057
De Terra, Helmut, 1282
Deussen, J., 697
de Valdés, Maria Elena, 1310
Deraux, Philippe, 1148
Deraux, André-A., 1140
De Veer, Albert C., 102, 149
Devereux, E. J., 443
De Vleeschauwer, H. J., 663
De Vooys, C. G. N., 218
De Vos, A., 2087
Dewey, John, 1642
De Wulf, M., 2050
Dharma Vir., 491
Díaz de Cerio, Franco, 513
Dibon, Paul, 369
Di Carlo, E., 1105, 1106
Dieckmann, Herbert, 391, 392, 394, 395
Diemer, Alwin, 670
Dienstag, Jacob Israel, 844
Diermanse, P. J. J., 522, 523
Di Giovanni, Vincenzo, 2245
Ditz, E., 1213
Dmitriev, E., 771
Dobbert, E., 1410
Doherty, Kevin F., 1082
Domet de Vorges, Cte., 26, 27
Dommeyer, Frederick C., 1652
Domonkos, L. S., 469
Donoko, Anton, 1985
Donzelli, Maria, 1326
Dortmund. Stadtbücherei, 910
Dorward, Alan, 1145
Douglas, Kenneth, 1679
Drahn, Ernst, 761, 875
Drake, Stillman, 479, 480
Draper, J. W., 1417
Dredge, John Ingle, 281
Dresden. Stadt-und bezirks bibliothek, 219
Drudin-Boldrich, Raimundo, 2104
Dublin University, 184
Ducassé, Pierre, 307, 2177
Dürr, Karl, 2034
Dufour, Théophile, 1123
Dulles, Joseph Keatley, 831, 832
Duncan, Elmer H., 1043, 1441, 1442
Dunlop, Jacqueline, 1166
Duràn, Estanislau, 817
Durbin, Jack D., 676
Durville, Hector, 2120
Du Saussay, André, 2095
Duval, André, 291
Dyer, Issac Watson, 277
Dyroff, A., 70

Easton, Stewart Copinger, 141
Ebisaka, Takeshi, 1163
Echard, J., 24
Eckhart, J. G. von, 723
Edie, Callistus James, 506
Edmunds, Heinz, 2305
Edwards, Paul, 1467
Egle, L., 1988
Eisler, M., 1243
Eisler, Rudolf, 2290, 2296
Ekowski, Felix, 758, 759
Ellenberger, H. F., 640
Embree, Ainslee T., 2131
Encausse, Gérard, 2119
Endara, Julio, 1623
Enslin, Theodor Christian Friedrich, 1803
Erdmann, Benno, 656
Ergin, Osman, 127
Erickson, Keith, 85
Ersch, Johann Samuel, 1801, 1871
Ernesti, Johann Heinrich Martin, 1734
Esquerra, R., 962
Eschmann, I. T., 43
Ettlinger, Max, 733
Evain, François, 1115
Evans, A. P., 2053
Evans, A. W., 1346
Evans, Joseph W., 870
Everett, C. W., 166
Ewing, A. C., 660, 1858
Eyring, Jeremias Nicolaus, 1799

Faber, F., 2239
Fabricius, J[ohann?] A[lbert?], 1723
Fabro, Cornelio, 687
Fann, K. T., ed., 116, 1380, 1382, 1383
Farkas, J., 2233
Farrar, C. P., 2053
Faucci, Dario, 292
Faust, C. H., 428
Favaro, Antonio, 471, 473, 474
Federn, R., 2335
Feigl, Herbert, 2035, 2231
Feinberg, Barry, et al., 1146
Felix a Mareto, 712, 1689
Ferreira, C., 45, 1661
Ferretti, Giovanni, 1175
Ferrier, Francis, 290
Ferro, Carmelo, 370, 744, 1760, 1951
Feys, Robert, 2014, 2031
Fichte, Johann Gottlieb, 1466
Fidlero, Daniele, 1635
Figueiredo, Manuel Versos, 1294
Filiasi, Carcano, 2228
Firenze. Biblioteca filosofica, 1686
Firpo, Luigi, 262, 264
Fisch, Max H. [et al.], 1036, 1037, 1039
Fischer, Hans, 2225
Fischer, G. H., 635
Fischer-Appelt, Peter, 585
Fitch, Brian T., 270
Flasche, Hans, 1031, 1816
Flo, Olav, 984, 985, 1077, 1305, 1388, 1390, 2113, 2114, 2115
Flora, Francesco, 319
Flors, Juan, 1778
Fock, Gustav (firm), 948, 1503
Folliet, G., 102
Fomin, Aleksandr G., 879
Fontinell, Eugene, 273
Forest, Aimé, 1766
Formigari, Lia, 1438
Fowler, Dean R., 537
Fraenkel, Abraham A., 2242
Fragata, J., 1285
Franchini, Raffaello, 328
Frankfurt, Usher I., 481
Franklin, Burt, 1232
Frauwallner, E., 1919
Frénand, G., 256
French Library (Prague), 1788
Freude, C. G. A., 2286
Freytag-Löringhoff, B. von, 630
Friedman, Maurice, 245
Fries, Horace S., 609
Frisius, Johannes Jacobus, 1708
Fritz, Kurt, 1066
Frobes, Johann Nikolaus, 1994
Frondizi, Risieri, 1978
Frudenthal, Jacob, 1244
Fülleborn, Georg Gustav, 1818
Fukuhara, Gyozo, 957
Fulton, John Farquhar, 232, 1074

Gabriel, Astrik L., 2238
Gabriel, Leo, 864
Gagné, Armand, 338
Gallagher, Donald A., 869
Gandhi, L. B., 1958
Gandhian institute of studies (Varanasi), 2110
García, Jesús, 824, 826
García Ramos, Dagoberto, 1578
Gardeil, H. D., 1826
Gardner, Frederick Leigh, 2121
Garin, Eugenio, 1551, 1687, 1952, 2056, 2089, 2207
Gassen, Kurt, 1223, 1607
Ganthier, Léon, 119
Gavin, Pierre, 1092
Gay, John H., 298
Gayley, Charles Mills, 1408
Gehlen, A., 736
Geiger, L. B., 1580, 1680
Geldsetzer, Lutz, 1781, 1790
Gemelli, Agostino, 293
Gentili, Elio, 482, 1283
Gerber, Adolph, 835
Gerlo, Aloïs, 1848, 1851
German Jewish publishers of New York, 86
Gerresheim, Eduard, 939
Gerth, H., 1351

Gesamteuropäisches Studienwerk e. V. Bibliothek, 1426
Gesner, Conrad, 1709, 1710
Getrich, Richard J., 1360
Geyer, B., 2135
Ghani, Abdul, 628
Ghio, M. Michaelangelo, 846
Ghuys, Walter, 1228
Giacon, Carlo, 357, 2052
Giannarás, Anastasios, 458
Gianturco, Elio, 1322
Gibson, R. W., 137, 972
Gietz, Ernesto G. [et al.], 1582
Gignon, Olaf, 1060, 1548
Gilles, B., 1650
Gilman, Richard C., 596, 597
Gilson, Lucie, 238
Ginori Conti, Piero, 1171
Giraldo Jaramillo, Gabriel, 1562
Girbal, François, 710
Givone, Sergio, 949
Glorieux, Palémon, 1604, 2337
Göldel, Rolf W., 1862
Gogacz, Mieczysław, 1610
Gohdes, Clarence L. F., 2338
Gollmann, Franz, 1838
Gómez Caffarena, José, 212
Gómez Nogalez, Salvador, 21
Gomperz, Neinrich, 512, 1234, 1235
Good, Paul, 941
Gopinath, Kaviraj, 2116
Gordon, Cosmo Alexander, 808
Gore, N. A., 2193
Gorfinkle, Joseph Issac, 842, 843
Gothie, Daniel L., 1666
Gotō, Shigeru, 1910
Gottron, Adam, 814
Gottsched, Johann Christoph, 726
Gottschlingio, Casparo, 1635
Gouhier, Henri, 849
Grabmann, Martin, 31, 71, 1045, 1372, 1520, 2011
Gracklaner, O., 1406
Grässe, Johann Georg Theodor, 1863
Grajewski, Maurice, 414
Grandi, Terenzio, 928
Grases, Pedro, 164
Gratton, Carolyn, 2157, 2326
Grau, Kurt Joachim, 1575
Gray, George J., 990
Gray, William, 196
Greaves, Charles, 806
Grégoire, F., 1540
Griffin, David, 1369
Grillo, Francesco, 261, 265, 266
Grin, T͡siliia Iosifovna, 919
Grisebach, Eduard, 1192
Grislis, Egil, 601
Grismer, Raymond Leonard, 1980
Groethuysen, Bernhard, 732
Grohmann, W., 1410
Grundé de la Croix du Maine, Francois, 1727
Grünbaum, Adolph, 2046
Grzegorczyk, Andrzej, 2161
Gudeman, Alfred, 72
Guérard des Lauriers, M. L., 2227
Guerinot, Armand Albert, 1957
Guerrieri, Guerriera, 1323
Gui, Śiva Chandra, 2220
Gumposch, Victor Philipp, 1735
Gunn, J. Alexander, 2294
Gunter, P. A. Y., 180
Guss, Allene, 1973
Gustafson, R. K., 1656
Gutiérrez, David, 99
Gutzwiller, Alois, 1485
Guzzo, A., 526, 2339

Hadas, Moses, 2169
Haering, Th., 549
Hainds, J. R., 952
Hall, Fitzedward, 1913
Hall, Manly Palmer, 532
Hall, Roland, 607, 796, 797, 798, 1450, 1692
Hamburg, C. H., 286
Hammond, William A., 1418
Hampton, J., 788
Hanayama, Shinsho, 1514
Handen, Ralph D., 159
Hanover. Stadtbibliothek, 1767
Harari, Jeané V., 2281
Hargreaves, Mary, 591
Harlow, Victor Emmanuel, 2197

Harman, Marian, 437
Harrassowitz, Otto, 1494
Harrison, John, 793
Hartmann, Wilfried, 1173
Hartshorne, Dorothy C., 538, 536
Harvard University, 1230, 1792, 2252
Hascall, Dudley, 956
Haulotte, Edgar, 342
Hauréau, Barthelemy, 602
Havet, Jacques, 1701
Hay, William H., 1357
Hayen, André, 207, 208
Heimsoeth, Heinz, 840
Heinemann, F. H., 2108
Heldt, H. L., 1507
Hellersberg (firm), 541
Henderickx, A. F., 1469
Henderson, James L., 1088
Hennemann, Gerhard, 580
Henning, Max, 1837
Henrichs, Norbert, 1812
Hensard, O., 1328
Herbert, Jean, 2129
Herbertz, Richard, 2291
Herchlova, L. [et al], 900
Hermann, Friedrich-Wilhelm von, 458
Hermann, Grete, 987
Herrmann, Friedrich Wilhelm von, 459
Herrmann, Ulrich, 402
Herscher, I., 13
Hervey, William Addison, 775
Herwig, Johann Just, 1398
Hespe, Roswitha, 811
Heumann, Christoph Augst., 1720, 1731
Heuss, Eugen [et al.], 2325
Heyde, J. E., 1648
Heydenreich, K., 1730
Heyer, Henri, 2324
Heynck, Valens, 1375
Hibben, J. G., 1643
Hickman, Larry, 2029
Higgins, Charles L., 2308
Hilarin de Milan, 1688
Hill, William Speed, 600, 601
Hillgarth, J. N., 824, 826
Hilsenbeck, Adolf, 1748
Himmelstrup, Jens, 689
Hinemann, F. H., 1302
Hintikka, Jaakko, 2232
Hissmann, Michael, 1729
Hoadly, Benjamin, 297
Hocedez Edgar, 1093
Hölzer, Anke, 757, 758, 759
Hofmann, Joseph Enrenfried, 994
Hoffman, Arthur, 1894
Hoffmann, Jean, 1750
Hogrebe, Wolfram, 2147
Holbrook, David, 2044
Holm, O., 829
Holst, P. A., 2032
Holt, Edwin B., 637
Holzman, Donald [et al.], 1960
Hope, Richard, 2298
Hornus, Jean-Michel, 1081, 1083
Horten, Max Joseph Heinrich, 1929, 1930, 1931
Hossfeld, Knut, 1393
Houtin, A., 801
Howald, E., 2179
Hoy, Peter Charles, 271
Hubert, F., 885
Hübner, Emil, 295
Hübscher, Arthur, 1208, 1209, 1210
Hughes, H. C., 785
Huisman, Denis, 2302
Hume, Robert Ernest, 2343
Hungerland, H., 1429
Hyppolite, J., 550
Hyslop, J. H., 1641

ÌÀkovenko [Jakovenko], Borīs Valentīnovīch, 165, 922
Ibáñez de García Blanco, L., 1309
Ijsseling, Samuel, 1008
Ilaha, Khwaja Nur, 628
In-Jae, Jeun, 1971
Isachenkova, Anna Ivanova, 1566
Institut des etudes augustiniennes, 112
Institut für Marxismus-Leninismus (Berlin), 890
Institut Karla Marksa i Fridrikha Engel'sa (Moscow), 878
Institut Marksa-Engel'sa-Lenina (Moscow), 769, 770

Institut V. I. Lenina (Moscow), 766, 767
Instituto Bibliográfico (Buenos Aires), 1461, 1462
Interamerican congress of philosophy, 1570
International association of theological libraries, 1771
International congress for philosophy, third, 1806
Internationalen institut (Freiburg), 2253
Ireland, A., 143
Israel. ha-Mahlakah le-tarbut toranit, 978
Istituto di studi filosofici (Roma), 1953, 1954
Istituto nazionale per le relazioni culturali con l'estero, 1947
Iturrioz, Jesús, 1268

J. L., 172, 1676
Jacob, Gertrude, 1144
Jacobs, Joseph, 1810
Jacobs, Wilhelm G., 456
Jacoby, Günther, 1052
Jagindar Singh, 1227
Jakovenko, B. V., 2216
Jalabert, J., 751
James, Henry, Jr., 637
Janauschek, Leopold, 190
Janeff-Sofia, Janko, 542, 543
Jansen, Wilhelm Albert, 1120
Jarque i Jutglar, Joan E., 1292
Jaryc, Marc, 2143
Jellinek, Adolf, 841
Jelonek, Eugenius, 1591
Jerphagnon, Lucien, 641
Jessop, Thomas Edmund, 188, 189, 593, 604
Jevons, William Stanley, 344
Jodl,Friedrich, 454, 455
Johnson, Edmund J., 2202
Johnson, Thomas H., 428, 429
Joliret, Régis, 683, 1675
Jones, Claude Edward, 1231
Jonsius Johannes, 1718
Joó, Tibor, 1855
Jørgensen, Aage, 692
Jost, Johannes, 128, 1176
Junta del centenario de Suarez (Spain), 2270

Kahl [Kahlis], Ludwig Martin, 1722
Kalfs, G., 1197
Kamm, Peter, 528
Kanazawa Bunko, 1962
Kandel', Efim Pavlovich, 883
Karutsin, Krŭstiu͡, 893
Kasiński, Ludwik, 2161
Katushkina, L., 333
Kaul, H. K., 114
Keeling, S. V., 348, 358, 1541
Keeler, Willy, 1352
Kempski, J. von, 424
Kennedy, Virginia Wadlow, 302
Kern, Iso, 618
Kern, Walter, 558, 561, 562
Kerschensteiner, Jula, 1549
Keynes, Geoffrey Langdon, 231, 794
Kiesewetter, Johann Gottfried Carl Christian, 652
Kleberg, Tönnes, 1546
Kleinen, H., 998
Kleinschneider, M., 667
Klibansky, Raymond, 285, 1589
Kline, George L., 1367
Klubertanx, George, 1672
Kluckhohn, Clyde, 1658
Klug, Ulrich, 1215
Kluge, Fr., 979
Kníazeva, L. G., 905
Knizhnik, Ivan S., 876
Knock, Ann, 398
Koch-Klose, Abel, 757
Koehler und Volckmar (firm), 1505
Kohlmeier, Johann, 123
Koller, J., 1399
Kommunisticheskaia akademii͡a (Moscow), 765
Kopf, Eike, 874
Kopreeva, Tatiana N., 1342
Korcik, A., 2013
Koren, Henry J., 2309
Korff, H., 1519
Kortholt, Seb, 1637
Kovachev, Velcho Vŭlkov, 435, 893
Kovalsky, Susan Joan, 490
Kowalski, K., 33
Koyré, A., 545, 551
Kraenzlin, G., 1172

Kraft, Margit, 704
Krallmann, Dieter, 666
Kremer-Marietti, Angèle, 179
Kristeller, Paul Oskar, 1553, 1845, 1987
Krońska, Irena, 559
Kropp, Gerhard, 782
Krüger, G., 359
Krug, Wilhelm Traugott, 1733, 2285, 2287
Krummel, Richard F., 1009
Krupa, H., 1187
Kruse, Margot, 1032
Kühler, Otto, 546
Küng, Guido, 2019
Kuhn, H., 659
Kuhn, M. A., 300
Kuno, Osamu, 1961
Kuntz, Paul G., 806
Kwee, Swan-liat, 1840, 2074

Lababi, Mohamed-Aziz, 625
Laban, Ferdinand, 1190, 1191
Labbé, Philippe, 61, 642
Labergie (firm), 35
Labrousse, Élisabeth, 157
Lachs, John, 912
Lacombe, Georgius, 75
Ladragne, A., 2118
Lal, P., 2041
Lalande, André, 708, 2229
Lambrino, Sc., 1550
Lameere, J. [et al.], 185, 605 605
Lamirande, Emillen, 108
Landes, Margaret Winifred, 970
Landesberg, Paul Ludwig, 906
Landolt, Eduard, 573
Lapointe, François H., 462, 779, 861, 866, 942, 944, 945, 1097, 1164, 1165, 1167, 1168
La Salle, Edmundo, 1979
Laslett, Peter, 790, 793
Laszlo, Ervin, 195
Lauf, Emile, 1848
Laugwitz, Detlef, 2021
Lecat, Maurice, 839
Leclercq, Jean, 194
Lechène, M. L., 1297
Ledos, Emile Gabriel, 1056
Lee, Harold N., 717
Leemans, Victor, 2344
Leger, Guy, 1826
Legowicz, Jan, 55
Lehmann, Gerhard, 662
Leisegang, H., 1538, 1544
Lenger, Marie Thérèse, 837
Lenoci, Michele, 931
Lepine, Joseph E., 1980
Leroux, E., 2178
Leroy, A. L., 186
Le Senne, René, 2304
Levallois, Marie Charles Henri, 735
Levi, Alexandro, 48, 1945, 1946
Lévin, L. A., 884
Levin, M. I., 2102
Lewy, C., 241
Leyds, J. J. C., 390
Library association (London), 2303
Library of Congress, see U. S. Library of Congress
Libreria Siglo XX, Bogotá, 1577
Lier, R., and Co., 475
Lufshits, I., 2024
Lillie, Robert, 1757
Lima-Alceu, Amoroso, 742
Lime, V., 411
Lindner, Frank, 933
Lipenius, M. Martinus, 1715
Lippert, J. F. Bookstore, 1487
Lipps, Theodor, 1409
Lisi, E., 91
Little, Janet Patricia, 1356
Livraria Universal de Echenique y Irmão, 1797
Livingston, Dorothy F., 136
Llavonia, Rafael, 943
Llinares, Armand, 825
Łódź, Poland, 314
Lohr, Charles H., 56, 82
London Science Museum, 1448
London University, 1020, 1782
Long, Herbert S., 78
Long, Philip, 789, 792
Longas, Pedro, 88
Longpre, E., 412
Loome, Thomas Michael, 1307
Lopez de Oñate, F., 1112
Loreaux, Max, 1007
Lotze, Hermann, 805

Lough, J., 786, 787
Lovi, Henrietta, 2185
Lowe, Elias Avery, 94
Lowe, Victor, 1363
Lowenberg, Jacob, 1137
Lubnici, N., 361
Ludovici, Sergio Samek, 1049
Lübbe, Hermann, 566
Lust, John, 1526
Lutosławski, W., 1824

McCormick, J. J., 1266
MacCosh, J., 2240
McCrimmon, James McNab, 952
McDermott, John J., 639
Macdonald, Hugh, 591
McGill University, 2315
Machado dos Santos, Mariana Amélia, 2247
Mackey, R., 2330
Mackintosh, James, 1638
McLean, George F., 1588
MacMaster, Robert E., 332
MacMinn, Ney, 952
McMullin, Ernan, 484, 485
Madoz, J., 2136
Madrid. Universidad, 1608
Maier, A., 738
Maire, Albert, 1027, 1028
Maison des sci[ences] de l' homme (Paris), 2145
Maisonneuve [Abbé], 1694
Malavassi, V., 1308
Malter, Rudolf, 665, 1225
Mandolfo, A., 257
Mandonnet, P., 29, 32
Manmohan Reddy, Vedre, 115, 1397
Mannheim, Karl, 2259
Manova, Nadezhda Vasileva, 1431
Mansion, Auguste, 79
Mantese, Giovanni, 999
March, Arthur Charles, 1508
Marcos, Benjamin, 1312
Marega, Isnardus M., 253
Margolin, Jean Claude, 441, 446
Margolis, Joseph, 1433
Marien, B., 1068
Markowski, Mieczysław, 57, 420
Martin, Hans Adolf, 666
Martin, Gottfried, 666
Martin, L. A., 1874
Martínez Gómez, Louis, 2271, 2272, 2274
Maschke, Gerhard, 618
Masson-Oursel, P., 2128
Matczak, Sebastian A., 606, 1664, 2313
Mathieu, V., 176
Matica slovenská, Turčiansky sv. Martin, 2307
Mattesini, F., 499
May, Otto Heinrich, 745
Mayer, Jacob Peter, 381
Mayer-Hillebrand, Franziska, 239
Mayerohoff, Milton [et al.], 383
Mayjonade, J. B., 845
Mays, Paul D., 1787
Mead, Herman Ralph, 182
Meade, J. E., 2133
Medellín, Colombia, 1986
Meersseman, Gérard Gilles, 8
Mehdawi, Yaha, 126
Meier, Ludger, 417
Meijer, Willem, 1246
Meiner, Felix (firm), 1499, 1501, 1502
Meister, Christian Friedrich Georg, 1989
Menagius, Aegidius [Menage, Gilles], 2349
Menard, R. J., 1402
Mencharca, José A., 1779
Mendia, Benito, 821
Menut, Albert, 1015
Merches, Dorina, 1443
Merker, Nicolas, 554
Merton, Robert K., 2236
Mitall, R. A., 677
Mette, Hans Joachim, 1004
Mettler, A., 1350
Metz, Rudolf, 603
México (City) Universidad nacional, 1427, 1432, 2079, 2080, 2081
Meyer, B., 1394
Meyerson, I., 339
Michelitsch, Anton, 30
Miladinova, Milka, 1437
Milchsack, G., 774
Milhaud, Gérard, 362
Millard, Richard M., 2201
Millas-Vallicrosa, J. M., 2226

Miller, Albert Jay, 1626
Millet, Louis, 173
Milne, Alexander Taylor, 168
Min-Hong, Choi, 1972
Minges, P., 408
Minio-Paleullo, Laurentius, 53
Mintŝ, G. E., 2024
Mioni, Elpidio, 51
Misharina, Vladilena Vasil' evna, 894, 1565
Mitcham, C., 2330
Mizuta, Hiroshi, 1233
Moede, Walter, 1379
Moine, Michel, 2189
Mommsen, Theodor E., 2205
Mondolfo, Rodolfo, 1554
Monfrin, Jacques, 505
Montelone, F., 1759
Montenegro, A., 2167
Montevideo. Universidad, 1316
Moog, Willy, 1890
Moore, C. S., 1920
Moore, G. E., 969
Moore, Russell Franklin, 2130
Moore, W. G., 682
Morando, D., 1111
Moraux, Paul, 50, 80
Morell, John Daniel, 2277
Morgan, S. R., 2191
Morra, Gianfranco, 1034
Morris, Charles, 2231
Moschitti, Andrea Mario, 1552
Moscow. Publichnaîa biblioteka, 772, 1655, 2282
Moskovskiĭ rabochiĭ, 768
Mossé-Bastide, R.-M., 174
Mostowski, Andrzej, 2047
Motta, E., 2319
Moubarac, Y., 923, 924
Moustoxydēs, Theodosios Mauroeidēs, 1416
Mudge, I. G., 170
Mühlbrecht, O., 2165
Müller, Hans von, 1334
Müller, Kurt, 753
Múgica, Placido, 1269
Muirhead, Arnold Meadowcroft, 167
Mukherji, P. K., 1916
Muller, Frederik, and Co., 1606
Munby, Lionel M., 907
Munk, Salomon, 122
Muñoz-Delgado, Vincente, 2022, 2109
Murray, J. Clayton, 1927
Musée pédagogique de l' État (France), 1700
Mussotter, Cos., 1497

Nadler, K., 547
Naficy, Said, 125
Natanson, Maurice, 929
National Art Museum, see South Kensington Museum
National book council, 2097, 2293
National book league, 2295
National Library of Wales, 1018
Nauchno-isseledovatel'skiĭ institut knigovedeniîa, 762
Naudé, Gabriel, 2094
Nebreda, R. P., 96
Nesselmark, 711
Nettlau, Max, 1451
Neu, Jerome, 1974
Neu, Theodor, 1255
Newberry library (Chicago), 1751
Newcastle upon tyne. University, 230
New York (City) public library, 1745
New York Society for Ethical Culture, 1651
Nicolas, Jean-Hervé, 2278
Nicolin, Friedhelm, 556, 576
Nicolini, Fausto, 320
Nicolosi, S., 851
Nielson, Edith Ortman, 684
Nihon Gakujutsu Kaigi, 1853
Niklaus, Robert, 396
Noguez, Dominique [et al.], 1537
Noica, Constantin, 560
Norsa, A., 836
North, Robert, 1022
Nottingham, Eng. Free public libraries and museums, 1 1640
Nowicki, M., 1831
Nuremberg. Stadtbibliothek, 557
Nuño Montes, Juan Antonio, 1555, 1774

Oehler, Max, 1005
Oettinger, E. M., 2318
Oko, Adolph S., 1249
Okuma Seishin Bunka Kenkyusho, 1963
Oldfather, W. A., 436
Olgiati, Francesco, 346
Olivier, Paul, 1324, 1325
Olmsted, Richard H., 1980
Ong, Walter Jackson, 1085
Oporto, Portugal. Biblioteca publica, 1737
Oppenheim, Frank M., 1139
Orecchia, Rinaldo, 343, 1013
Orellá, José L., 1966
Orlando, Pasquale, 1078, 1155, 1275
Orlov, S. M., 905
Ortega, Eusebio, 1312
Ortloff, Johann Andreas, 1732
Ostrowski, Jean J., 450
Ostwald, Friedrich Wilhelm, 306
Otilío del Niño Jesús, 2217
Ottaviano, Carmelo, 818
Otto, Anneliese, 2310
Ottonello, Pier Paolo, 1217

Pacchi, A., 592
Palacz, Ryszard, 1259
Paliard, Jacques, 1568
Palmer, George Herbert, 584
Pan american union, 1983
Parker, Franklin, 1365
Parkinson, G. H. R., 752
Parra, Caracciolo, 2348
Pasquali, Alberto, 1707
Pasquinelli, Alberto, 279
Passmore, John A., 329
Patocka, Jan, 610
Patrick, J. Max, 139
Patton, M. M., 136
Paumen, Jean, 152, 568, 2260
Pavlov, Andrei [Pawlow, Andrej], 1596
Pavlova, L., 1665
Payen, Jean François, 961
Peignot, Gabriel, 1335
Pelikán, Bohumil, 773
Pellegrino, G., 504
Pelseneer, Jean, 992
Pelzer, Auguste, 1042, 2088, 2332
Pereboom, Dirk, 571
Perez Martinex, Lorenzo, 823, 826
Perini, D. A., 98
Perler, Othmar, 2137
Pernoud, Mary Anne, 1377
Perry, Ralph Barton, 638
Peters, C. H., 1074
Petrova, Galina Aleksandrovna, 1439
Peyre, H., 1029
Pfanmüller, D. G., 1932
Pfeiffer, K., 1196
Philippe, Marie-Dominique, 76
Picaret, François, 1875, 2105
Piersol, Wesley, 983
Pilz, Kurt, 303
Pin, Emile, 2261
Pinilla, Norberto, 1420
Pinto, O., 1274
Pisarzy, Słownik, 2163
Placer, Gumersindo, 1395
Planty-Bonjour, G., 918
Plott, John C., 1787
Poëy, Andre, 2176
Polanyi, J., 1069
Polgár, László, 1284
Polin, R., 590
Pollin, Burton R., 507
Polska akademia nauk, 2164
Pompa, Raffaele, 1943, 1944
Pontara, Giuliano, 489
Poortman, J. J., 1622
Popp, K. R., 216
Porter, H., 2001
Pos, H.-J., 364
Potter, Karl H., 1923, 1924
Pouget, H.-M., 1455
Poulin, Daniel, 1286
Poulos, Kathleen, 389
Powell, John P., 1627
Poznanski, Marceli, 311
Prantl, Carl von, 2004
Preiss, Th., 681
Preto, E., 1014
Preussische staatsbibliothek (Berlin), 74, 97, 162, 1959
Price, Harry, 2187
Primakovskiĭ, A. P., 2016
Proost, K. F., 1621
Prümm, Karl, 2351
Przymusiała, Andrzy, 702

Quadri, G., 1936
Quasten, J., 451
Queen's college library (Belfast), 2071
Quérard, Joseph Marie, 965
Quérard, Joseph Marie, 1336
Quetif, J., 24
Quinton, A. M., 1585

Rabus, Leonhard, 2003, 2005, 2007
Rader, Melvin, 649
Radhakrishnan, Savepalli, 1920
Raes, Jean, 612
Raffelt, Albert, 213
Rakhnev, Slavi, 435
Rand, Benjamin, 1138, 1742, 1743, 1820
Ravier, Emile, 739
Ravisson, Félix, 1693
Read, J., 1447
Reck, Andrew, 930
Redmond, Walter Bernard, 1984
Rees, D. A., 1653
Reeves, Gene, 1369
Reeves, Jesse Siddall, 519
Regamey, C., 1512
Régnier, M., 1100
Reichert, Herbert W., 1006
Reichke, Rudolph, 655
Reiffenberg, Frédéric Auguste Ferdinand Thomas, baron de., 2000
Reilly, James P., 1376
Reimmann, Jacob Friedrich, 1534
Reims. Bibliothèque, 1738
Renoir, Edmund, 1698
Renou, L., 1917, 2345
Rescher, Nicholas, 15, 20, 2030
Reuter, Ottfried, 151
Revilla, H., 1542
Reynolds, Michael M., 1614
Rhode, Gisela, 81
Ribeiro, Alvaro, 301
Riccardi, Pietro, 470
Rice, Frank A., 1973
Richot, B., 748
Richou, Gabriel Charles Marie, 964
Richter, Günter, 669
Richter, Liselotte, 746
Richter, Richard, 1784
Riedl, John O., ed., 2208
Riepe, Dale, 1918, 1921
Risse, W., 2025
Ritter, H., 1456
Ritter, Joachim, ed., 1791
Ritter, Paul, 730, 734
Riva, Clemente, 233, 234
Rizzo, Nicholas D., 196
Roback, A. A., 1522
Robberechts, L., 982
Robert, Jean-Dominique, 1629, 1632, 2230
Robertson, John M., 144
Robin, Richard S., 1038
Robinet, André, 749, 850
Robinson, A. L., 834
Robinson, D. S., 366
Robson, J. M., 956
Rocco di Torrepadula, Giampaolo, 478
Rodenberg, Julius F. W. A., 1753
Rodi, Frithjof, 222
Rodis-Lewis, Geneviève, 372, 1065
Roeming, Robert F., 272
Rogent, Elíes, 817
Rogge, Hendrik Cornelis, 518
Roig, Arturo Andres, 632
Romein, Jan, 1621
Ronchetti, Emanuele, 1850
Rondet, Henri, 101, 106
Rondet, Louis, 40
Rorty, Richard, 1974
Rosen, Edward, 312
Rosenkranz, Karl, 539
Rosenmeyer, T. G., 1061
Ross, W. David, 1277
Rosselet, Claire, 1131
Rossi, Giovanni Felice, 42
Rossi, Paolo, 138, 887
Rossmann, Kurt, 645
Rost, Hans, 2321
Rothenfelder, Ludwig, 679
Rotta, Paolo, 996, 1547
Rouse, Richard H., 2064
Rousseau, Jean-Jacques, 1133
Roussos, Evangelos N., 581
Royce, Josiah, 2327
Rozanov, Íakov S., 877
Rozanov, J. S., 1814
Rozenfeld, Boris, 2048
Rubel, Maximilien, 892
Ruge, Arnold, 1887

Ruiz, Félix, 1035
Rukser, Udo, 1017
Rule, John C., 159, 1304, 1830
Rummens, Jean, 129, 2206
Russo, François, 486
Ruybinx, J., 1364
Ryan, James Hugh, 2106
Rybalka, Michel, 1162
Ryle, Gilbert, 2133

Saavedra, Modesto, 1993
Sacki, Ryōken, 2026
Saffrey, H. D., 1826
Saf'ián, Hdaliĭ Maĭseevich, 913
St. Marin, Demetrio, 1435
St. Pierre, Jules A., 1371
Saisset, E. E., 1822
Saitschick, Robert, 1153
Sakharova, Eugeniia Mikhailovna, 1428
Sales, Michel, 694
Salomon-Bayet, Claire, 1134
Salvestrini, Virgilio, 243
Sanchez, J., 45
Sánchez Morales, Narciso, 1080
Sanchez-Ruiz, José, 1630
Sanders, Charles Ríchard, 278
Saner, H., 648
Sangin, M. A. F., 1465
Sankey-Jones, Nancy E., 2098
Santinello, G., 1258
Santoro, Caterina, 2124
Santos Escuerda, Ceferino, 1157
São Paulo. Universidade., 2221
Sartiaux, F., 801
Sass, Hans-Martin, 570, 1809
Saštrī, G-Krsna, 1914
Śástrí Hrishikeśa, 2220
Sauvaget, Jean, 1939
Savérien, Alexandre, 1728
Savin, Maurice, 4
Schaarschmidt, C., 727
Schadewaldt, Wolfgang, 633
Schäfer, Odulf, 418, 419
Schaller, Karl August, 1802
Schaller, Toni, 426
Scheive, Urbain, 407
Schelle, Johann Christian, 1636
Scheurl, Heinrich Julius, 1633
Schiavone, Michele, 1216, 1846
Schiffers, N., 988
Schinz, Albert, 1124
Schitlowsky, Ch., 1877
Schlechta, Karl, 1006
Schlegel, Gustaaf, 1184
Schliebitz, Hans, 1883
Schliebitz, Hertha, 1883
Schmandt, Jürgen, 1119
Schmid, Günther, 509
Schmied-Kowarzik, Walther, 1414, 1415
Schmidkung, H., 1572
Schmidt, M. A., 421
Schmidt, Raymond, 1573
Schmidt-Koch, Ria, 2276
Schmitt, Charles B., 83
Schneeberger, Guido, 567, 569, 1178
Schneemeicher, Wilhelm [et al.], 2140
Schönmetzer, Adolf, 1040
Schoeps, Hans Joachim, 1828
Scholem, Gershom Gerhard, 2096, 2099
Scholtz, Gunter, 1817
Schonborn, Charles von, 1002
Schooyans, Michel, 12
Schottlaender, Rudolf, 1657
Schrâder, Otto, 1914
Schrecker, Paul, 741
Schreiber, Ch., 1881
Schröder, Ernst, 2008
Schröter, M., 1177
Schüling, Herman, 1996
Schuhl, P.-M., 926
Schum, M., 1706
Schwab, Moïse, 69, 932
Schwitzer, R., 413
Sciacca, Michele Federico, 100, 1058, 1059, 1586, 1949
Scott, F. N., 1408
Scott, J. W., 1900
Scribner [firm (Charles Scribner's Sons)], 1493
Scarles, Herbert L., 1183
Sears, Minnie Earl, 1484
Sebba, Gregor, 374, 376, 378 852, 853
Segovia, A., 629
Seifert, Siegfried, 776

Semenova, V. A., 2263
Sénelier, Jean, 1126
Servetti de Torrano, Matilde, 1681
Sexauer, A., 1752
Sharma, Jagdish Saran, 488
Shanghnessy, Amy E., 1613
Sheldon, W. L., 1645
Sheldon-Williams, I. P., 449
Shepard, Herbert A., 1595
Shepherd, Richard Werne, 275
Shields, Allan, 1183
Shields, Margaret C., 432
Shin, Kee See, 1370
Shneerson, Boris S., 763, 764
Silvin, E., 2257
Simon, Anthony O., 1226
Simon, I., 1536
Simoniti, Primož, 2250
Siwek, Paul, 52
Skrupskelis, Ignas, 1142
Slosiar, Dezider, 2248
Smart, James P., 1143
Smeets, Uriel, 415
Smith, Gerald, 1267
Smith, May, 833
Sneessens, Germaine, 199
Société Jean-Jacques Rousseau, 1135
Society for psychical research (London), 2183, 2190
Solá, Francisco de P., 1270
Sola, José, 1941
Sollitto, Sharmon, 2254
Solmitz, W., 285, 286
Sonnenschein, William Swan, 1747
Sortais, G., 1571, 1823
South Kensington Museum (London), 1403
Spach, Israel, 1712
Spaemann, Robert, 1808
Spätling, Luchesius, 1067
Spalding, Johann Joachim, 1239
Spedding, James, 135
Spencer, Claude E., 268
Spurlin, Paul M., 1127
Staal, J. F., 197, 198
Stäglich, Hans, 510, 1896, 2150, 2151, 2152, 2153, 2154
Stainton, Elsie Myers, 251
Stammhammer, Josef, 2256
Starfelt, Eric, 1012
Steenberger, C.-A., 364
Steinhofer, Johann Ulrich, 725
Steinkraus, Warren E., 1859
Steinschneider, Moritz, 2117
Stella, Vittorio, 323
Stéphanou, E., 1518
Stewart, Dugald, 2070
Sticker, Bernhard, 754
Stieler, G., 854
Stockhausen, Johann Christoph, 2283
Stokes, W. E., 1366
Stolle, Gottlieb, 1719
Strenger, Irineu, 951
Stroll, Avrum, 466
Struve, Burkhard Gotthelf, 1717
Suchorzewska, J., 1824
Sully, James, 2149
Sullivan, Frank, 971, 973, 974
Suzuki, Michihiko, 1163
Svatošova, Miluše, 920
Sweeney, Leo, 1926
Swiezawski, Stefan, 2062
Swinne, Axel Hilmar, 259
Syracuse University, 2146

Tagart, Edward, 783
Talbot, C. H., 192
Tannenbaun, Samuel Aaron, 963
Taylor, Alfred Edward, 236
Taylor, Archer, 1780, 2203
Tennemann, Wilhelm Gottlieb, 1054, 1821
Ter Meulen, Jacob, 520, 522, 523
Terzian, Shonig, 1156
Tetsugaku Meicho Kaidai, 1769
Teuffel, Wilhelm Sigismund, 1055
Theosophical society in England, 2123
Theunissen, Michael, 688
Thévenaz, Pierre, 1298
Thomas, Milton Halsey, 385, 386
Thomasius, Jacobus, 2049
Thulstrup, Niels, 684, 685

Tice, Terence N., 1185
Tilliette, Xavier, 1180
Titchener, E. B., 1347
Todd, William Burton, 248, 250
Toerey, Norman L., 394
Toledano, Jacob Moses, 1086
Tomas, Vincent, 1424
Tonelli, Giorgio, 2073
Totok, Wilhelm, 1776, 1777, 2306
Touchlík, Karol, 917
Toulois, Pedro, 1506
Trinity College Library, see Dublin University
Tritheim, Johann, 2333
Troisfontaines, Roger, 860
Tübingen. Königlichen universitätsbibliothek, 1736
Tugov, Yu. M., 1565
Tumarkin, Anna, 1413
Turbayne, C. M., 187
Tvrdy, A., 2352
Turich, Irina Mikhailovna, 1434
Turnbull, H. G. D., 1240
Turina, Irina A., 481

U. S. Library of congress, 1003, 1758, 1915, 2122, 2300
Ueberweg, Friedrich, 1754
Uebinger, J., 995
Ullman, B. L., 997
Un-Aham, Han, 2132
Universidad de los Andes (Venezuela), 2347
Universidad Nacional (Córdoba), 1965
Universidad Nacional (La Plata), 1459
Universita cattolica del Sacro Curore, 1761
Università Karlova, see Charles University
Université Laval (Quebec), 1789
University of Pennsylvania, 62
University of Southern California, 1755, 1783
Untermoehlen, Gerda, 755
Urano, Kinuko, 1163
Usai, Roberto, 1368
Ústav dějin kommunistické strany Československa, 881
Ústřední ekonomická knihovna, 1564
Utz, A., 1668
Utz, Arthur, 1662

Vade, Yves, 1279
Vaihinger, Hans, 655
Vajda, Georges, 5, 1967
Valadier, Paul, 1010
Valdés, Mario J., 1310
Valenti, E., 1024
Valente, Umberto, 1303
Valentiné, Francesco, 1683
Valori, P., 615
Van Luijk, H., 1102
Valverde Tellez, Emeterio, 2075, 2076, 2077
Van Bavel, Tarsicius J., 105, 110
Van Breda, H. L., 613, 614
Van de Vyver, E., 425
Van den Berg, J. H., 1313, 2069
Vander Haeghen, Victor, 503
Van der Haeghen, Ferdinand, 439
Vander Kerken, L., 1682
Van der Linde, A., 1248
Van de Wiele, R., 380
Van Gassel, E., 191
Van Langenhove, Fernand, 1315
Van Leeuwen, A. P., 19
Vannérus, A., 2323
Vansina, Dirk F., 1095, 1096, 1098
Van Steenberghen, Fernand, 9, 36, 804, 2054, 2060, 2066
Van Steenkiste, C., 46, 1471
Van Tricht, Victor, 1964
Varenychenko, K., 914
Varet, Gilbert, 1624, 1770
Varisco, Bernardino, 1945
Vaschide, N., 1744
Vasoli, Cesare, 2065
Vásquez, Juan Adolpho, 1981
Vatican, 226

Veatch, Robert M., 2254
Vennebusch, Joachim, 121
Vera, Francisco, 1385
Verbinc, Franc., 2249
Vercruysse, Jeroom, 598
Verderius, Antonius [Antonio Verderio], 1711
Vereeniging "Het Spinozahuis", 1250
Vergé, H., 1878
Verlière, A., 2194
Vervliet, Hendrik D. L., 1851
Vicentini, José I., 1477
Vickers, Brian, 140
Victoroff, D., 1650
Vidart, Luis, 2268
Viel, A., 28
Vigil, José María, 2082
Vinet, Ernest, 1405
Vismara, Silvio, 476
Vitier, M., 1593
Vleeschauwer, Herman Jan de, 77
Voise, Waldemar, 756
Voisine, Jacques, 1132
Voumvlinopoulos, Georges E., 1811
Vrtacic, Ludvik, 921
Vŭlchev, Velichko, 886
Vurgey [i.e., M. Bouillot], 1412

Wachsmuth, Guenther, 1261
Wagner, Gustav Friedrich, 1195
Walch, Jean, 1152
Walford, Albert John, 1785
Walgrave, J. H., 1670
Wallich, Paul, 1334
Walsh, Edward J., 1617
Walters, LeRoy, 1667
Waltmann, H., 524
Walzer, R., 1456, 1457, 1458
Wangermann, Ernest, 907
Warda, Arthur, 654, 658
Ware, C. S., 371
Ware, Robert S., 187
Warner, J. H., 1125
Warnotte, D., 2155
Warrender, J. H., 2166
Warwrzinek, Utta, 1816
Wehr, H., 1937
Weigand, Georg, 160
Weil, Eric, 659, 1355
Weimann, Karl-Heinz, 1023
Weinhandl, F., 508
Weiss, Frederick G., 563
Weiss, Melchior, 7
Wells, Rulon, 1063, 1064
Welsh, David, 242
Weltsch, Robert, 246
Wenin, Christian, 225
Weser, Adolf, 1311
Wetlesen, Jon, 1251
Wheare, K. C., 2133
Whitmore, Frank Hayden, 1646
Wigny, P., 1649
Willers, Dietrich, 1306
Williams, Harry, 2057
Wilson, John Cook, 1378
Wingate, Sybil Douglas, 54
Winn, Ralph B., 2341
Wirth, Ingeborg, 535
Wise, Thomas J., 1143
Witschi-Bernz, Astrid, 1835
Wlodek, Sophie, 2063
Wolf, Abraham, 1247
Wolf, Gustav, 2289
Wolff, Kurt H., 1224
Wolfson, H. A., 118, 120
Woodcock, George, 1452
Woodger, Michael, 1387
Woodward, Parker, 134
Woolhouse, Roger, 796, 797
Wren, Thomas E., 204
Wright, Georg Henrik von, 1384
Wtodek, Zofia, 420
Wundt, Eleonore, 1389
Wurgaft, Lewis D., 1832, 1833
Wust, Peter, 1317
Wyser, Paul, 38, 39

Yakovenko [Jakowenko], Boris, 1596
Yanitelli, Victor R., 1678
Yela, Juan Francisco, 1756
Yoo, Yushin, 1516
Ysart, F. X., 2269
Yuan, Tung-Li, 1531

Zahn, Manfred, 457
Zamarriego, Tomas, dir, 1778
Zambonini Corona, Olga, 1392
Zampetti, Enrico, 1476
Zarco, Miguel Angel, 871

Zavalloni, Roberto, 1094
Zawadzki, Jane, 1436, 2043
Zea, Leopoldo, 2078
Zeeck, Hans, 400
Zíâtkova, Líudmila Ivanovna, 1631, 2316
Ziegenfuss, Werner [et al.], 1765
Zimny, Leo, 161, 1079
Zoccoli, Ettore, 1193
Zorab, George, 2134
Zorcolo, B., 497
Zucker, Arthur, 1396
Zumkeller, Adolar, 94

About the Editor

Herbert Guerry has taught at Idaho State University and Pembroke State University. In 1976-77, he was a postdoctoral student in the Department of Population Planning at the University of Michigan. He has written articles for such journals as *Cirpho Review, Journal of Philosophy,* and *Analysis.* He is currently doing research for a book on population ethics.